SANCTUARY

SANCTUARY

A Story of American Conscience and the Law in Collision

BY

ANN CRITTENDEN

Weidenfeld & Nicolson
New York

PUBLISHED BY WEIDENFELD & NICOLSON, NEW YORK
A DIVISION OF WHEATLAND CORPORATION
841 BROADWAY
NEW YORK, NY 10003-4793

PUBLISHED IN CANADA BY GENERAL PUBLISHING COMPANY, LTD.

The photographs in this book appear courtesy of the following:
HARVEY FINKLE: John M. Fife greeting congregant; Ricardo Elford and child; Ramón Quiñones at home for aged; Philip and Ellen Willis-Conger; Darlene Nicgorski at convent; María Socorro Aguilar; Joel Morelos and Lucy; demonstrators in front of Federal Building; Fife at St. Augustine Catholic Church; Nena MacDonald and daughter; Mary K. Espinosa and Ken Kennon at Nogales demonstration; Ken Kennon with William Johnston outside Federal Building. *ARIZONA DAILY STAR:* James A. Corbett in desert; Anthony Clark; Corbett assisting Álvarez over fence; Donald M. Reno; Judge Earl H. Carroll; Fife with reporters following trial. *TUCSON CITIZEN:* The Reverends Sinner, Elford, and Kennon conducting services; sanctuary declaration at Southside United Presbyterian Church. RICARDO VALDIVIESO: James A. Rayburn; James J. Brosnahan; Robert J. Hirsh; A. Bates Butler. DARLENE NICGORSKI: Jesus Cruz and James Oines at Alzona Evangelical Lutheran Church. *NATIONAL CATHOLIC REPORTER*/MARK DAY: Espinosa, Clark, LeWin, Flaherty, Corbett, and Nicgorski during pretrial hearings.

Library of Congress Cataloging-in-Publication Data

Crittenden, Ann.
Sanctuary.

Includes index.
1. Sanctuary movement. 2. Refugees, Political—
Central America. 3. Church work with refugees—United
States. I. Title.
HV645.C75   1988   261.8′32   88-118
ISBN 1-55584-039-6

MANUFACTURED IN THE UNITED STATES OF AMERICA
DESIGNED BY IRVING PERKINS ASSOCIATES
FIRST EDITION
10 9 8 7 6 5 4 3 2 1

To John and James

To John and David

Acknowledgments

THIS UNDERTAKING TO record the story of the Arizona sanctuary workers would not have been possible without the assistance and cooperation of the participants themselves. Above all, my gratitude goes to the defendants, most of whom gave generously of their time and shared their personal histories at a difficult and stressful moment in their lives. Reporting on the book began a few weeks before the end of their trial, and the first two rounds of interviews took place in the late spring of 1986, during the final arguments and between the verdict and the sentencing. That the defendants were willing to tell their stories in great detail at a time when they were facing prison sentences testifies to their enduring faith not only in their cause but in the willingness of the public to hear them.

By the same token, I am deeply grateful that Don Reno, the prosecutor in the sanctuary trial, shared so fully his thoughts, feelings, and strategies in the case. A full and accurate presentation of events would not have been possible without the government's cooperation and assistance.

Several other individuals, experts on United States refugee policy and the Central American refugee crisis, gave generously of their time and understanding of these complex issues. I especially want to thank Doris Meissner, who left the Immigration and Naturalization Service in 1985 to join the Carnegie Endowment for International Peace in Washington, D.C.; Patricia Weiss Fagen, now with the United Nations High Commission on Refugees; the Refugee Policy Group in Washington, which made available its archives; and Arthur C. Helton, of the Lawyers' Committee for International Human Rights in New York City. Any errors that may remain are entirely my own.

I also want to express deep appreciation to my agent, Al Lowman, for encouraging this project from start to finish; my editor, John Herman, for his support; and Lynn Omlie, for applying a sharp and sensitive judgment to the manuscript as it evolved.

Thanks go as well to my neighbors at the National Security Archives, who rescued me from occasional computer crises, the bane of writers under deadline; and a very special thanks to Dorothy Breen and Anja Pritzkow, who kept my household afloat while this book was under way.

Most of all, thank you to my husband, John Henry, and son, James Crittenden Henry, for understanding that I would, in the end, come back.

Notes on Sources and Points of View

THIS BOOK IS based primarily on several hundred hours of interviews with participants in and opponents of the Arizona sanctuary movement. More than one hundred people were interviewed, some repeatedly. Several of the principals, including Jim Corbett, John Fife, and Phil Willis-Conger, also read those parts of the manuscript that had to do with them and were given an opportunity to correct any inaccuracies. In addition, prosecutor Don Reno, who was interviewed for fourteen hours over two days, and defense attorney Bates Butler vetted those chapters covering the trial, so that both sides in a bitter and contentious case were able to prevent any misinterpretation of their statements and actions.

The other principal materials used for research in this book were the court records of the sanctuary trial; the notes made by government agents during the course of a nine-month undercover operation; internal memoranda of the defense attorneys; and 40,000 pages of transcripts of the ninety-one hours of secret tape recordings made by the government during the investigation. There were several versions of tape transcripts made, and discrepancies showed up among them.

While some dispute remains over what was said on some of the less intelligible tapes, the documents used here to report conversations are considered by both parties to be as accurate as any available.

I also relied heavily on the largely unpublished writings of Jim Corbett, and on the extensive press coverage of the underground railroad and the trial of its founders.

Wherever the text refers to an individual's thoughts or feelings, that statement is based on his or her comments to the author. Wherever a conversation is recorded, or an incident involves more than one person, an attempt was made to corroborate the account with all parties involved. If that was not possible, the single source is identified in a source note.

This is not "New Journalism," with reconstructed conversations and imagined states of mind. It is an old-fashioned, powerfully human story, told as accurately and as evenhandedly as possible. Since the subject of sanctuary has aroused passionate partisanship, I have attempted to set down a narrative that people on both sides of the issue can rely upon as fair.

At the same time, there is no such thing as perfect objectivity, and I do bring to the book my own personal feelings and point of view. The reader is entitled to be aware of my particular set of biases.

First and foremost is a commitment to fairness. I believe a society can and should be judged by the way it treats its less fortunate members.

Secondly, I confess to a pronounced distaste for doctrinal authority and the kind of knee-jerk anticommunism that turns other people and even entire nations into objects of enmity, to be stamped out like so many garden pests. In her memoirs Simone de Beauvoir recalls a conversation between her parents when she was five years old and World War I was raging. They were talking about the dreadful Germans and she asked if Germans were people. When assured that they were she thought: Well then, whatever happens, people will win the war.

It is particularly hard for me to view Central America through Red-tinted glasses. I first traveled through the region in the late 1960s as a journalist, and was told by virtually everyone that the deep inequities there, especially in El Salvador, would sooner or later explode into revolution. I will never forget an evening in San Salvador, talking with American businessmen in one of those houses with walls around them topped by bits of broken glass. No company would invest here, they said, unless it was certain it could earn all of its money back within a year and a half. Even in that relatively calm period there was no "long-term" in Central America, and the Russians and Cubans and all the other bogeymen had nothing to do with it.

In my view, the best way to ensure Communist influence in this hemisphere is to deny and oppose the legitimate grievances of the majority of its people.

Finally, I have a very pragmatic, secular turn of mind; religiously motivated individuals, no matter how well-meaning, are no more likely to convince me that the world is black and white than an ideological government can. Robes of self-righteousness are not becoming, whoever wears them. The older I get, the more I agree with the late French filmmaker Jean Renoir, who, in his classic *The Rules of the Game,* has a character declare that "every man has his reasons." I hope that that tolerant spirit, of trying to understand rather than merely condemn, informs this essay in contemporary history, despite its unavoidable judgments.

When the Son of Man comes in his glory, escorted by all the angels of heaven, he will sit upon his royal throne, and all the nations will be assembled before him. Then he will separate them into two groups, as a shepherd separates sheep from goats. The sheep he will place on his right hand, the goats on his left. The king will say to those on his right: "Come. You have my Father's blessing! Inherit the kingdom prepared for you from the creation of the world. For I was hungry and you gave me food, I was thirsty and you gave me drink. I was a stranger and you welcomed me, naked and you clothed me. I was ill and you comforted me, in prison and you came to visit me." Then the just will ask him: "Lord, when did we see you hungry and feed you or see you thirsty and give you drink? When did we welcome you away from home or clothe you in your nakedness? When did we visit you when you were ill or in prison?" The king will answer them: "I assure you, as often as you did it for one of my least brothers, you did it for me."

Matthew 25:31–40

Introduction

IN THE EARLY 1980s a small group of individuals in southern Arizona, most of them clergy and lay church workers, were confronted with a profound moral dilemma: What should they do if they believed that their government was breaking its own laws and endangering the lives of desperate people? How were they to choose between their conscience and the civil authority?

This is one of the oldest problems in political philosophy, and since the Holocaust, one of the most compelling ethical dilemmas of our time. But for these particular Americans, the issue was not academic. They lived near the border, and stumbling into their churches and turning up in their jails were thousands of people driven from their homes by the wars and the death squads of Central America. The men and women in this book decided that they had no choice. They defied their government and took the law into their own hands.

Thus was born a new underground railroad, even larger than its celebrated predecessor in the nineteenth century: a chain of churches helping refugees from El Salvador and Guatemala find safe haven in the United States. In a couple of years the tiny band of good Samaritans

had grown to become the national sanctuary movement, a loose network of several hundred churches, hundreds of activists, and tens of
thousands of supporters from the state of Washington to south Texas
to the mountains of Vermont. By the mid-1980s sanctuary had become
the largest grass-roots civil disobedience movement in the United States
since the turbulent sixties, and one of the few expressions of moral
protest against the Reagan administration's bellicose crusade in Central
America.

The sanctuary story is a tale of heroism and foolishness, moral courage and betrayal. It is an ultimately frightening story of how the most
powerful government in the world sent informants into the homes and
churches of peaceful dissenters and set about trying to silence them.
They had broken the law, as it was interpreted by an administration
soon to be revealed as one of the most contemptuous of law in American
history. Less than three years after the government first moved against
the underground railroad, more than 125 of the President's close associates had been convicted or were under criminal investigation, including
the nation's chief law-enforcement officer. Never were the words of
Justice Louis Brandeis more apt: "If a government becomes a lawbreaker, it breeds contempt for the law; it invites every man to become
a law unto himself."

The American sanctuary movement was a response to the largest
displacement of peoples in the western hemisphere in modern times.
Between 1980 and 1983, 1 million to 1.5 million people in Central
America were driven from their homes by violence and civil war.[1] Many
of these people remained in refugee camps and temporary shelters in
their own countries, but hundreds of thousands more made their way
north into Mexico and on into the United States. Pouring across the
nation's southern border were an estimated 500,000 to 750,000 Central
Americans, including 400,000 to 500,000 Salvadorans—almost a tenth
of the population of the country. The *New York Times* called their flight
one of "the most determined and concentrated migrations of any national group to the United States in recent history."[2]

The most apt comparison is with the flight from Indochina in the
1970s, which by a remarkable coincidence involved almost the same
number of refugees and roughly the same number of people—some
750,000—who eventually entered the United States.

But there was a tremendous difference in the reception accorded the
two different groups of refugees. The Southeast Asians came in legally,

with the blessing of the American government as well as its people, while the Central Americans had to enter illegally and remain by stealth. They were officially labeled "economic migrants," although their stories, their scars, and common sense said otherwise. They were greeted as if they were criminals, arrested and thrown into detention camps when they showed up at the border, and offered the choice of returning, voluntarily or involuntarily, to the maelstrom of the death squads, the guerrillas, and the military sweeps. The welcome they received was not that of a good neighbor.

But the official response was not the only response. Ordinary citizens, coming face-to-face with the refugees, stepped into the government's shoes and welcomed the sojourners in their midst. In this they represented their country at its best. As the *Arizona Daily Star,* a Tucson daily newspaper that was sympathetic to the underground railroad, commented, "America at its greatest has always been America as a refuge from persecution, as a protector of the helpless, and a voice for justice. America has won wars and flexed its military power, but it's the enlightened attitude toward basic human freedom that gives us our special status in the world."[3]

Yet the issues the sanctuary movement raised were anything but simple. Was this really a "civil initiative" in defense of just laws being violated by an administration with scant respect for law? Or were these men and women simply too impatient to work within the rules to change them?

And how should a government react to peaceful civil disobedience? Does it have an obligation to come to terms with the concerns of its moral leaders, including almost every mainstream church denomination in the country? Or should it confront and prosecute those who would try to circumvent its statutes in the name of a "higher law"?

Did the government have a right to go further and engage in undercover operations against domestic dissenters, sending spies with secret tape recorders into their homes and offices and places of worship, as the Justice Department ultimately did? Where is the line between nonviolent dissent and a national security risk? And who is to decide what is religion and what is politics: the citizen or the state?

Finally, how is the United States going to deal with a fundamental shift in its history as a refugee nation? The refugees of the future are not likely to be abstractions, huddled in camps thousands of miles and an ocean away, but our own neighbors, knocking at our very gates. The

Salvadorans today may be the Mexicans of tomorrow. One of the lessons of the sanctuary story is the need, completely unaddressed by the immigration reform of 1986, to put in place a coherent refugee policy at our borders.

A deeper moral of this tale is that there can be no neat military solution to the civil wars in Central America that won't recoil in the United States itself. War has its inevitable human cost, and the victims will arrive, filling our cities and dividing us against one another. Sanctuary, like the Iran-contra affair, demonstrates that controversial wars have a nasty way of coming home to roost and of driving well-meaning citizens of all persuasions to "go beyond the written law."

In the end the sanctuary story is about a battle between Americans, between two radically different visions of the kind of country we are and our place in the world. In the words of Aleksandr Solzhenitsyn, the contest for the future is radically a contestation of the spirit. It is on the battleground of the spirit that the contest will be decided.

SANCTUARY

Chapter
One

Can we doubt that only a Divine Providence placed this land, this island of freedom here as a refuge for all those people who yearn to breathe free? Jews and Christians enduring persecution behind the Iron Curtain; the boat people of Southeast Asia, Cuba, and of Haiti; the victims of drought and famine in Africa; the freedom fighters of Afghanistan.
> —RONALD W. REAGAN,
> in his acceptance speech for the Republican nomination
> for president, July 17, 1980, in Detroit, Michigan[1]

ONLY TWO WEEKS before Ronald Reagan's acceptance speech, the phantasmagoric violence in Central America cast its first shadow in the United States. On the evening of the Fourth of July a sheriff's deputy and several Border Patrol agents found three men, nearly delirious and close to death, lying in the 120-degree heat of the vast Sonoran desert. In the next two days some twenty-seven Salvadorans—thirteen of them dead of dehydration—were discovered in the virtually waterless wilderness of the Organ Pipe Cactus National Monument, where, as one local put it, "everything you touch either bites or sticks." The story of the deaths quickly became national and even international news, not least because most of the ill-fated wayfarers were not destitute farm workers but well-dressed, obviously middle-class men and women traveling with Bibles, cold cream, and toilet water.

The press immediately undertook to investigate why such people, so much like average Americans, would have chanced crossing a desolate wasteland on foot. As the survivors' stories gradually emerged, they described a country in absolute terror. One seventeen-year-old boy, a university student in agriculture, said that he had seen five close friends killed in the street. Though he himself had not been political, his cousin, who had flown in from San Francisco to be with him, told reporters that "there is definitely death waiting for him if he returns."[2]

Others claimed that so many Salvadorans were trying to get out of the country that they hadn't even been able to get inside the American embassy to obtain a temporary visa. So many people were trying to meet with embassy officials, they said, that people were sleeping outside the building to be first in line the next day.

For days Pima County Sheriff Clarence W. Dupnik, a pleasant, easygoing man in his forties, heard dozens of such stories, from survivors and everyone else professing to be knowledgeable about Central America. A veteran of twenty-two years of law enforcement, Dupnik also felt uneasy about the Salvadoran consul's exceptional interest in the case. The official, named Hugo Orantes, had flown in from Los Angeles, demanding to see all the reports of Dupnik's investigation and pictures of the thirteen who had died. Why on earth would he want pictures? Dupnik asked himself.[3] Orantes's explanation—that the government could publish them in Salvadoran newspapers so that relatives could come forward and claim the bodies—was not credible to the sheriff. It became even less so when five families who believed that their relatives were among the dead sent a chilling message. Please cremate the bodies, they pleaded, so they would not be recognizable when they were sent back to El Salvador.[4]

Dupnik decided to freeze Orantes out of the case, and at the same time he asked Carla Ewald Pedersen, his campaign manager and the wife of a prominent local attorney, to find a place other than the jail for the survivors. To reporters, Dupnik announced that it was becoming clear that "the tragedy unfolding here in the desert is due in part to social and political problems in El Salvador . . . this is not an ordinary illegal entry situation. . . . I don't think the legalistic approach would be the appropriate response from our government."[5]

Orantes was furious. He complained publicly, and privately he dropped his mask of cordiality with the sheriff. He warned Dupnik, as the sheriff put it later, "that something bad was going to happen to me and the State Department was going to do it."[6]*

---

*About two weeks after this threat Dupnik received a call from someone in the State Department who told him that he had done the right thing.

In the meantime, throughout southern Arizona people reacted to the tragedy with spontaneous generosity. Money was collected to send telegrams to the state's congressional delegation and other federal officials, urging that the refugees not be sent back. Carla Pedersen's phone calls helped launch a major effort to free the refugees. The Reverend David ("Dave") Sholin, the pastor of her church, St. Mark's Presbyterian, immediately called members of the session of the Presbyterian Church in Arizona and the Catholic diocese in Phoenix to raise the necessary bond money. "We consider the mess in El Salvador to be so dangerous that anybody who could get out would want to," Sholin declared.[7] Within days the churches, aided by local businessmen, politicians, and lawyers, had raised $2,000 to free the fourteen survivors. A representative of the German magazine *Der Stern* offered to post the entire bond in return for exclusive interviews with the refugees, but one of their attorneys angrily refused the offer. "I don't sell my clients," she told the Germans.

One of the first ministers contacted was the Reverend John Fife, the tall, razor-thin pastor of Southside Presbyterian Church, a small congregation in the barrio of south Tucson. Of all the activist clergy in Tucson, John Macmillan Fife was the most visible and indisputably the most charismatic. A warm, open man with a ready smile, a trim beard, and an ever-present cigarette, the forty-year-old minister wore his calling with a western sense of style. His habitual uniform was a clerical collar atop a dark shirt, a large silver cross, a big turquoise belt buckle, skintight jeans, and cowboy boots. At six feet four inches and 145 pounds, he looked like a lanky cowboy in clerical drag. In fact, Fife was from western Pennsylvania, but he was spiritually and emotionally at home in the West, with its white-water rivers, its relaxed informality, and its outspoken citizenry.

Fife's casual, iconoclastic temperament was particularly well suited to Tucson, where he had settled some ten years earlier. The liberal university town of some half a million people had never been dominated by one industry or a tightly organized power structure. Its economic community had always been relatively democratic, and Tucsonians were accustomed to ready access to their political leaders. It was a town of professionals, service workers, and small businessmen; retirees and students; and not a few maturing flower children of the sixties who had chosen the city not just for its climate but for its free spirit and lively arts scene. Despite the new office buildings going up downtown and the spreading urban sprawl, the city's self-image remained that of a frontier community. Eastern visitors were often struck by the independent they-can't-tell-me-what-to-think-or-do spirit of the place.

Throughout the 1970s there had been a very strong political movement in Tucson oriented to the environment and aimed at controlling growth. Many local churches had also taken the lead in what activists called "peace and justice" issues. Fife had been in the forefront of many of those campaigns, and when Dave Sholin had called about the desert survivors, he had immediately responded by helping raise money.

Like other disaster stories, the news of the tragedy quickly faded out of the media. But the episode had a lasting effect on the community and gave the citizens of Tucson, unlike the great majority of other Americans, an education on the troubles brewing in Central America.

The desert incident hinted at a massive violation of human rights on the very doorstep of the United States. Fife, peering around the corner at middle age, had been thinking of cutting back on his hectic schedule to spend more time with his wife and two teenaged sons. But the appearance of the refugees was not the kind of thing he could ignore. The minister's entire career had been a microcosm of the social activism that had swept the country during the 1960s and 1970s, and he wasn't about to change in 1980, although the country itself was poised to do just that.

John Fife hadn't set out to become an advocate of the poor and downtrodden. The son of a conservative Presbyterian minister in rural western Pennsylvania, he had grown up absorbing all the values of what he later described as a Norman Rockwell existence, bounded by God, country, and the Boy Scouts.[8] The idyll had ended when he was nine and his father died, leaving his mother to support two children on a high school Latin teacher's salary. By the time he became a scholarship boy at Washington and Jefferson College, a men's school near Pittsburgh, John Fife was determined to make his way in the world, have a good time, and never be poor again.

In no time the skinny eighteen-year-old was a fraternity man in a button-down shirt, traveling to national conventions and rubbing elbows with corporate lawyers and businessmen. He thought he had arrived, and he planned to become a doctor because doctors seemed to have more money than anyone else he had ever met.

"I loved it; I was having a ball," the minister later recalled. "But one of the sidebars to that was that I did a lot of drinking. In fact, I got to the point about my junior year where I was putting a can of beer by my bed at night to get going the next morning. I'd wake up and crack it and drink it so I could make it to the shower. One morning I did that and said to myself, 'You're not going to live a long time, buddy, if you keep this up.' At that point I started to raise all the questions that some college people do. 'What are my values? What do I really want to do with my life?'—That sort of thing."

The identity crisis ended with a decision to drop medicine and return to the church, and from his first year at the Pittsburgh Theological Seminary, John Fife's course was set. Years later he recalled that many of his teachers were German theologians and biblical scholars who again and again, to illustrate a point, referred to the passivity of the state-dominated German Protestant churches of the 1930s and 1940s, which had largely ignored Hitler's persecution of the Jews. The church's moral obligations and social responsibilities became central to the young seminarian's faith just as a rare and heady moment in American history was beginning, a time when morality and politics came together.

Fife was on the historic civil rights march from Selma to Montgomery, Alabama, in the spring of 1965. He was arrested in sit-ins to integrate whites-only public facilities in Pittsburgh and was booked for picketing the suburban lawns of slum landlords. He spent his summers on an Indian reservation in Arizona, where he courted his future wife, and his first real job was a ghetto ministry in the black slums of Canton, Ohio. As his black parishioners might have put it, he was "baaad" in the name of good. All this had come together in 1970, when the thirty-year-old pastor took up the challenge at Southside Presbyterian in Tucson.

John Fife's new church had begun in 1906 as an Indian mission project on the outskirts of town in an Indian shantytown called Papago-ville, after the largest tribe in the area. The Papagos and the Pima Indians in Arizona had been Christianized and educated by the Presbyterians, and as the tribesmen gradually drifted into town for work, they identified themselves as Presbyterians. Their arrival prompted the members of the existing Presbyterian church to raise funds for the Indians to build their own church in their own neighborhood.

"They wanted to make sure the Indians wouldn't come to their nice respectable church," Fife related, "and that was the auspicious beginning of Southside."

Southside had always been a national mission project of the Presbyterian Church, one of a number of churches partially supported by contributions from the national denomination. The congregation had never generated enough income to pay its expenses, including the minister's modest stipend of $14,000. But it served a minority population with special needs and fulfilled certain responsibilities in the community that the Presbyterian Church believed were important. As a member of one of the governing councils of the church later put it, "Churches like Southside help the Presbyterian Church stay a church."[9]

One of Fife's predecessors at Southside had been the black leader of Tucson in the late 1950s and early 1960s, a figure in all the civil rights struggles in the city. "So this church, early on, had a very clear commitment and understood that their pastor ought to provide some leadership to the community in terms of social justice issues," Fife related during a conversation in the living room of the rectory at Southside, a small room dominated by a large bronze sculpture of a Guatemalan refugee woman.

"That was my frame of reference. I knew that this had been one of the best urban congregations in the country, and I wanted to be the pastor of that congregation. It was diverse; it had blacks, Hispanics, and Indians; it was in the Southwest, which I loved; and it was a perfect location for an urban ministry. Right next door to downtown, right in the middle of the barrio, where the ministry is obvious—you don't have to agonize about what to do next."

The church building, with its three-foot-thick adobe walls and simple whitewashed bell tower, dated back to 1911 or 1912. The new minister freshened up the tower with a coat of bright blue paint and a new bell, which he took to ringing ceremonially at the end of every Sunday service. Inside the small sanctuary a large wooden cross, draped with a white cloth or occasionally an Indian textile, stood behind the pulpit. Three rows of chairs lined both sides of the chapel, and an organ completed the Spartan decor.

Fife's first task was to rebuild the congregation, which had dwindled to a mere two dozen people. He made calls all over the neighborhood, sitting in the modest houses and apartments, trying to convince skeptical poor people that they should listen to this smooth-talking stranger every Sunday. In a stroke of theatrical genius he persuaded a powerful black organist to leave her Baptist church and play for Southside, and he had no doubt that her booming gospel rhythms and Mahalia Jackson-like voice probably attracted more new parishioners than his own earnest appeals.

At the end of two years Southside still had only a handful of regular members, maybe 100 or so, but that was enough to persuade the national presbytery that the mission should continue. By that time the new pastor was already involved in more good causes than even he could handle. He helped put together a group of young Indians concerned about treaty violations. He became involved in a fight for public housing in the neighborhood, a dreary expanse of run-down houses, boarded-up shops, and government housing projects within walking distance of the clean and prosperous center of the city. He was instrumental in forming a community food bank and helping the farm workers organize.

One of Fife's colleagues in these struggles was Father Ricardo Elford, a Catholic priest who had arrived in Tucson at around the same time. Father Ricardo, a small white-haired man in his early forties, was a member of the Redemptorists, a Catholic order devoted to the poor, and St. Francis himself was no more fiercely dedicated to the cause of the underprivileged. Elford was like an armadillo: Underneath his deceptively frail exterior lurked one of the toughest animals in the desert.

The priest had been assigned the task of becoming the presence of the Catholic Church in the South Side barrio. Fife recognized that a Protestant couldn't operate in a Mexican-Indian barrio unless he had some working understanding with the Catholic Church, and inevitably the two men became friends and comrades-in-arms.

One of their first campaigns involved a golf course that the city had put right in the middle of the barrio.

"All of the business people and lawyers and doctors in the downtown area would just bop over there in five minutes and play golf," Fife recalled later, with undimmed, almost boyish enthusiasm. "It was a very nice golf course, called El Rio, but there was nothing there for the barrio. One of the first things that happened after I got here, back in 1970 or 1971, was the mobilization of the whole barrio to get the city to put a community center and a park and education facilities in that golf course area. That was where we all came together and acquired some experience and had a success under our belts. It was pretty heady stuff. We found out that by golly, not only could we work together, but we could change things. And that spilled over into all kinds of things throughout the 1970s."

During the next few years in Tucson a small group, including Fife and Elford, became seasoned social reformers who knew how to take into consideration each other's strengths and weaknesses and effect real change. In retrospect, Fife believed that the experience was a major reason why Tucson was able to respond as it did when the refugee crisis arrived.

At the same time John Fife was becoming a national figure within the Presbyterian Church. In 1973 he was elected the representative of the Presbyterians of Arizona and New Mexico on the national policy-making council. That body of forty-six individuals, half clergy and half laity, has responsibility for national programs and budget and the international mission of the church. (The Presbyterian Church is organized on a representative basis, with power shared by the clergy and the laity.) The council met at 475 Riverside Drive on the Upper West Side of Manhattan, in a tall white building known as the "God Box" because of the numerous religious organizations headquartered there. From 1974 to 1981 Fife was in New York City almost monthly as part of his work on the council.

He became acquainted not only with the leadership of the Presbyterian Church but with most of the other individuals working nationally on social policy issues. He was chairman of the committee that reviewed all the investments of the Presbyterian Church and filed shareholder resolutions. For several exhilarating years he was one of those who negotiated with corporations over changes in business practices that the church questioned on ethical grounds. A Savonarola of the boardrooms, he was involved in almost every corporate responsibility issue that came up, from South Africa to nuclear power plants to the sale of computers to Argentina and Chile. He helped organize the Nestlé boycott, protesting the company's sale of infant formula in the third world, and negotiated with Coca-Cola to buy out the controversial manager of a bottling plant in Guatemala.

"Most churches do that whole shareholder resolution thing as a symbolic gesture. We did not," Fife later recounted proudly. "I think we had an influence on Exxon's decision not to invest in uranium mines in South Africa. One of the more interesting experiences came out of our annual negotiations with General Motors over their South African policies. Somebody inside GM anonymously leaked to us a whole series of communications between Detroit and General Motors managers in South Africa, about how they were organizing their white employees in a paramilitary group to defend the plant in the event of a revolution.

They also had a secret agreement with the South African government to convert to military production immediately in that event. We released the documents immediately to the press in Detroit, at which point Tom Murphy [then the chief executive officer of GM] called me and said, 'How can you do this to us?'

"I said, 'Tom, you've been talking to us for five years now, and you assured us that you abhorred apartheid and that you were certainly not cooperating with the government in any way. Now we get these documents. The point is, you've been kidding us, fella, not the other way around. Of course, we're still open to talking with you, but we're going to do this straight up if we're going to do it again.'

"Three days later I was sitting in the GM boardroom having a serious discussion. And we were able to get them to make some significant changes in terms of black union recognition, desegregation of facilities, training programs for blacks in the organization.

"I had to do my homework for all of this. I was involved not only with the ministry here, but I also had to be prepared enough to sit down with the CEO [chief executive officer] of General Motors throughout that period. I was literally bouncing back and forth between the boardroom and the barrio. It was a fascinating kind of existence. We were also involved in Washington with coalitions trying to affect public policies on things like Agent Orange. All this and dealing with the policies of our church generally. In retrospect I think that it was all one hell of a training program for when the refugees started showing up."

In all this activity John Fife had acted not simply as an individual, but as an executor of the national policies of the Presbyterian Church. He was typical of the many pastors and lay leaders in the mainstream Protestant denominations who believe that they have a responsibility not just to represent their congregations but to exercise a broader moral leadership, to be, in other words, prophetic, no matter how unpopular their message might be.

This strain in American Protestantism is at least as old as the Social Gospel of the late nineteenth century, with its challenge to the excesses of unrestrained industrial capitalism. Woodrow Wilson, the son of a Presbyterian minister, represented that tradition in public life. But the events in Germany in the 1930s gave new life to the prophetic calling. Most German Protestant leaders had watched the triumph of the Nazis in silence or, in some cases, had actively supported Hitler's rise to power, and that unhappy history gave rise to a "never again" consensus in the mainstream American religious community that the church must take a position on issues that raise important ethical questions.

The clergy of many mainline denominations were in the forefront of social change in the 1960s and 1970s. They were clearly to the left of the average congregation in this, a fact that may at least partially explain the relatively rapid growth of more conservative fundamentalism. In any event, by the 1980s, when the secular left virtually evaporated in the face of the popularity of Ronald Reagan, the mainline churches were left virtually alone as the only outspoken opposition party in the United States.

While the press celebrated the Reagan magic, and the public turned to its own concerns, religious leaders challenged almost every aspect of the administration's policies, from military spending to cuts in social services. They took these stands despite the fact that most of their members were more conservative than they, prompting theologian Martin Marty to quip that American Protestantism had become a "two-party system."[10]

Yet in the eyes of men like John Fife the principle was unambiguous: The church was morally bound to do what it could to resist injustice, despotism, and terror.

Chapter
Two

When I feed the poor, I am called a saint. When I ask why the poor are hungry, I am called a Communist.
—DOM HELDER CAMARA,
retired Bishop of Recife, Brazil

E L SALVADOR, IN the late 1970s, was a very sick place. A Peace Corps volunteer, who later became a poet, was invited to dine at the home of a colonel in those years, and after the lamb and the French wine, to impress his seriousness upon her, he brought out a fistful of human ears he kept in a sack.[1]

El Salvador had always been a country dominated by a very few wealthy families and their armed enforcers, lording it over a scorned and impoverished majority.* For most of its existence no one had paid much attention to the suffering, for El Salvador is a very small country, barely the size of Massachusetts and smaller than Pima County, Arizona, where the Salvadoran travail was soon to become a burning issue.

For years observers had been warning that one day the overcrowded country would blow up like one of its smoking volcanoes. "I imagine

---

*"For hundreds of years there were very few who were so wealthy they had everything. The rest of the people had to pay for it, and they paid in misery and injustice . . . we cannot ignore this is the reason we have the violence in my country," Salvadoran President José Napoleón Duarte declared in a speech before the National Press Club during a state visit to Washington, D.C., on October 15, 1987.

13

Ann Crittenden

the situation in El Salvador today is very much like France was before its revolution, Russia before its revolution and Mexico before its revolution," wrote one visitor. "A socialist or communistic revolution in El Salvador may be delayed for several years, ten or even twenty, but when it comes it will be a bloody one."[2]

This gloomy forecast was made back in 1931 by one Major R. A. Harris, then the U.S. attaché for Central American military affairs. Less than a year later a peasant revolt did break out and threaten to become the much-feared upheaval before it was brutally put down by the military. To ensure that the countryside would never again support such a rebellion, the authorities, in an event that became known as *la Matanza* ("massacre"), hunted down and killed thousands of peasants and Indians, virtually eradicating the country's rich Indian language, dress, and culture. No one knows how many people died, but the most commonly cited estimate is 30,000.

For the next fifty years a partnership of the military and the oligarchy ensured that there would be no more free elections, no independent judicial system, no reforms. The slightest efforts to redistribute land or income or to establish democratic institutions were labeled Communist or Communist-inspired.

Inevitably in such a climate resistance groups began to form. After the military overturned the presidential election of José Napoleón Duarte in 1972 and as the economic situation worsened,* popular organizations of students, workers, and peasants became increasingly militant.

Public demonstrations against the government became more and

---

*After a period of relative prosperity in the 1960s, conditions in the rural areas had become worse in the late 1970s than they had been in decades. The same few families still dominated production and processing of the three principal crops: coffee, cotton, and sugar. A handful of interests owned the largest banks, insurance companies, and utilities, the choicest real estate, the most important construction and manufacturing companies.

At the other end of the economic spectrum, the poorest 40 percent of the population, jammed into one of the world's most crowded countries, made do with 7.5 percent of the national income. The statistics sanitize the brutal reality: In the late seventies 40 percent of the peasantry had no land, even to rent or to work as sharecroppers, three-quarters of rural children were malnourished, three-quarters of the people had no access to safe water, two-thirds of the people were illiterate, and only 8 percent of children aged thirteen to fifteen went to school. In two provinces there was a total of 5 doctors, or 1 for every 90,000 inhabitants, and in those places 1 of every 10 children died before his or her first birthday.

more frequent, and people were caught up in protest like dry leaves in a fire. Guerrilla groups began to proliferate, kidnapping and threatening the elite. The military government reacted with brutality, and political assassination, disappearances (describing those who are picked up by the police, the military, or death squads and never seen again), and torture were rampant.

One of the principal targets of the savage repression was the Catholic Church. After centuries of alliance with the status quo, by the late 1960s the church in Latin America had begun to stir. Increasingly, priests and even bishops were raising questions about the morality of existing political and economic arrangements. In 1968, at a meeting in Medellín, Colombia, the bishops of Latin America seemed to ratify the grass-roots appeal from within the church for a new commitment to the poor. Their final statement declared that the Christian "is not unaware that in many places in Latin America there is a situation of injustice that must be recognized as institutionalized violence, because the existing structures violate people's basic rights: a situation which calls for far-reaching, daring, urgent and profoundly innovative change."

Nowhere did this liberation theology fall on more fertile ground than in El Salvador. Parish priests began to live in the villages, teaching a new kind of Christianity that challenged the traditional fatalism of the peasantry. Following a growing practice throughout Latin America, priests conducted nightly meetings at which the Bible was read and discussed. The parishioners were encouraged to explain what they thought its passages meant in terms of their own daily lives. In the 1970s the ratio of parishioners to priests in El Salvador was 10,000 to 1, so the priests would move on to another village after two weeks, electing lay preachers (Delegates of the Word) to continue the Scripture readings and discussions.

These Christian base communities *(communidades de base)* sprang up all over El Salvador. Informal gatherings led by lay church workers, teachers, and catechists, they were part religious service, part political discussion, and part town meeting, where local problems and possible solutions were aired. The Bible study, and the liberation theology that guided it, proved to be revolutionary. The Gospel teachings that all people are the children of God and that all are loved equally by God awakened a new hope and anger in the poor. It was inevitable that the powers that be would see it all as Communist-inspired sedition. In fact, it had nothing to do with Marxist-Leninism; it was a new vision of

Christianity. But the governments were right: it was profoundly subversive.

One by one the activist priests, including numerous foreigners, were picked up, tortured, and murdered. Between February and July 1977, seven priests were refused reentry into El Salvador, eight were expelled, two were killed, two tortured, one beaten, two imprisoned, and four threatened with death. All protests, demonstrations, land occupations, and kidnappings by the rapidly growing guerrilla forces were blamed on the Catholic Church. In March 1977 Father Rutilio Grande, a Salvadoran Jesuit who had pioneered the base community movement there, was machine-gunned to death while driving to mass in his Land-Rover. Two months later the priest's village of Aguilares, a town of 10,000 in a valley of absentee-owned sugarcane plantations, was invaded by the army, shot up, burned, and occupied for a month. In the aftermath 50 people were killed, and hundreds more, including many women and children, disappeared. The military dubbed the massacre Operation Rutilio.

In all, sixteen Catholic religious leaders—roughly 3 percent of the Catholic clergy—were murdered in El Salvador between the killing of the popular priest and December 1980. And that month four American women church workers—three nuns and a lay church worker—were found raped and murdered. They had been shot by Salvadoran national guardsmen who believed that the women were "subversives."

Shortly before Father Rutilio's death a new archbishop had been appointed in El Salvador. A man with a conservative reputation, Archbishop Oscar Arnulfo Romero gradually became the principal spokesman against the repression and the most popular political figure in the country. As the violence mounted, Romero became increasingly outspoken, to the point where U.S. officials, who feared that his attacks would weaken the governing junta and by extension the war against the guerrillas, tried to persuade him to moderate his position.

On March 24, 1980, Romero paid the price for his courage. The day before, he had conducted a four-hour mass in which he issued a special appeal to the men of the army, the National Guard, and the police. "Brothers," he cried, "you are part of our people. You kill your own peasant brothers and sisters. And before an order to kill that a man might give, the law of God must prevail that says: Thou shalt not kill! No soldier is obliged to obey an order against the law of God. No one has to fulfill an immoral law." The next day, as he was reciting the

Twenty-third Psalm at mass, the archbishop was shot dead, a bullet through his heart.[3]

The assassination of the archbishop signaled an all-out war. Hard-line army officers had gradually taken power within the governing junta, and they were determined to crush every effort to wrest power from the traditional elite. Leaders of the reformist political parties were murdered. Students, professors, and teachers, clergy and lay church workers, village leaders, union organizers, and agrarian reform work-ers—everyone who might even be a potential member of the opposi-tion—came under suspicion and the scrutiny of the death squads, and many of those who weren't killed ultimately decided that life was no longer possible in their country.

At the same time, in January 1981 the growing guerrilla forces launched what they claimed would be their "final offensive," and two-thirds of the country became the scene of major military actions. A long and bloody war of attrition began, with its principal victims, as always, the civilian noncombatants.

According to the legal aid office of the Roman Catholic Church in El Salvador, at least 40,000 civilians were killed between October 1979 and the beginning of 1984.* An estimated half million more people were driven from their homes and villages between 1980 and 1982. Many of the displaced persons remained within El Salvador, in refugee camps and slums around the capital city. Others fled to camps in neighboring Honduras and in Mexico. But in those first two years of the 1980s more than 100,000 people made the trip north to seek entry through the golden door into the United States, the fabled haven of the world's oppressed.

. . .

The Salvadorans could not have picked a worse time to test the quality of mercy in American immigration policy.

Just when they began turning up along the U.S.-Mexican border, hundreds of thousands of other refugees were suddenly seeking safety in the United States: Iranian students, Haitian peasants, Nicaraguans

---

*By 1987 the civilian casualties were estimated at 60,000, or more than 1 percent of the total population. An estimated one-third of the country was still a war zone, after seven years of conflict. As a point of comparison, by 1987, six years after the first AIDS case had been reported, an estimated 33,000 people in the United States had contracted the disease, or 0.00015 percent of the population.

fleeing the new Sandinista regime, and, above all, Cubans. In the spring of 1980 a flotilla of boats, carrying more than 100,000 people, set out of Havana's Mariel Harbor bound for South Florida.

The infamous Marielitos, including the dregs of Cuban prisons and mental institutions, were able to stay, although many remained in detention. Iranian students, trying to escape the clutches of the ayatollah who had recently come to power in Teheran, were allowed to remain. The Nicaraguans were given a temporary safe haven. All were fleeing regimes the United States considered enemies. But the Haitians and the Salvadorans, victims of governments that Washington counted as friendly, found America's gates shut firmly in their faces.

This was nothing new. The United States is a rightly celebrated haven for the displaced and the persecuted. It has accepted more refugees than the rest of the world combined—more than 2 million people—since World War II alone, and is a major contributor to international refugee agencies. In addition, more than 400,000 people are accepted yearly under regular immigration procedures. Yet that is not the whole story. As the authors of *Calculated Kindness*, a meticulous study of postwar refugee policy, point out, "For each statistic of welcome, there is another of exclusion, for each example of the open door, there is another of the door banging shut."[4]

The other part of the story is that *more than 90 percent* of those 2 million refugees admitted outside the regular immigration system since World War II were from Communist countries. Cold war ideology has dictated who, of all those fleeing persecution, would be embraced by Lady Liberty. Those who were principally excluded by this "politics of escape" were mostly our closest neighbors, the hundreds of thousands of Salvadorans, Guatemalans, Haitians, Chileans, and Argentines fleeing civil war and brutal repression in recent years.

The numbers tell the tale by themselves. Between 1952 and 1968, 232,711 refugees from Communist countries, most of them Cubans, were admitted into the United States, compared with 925 refugees from non-Communist countries. Even after the United States had became a party to the United Nations 1967 Protocol Relating to the Status of Refugees, thereby binding itself to a nonideological definition of a refugee, anticommunism still determined who was granted a safe haven and who was not. The United States admitted only 7,150 refugees from non-Communist countries between 1968 and 1980, compared with 608,365 people fleeing Communist regimes (including 290,075 from

Indochina and 232,666 from Cuba). Only 4,400 refugees were admitted from all the rest of Latin America in that period, despite the advent of authoritarian regimes in Chile, Argentina, and Uruguay and continual human rights abuses in Central America and Haiti. As one refugee expert put it, "the parole power was used almost exclusively to bring in those fleeing communism."[5]

The Reagan administration found this cold war approach to refugee policy completely congenial and continued it with zeal. In the opinion of some experts on refugee policy, the virulence of the government's campaign against Haitian and Salvadoran asylum seekers in recent years has been unmatched.[6]

By 1982 more than 1 million people had fled rightist governments in Central America, yet Elliott Abrams, then the assistant secretary of state for human rights, in a speech that year managed to assert that "it is Communist rule that caused the greatest refugee flows of recent years."[7] At a time—between 1980 and 1982—when the illegal Salvadoran population in the United States suddenly shot up from an estimated 94,000 to between 300,000 and 500,000[8] and when Guatemalans were streaming into Mexico at the rate of 2,000 to 3,500 people a week,[9] the man responsible for humanitarian affairs in the State Department maintained that the exodus was purely economic.

Ideology and geopolitics were reinforced by the "floodgate" argument: that if the United States decided to admit all those fleeing war or repression in this hemisphere, an entire subcontinent might walk in in their wake. This fear of the so-called magnet effect—that for every person admitted, a horde of friends and relatives would follow—accounts for much of the discrimination against refugees from neighboring countries.

It is a very real fear. Salvadorans can earn wages five to ten times higher in the United States than in El Salvador, if they are lucky enough to find jobs there at all. One poll often cited by the Reagan administration asked 4,000 Salvadorans the question "If you had the opportunity, would you emigrate to the United States?" Sixty-seven percent answered yes. With complete, and some would call uncharacteristic, candor, Assistant Secretary of State Abrams told Congress in 1985 that El Salvador's proximity to the United States and its history of illegal economic migration were reasons why the Reagan administration opposed giving Salvadorans a safe haven in the United States.[10]

Thus, anticommunism and fears of massive immigration combined to stack the deck against ill-fated refugees from Central America and the Caribbean.*

From mid-1980, soon after the civil wars in Central America began, to mid-1985, a grand total of 626 Salvadorans was granted political asylum in the United States, out of more than 10,000 that applied.[11] From mid-1983 to September 1986, 14 percent of Nicaraguans, 2.6 percent of Salvadorans, 1.8 percent of Haitians, and 0.9 percent of Guatemalans who requested political asylum were granted it, compared with 60.4 percent of Iranians, 37.7 percent of Afghans, 34 percent of Poles, and an average approval rate for all nationalities of 23.3 percent (see chart).

This discrimination was supposed to have been eliminated by a refugee act passed in 1980. Congress in that year passed a new law establishing a humanitarian, nonideological definition of a refugee. Before 1980 U.S. refugee law had been blatantly political. It had specified that refugees *had* to come from Communist countries or the Middle East; if the government wanted to admit any exceptions the attorney general had to use his discretionary parole authority. The Refugee Act of 1980 tried to introduce a fairer system by incorporating the United Nations definition of refugee into U.S. law, defining as a refugee *anyone* with a "well-founded fear of persecution" for reasons of "race, religion, nationality, membership in a particular social group or political opinion. . . ."**

But the new U.S. law was not as completely neutral as some refugee advocates later argued. It referred to the admission of refugees "of special humanitarian concern to the United States," in effect enabling the government to give preferences to certain refugee groups. Moreover, according to the operating instructions that accompanied the new

---

*A report in late 1982 by the Refugee Policy Group, a nonpartisan research organization based in Washington, D.C., summed up the rationale for the Reagan administration's refusal to grant the Salvadorans a safe haven: "The U.S. position is probably based on two considerations. If U.S. officials were to grant large scale political asylum or extended voluntary departure status to Salvadorans, these actions would constitute an admission that the Salvadoran government is both unable to defeat the guerrilla insurgents and unable to control its own security forces. Second, such actions would encourage an even larger scale Salvadoran entry, and oblige the U.S. to grant legal status and benefits to the entrants."

**This language originated with the 1951 United Nations Refugee Convention; hence the term *Convention refugee* is sometimes used to refer to individuals with a "well-founded fear of persecution."

Asylum Cases Filed with INS District Directors, Approved and Denied, by Nationality, June 1983 to September 1986

Country	Approval Rate for Cases Decided	Cases Granted	Cases Denied
TOTAL	23.3%	18,701	61,717
Iran	60.4%	10,728	7,005
Romania	51.0%	424	406
Czechoslovakia	45.4%	99	119
Afghanistan	37.7%	344	567
Poland	34.0%	1,806	3,495
Hungary	31.9%	137	292
Syria	30.2%	114	263
Ethiopia	29.2%	734	1,774
Vietnam	26.0%	50	142
Uganda	25.3%	75	221
China	21.4%	84	307
Philippines	20.9%	77	291
Somalia	15.6%	74	399
Nicaragua	14.0%	2,602	15,856
Iraq	12.1%	91	655
Yugoslavia	11.0%	31	249
Liberia	8.4%	20	218
Pakistan	6.5%	26	370
Cuba[a]	4.9%	99	1,906
El Salvador	2.6%	528	19,207
Honduras	2.5%	6	234
Lebanon	2.4%	34	1,338
Haiti[b]	1.8%	30	1,631
Guatemala	.9%	14	1,461
India	.3%	1	311
Egypt	.2%	2	703
Bangladesh	.0%	0	403

[a]There were 89,606 cases from Cuba pending at the end of FY 86.

[b]There were 2,042 cases from Haiti pending at the end of FY 86.

Source: Immigration and Naturalization Service (INS)/U.S. Department of Justice.

Note: Starting in May 1983, the Immigration and Naturalization Service kept asylum statistics by number of cases. Each case, or application, may include more than one individual. From June to September 1982 and October 1982 to April 1983, INS asylum figures were for actual number of individuals. To avoid inconsistency, this chart includes data only since INS data was based on number of cases. Nationalities shown are those that had 100 or more cases decided in any one of the fiscal year periods included. The total includes all nationalities.

This chart is based on data for asylum cases filed with INS district directors only. Many applications for asylum are filed with immigration judges, particularly in the context of deportation proceedings. The Office of the Chief Immigration Judge is developing a data system, but asylum statistics are not now available.

procedures under the act, applicants from the Soviet Union and Eastern bloc nations were to receive immediate action. Even under the 1980 law, then, all refugees were to be considered equal, but some were to be more equal than others.

Most important, the new law did not mean that many or even most of the Salvadorans, Guatemalans, and Nicaraguans fleeing their war-torn countries automatically qualified as refugees. The United Nations refugee definition that was adopted into U.S. law *excludes* people displaced by military operations, civil strife, or natural disasters. Thus many immigration experts argue that most Salvadorans do not qualify for political asylum in the United States because they are fleeing a generalized climate of terror and violence rather than specific threats to their lives.

The new law also failed to foresee a historic development: that future refugees were likely to be physically at the border rather than at camps thousands of miles away. In the past the United States had always been a country of "second asylum," admitting refugees like those from post-war Europe or Southeast Asia after they had already left their home-lands and made their way to "first asylum" countries. The United States has had the luxury of screening potential refugees and choosing those it wanted to allow to enter the country.

Assuming this situation would continue, the Refugee Act of 1980 provided for political asylum—the admission of someone who was already within or at the U.S. border—almost as an afterthought and only after strenuous lobbying by various human rights groups and the urging of the United Nations High Commissioner for Refugees. The granting of asylum was made discretionary. The act requires that the U.S. attorney general "shall establish a procedure for an alien physi-cally present in the U.S. or at a land border or port of entry, irrespective of such alien's status, to apply for asylum, and the alien may be granted asylum at the discretion of the Attorney General if the Attorney Gen-eral determines that such alien is a refugee within the definition (pro-vided in the Act)."

The new law was signed on March 17, 1980. One month later the hurricane struck. On April 20 the first boats carrying Cubans out of Mariel Harbor began arriving in Miami. The invasion didn't stop for five months, and when it had ended, there were 125,000 additional Cubans on U.S. soil, all demanding safe haven. It was an event that had been completely unforeseen by the new law.

American officials responded by instructing the Marielitos to submit individual claims for asylum. More than 50,000 of them did.

The same year the Immigration Service advised Iranians in the United States whose visas had expired and who did not want to return home to file claims for political asylum. There were in the United States about 225,000 Iranian students, the largest contingent of foreign students in the country, and many of them eventually sought asylum.

In the fall of 1980 the Immigration Service also advised Nicaraguans in the United States who were unwilling to return and live under the Sandinista government to file asylum claims.

As a result of these three events, within six months of the passage of the 1980 act, more than 100,000 claims for political asylum had been filed. All this had happened before the beleaguered bureaucrats in the Immigration Service had even begun to analyze the new reality: that the United States had become a country of first asylum and that it had to put in place machinery to process refugees arriving directly at the border.

The thinking within the INS bureaucracy in 1980 was that there were countries of refugee origin—Vietnam, Cambodia, the Soviet Union, Poland, Afghanistan—and countries of illegal economic migration—Mexico, El Salvador, Haiti. The Immigration Service was not comfortable with the complex notion that some countries might produce both refugees and economic migrants. It could deal even less with the messy fact that many people on the move, be they Poles, Salvadorans, or Southeast Asians, were leaving their homelands for a complicated mix of economic and political reasons.

The Salvadorans in particular had a history of migrating north for jobs. It was hard for immigration officials to recognize that among the sudden flood of newcomers might be many authentic refugees, who were fleeing bullets, bombs, and men in unmarked cars. The last thing the beleaguered INS wanted to do was to establish procedures to sort the genuine refugees out from the chaff of the economic migrants, to generate *more* asylum applicants.[12]

The new Republican team in the Justice Department, of which the Immigration Service is a part, found it particularly easy to dismiss the Central Americans as "economic." In January 1981 Justice had been taken over by conservative Californians determined to establish tighter border control. They believed that their predecessors in the previous administration had been pitifully lenient on immigration in general and were convinced that Jimmy Carter's open-door policy toward the Cubans had helped lose the 1980 election for the Democrat. There was a we're-not-going-to-let-those-illegals-take-advantage-of-us-again mentality among the newcomers that continued throughout the administration.[13] Despite Ronald Reagan's generous rhetoric, a harder line was quickly taken against refugees from *all* countries, and the number of proposed refugee allocations steadily declined, from 173,000 in 1981–82 to 70,000 in 1985–86.

The Justice Department and the Immigration Service were traditionally the hard-boiled naysayers on refugee admissions, while the State Department had historically acted as the soft guy, usually because admissions served broader foreign policy goals. In the case of the Central Americans, however, that normal balance broke down. The new men responsible for Central America at State tended to be ideological hard-liners who saw the conflict in the region as an East-West struggle for power.* They were anxious to support the Salvadoran and Guatemalan militaries in their struggle against leftists and as a bulwark against the Sandinistas. As a result, State as well as Justice stood against the refugees in a united front that was fatal to their cause.

*It was recently reported that the CIA and American officials in El Salvador knew in 1980 or 1981 the names of those implicated in death squad killings, including the murder of Archbishop Romero, but did nothing. Asked why, an American who had served in El Salvador at the time replied, "The CIA didn't mind what was going on so long as they were killing Communists."[14]

Chapter
Three

Do not neglect to show hospitality to strangers, for thereby some have entertained angels unawares. Remember those . . . who are ill-treated, since you also are in the body.

—HEBREWS 13:1–2

JOHN FIFE AND Ricardo Elford had no way of knowing how formidable the odds against the Salvadorans were. They had been learning about events in Central America through their respective church grapevines, a reporting network made up of the hundreds of American missionaries, priests, and nuns stationed in the area. The clergy were in effect a private diplomatic corps with deep ties to the people of the region, and that fall and winter of 1980 the word sent back to thousands of churches in America was that, contrary to what American officials were saying, a bloodbath was going on. It appeared that the liberation church in El Salvador and Guatemala was rapidly being purged out of existence.

Like many other religious activists in the United States, Fife and Elford were deeply attracted to liberation theology, with its cry for social and economic justice and a new political order, and their immediate fear was for the survival of the movement. For months the two clergymen talked about what they could do to attract public attention to the bloody drama unfolding to the south. Trying to recall what had worked for them in the past, they remembered a recent victory on behalf of a young Yaqui Indian, who had been shot in the back by a policeman. Elford had tried unsuccessfully to have charges brought against the officer, and when the county and the state refused to take action, he had organized a thirty-minute prayer vigil with the family. After several weeks the federal authorities had finally brought violation of civil rights charges against the officer.

"Why not organize another prayer vigil?" the priest suggested. "You get some people from your congregation and I'll find some people and we'll see what happens."[1]

The vigil began on the afternoon of February 19, 1981. As the first office workers were beginning to trickle home, some twenty people, carrying placards and signs, paraded in a slow circle in front of Tucson's new Federal Building. At 5:00 P.M. Father Ricardo, as he was known to the community, spoke about events in Central America, read a lesson from Scripture, and offered a prayer for the people and the church of the region. It was all over in thirty minutes. The organizers of the modest event would have been astounded had they known that the vigil would become the longest-running continuous demonstration in the United States and that more than six years later it, like the war it protested, would still be dragging on.

Among those who regularly showed up at the demonstration were Margo Cowan and Lupe Castillo, two political organizers with formidable experience in *mano a mano* combat with officialdom. Both women were with the Manzo Area Council, a private social service agency that assisted undocumented Hispanics, mostly Mexicans, with their immigration problems.

Manzo, originally a child of the War on Poverty, had had a brief brush with the law once, in 1976, when four of its female staff members had been indicted by the Justice Department on charges of transporting and aiding and abetting the presence of illegal aliens in the United States. Essentially what they had been doing was advising undocumented Mexicans of their legal rights, driving them to appointments, and otherwise facilitating their lives in Tucson, without alerting the federal government to their presence. As Manzo saw it, the basic issue was whether social agencies in the United States had the right to help undocumented people and whether, if they did so without reporting them, they were guilty of violating the law.[2]

The issue was never put to a test in court, for as it happened, the election of 1976 brought the Carter administration into office. Cowan, who had been trained by Cesar Chavez, and the others put pressure on the Democrats coming into the Justice Department to have the charges against them dropped. Not only was the case dismissed, but the new commissioner of the INS, Leonel J. Castillo, shortly thereafter certified Manzo to represent undocumented aliens before the immigration courts. The group thus became one of the first grass-roots organizations in the country legally certified to assist aliens, as part of Leonel Castillo's efforts to give immigrants greater access to the legal process.

In 1979 the first few Central Americans began to show up at Manzo's headquarters in an old house near downtown Tucson. One day a man from El Salvador appeared in Lupe Castillo's office, bleeding from a fresh bullet wound, asking how he could avoid deportation. Castillo, a large, deliberate Indian-looking woman, commented years later that "that really dramatized the problem for us."

Manzo did not advise the refugees to apply for political asylum. Since most illegal aliens are never caught, they advised their clients to try to stay undetected. Most of the Central Americans wanted to move on to Los Angeles, where a large community of émigrés was forming, and Manzo wasn't about to tell them to do otherwise.

Like many people living near the 1,900-mile U.S.-Mexican border, Castillo, whose family had emigrated many years before from Mexico, took a decidedly relaxed view of movement across national boundaries. She and her colleagues viewed illegal crossings as routine, part of a massive labor flow that both countries depended upon heavily.

Every night the Border Patrol in the San Diego sector, just across from Tijuana, rounded up several hundred people, a fraction of those on their way to work in the fields, restaurants, and sweatshops of California. Three states away in Texas, middle-aged Mexican women carefully waded across the Rio Grande every morning on their way to housecleaning jobs in El Paso. And along the Arizona border it was well known that growers sent their foremen into Mexico to recruit labor, in a practice that the Border Patrol had never been able to curb.

The border, in short, was porous as a sieve. "This border has always been open," Lupe Castillo told a visitor to her office in 1986, against a backdrop of books, stacks of documents and immigration forms, posters, and bumper stickers (EL SALVADOR IS SPANISH FOR VIET-NAM). "Everyone in this county has helped someone across at one time or another. That's been true since the Mexican War in 1848. It was true before and after the Mexican Revolution in 1910; it was true in World

War Two, when the U.S. needed workers. That's part of the tradition at the border, of the history of this area."

By 1980 more and more Central Americans were showing up in this traffic. Visiting local prisons to see their Mexican clients, the social workers were besieged by frightened Salvadorans and even Guatemalans, grabbing at their sleeves and begging for help against deportation. Manzo worked out an arrangement to give the names of these people to a small group of ministers, including Fife and Elford, who would then go to the local INS office and have them released while Manzo helped them apply for political asylum.

Before long the Tucson Ecumenical Council (TEC), a coalition of some sixty local churches, became involved in the effort. The churches set up a new Task Force on Central America and hired Timothy Nonn, a young college graduate, as a part-time staffer for the lush sum of $500 a month.

In the beginning no one had a terribly clear notion of just what the TEC task force would do. St. Mark's Presbyterian, a whitewashed Spanish-style church in a prosperous part of northeast Tucson, had taken the lead on the refugees found in the desert the previous summer, and had had experience in helping resettle refugees from Southeast Asia, Cuba, and Chile. Its pastor and the other ministers in the TEC did not imagine that their initiative on behalf of the Central Americans would operate all that differently.[3]

· · ·

On May 4, 1981, almost the same day that the task force was formed, a Quaker from Albuquerque named James Dudley, driving through the country south of Tucson in a borrowed van, spotted a lone hitchhiker. The area was remote and forbidding, and the driver decided to stop and pick up the man, who turned out to be a young Salvadoran who had just walked across the border. Before Dudley had a chance to hear his story, the van was stopped at a Border Patrol roadblock in a canyon, a few miles to the north, and the hitchhiker was arrested and taken away.

When Dudley turned into the unpaved road leading to the house of his friend and fellow Quaker James Corbett, he was visibly shaken. While Corbett's wife, Pat, fixed dinner, the three speculated on the man's fate. None of them then had any special knowledge of Central America, but they had heard a rumor that a whole planeload of deportees had been shot by one of the Salvadoran military's death squads soon after they arrived at the airport in San Salvador. They talked about the anonymous Salvadoran long into the night, and Corbett, a small, wiry man with a grizzled goatee, expressed the hope that he had managed to escape. The Quaker shared Lupe Castillo's attitude toward borders; he often thought that if the human race made it into the twenty-first century, it would look back on national boundaries in much the same way as it now viewed slavery. It was barbaric, he believed, to put roadblocks in the way of people fleeing intolerable situations.[4]

The forty-seven-year-old Quaker's views on nationalism were typical of his iconoclastic opinions on life. A Harvard-educated former philosophy student, librarian, and rancher, Corbett had been forced to give up cattle raising by a severe collagen disease that had crippled his hands and feet and left him as gnarled as a mesquite tree (although he was quick to point out that despite his affliction, he could still do all the things he really needed to do: milk goats, drive a truck, saddle a horse, and type).

At the time of Dudley's visit Corbett was living on a scraggly one-and-a-half-acre property in northeast Tucson with his wife, trying to develop a breed of goats specially adapted to the desert and working on a philosophical treatise on goat ranching and desert survival. Quiet and dignified, scholarly and modest, he more than slightly resembled Don Quixote, and in some ways he was an indigenous version of that impoverished European nobleman who lived off his meager estate, read seriously and widely, and occasionally took off on an admirable, if utopian, quest.

Corbett went to bed that night feeling helpless, assuming that there was nothing he could do. The next morning he awakened determined to act. He first called the Border Patrol and the INS and was told that he could be given no information unless he had the name of the man he sought. Then, remembering that his own name was the same as that of a well-known former mayor of Tucson, he called again, and this time found out that the hitchhiker was being held in the Santa Cruz county jail in Nogales.

The rancher made a few more calls and got the name of Father Ricardo Elford, a priest who might help. But Elford, and all the paralegals on the Manzo staff, were busy that day with a group of fourteen Salvadorans who had just been caught on the 2.7-million-acre Papago Indian Reservation west of Tucson.

"Why don't you go down yourself?" the Catholic priest suggested when Corbett called. "You can do anything we might be able to do."

Father Ricardo explained that the immediate danger facing any arrested refugee was that he or she might be persuaded to sign a voluntary departure statement, waiving the legal right to a hearing before deportation. Many didn't understand enough English to know what they were signing, and before they realized what was happening, they were whisked onto a plane back to El Salvador. A G-28 form would designate Manzo as the man's legal counsel and indicate that he intended to apply for political asylum. Legally it should automatically retract anything he might have previously signed and guarantee him a hearing.

Corbett climbed into his old '61 Chevy pickup, swung by the Manzo office for a G-28 form, and headed south on the hour-long drive to Nogales, a border town named by Spanish explorers for the deep green groves of walnut trees covering the surrounding hills.

The Santa Cruz county jail was a one-story adobe structure a few blocks off the town's main street. There, behind bars in a spare concrete cell, Corbett found the hitchhiker, along with two other Salvadoran men. He spent about an hour interviewing the hitchhiker and then went off to the nearby Border Patrol office to get G-28 forms for the two others.

"We've run out," one of the patrolmen on duty told him.

"Oh. Well, maybe I can just write up something that might be an equivalent," the rancher responded.

"Well, we may have some more forms, but we'll have to look for them," the officer said. "You'll have to wait awhile."

After about half an hour the patrolmen on duty said they had finally located some forms, and grabbing them up, Corbett hurried back to the jail. He asked to see the two Salvadorans.

"They'll be up in a minute or two," the jailer told him.

After another long delay Corbett asked what was going on. He explained that he had to get back to Tucson to file the forms.

"Who was it you were looking for again?"

Corbett told him.

"Oh, I'm sorry, you want to see those guys? The Border Patrol came and got them thirty minutes ago. There's no way to know where they went," said the jailer with a hint of satisfaction.[5]

The next day Lupe Castillo tried to track down the two men and found not a trace, although she did discover seventeen more Salvadorans in detention, including four women and a child incarcerated in a trailer owned by a fundamentalist sect called the House of Samuel, near Sahuarito.*

In the meantime, the young hitchhiker was transferred as well, to the south Tucson jail. Before Corbett was able to bond him out, he was moved a third time, to the INS detention center at El Centro, California.

A few days later, on May 12, 1981, Corbett wrote an open letter to some 500 Quakers and Quaker meetings around the country, in the first of what became a steady stream of letters. The epistle was full of useful suggestions and coolheaded in tone. The Quaker stressed that members of the Border Patrol and the INS were not "SS goons" engaged in some evil conspiracy and delighting in sending undocumented refugees to their fates. "The game," he wrote, "seems to be the moving of bodies through deportation channels as fast as possible—Expulsion must equal intake to keep the channels from clogging; it's a simple matter of efficient administrative plumbing."[6]

Corbett's analysis was right on the mark. The perennially over-stretched and underfunded Immigration Service was trying to hustle the undocumented Central Americans through its overcrowded facilities as quickly as possible.

But underneath Jim Corbett's rational analysis of the situation ran a deep wellspring of emotional outrage that had been tapped by the treatment of the Central Americans. In that very first letter he warned his fellow Quakers that "active resistance" to the government might become necessary.

"Speaking only for myself," he wrote, "I can see that if Central American refugees' rights to political asylum are decisively rejected by the U.S. government or if the U.S. legal system insists on ransom that exceeds our ability to pay, active resistance will be the only alternative to abandoning the refugees to their fate. The creation of a network of actively concerned, mutually supportive people in the U.S. and Mexico may be the best preparation for an adequate response.

"—A network?" he wrote. "Quakers will know what I mean."[7]

---

*The Immigration Service routinely separates men and women captured at the border, a practice that makes it more difficult for families to coordinate legal assistance. Because of the shortage of federal detention facilities, often women and minors are held by private organizations operating under contract to the federal government. In Arizona these privatized jails were run by the Salvation Army and the House of Samuel, among others.

Within a week of his encounter with the hitchhiker, Jim Corbett had already envisioned a new underground railroad for the "feet people" of Central America, modeled on the nineteenth-century band of abolitionists and Quakers who smuggled slaves up to freedom from the antebellum South.

Nothing if not determined, the Quaker decided to go to El Centro himself, to try to locate some of the people who had been "disappeared" out of Tucson. Once in Southern California, he realized immediately that an almost completely unpublicized, full-scale exodus from El Salvador was occurring. The Latin neighborhoods of Los Angeles were teeming with new arrivals, and Central Americans were rapidly transforming the black neighborhood of Pico-Union into a Spanish-speaking enclave. A new legal aid agency named El Rescate ("Rescue") had just been set up for Central Americans on Eighth and Union, and Corbett gave it a hand, distributing the agency's newly printed legal rights cards in stores all over the barrio.

He made the rounds of government detention centers and found that several Salvadoran women for whom Manzo had filed G-28s had been flown back to El Salvador with no notice to Manzo, the women's legal representative.[8] At El Centro his inquisitiveness provoked a nasty incident with an INS jailer.

The big prison camp, located some two hours east of San Diego in the Imperial Valley, just north of the Mexican border, was the main INS detention center for Central Americans. Corbett located a few of Manzo's missing refugees there, but still on the trail of the hitchhiker, he interrogated a camp official as to his whereabouts. The jailer, J. E. Aguirre, insisted that there was no record of the man, when one of the other Salvadorans present piped up and said that the man had indeed been in El Centro and had already been deported.

Aguirre immediately ordered that all the Salvadorans in the room who were waiting to see Corbett be taken away. He informed his unwelcome visitor that under no circumstances would he be allowed to speak with anyone else at the camp.

In the ensuing showdown the rancher reminded the jailer that refugees could hardly exercise their legal rights if they were deprived of their right to see their legal representative, a lecture that drove Aguirre out of the room in a rage. He finally returned, only to discover that Corbett's companion, a Salvadoran named Rubén, had tape-recorded the entire incident, official threats and all. With Aguirre now seriously interested in the tape, Corbett decided that it was finally time to go. But before he could edge out of the room, the burly jailer ordered an associate to lock the reception area's electronic doors and to keep them locked until the two visitors handed over the recorder.

Corbett, the physically disabled bibliophile, then notified the towering prison official that he would have to resort to force to get the tape. "We are being held prisoner solely because you want to seize the evidence we have obtained," he declared, indulging himself in one more lecture, "evidence that conclusively proves that the INS is violating the rights of Salvadoran refugees to counsel and asylum. . . . This tape is my personal property and it can be taken away from me only by physical force."[9]

"There is no way you are getting out of here until you give me that tape," Aguirre retorted. And like two dogs frozen in the second before snarling mayhem, the two men stared at each other. Finally Aguirre picked up the telephone and called Harry Malone, the camp commander. After a whispered conference he hung up and told Corbett and Rubén that they could leave.

Back in Tucson in early June, Corbett sent out a news release about the incident, prompting Representative Morris Udall (Democrat-Arizona) to query the INS about its procedures. But the most significant outcome of the confrontation was the way it had hardened Jim Corbett's attitude toward the government. He wrote in his statement to the press:

Only a few weeks ago I thought that the systematic violation of Salvadoran refugees' human rights by the Border Patrol and I.N.S. was just a symptom of bureaucratic priorities. . . . I now know that I was wrong. . . . Rather, just as the ultra-rightist forces that rule much of Latin America are now being heavily armed by the U.S. . . . the Border Patrol and I.N.S. are being developed to shut off the escape route created by the possibility of asylum for Latin Americans in the U.S. . . .

The scrapping of human rights priorities and the rush to arm ultra-rightist forces throughout Latin America clearly signals that, in common with client states such as Guatemala, El Salvador, Honduras, Chile, Argentina, and Brazil, the U.S. administration has decided that the status quo can be preserved in Latin America only by a hemispherically organized reign of terror.

Chapter
Four

We are the people above all others who must stand in the gap.
                                                    —WILLIAM PENN,
                                                    speaking of Quakers[1]

IN MANY WAYS Jim Corbett and John Fife could not have been more different. Where Fife was gregarious and expansive, a sort of liberal good old boy, Corbett was soft-spoken and shy to the point of self-effacing. Where Fife was casual and athletic, a white-water rafter and a hunter of the javelina, the wild pig of the desert, Corbett was meticulous and bookish, a model of the nonviolent pacifist. And while Fife was part of the mainline church establishment, Corbett had always been a loner and what he called an "unbeliever."

Yet both men shared the gift of outrage and were fired by a passion against the abuse and misuse of power. The first time that this had become apparent in Corbett's life was in 1947, when he was thirteen and working for the summer in a store in Yellowstone National Park. He and the other young employees were housed above the store in dormitories segregated by sex. One night the boys decided to raid the girls' quarters, and in the ensuing melee the housemother was locked up. When she finally emerged, she demanded that heads roll.[2]

The management of the concession was reluctant to sacrifice its scarce labor force, so it decided to take a symbolic action. Casting about for a scapegoat, its gaze fell on one young man known to all as Ersatz.

34

A slow, clumsy fellow who could barely operate the cash register, he was studying to be a Baptist preacher, and every time he started to say a swearword, he would say "ersatz" instead. He hadn't even been involved in the incident, but his bosses decreed that he was the one who had to go.

In protest the rest of the summer staff announced that if Ersatz were fired, they, too, would depart. But one by one their resolve weakened, until finally only Jim Corbett, supported by his loyal older sister, stood by Ersatz. In the end all three of them lost their jobs and hitchhiked out of the park by themselves.

That episode was the first of a recurring pattern of what were usually one-man stands for the underdog. Corbett attributed at least part of his passion for justice to the influence of his father, a country lawyer from the Missouri Ozarks and the son of a full-blooded Blackfoot woman.

At age twenty-two his father was county attorney, a post that required considerable courage in the Prohibition-era Ozarks. But an accident damaged Raymond Corbett's eyesight and cut short his legal career. He moved to Wyoming, took up schoolteaching, and eventually became a member of the State House of Representatives and chairman of its Judiciary Committee. He was a pure New Deal Democrat and, as Corbett remembers him, "a very socially concerned person."

One anecdote illustrating his father's character occurred when the old man was already retired and living on an Arizona ranch. The property included a trailer court. One day a man came to the house and said that there was a black family looking for housing in the area. Raymond Corbett offered to let them move into an apartment above his house. Now there were a number of southerners living in the trailer court, and in no time a delegation appeared and informed their landlord that they would have to leave if the blacks ever presumed to swim in their swimming pool. Without hesitation the elder Corbett told them to hit the road.

Corbett's mother, too, was a child of the Ozarks, the daughter of one of the most notorious mule traders in the mountains. She was reared like a boy and was as tough and unsentimental as a horsewhip. Later she went into horse trading herself, with money her husband gave her for a pretty dress, and at eighty-four she was still showing Appaloosas and living alone on a ranch amid trophies and boxes of dusty prize ribbons. Jim Corbett had never been very close emotionally to his father, and he was even less close to his mother.

The family was living in Casper, Wyoming, when Corbett was born on October 8, 1933, and though they were not poor, they had very little money. When she could, his mother would spend a week or two substitute teaching, and since she couldn't afford a baby-sitter, she would leave the two-and-a-half to three-year-old boy alone for half a day. She would order him to stay on the bed and not get off until she got back.

One of Corbett's earliest memories is of those long hours on the bed waiting for life to resume and trying to amuse himself in various ways. Once he asked his mother if a pet cat could stay with him and keep him company, and she agreed. But when he tried to cuddle the cat, it scratched him and jumped off the bed.

"I was in an agony trying to decide whether to get off the bed and get that cat or not," he recalled fifty years later during an interview in his office in the Pima Friends Meeting House, a pre-World War I house near the campus of the University of Arizona. "I wanted to so badly. Finally I did, but I felt terribly guilty. And it scratched me again."

Corbett grew up shy but able to fend for himself. His parents moved every summer to the nearby Shoshone Indian reservation or to the Tetons, where they camped and fished for trout and picked berries, like 1940s forerunners of live-off-the-land hippies. Years later he re-created the experience of wilderness life by teaching a course for a Quaker school that showed college-bound teenagers how to subsist in the desert, living off goat's milk and whatever they could forage in the wild.

A junior high school teacher informed Corbett's parents that the laconic child wasn't high school material. By the time he was a senior, however, he was a straight A student. He applied for and won a scholarship to Colgate University in Hamilton, New York, a feat his family learned about when they read it in the local newspaper.

He majored in philosophy, and one professor remembered him as the "one of the half dozen most brilliant students I encountered in 35 years of teaching." Another of his professors recalled that "he was probably the only straight A student we ever had in philosophy. It was ideas that mattered . . . he thought for himself. At the time I didn't realize he would have such a passionate concern for victims. . . . Those were not things we were thinking about then."[3]

Earning a degree at Colgate in just three years, Corbett went on to Harvard on a Woodrow Wilson fellowship and finished a master's degree in one year. Realizing that he didn't want to teach philosophy, he quit school, married a Casper girl who had gone to Wellesley, and was promptly drafted into the army. After his twenty-one months of military service the young couple returned to Corbett's parents' ranch in Cochise County, Arizona, a few miles north of the Mexican border, and raised beef cattle, traded horses, and had three children in rapid succession.

Within a few years the marriage broke up, and the summer after his divorce the first sign of Corbett's unusual crippling disease appeared. For years he was plagued by recurring ill health, and several times he was told that the disease, which was similar to arthritis but sufficiently different to have been misdiagnosed, was going to kill him. At one point he holed up on a mountaintop on his family's ranch in the Huachuca Mountains and taught himself how to read Bahasa Indonesia, the language of a culture he had never seen on the opposite side of the earth.

Finally, as he approached thirty, he decided to study to become a librarian. He enrolled in the University of Southern California and there met Pat Collins, the tall blond daughter of a prosperous Republican lawyer in Los Angeles. She says she "only started asking Jim home to dinner because he looked so hungry," but she shared his quiet shyness, his love of horses and the desert, and his stubborn integrity. In 1963 the two were married and returned to Arizona, where Corbett took up a position as head librarian and philosophy instructor at Cochise Junior College.

The college was in the southeastern part of the state, an area dominated by the huge Phelps Dodge copper company, and according to Corbett, the corporation's reach was so long that the local libraries in Bisbee and Douglas were actually owned and staffed by Phelps Dodge. The librarians submitted their purchases to the company's public relations department for approval. One of the Corbetts' friends from Bisbee once offered the library his copies of the *Nation* and the *New Republic* as soon as he had read them, and the offer was politely declined with the comment that the librarian didn't really think the people of Bisbee were ready for that sort of thing.

On another occasion Pat went in to see if the local librarian in Douglas would want a friends of the library group to buy more books for her, because the existing collection mostly consisted of nineteenth-century novels "and other very safe stuff," as Corbett put it. The Douglas librarian demurred as well.[4]

In such a climate a clash was virtually inevitable, and within a year Corbett had become embroiled in a series of disputes that cost him his job. First the school tried to ban a book that was on an instructor's reading list, provoking the new librarian to object. Then the college administration tried to exclude the paintings of a member of the John

Birch Society from an art exhibit planned for the library. Corbett reported the incidents, and the American Civil Liberties Union (ACLU) denounced the school. At the end of the year his contract was not renewed, and the Corbetts headed back to Los Angeles, where he could get medical treatment.

By that time the Vietnam War was heating up, and for a while Corbett ran a small office in the eastern part of Hollywood for the Fellowship of Reconciliation, one of the first groups to protest the war. By June 1966 he had recovered enough to return to Arizona to help his parents operate a new ranch, and there he had his first experience with civil disobedience.

During the Vietnam conflict American Quakers ran one of the most effective relief programs in South Vietnam, and the medical aid program of the Canadian Friends Service Committee aided noncombatants in North as well as South Vietnam. The United States government had decreed that Americans who contributed to the Canadian program would be in violation of American laws and could be imprisoned for up to ten years and fined as much as $10,000. Speaking at an antiwar rally in Tucson in 1967, Corbett declared that he had informed the U.S. Treasury in writing that public donations to the Canadian medical aid program would be made at the rally. In a reply to his letter the director of the Bureau of Foreign Assets Control said that she was referring "appropriate" cases to the Justice Department with a recommendation of prosecution, but that was the last he heard of it.[5]

After a couple of years Corbett started another new job, as social science librarian at Chico State College in California. Here the cyclical pattern of losing a job in a one-man stand over principle caught up with him again. A popular sociology professor, who had been an adviser to the Students for a Democratic Society and was himself considered a radical, failed to have his contract renewed for the academic year of 1969–70. Corbett tried to persuade the faculty rights committee to take action against the school, and when it refused, he went out on strike by himself.

That was the last of Corbett's academic posts, and when the progression of his disease made active ranching impossible as well, he moved into Tucson. Living on Social Security disability checks, Pat's salary as a part-time research assistant at the University of Arizona, and rent from the trailers scattered about their property, he turned to a series of projects. He wrote a study of bees and invented a specialized hive designed for use in the third world. He became fascinated with systems of nomadic agriculture and the nomad's harmonious adaptation to the land. He wrote a 300-page treatise on "goat walking" and desert survival and shared information from his goat-breeding program with Mexican goat herders in Baja California.

All the while he immersed himself in political philosophy. Among other things he developed an unlikely fondness for Thomas Hobbes, the crusty seventeenth-century English author of *Leviathan,* a treatise justifying the need for strong authoritarian government and famous for its assertion that life is "solitary, poor, nasty, brutish, and short." Corbett thought Hobbes was misunderstood. "He was a timid man with a great deal of courage," the rancher commented once. "Reading between the lines, you can see he is quite compassionate but wants to look at things realistically. I really like him."[6]

The strongest influence on Corbett's thinking, however, was the Quakers, that gentle, stubborn sect that had suffered recurring persecution in seventeenth-century England and, with other nonconformists, fled to the New World in large numbers.

In the United States Quakers had continued to be influential far beyond their numbers, as pioneers in the abolitionist movement, in the Underground Railroad for escaping slaves, in turn-of-the-century social reform efforts, and during the Vietnam War, when many were conscientious objectors. Corbett became a member of the Religious Society of Friends in the early 1960s and was one of the approximately 30,000 "unprogrammed" Quakers in the United States. He deeply shared the faith's belief in a life of moral example and many contemporary Quakers' distaste for doctrines, party lines, and all the other accoutrements of authority.

The Quakers believe that every individual—and community of individuals—must act as if the good already prevailed. That is the only way the world can be perfected—through acts of conscience. Means and ends are one. Once, in a letter attempting to diagnose the madness of his patron saint Don Quixote, who jousted with windmills and dreamed of reviving the ethics of knighthood, Corbett endowed the Man of La Mancha with the attributes of the Quaker: If poor Don Quixote "fails to *live* chivalry into creation, who will? And he does fail, repeatedly, comically, inevitably—yet, even in his worst defeats, quixotically. And the quest survives."[7]

Fundamentally, however, Jim Corbett, with his stubborn integrity and uncompromising spirit, was an authentic American original. His message was like the serpent's on the early revolutionists' banner: "Don't tread on me."

Corbett wrote a second long epistle on July 6, 1981, this time addressed to "friends," instead of "Friends." He sent it not only to the Quakers who had received his first letter but also to other individuals and denominations around the country. The letter had all the hallmarks of his thinking and writing: his abhorrence of American support for the brutal regimes in Central America; his distaste for 1960s-style hierarchically organized political protests; and his Quaker belief that political change occurs only when people *act out* their moral convictions. He wrote:

> *Whatever my emotional weaknesses, the refugees themselves bring strength and renewal. They share their joys and their hopes as well as their griefs, and one soon learns that a new religious awareness has been spreading through Latin America, a revolutionary religious consciousness taking root in basic communities that are determined to live the freedom, peace, and justice of the Kingdom into actuality. There is, indeed, a force at work that threatens to sweep away the established powers of this hemisphere, and it is far more radical than the state capitalism of Cuba or Russia. . . .*
>
> *Because the refugees are here, the war against the people of Latin America is being waged here as well. Yet, because the refugees are among us, the basic communities capable of waging the peace can also emerge here. Such communities are not merely possible, they are essential if our stand for peace is to be more than just another petition addressed to those who command the war machine. (Peacemaking in the '80's isn't likely to bear much resemblance to the ephemerally fashionable anti-war happenings of the '60's.)* [8]

Corbett added that merely verbal attacks on "those that run the war machine" often struck him as the "ritual venting of gripes, simply releasing pressure and permitting the dissenter to go about his daily business while ignoring the refugees in his midst." He went on:

> *. . . If we do give up our position of privilege, a place to stand with the dispossessed and serve the peaceable kingdom can only be found in a special kind of community that dedicates itself to such service.*

During recent weeks I've been discovering this catholic church that is a people rather than creed or rite, a living church of many cultures that must be met to be known.

Corbett warned that the danger in opposing the Reagan administration's radical Central American and refugee policies was to counter it with another, but similarly rigid, ideology:

Identifying unacceptable violence with a particular ideology, one chooses the way of violence under cover of a contrasting ideology.
   In contrast to ideologies, which we fashion out of words in order to justify ourselves, the way of the Cross is communicated by being lived. It is met in those who point the way with their lives.

The "unregenerate Quaker" ended his letter with a poem that he himself had written:

> *Give me, then, my share of pain,*
> *survivor's grief and unnamed ills,*
> *the slow decay that yet may maim*
> *and torture years before it kills.*
> *Burn us with their mark of Cain,*
> *the outlaw brand the powers despise,*
> *and freeze us with the misfit shame*
> *that touches ice in knowing eyes.*
> *Bind us with the pauper's chain,*
> *here where life and health are sold*
> *by those who play the money game*
> *and fashion God of Mammon's gold.*
> *And let our sense be clear and sane,*
> *unnumbed by drugs or pious lies*
> *unpoisoned by the urge to blame,*
> *undrained into self-pity's sighs.*
> *Let it be that this, our fate,*
> *reveals the working of Your grace,*
> *that we can bear the hurt and hate,*
> *to grow love's realm, in this pain's place.* [9]

Chapter
Five

The history of liberty has largely been the history of observance of procedural safeguards.

—JUSTICE FELIX FRANKFURTER

ONE BLAZINGLY HOT Sunday afternoon in late June 1981 the new Religious Task Force on Central America, with Jim Corbett in attendance, held a meeting at the Picture Rocks Retreat, a 100-acre religious center in the Tucson Mountains, some thirty minutes' drive northeast of the city. Picture Rocks, named after Indian rock carvings chiseled some 800 years ago by the Hohokam tribe, was owned by Father Ricardo Elford's order, the Redemptorists, and the priests living at the retreat house ran an outreach program in Tucson's prisons and poorer neighborhoods. The magnificent desert setting, a favorite spot for European film crews shooting commercials, also provided visiting members of the international order with a place to recharge their batteries and revitalize their commitments to social justice.

The meeting had no sooner begun than the planned agenda was sidetracked by a report from Margo Cowan and Lupe Castillo, who had just returned from their first trip to El Centro. Like Corbett, the two women had gone in search of refugees—in this case two Salvadoran students—who had been arrested and shipped out of Arizona before they had had a chance to file for political asylum.

The two organizers held the assembled ministers spellbound by their description of the conditions at the detention center. They had found about 200 Salvadorans, including some who had been incarcerated for as long as nine months. The prisoners had no access to lawyers and were being told to sign papers, printed in English, stating that they agreed to return voluntarily to El Salvador. If they balked at signing, they were reminded that they faced months in detention and would probably be deported back to El Salvador in the end anyway. Once they did sign, they were put on buses to Los Angeles and from there flown to San Salvador.*

The ministers immediately agreed that their first priority had to be to help Manzo bail out every Central American in the camp.[1] And in what became a hallmark of the Tucson activists' strategy, they decided to try to attract as much publicity as possible. A mass bailout, they reasoned, would capture the media's imagination and alert the public to the refugees streaming across the border. That afternoon they agreed to send a delegation of twelve to fifteen people to El Centro at once. Manzo would interview and fill out asylum applications, while the churches would provide volunteers and raise money for bail bonds and expenses.

The next day a crash recruiting drive was launched. Manzo staffers and an elder of the Southside Church, Susan Parrott, organized typists, paralegals, and Spanish speakers to do the interviews. Tim Nonn got on the phone and tried to recruit, among others, Ken Kennon, the pastor of the Broadway Christian Church, another congregation with experience in working with refugees. Kennon was a burly black-bearded Missourian whose solid frame, usually clad in a Cuban shirt, had been present at most of the social action campaigns in Tucson.

Kennon first begged off going himself, but after Nonn came over to his house and explained how the Salvadorans were being shipped back to possible torture or worse, he thought of the Jews trying to get out of Nazi-occupied Europe and being turned away from the ports of the

---

*These allegations were later supported by voluminous evidence presented in subsequent court cases, particularly *Orantes-Hernández et al.* v. *William French Smith et al.*, District Court for the Central District of California. By having someone sign a voluntary departure statement, the INS was saved the trouble of formal deportation, while the individual got no black mark on his or her immigration record that would jeopardize his or her chances of reentering the United States legally. The procedure was devised and worked well for Mexican illegals, not for the completely new phenomenon of refugees, many of whom feared for their lives.

United States. Can this be happening all over again? he wondered. Is it possible we haven't learned a damn thing from that history? "Well," he told Nonn, "I can type."

On July 10, 1981, Kennon headed for California, traveling with three companions: an actress, a Quaker, and a professor of drama from Pima Community College, Barclay Goldsmith. (Goldsmith later helped his students write and produce an original drama about the experience, which was performed on several occasions throughout Arizona.) Some two dozen people, including Jim Corbett, made the 210-mile drive to El Centro and launched the most massive bailout that the Immigration Service had ever seen.

The group stayed at the Golden West Motel, a third-rate establishment whose main attraction was its cheap rates. The clean, if somewhat seedy, rooms were arranged in a horseshoe around an expanse of asphalt relieved by a tiny pool. The owners were a Chinese refugee couple who were sympathetic to their unusual guests and allowed them to crowd three and four into a room for the regular daily rate.

The Golden West was the Crillon, however, compared with what the delegation found in El Centro. The camp, built in 1973 to house 250 undocumented Mexicans for a few days at most, was bursting at the seams as a result of a new Reagan administration policy that all aliens captured on the border had to be detained. The facilities consisted of twelve buildings, including four brick barracks surrounded by electrified mesh fences topped with barbed wire. During the day the 300 to 400 prisoners were locked in a corral inside the barracks compound, where they had to remain outside all day, like cattle, in temperatures that reached 110 to 120 degrees in summer. The only shade was provided by a couple of open-sided lean-tos, where swarms of flies gathered around the few sweating prisoners who managed to crowd under the tiny tin roofs. The camp had neither a doctor nor a nurse.[2]

When Corbett and several others complained to the camp guards about these conditions, they overheard one guard joking with another. "I've seen a lot of them get pretty withered, but I've yet to see one die of dehydration."[3]

Conditions were so bad that all but the most desperate refugees were likely to prefer to take their chances back in El Salvador. The detainees interviewed by the Tucson volunteers claimed that infractions of rules carried the risk of solitary confinement. All reading material except the Bible and all writing materials were denied. The number of pay phones, the prisoners' only link with the outside world, had been cut from three to two in 1981. Even if a person did manage to contact a lawyer, El Corralón, as the detainees called the "big corral" of El Centro, was a two-hour drive from San Diego, three hours from Los Angeles, and more than four hours from Phoenix and Tucson, the nearest cities with organized legal and paralegal services for aliens.

To complicate matters even further, many legitimate refugees feared giving unsympathetic INS officials details of their political problems, out of concern that the information would be sent back to El Salvador and endanger their families.

Harry Malone, the supervisor in charge of detention and deportation at El Centro, seemed at least as unhappy as his Latin charges. He had previously barred all reporters and cameramen from the camp and from deportation hearings, and now a pack of journalists had descended on him, determined to expose conditions on his watch. One enterprising cameraman from a Tucson television station even bought beer for some local linemen for the privilege of borrowing their cherry picker to shoot pictures over the camp fence.[4]

It took a federal court action before Malone relented and allowed the representatives from Manzo and the TEC to interview the Central Americans who wanted to file asylum petitions. Even then, one activist wrote, "countless impediments were put in their path."[5] When the volunteers arrived at 8:30 A.M., as agreed in the court order, the camp authorities started a roll call that wasted two hours. Interviews were conducted in a room approximately 100 square feet in area, into which were crowded eight Central Americans, eight interpreters, and two to four additional helpers. Sitting on the floor, the volunteers interviewed a steady stream of inmates, each for more than an hour, taking down the information that was needed to file the claims for political asylum.

Camp authorities had refused to give the social workers a list of the Central Americans who wanted to claim asylum. So those whose names Manzo already had were told to bring with them the names of others who wanted help, and they did, scribbling them on cigarette wrappers and pieces of the camp Bibles. The process continued for days, until the volunteers in the tiny, crowded room had interviewed some 150 people, each with an individual tale of woe.

"Most of us had not heard these horror stories before," Ken Kennon later recalled. "We'd go back to the motel and start typing our notes out on the I-five-eight-nines—the asylum application forms—and it was a real eye opener for us. We were reading and learning at the same time, one after another, these stories from people across the spectrum. We had one fellow who'd deserted from the army in Salvador; he'd been a torturer and couldn't stand doing it anymore. We had people who had been in the guerrilla forces. More than anything else we saw people caught in the middle, who'd lost members of their immediate family, seen their mutilated bodies. We were shocked."[6]

Young Tim Nonn couldn't believe that what he saw in El Centro could be happening in the United States. After one visit to the detention center he walked through the broiling hot parking lot of the Golden West, his shoes sinking into the melting asphalt. Why are we imprisoning these people, he thought, instead of offering them refuge?[7]

As the numbers of those seeking asylum grew, the shabby motel came to resemble a political campaign headquarters, bustling around the clock with people typing furiously and paper strewn everywhere. The church volunteers were constantly working the phones, trying to raise more bail bond money, lining up medical visits, figuring out how to put the refugees up temporarily. Kennon called his church's home office in Indianapolis and persuaded it to send enough money to charter two buses. "Somehow the money always came through," he recalled.

One night, as if to demonstrate that the massive bailout couldn't really change anything, camp authorities ordered fifteen of the men who had filled out asylum applications dragged out of the camp, screaming, kicking, and crying. A few hours before the incident Jim Corbett had completed the application for one of them, a Salvadoran campesino who had worked all his life to build a herd of fifteen Holsteins. He'd had to abandon his animals when he left the country, but Corbett told him he could probably get him a job working cattle in Arizona when he got out of El Centro. At least he would be safe until things changed and he could return home, the rancher told him. They had talked cows for a while and parted laughing.[8]

A total of 50 to 60 rotating volunteers spent some two weeks at the detention center. With the exception of the 15 men who had been taken away, the Salvadorans and Guatemalans held at the camp—more than 150 people in all—were freed on bonds provided by the Tucsonians. Gary MacEoin, a Tucson-based writer, lawyer, and activist who was also a former priest, put up his house as collateral. Jim and Pat Corbett put up their trailers. Dick Sinner, a Catholic priest from Phoenix whose family owned property in North Dakota and whose brother later became governor of the state, put up his land as collateral. Altogether the civic and religious volunteers turned over some $16,000 to a Tucson bail bond firm to secure the releases and raised another $175,000 in collateral.

To the very end Harry Malone and the other camp authorities did their best to frustrate the operation. According to Ken Kennon, "He limited the number of people we could interview at one time, and he made us wait long stretches of time between interviews. Even after we had posted bond, he refused for three days to release the men." After the first few Central Americans were released, Malone angrily denied the charges.

"There has been no stalling here," he told the press. "I had to miss my July barbecue with the Lions Club over this [the late release], if that means anything to you."

Malone also denied several Central Americans' allegations that they had been told to sign voluntary departure statements, without being informed that that meant being sent back to El Salvador. "I don't lend credence to all that," he told a reporter for the *Tucson Citizen.* "I am not saying it couldn't happen, but I don't lend credence to it."[9]

After the mass bailout the Central Americans, with the continuing help of the Tucson volunteers, went their separate ways. Jim Corbett, Margo Cowan, and Lupe Castillo accompanied two busloads to Los Angeles, where a black church in Watts offered its gymnasium as a temporary shelter for about eighty people. Others went on to San Francisco in a station wagon donated on the spot by a local industrialist, and still others headed for Phoenix and Tucson. Before the sojourners left El Centro, Margo Cowan and Lupe Castillo warned them that it might take years before the Immigration Service and the State Department decided their cases. Filing the asylum applications, they said, was at best "a tactic to buy time."[10]

Chapter
Six

*Look, my country, what you've done to me, what I have to do
to live with myself.*

—E. L. DOCTOROW,
Lives of the Poets

JOHN FIFE, WHO had been on a long-planned river trip in Utah
when the big bailout began, came home to welcome almost a dozen
refugees from El Centro to Southside. It was the largest single group
staying with one congregation, but other congregations all over the city
joined the little Presbyterian church in the unglamorous work of finding
the sojourners jobs, homes, emergency clothing, and medical treatment.

It was classic refugee resettlement work, the kind the government
had paid churches to do when the Vietnamese, Cambodian, and Lao-
tian refugees had arrived in the 1970s. This time, however, the churches
were operating on their own. Ironically, the Reagan administration's
unwillingness to assist the latest victims of war and revolution gave
birth to a very Reagan-like response: a private-sector initiative perform-
ing a service that had previously been endorsed and underwritten by
the government.

Every one of the Tucson activists played a role. Tim Nonn, the only
real staff member of the Tucson Ecumenical Council, moved a mattress
into his office at St. Mark's and put in eighteen-hour days, seven days
a week, handling everything from resettlement to fund-raising to dealing with the press.

Margo Cowan and Lupe Castillo worked day and night, preparing asylum applications for those released and filing new ones for the dozens of refugees pouring into El Centro every week. The churches in the TEC, for their part, set about raising enough bond money to bail ten refugees out of detention every week, a scheme that would cost as much as $2,000 a week (based on an average bond of $2,000 and a 10 percent down payment on each bond; later a 25 percent payment was required).

John Fife felt that his most important contribution would be fund-raising, by tapping as many of his national contacts as he could. And the money did flow in. The Presbyterian Church, the Lutherans, the Episcopalians, the United Church of Christ, the Disciples of Christ, the Church World Service, and several Catholic orders were among those that gave generously and regularly to the Arizona and other refugee efforts, including the crowded refugee camps in Central America itself.* In the next few years the outpouring of cash and kind, legal and social services, for the displaced people of Central America was surpassed only by the multimillion-dollar donations for African famine relief.

Jim Corbett, in the meantime, was marching to a different drummer.

One night in early June the telephone rang at the Quaker's house while he was hosting the regular weekly meeting of his goat-milking cooperative. (He had dubbed the group Los Cabreros Andantes, a play on the Spanish *caballero andante,* or "knight errant." It was also a play on Corbett's identification with the sixteenth-century caballero Don Quixote.)

The call was from a Salvadoran woman in Phoenix, who said that her brother and cousin were hiding under a house in Nogales, Sonora, and didn't know what to do next. She knew that Corbett had been working with Central American refugees and wanted to know if he could help.[1]

Corbett and two other members of the group immediately decided to drive down to Nogales, and a couple of hours later they were prowling through the red-light district of the gamy little border town, looking for two frightened refugees. They found the Salvadorans hiding in a basement and told them to sit tight for a little longer.

The next morning Corbett asked around how "folks went through."

*See Appendix I for a summary of the national response to the Central American refugee crisis at this time and for the criticisms, particularly from the United Nations and from within the Immigration Service itself, of the official response.

He learned that it was a fairly simple matter to walk through one of the countless gaping holes in the international fence dividing the twin cities of Nogales. The chain-link fence snaked through the central business district, and Mexican children routinely slipped back and forth to beg at the McDonald's on the American side. The trick for anyone who really wanted to enter the United States was to get past the roadblocks and the surveillance on the highways heading north.

Public transportation was very thoroughly checked by the Border Patrol, so illegal immigrants often arranged to rendezvous in the public park in Nogales, Arizona, with coyotes, or smugglers who would guide them on up to Tucson or Phoenix. Corbett, who thought that the park was too exposed a meeting place, noticed a large Catholic church on a hill on the American side, its gleaming white walls and red-tiled roof clearly visible from Mexico. He decided to go over to Sacred Heart and see if the door was kept open.

The rancher had been in a Catholic church only once before in his life, as a child, and as he walked into the sanctuary, the religiosity of the place, with its candles and icons and the smell of incense, almost made him hesitate. Still, he thought, the place was perfect: open to all and a quiet safe spot for the two men to land. He went back and instructed the Salvadorans to meet him at the church after they had made their way over the international line. Sacred Heart, in the subsequent language of the Immigration Service, became a safe house.

Next Corbett called Lupe Castillo and Father Ricardo Elford. The two drove down from Tucson together, and while Castillo prepared asylum applications for the two men, Elford introduced Corbett to a priest at Sacred Heart who was sympathetic to the plight of the refugees. He suggested that the *norteamericanos* might go talk to a Mexican priest on the other side who was an "ultratraditionalist" and a "reactionary" but who might be willing to help Central Americans.

That same day Corbett and Father Ricardo paid a call on Father Ramón Dagoberto Quiñones, the priest of Our Lady of Guadalupe in Nogales, Sonora. Quiñones, a handsome, black-haired man of forty-five, was the epitome of the old-fashioned Mexican priest: dedicated to his faith, his bishop, and his flock, and too busy to concern himself with the radical theories of liberation theologians. Yet Quiñones's work went far beyond the traditional consolations of the mass, confession, baptism, and the last rites. In Latin America, a region with limited welfare services, people frequently turned to the church during natural or personal disasters, and in keeping with that tradition, Quiñones had turned Our Lady of Guadalupe into an all-purpose social service agency.

The church dispensed free hot meals every day and milk for children. It operated a nursing home with thirty-five beds for homeless old people. It ran free medical and dental clinics that treated several hundred patients a month. And Father Quiñones had recently begun a ministry for the Central Americans who were increasingly showing up in Nogales. He allowed the sojourners to rest for a while at the church, and on the day of the rancher's visit, seventeen guests from Central America were staying there. He had also begun regular visits to the Central Americans detained in the Nogales penitentiary, the Centro para Readaptación Social.[2]

At that first meeting the Mexican priest invited Corbett to accompany him on his prison visits, and a few days later the rancher, dressed in black pants and a white shirt to simulate clerical garb, made the first of many weekly trips to the forbidding stone and concrete building on the southern outskirts of town, just off the main highway leading south toward Hermosillo. Father Quiñones and another volunteer, María del Socorro Pardo de Aguilar, a housewife in her mid-fifties who was one of the priest's most devoted parishioners, called the Quaker "Father Jim" and the guards were fooled into thinking the American was a priest.

The three volunteers were allowed into a large open-air half-roofed holding tank where the Central American men were held. A gigantic cross cast its shadow over the yard, where those imprisoned sat or strolled or just stared during the long, idle days. At night they slept on the floor, with no beds, no mattresses, and no blankets to ward off the chill of the desert. Among the prisoners were many children, including some as young as six, and several frightened youngsters who had been separated from their parents.

The volunteers distributed food, warm clothing and blankets, soap, and writing materials and took messages to relay to relatives in the United States and El Salvador. Corbett, who was fluent in Spanish, later prepared for distribution a one-page leaflet, explaining the definition of a refugee in American law and outlining how to request political asylum in the United States. It listed legal aid organizations and Corbett's own name and telephone number as contacts for help on the American side.

The visitors were told that about 150 Salvadorans were being deported out of Mexican prisons every week; put on buses and dumped back on the Mexican-Guatemalan border. Many of the Salvadorans whom Corbett spoke with on that first visit, particularly those who were traveling without money or proper documentation, were terrified about being sent back. They claimed that anyone who returned to El Salvador without identification was automatically suspected of having been with the guerrillas and risked being interrogated, tortured, and killed by security forces.

Those prisoners who had managed to get as far as the American port of entry at Nogales told the visitors that it was impossible to apply for political asylum there. Corbett spoke with one man in the penitentiary who told him that, knowing no better and in fear for his life, he had gone up to the U.S. inspector at the port of entry and explained that he was Salvadoran, that he was in great danger, and that he wanted to apply for asylum in the United States. The inspector told him to wait a minute and then returned with a Mexican immigration official, who hauled him off to the prison.[3]

Quiñones had checked out these stories with Mexican immigration officials, and they confirmed to the priest that Central Americans appearing at the port of entry without papers were detained by U.S. immigration until the Mexican authorities were notified.[4] The U.S. authorities then turned them over to the Mexicans. There were simply no procedures for anyone to apply for political asylum at the American border.

Corbett and the other refugee workers concluded that a person could apply for political asylum only *after* he or she was already in the United States.

With that in mind, the rancher devised a plan for the two Salvadorans he had helped into the United States. He would drive them up to Tucson, hoping that if they were stopped by the Border Patrol, their I-589 forms, requesting asylum, would make it clear they were legally on their way to an INS office.

The trip was made without incident, and on June 27, 1981, Corbett escorted the two men, and a third Central American who had been staying on his property, into the office of the Immigration and Naturalization Service in Tucson.

The officer in charge was William N. Johnston, a fifth-generation New Yorker who had just been transferred from the busy border station in San Ysidro, south of San Diego. A tall, dark-haired, good-looking man of forty, Bill Johnston was a practicing Catholic, and in his youth he had been opposed to the war in Vietnam. After military service he had worked as a cabbie in New York City, and he liked to joke that getting into the lower middle class was his goal. He had a master's degree in Latin American studies from the University of Texas, and he was familiar with the causes of the violence ravaging Central America.[5]

For several months Johnston had been releasing captured undocumented Salvadorans to the small group of local ministers who guaranteed that they would show up for their hearings. Their relations were pleasant; his daughter went to the same school as John Fife's son, and he was sympathetic to the refugees' plight. On the day Corbett came in he remarked that any Cuban rapist or Russian ballerina would be given asylum, but he had yet to see a Salvadoran request that would be approved.

Johnston had added, however, that as far as he was concerned, if Salvadorans were being tortured and murdered by their government, they ought to take up arms and fight rather than run away. Still, Corbett had no reason to believe that there would be any problem when he took the men in that day to start the long asylum process.

He was wrong.

A clerk took the three asylum applications back to Johnston, and after a few minutes the INS official appeared and ordered the men put under arrest and placed under $3,000 bond each.

Johnston had run the men's names through the INS computer and found that at least two of them had been deported before. That in itself was grounds for exclusion from the United States, and in keeping with guidelines requiring detention if the likelihood of absconding seemed high, Johnston had taken the men into custody. He had taken the additional precaution of setting high bonds. If they were legitimate refugees, he reasoned, they would still have a chance to ask for asylum at their hearings.*

Jim Corbett saw another set of facts. The $3,000 bonds were unprecedented; at the time bonds of $1,000 had been routine, although they had

---

*Aliens caught illegally in the United States are entitled to a deportation hearing, where they can show cause why they should not be deported. At the hearing the refugees can declare that they want to apply for political asylum, at which point the hearing is ended and a second hearing on the merits of the asylum application is scheduled.

begun to rise. For an hour the *cabrero* argued with the bureaucrat, explaining that if refugees could no longer "affirmatively file" for asylum with the INS without being placed in detention, he and others trying to help them would have no way to work within the system. He explained that the church workers did not have enough money to bail out every refugee who turned up and that if it came to a choice between having the refugees imprisoned for months and then probably returned to El Salvador or helping them find safe haven outside proper immigration channels, they would have no choice. They would be forced to go underground.

"To stand by and do nothing would constitute a fundamental betrayal of our faith," Corbett said later, "so I described to Mr. Johnston in considerable detail the program of underground activities to aid undocumented refugees that would certainly develop as a result of the government's closing off all practicable options within the system. In this sense, the Tucson 'evasion services' that later developed were never clandestine."[6]

In Jim Corbett's mind the conversation was a turning point, marking the beginning of an underground railroad. Asked about it years later, Bill Johnston said he couldn't remember Corbett's warning. He doubted whether the conversation had even taken place.

· · ·

After the incident in Johnston's office Jim Corbett decided what he had to do. He told some of the ministers helping the refugees that they were working at the wrong end of the problem. Helping people who had been captured and imprisoned was fine, but his ethical conclusion was that their greatest need was to avoid capture in the first place.

Putting to use his intimate knowledge of the mountains and the desert, the riverbeds and gullies of the border terrain, the soft-spoken rancher began that summer to guide undocumented Salvadorans over the line himself. He put together a small group of Quakers and others to help him with his *pro bono* coyote operation. The group named itself the "tucson refugee support group," which was spelled with lower case letters because Corbett, a libertarian, didn't believe in organizations. The brigade of middle-class housewives, students, professional men, and retirees, often carrying binoculars for their "bird-watching" expeditions, was soon doing a brisk traffic across a border that was more familiar with the bustlings of drug dealers and smugglers of cheap labor.

The ministers of the eminently respectable Tucson churches who were involved in the refugee effort were extremely hesitant to follow in such problematic footsteps. Those who were aware of Corbett's initiative believed it would be considered a violation of law by the INS, and no one was remotely interested in breaking the law.

Nevertheless, in their frequent debates about what they should do about Corbett, the small band of pastors recognized that at some point they might have to walk down the same path. Of the approximately 13,000 Salvadorans apprehended at the border between mid-1980 and mid-1981, more than 10,000 were returned after signing "voluntary departure" statements. Almost all the remainder were deported, back into a country where 9,000 civilians died by political violence in 1980 alone, according to the conservative estimates of the State Department. In the minds of the ministers, being turned away was a death sentence for some refugees. At best, capture and detention were the first steps down a path to a dread, uncertain fate.[7]*

The ministers agreed that if there came a time when they had to begin transporting refugees, men and women of the cloth should do it, to counter any accusations that the work was anything other than humanitarian.

John Fife, in particular, wrestled with his conscience. Should he be helping Corbett? Another self answered back: What good would you be at border work? Your work is raising bond money and organizing. You don't even speak Spanish. If you got involved in what Jim is doing, who would do what you're doing? The inner debate raged on, and for several weeks Fife's cautious side won out.

Then one night in early October the Presbyterian pastor had to stop by the rancher's place on his way to the hospital to visit an ailing parishioner. There in the dusty compound of small houses and trailers he found twenty-one Salvadorans, camped in a little adobe house that Corbett had set aside for the refugees. It was a squalid scene, with the people crowded into two tiny rooms, constantly quarreling, sleeping wall to wall, and all sharing the same filthy bathroom. Pat Corbett was

---

*By 1982 human rights organizations estimated that since 1979, 30,000 civilians had been killed and another half million displaced from their homes in El Salvador (figures quoted in Ronald Copeland and Patricia Weiss Fagen, *Political Asylum: A Background Paper on Concepts, Procedures and Problems* [Washington, D.C.: Refugee Policy Group, December 1982], p. 43). See Appendix II for an analysis of the dangers faced by returnees to El Salvador.

at her wits' end and threatening to leave if something wasn't done soon
to move out the ragtag band. That night Corbett took Fife aside.

"Pat's going to drive them or me out," he confessed. "I don't know
what to do, but I've got to do something. What about using your
church? You've been using it for people that are bonded out; how would
you feel about my bringing some folks over there after I've brought
them up from the border, just for a few days until they find something
else?"[8]

It was Fife's moment of truth, but he still played for more time. "I
don't make decisions for our church," he told Corbett. "The elders of
the session do. We have a meeting scheduled for next Monday night,
and I'll bring it up then."

By that Monday Fife's mind was made up. He had decided that as
a matter of faith he couldn't duck the issue anymore and that as a
minister he had no choice. Ethically and theologically he felt Corbett
was right.

The meeting of the session started at 7:00 P.M. and continued until
midnight. The minister read a statement by Corbett explaining how the
rancher saw the issue:

> *Because the U.S. government takes the position that aiding undocu-*
> *mented Salvadoran and Guatemalan refugees in this country is a*
> *felony, we have no middle ground between collaborating and resis-*
> *tance. A maze of strategic dead ends can be averted if we face the*
> *imperative nature of this choice without attempting to delude our-*
> *selves or others. For those of us who would be faithful to our alle-*
> *giance to the Kingdom, there is also no way to avoid recognizing that*
> *in this case collaboration with the government is a betrayal of our*
> *faith, even if it is a passive or even loudly protesting collaboration*
> *that merely shuts out the undocumented refugee who is at our door.*
> *We can take our stand with the oppressed, or we can take our stand*
> *with organized oppression. We can serve the Kingdom, or we can*
> *serve the kingdoms of this world—but we cannot do both. Maybe,*
> *as the Gospel suggests, this choice is perennial and basic, but the*
> *presence of undocumented refugees here among us makes the*
> *definitive nature of our choice particularly clear and concrete. When*
> *the government itself sponsors the crucifixion of entire peoples and*
> *then makes it a felony to shelter those seeking refuge, law-abiding*
> *protest merely trains us to live with atrocity.*

With Fife a strong advocate of assisting Corbett, the four-hour discussion at Southside wasn't so much over whether the church should shelter refugees as over the probable risks. The group didn't know how the INS would view the matter: Was it a violation of immigration law or not? Although the INS considered harboring undocumented aliens illegal, many others in the community did not believe that housing refugees, some of whom had obviously been tortured, was a crime. On the contrary, for many it was a moral obligation. No one was certain just exactly what the church might be getting into.

In the end the session agreed that it had to open the doors of the church to the strangers in its midst. As Fife put it, "We do not check green cards at the door; we meet people's needs. We will provide hospitality at this church to anyone who needs it."

There were two abstentions from the vote of the session, both by federal employees who felt that they could not support the resolution but did not want to vote against it. All the elders agreed that their actions should be taken as quietly and as unobtrusively as possible.

The decision was announced to the congregation the following Sunday. Fife told his parishioners that they could expect to see, living at the church, Salvadorans and perhaps Guatemalans who had not been bonded out but who had been brought to Southside by a friend. The next day, after a meeting, Fife spoke to Corbett.

"Hey, I'm not one to sit around and watch you do all the legwork and just be a doorkeeper," he announced. Corbett asked him if he could drive a truck. "I've got a pickup truck," Fife replied, "and you can educate me. Sign me up—we're in this together now, fella."[9]

For the rest of the year, once or twice a week or whenever Corbett called, Fife hopped into his white Chevy Luv pickup with its four-wheel drive, overload springs, and tinted glass windows and drove down to Sacred Heart. He picked up his human load, said a little prayer, and took off down the main highway heading north. Looking back, he thought he had been insanely reckless. He didn't know where any of the Border Patrol roadblocks were; he hadn't tried to take every possible precaution; and he hadn't really thought through the consequences. At some point, he figured, we'll get caught, but hell, let's do it.

Fife didn't publicize his border runs, but he did make public statements to the effect that his congregation was providing refuge for Central Americans. Whenever there were refugees in the church, he would announce to the congregation at regular Sunday services that it was providing hospitality to undocumented people who were fleeing violence and terror in their homeland. He invoked the Bible as a guide: "And if a stranger sojourn with thee in your land, ye shall not vex him. But the stranger that dwelleth with you shall be unto you as one born among you, and thou shalt love him as thyself; for ye were strangers in the land of Egypt: I am the Lord your God."[10]

Fife then posed the question anew: "What do you think the faith requires?" The tiny congregation of 120 souls always agreed to keep up the work.

Chapter
Seven

ONE OF THE first of several lawsuits challenging the treatment of the refugees was on behalf of a young man named Crosby Wilfredo Orantes Hernández.[1] Orantes had fled El Salvador after he had been beaten by the National Guard, seen his mother's face smashed in with a rifle, and had two uncles abducted. Their bodies were found later, with their heads mutilated and their sexual organs cut off. Orantes had entered the United States without documentation and been picked up by the INS in Culver City, California. He claimed that he had been roughed up at his arrest and that for several days officers had tried to persuade him to sign voluntary departure papers. He was never advised of his right to consult with counsel, of the availability of free legal services, of his right to a deportation hearing or to apply for political asylum. Only after he was finally moved to El Centro was he able to call a friend, who arranged for a lawyer.

Orantes and the other early cases were only one prong of a major legal effort on behalf of the fleeing Salvadorans. Another prong of the legal attack was the tactic, used by Manzo at the mass bailout, of filing asylum applications for every Salvadoran who turned up. Anyone could apply, and since no one could be deported while the application was pending, the tactic bought time in the United States for those without serious claims. It also gave refugees the opportunity to prepare the lengthy documentation necessary to prove their claim. Immigration lawyers knew that the more claims they filed, the bigger the backlog would become, and time might stand still for as long as three or four years, while the applicant had the right to remain in the United States.

So the immigration lawyers flooded the INS with paper. Many of the forms stated no to all forty-four questions about the reasons why the person feared persecution. At the bottom the applicants would explain that they would reveal their fears when they had their asylum hearing. Not surprisingly, the State Department and the Immigration Service viewed many of these applications as fraudulent.[2] The message went out to the field offices that asylum was a loophole in the immigration laws, and the order was "plug that loophole." The right to asylum, in other words, became a crisis for the Immigration Service rather than a challenge requiring a humanitarian response.[3]

The need to focus on the litigation allowed the lawyers in the INS, rather than those with responsibility for the refugee, asylum, and parole program, to take the lead on the asylum issue. The general counsel of the agency was Maurice C. Inman, Jr., a former real estate lawyer from Los Angeles. Inman had no experience in immigration law, and very little in criminal law, but he was a litigator and a loyal Reaganite.* His deputy was the associate general counsel, Victor A. D. Rostow, a red-haired young man with a distinguished political lineage. He was the son of Eugene Rostow, who had served as undersecretary of state in the mid to late 1960s, and the nephew of Walt Rostow, Lyndon Johnson's political adviser during the Vietnam War. Victor Rostow, who later went on to become a legal counsel to Assistant Secretary of Defense Richard Perle and director of long-range policy in the Defense Department, was, like many young federal bureaucrats, ambitious, hard-working, and utterly unsentimental about the people affected by his decisions. He monitored all of the INS's litigation with a single-minded intensity that recommended him highly to his superiors in the Reagan administration.

Under Inman and Rostow the INS took a confrontational attitude

*"I'm nowhere near as conservative as Ed Meese," Inman said in a telephone interview with the author in November 1987. "I'm a Republican but not one of these extra-chromosome conservatives, as they call them in Washington."

toward the Central Americans' claims, and the name of the game became "winning" rather than designing an asylum program to meet the new realities. Internal suggestions that the Immigration Service try to approve at least 10 to 15 percent of the Salvadoran applications—enough to mollify the agency's critics—were spurned. Inman labeled a critical internal INS report the "big Red Book" and told its originator, Doris Meissner, that she should "deep-six" it.[4]

"We were going to the mat trying to defend those cases, and we didn't recognize that we had a new thing on our hands: refugees at our own borders, and a commingling of economic and political reasons for their flight," said Meissner later.[5]

At the end of 1981 the Immigration Service realized that it had another, even more unprecedented problem on its hands. INS officials in Tucson had picked up rumors that the city's ministers were more or less openly defying the immigration laws.

Right before Thanksgiving Margo Cowan was at the Federal Building in downtown Tucson for an asylum hearing. An INS attorney took her aside. "We're not sure what Fife and Corbett are up to," he confided, "but tell them to stop or we'll indict them."[6]

The warning prompted an emergency meeting in John Fife's living room during the last week in November 1981. Fife, Corbett, Margo Cowan, Lupe Castillo, Ken Kennon, Father Ricardo Elford, and a few others debated the dangers of their position. As Fife saw it, they had few options. They could stop what they were doing, and none of them believed that was ethically possible. Or they could continue and be charged with a criminal offense, an equally unappealing prospect.

The religious activists were particularly worried that the government might call a grand jury and offer them immunity in return for their testimony. If they testified, they might be forced to disclose the names and whereabouts of the refugees and others in the movement. If they refused to testify, they could be held in contempt and jailed without a trial for the duration of the grand jury. (Persons granted immunity cannot refuse to testify by claiming their privilege against self-incrimination.) That would be the worst of all worlds: They could end up behind bars for a year or more, with no opportunity to explain their actions to the country.

Fife argued that "the only choice we have is to beat 'em to the punch." They could go public about the underground railroad and try to build support for it within their national churches. Then, if they were indicted, at least the church community would understand the issue.[7]

Up to then there had been very little press coverage of the refugee crisis, other than a few stories about the bailout at El Centro. Whenever Fife or others urged local journalists to write more about the plight of the refugees, they were told, "Oh, we already did that story last summer." And despite the national efforts of ministers, human rights advocates, diplomats, and lawyers, there was, during the honeymoon period of the Reagan administration, little will in Congress to challenge the executive branch.

John Fife felt that the time had come to speak out, and Jim Corbett agreed that they were "obliged to speak truth to power."[8] The rancher had always been an advocate of openness; secrecy, he believed, was first cousin to the lie. He wanted to build a grass-roots faith community that would empower people to act in accordance with their consciences, and in his view, secrecy would smother the opportunity to develop such a consensus.

The discussion turned to ways to get the story out to the American people. At that point Fife had what he later described as the only original thought in his life. They were talking about the religious tradition of sanctuary. Why not announce that they were declaring sanctuary for undocumented refugees?

The tradition of sanctuary was as old as the Bible. The ancient Hebrews had allowed temples and even whole cities to declare themselves places of refuge for persons accused of a crime, a practice that allowed those wrongfully accused to escape swift and harsh retribution until the matter could be resolved. In the late Roman Empire fugitives could be harbored on the precincts of Christian churches. Later, during the medieval period, when canon law rivaled the secular authority, churches in England were recognized sanctuaries, offering safe haven for a temporary period to accused wrongdoers. Sanctuaries were widely used in the fourteenth, fifteenth, and sixteenth centuries, but the privilege, which had originally protected fugitives from blood revenge, came to be abused by debtors and common criminals and was abolished by Parliament in the early seventeenth century.[9]

The sanctuary privilege never became part of American common law or statute, although it could be argued that the continent itself was a sanctuary, a new Promised Land for the early colonists. The first practical provision of anything like sanctuary occurred in the years before the Civil War, when the Underground Railroad came into being to help slaves flee the South to safety. Clergymen, Quakers, and abolitionists set up a network of way stations where fleeing slaves could hide, in direct violation of the Fugitive Slave Law of 1850, prohibiting the harboring or assistance of runaway slaves anywhere in the United States. (Before that law was passed, a slave who had made it into the free states of the North was safe; the 1850 law meant that there was no safe haven in the entire United States, and fugitives could not rest until they reached Canada.)

Slaves were hidden in cellars, barns, churches, old mills, offices, and caves, and an elaborate system of passwords, codes, and special calls was developed to help them elude detection. Harriet Tubman, perhaps the most famous of all the Underground Railroad "conductors," would sing gospel verses as she passed slave cabins. One set of lyrics meant that a run was not possible that night; another signaled "all is ready." Others transported slaves in the false bottoms of wagons, and one train porter hid runaways in the sleeper car between Cairo, Illinois, and Chicago. Clerics and church communities were an integral part of the network, and some paid a very high price for their civil disobedience. A New England minister, Charles Torrey, died in prison after helping some 400 slaves escape servitude. The Presbyterian minister John Rankin maintained a refuge in Ripley, Ohio, across the river from the slave state of Kentucky. Slaveowners offered rewards of as much as $2,500 for Rankin's abduction and assassination, and his family had to carry arms to protect his life.[10]

It was not until the Vietnam War that sanctuary was explicitly invoked in the United States. Numerous churches and campuses all over the country, including Hawaii, sheltered draftees and servicemen seeking to avoid military service in Vietnam, although no claim was made to legal recognition of the activity. It was seen as an act of civil disobedience, rooted in moral opposition to an unjust war, a political protest dramatizing a conflict between individual conscience and government. In all cases the sanctuary seekers were arrested—many within the churches themselves—or surrendered voluntarily, and all were prosecuted by civil or military courts. The sanctuary concept was never tested in court, for all the defendants accepted their sentences as consequences of their actions. None of the sanctuaries themselves were ever prosecuted.[11]

The Tucson ministers were aware that other churches were groping toward a revival of the sanctuary idea. In October, for example, the

Lutheran Social Services of Southern California had sent out a letter suggesting that it was time for the church to reintroduce sanctuary as a means of seeking justice for those denied it. The letter described how a man being chased by an INS officer had run into a downtown church. The officer had pursued him through the nave and finally caught him in an upstairs loft. Handcuffed, he had been led away to probable deportation. After a complaint had been lodged with the local INS director, church representatives were told that an administrative order would be issued to all immigration officers that under no circumstances was a person to be pursued if he or she entered a church, hospital, or school. The order in effect said that these institutions were sanctuaries.

No one at the TEC meeting knew how the government would react if a number of churches proclaimed that concept. But even the most conservative had reluctantly concluded that the legal system just wasn't working for the refugees. The task force had already raised something like $750,000 in cash and collateral since the summer for bonds, and it could not indefinitely keep paying what it viewed as ransom.

Moreover, it was slowly becoming apparent that in the end even the most deserving refugees were being rejected. By mid-1981, exactly *two* Salvadorans had been granted political asylum. The Tucson task force had filled out hundreds of asylum applications, and not one of the requests had been granted. Already asylum applications with more than 100 pages of documentation had come back from the State Department denied, suspiciously quickly. Unless a refugee had *written* evidence that he or she would be persecuted, like a death list with his or her name on it, asylum was refused. (A Doonesbury cartoon showed a refugee asking an INS official what he needed to prove his fear of persecution. "A note from your dictator," the bureaucrat replied.)

One of those denied was Alejandro Hernández, a young man who had been working as a janitor at St Mark's Presbyterian after being bailed out of El Centro. Hernández, a student activist, had survived an ambush that killed several colleagues, lived underground for two years while being pursued by death squads, and had a brother, an uncle, and a cousin brutally murdered. Still, his asylum application came back denied, with no reason given.*

---

*Hernández resubmitted his asylum request after locating an old *New York Times* newspaper clip describing the massacre and obtaining an affidavit from another survivor of the shoot-out. He was finally granted asylum in Tucson in 1985, four years after his first application had been filed. He was one of the first refugees assisted by the Tucson church workers to receive asylum.

Why should we keep up this charade? Mike Smith, the pastor of St. Mark's, wondered aloud. We've busted our rear ends to use the system, and it turns out to be a kangaroo court.[12]

Ken Kennon had talked to the staffs of several congressmen's offices, but nothing had come out of it as far as he could see. The minister had also had several talks with Bill Johnston, and it was always the same. The official would tell him about his Catholic faith and about how horrible he knew things were in Central America, but when it came to INS policy, Johnston flip-flopped. He told Kennon that this was none of the churches' business, that they were sticking their noses in where they didn't belong. He referred to the refugee supporters as "goody two-shoes." It got to where Kennon avoided seeing the man. Talking with him felt like hitting a pillow, and his remarks reminded the minister of the "good Germans," who just did their job and helped send millions of Jews to their deaths.[13]

Father Ricardo had tried the political route as well. He had spent hours writing Arizona congressmen, but nothing ever seemed to happen. He felt a need to do more. In his mind, if a country was financing the planes that were bombing Salvadoran children, the citizens of that country had an absolute moral obligation to help the victims to escape. He recognized that we couldn't help everyone in the world, but he thought, if the crazies in our country are bombing, we can't just stand by and watch. It's necessary reparation.[14]

Only the Manzo people were dubious about a declaration of sanctuary, which they feared might mean a pulling away from the legal effort to help the refugees. If the churches despaired of the legal system, who would be left in Tucson but themselves, overwhelmed and swamped with an impossible caseload, to fight the necessary fights through the immigration courts?

The sentiment for sanctuary carried, however, and Fife outlined his idea. They would try to persuade one church in every large metropolitan area to join with the Tucson churches in announcing sanctuary for Central American refugees. Each church would locate a refugee family that would stand up and tell its story, to personalize the crisis. That was, after all, how the Tucson people had been drawn into the issue: by seeing that the Central Americans were not nameless, faceless "illegal aliens" but fellow human beings in distress.

Fife argued that such a declaration would generate much more publicity than simply calling a press conference about the TEC's work. It would probably stir up a fair amount of regional attention, he thought, at least in Arizona and California. Then, even if the Tucson activists were arrested, they would have wider support and the refugee issue could not be swept under the rug.

The group talked for a while about which congregation in Tucson should publicly declare sanctuary. It was clear that Southside was already a de facto place of refuge. John Fife estimated that as many as 300 to 350 Central Americans had passed through the church, staying behind the chapel in a tiny room equipped with one cot, a sink, and a refrigerator; with a makeshift shower rigged up in the furnace room next door. As many as 20 people had been in the church at one time, on cots that spilled out into hallways and into church offices. Fife agreed to take the proposal to his congregation.

During his next Sunday service the minister announced that he was going to bring up a proposal that the church declare itself a sanctuary at the next annual meeting, in late January. For the next two months his parishioners had a cram course on the implications, with law professors addressing discussion groups on the finer points of refugee statutes and Bible study classes immersing themselves in INS policy and the history of sanctuary.

But the decision was for all practical purposes made that Christmas Eve. One of the Salvadorans who had been bonded out of El Centro had left his country within hours after learning that the death squads were coming for him. He had left his pregnant wife behind. She had since had the baby, and Corbett had offered to help them join the father. On December 24 the rancher went down to Nogales to bring the pair across the border. An American woman carried the baby across the port of entry in the bustling Christmas crowd, and the Border Patrol didn't give a glance at the little bundle in her arms. The mother was coming through the border fence on her own, and Corbett found himself sitting in Nogales cradling the baby and waiting for her, praying that the child would stay asleep until she arrived.[15]

He couldn't help remembering the grief-stricken face of a nun he had met on Mexico's Guatemalan border two weeks earlier, as she told him of just such a baby boy, nine months old, whom Guatemalan soldiers had mutilated and slowly murdered while forcing his mother to watch. The victim might have been the baby in my arms, he thought, and he might still be, if he gets caught and sent back—his father was known to be opposed to the military rulers of El Salvador. He's a deportable illegal alien to the same government that is supporting the military terrorists that forced this family to flee, Corbett thought bitterly.

The mother arrived, flushed with excitement and relief. At four in the afternoon Corbett delivered them at Southside, and by nightfall the family was reunited in a little house in the Tucson barrio that a Hispanic family shared with refugees, a house so crowded that sometimes people had to sleep in cars parked in back. That evening at a candlelight service Fife stood up before the congregation and said, "I'm supposed to say something about the Gospel text tonight, but I think there is no doubt that we have seen the Gospel tonight." He told them about the latest refugees. "This is what the Bible calls a sign," he said. "Christ is present in the refugees and in sanctuary."[16]

The same Christmas Eve Jim and Pat Corbett attended the forty-fifth weekly prayer vigil for social justice in Central America at the Federal Building. By chance Corbett was asked to read the following passage: "She gave birth to her firstborn son and wrapped him in swaddling clothes and laid him in a manger, because there was no room for them in the place where travelers lodged. There were shepherds in that region, living in the fields and keeping night watch. . . ."[17]

Almost a month later, on the last Sunday in January 1982, Southside Presbyterian held its annual meeting. At this gathering the church routinely made its central policy decisions, adopted an annual budget, and elected the elders and deacons who made policy in session during the rest of the year. The sanctuary proposal dominated the discussion. Fife's plan was heatedly debated for four or five hours. Only one man was flatly opposed to the idea of sanctuary, but many people were reluctant to violate the law of the land. One man stood up and told the group that he had grown up believing that there was no conflict between being a good citizen and a good Presbyterian, and he still couldn't believe that the two were not synonymous. He had been an active Boy Scout and had fought in World War II. Something must be wrong with the way they were approaching this thing.[18]

Others wondered how they should vote on the decision. Should it be by majority or two-thirds vote? Fife said he didn't know but suggested that they take a vote and see what the feeling was first. At that point one woman stood up and reminded the congregation that Southside did not have to be the only church to declare sanctuary; why couldn't other congregations declare themselves at the same time? Fife realized that he had thought so much about organizing his own congregation that he had forgotten his original notion. Recognizing the possibility of strength in numbers, he immediately agreed. Depending on what the congregation decided, it would write letters to other churches asking them to join with Southside as sanctuaries.

The vote was by secret ballot. Fife thought, this is the way the faith works. We don't ask bishops, cardinals, or pastors what to do. We decide ourselves, and we decide together. The vote was 79 to 2, with four abstentions.

Not a few misgivings were expressed that night. Fife himself had a twinge; there were homeless people right here in the United States, even in Tucson. Was it really so clear that the church should set that ministry aside for the Salvadorans and Guatemalans? More than one person seemed anxious; many had families and jobs. Would this put them in jeopardy? There were jokes to ease the tension:

"Some of us are going to be indicted."

"That's OK; we'll volunteer our pastor as a scapegoat."

When the vote was announced, Fife immediately suggested that they talk about what "this means." Everyone agreed that wasn't necessary; everyone knew what it meant. Fife was instructed to prepare the letter to other churches, and the exact timing of the announcement would be left to the session to determine.

The next few weeks were the tensest that Fife had ever lived through. He was constantly anxious that he or someone else might be picked up by the Border Patrol or INS, wrecking the task force's plans to seize the initiative. Things were also tense at home. Ever since the summer Marianne Fife had been urging her husband to back off the refugee issue. A pretty blond woman in her late thirties, she had married John Fife while still in college and had their first child while he was still in seminary. She had been with him through the civil rights battles and had lived for years in run-down neighborhoods and barrios while he pursued his calling. Now he was running the risk of going to prison.

At every step of this new ministry he had assured her that what he was doing was perfectly safe. "I'm just bonding out refugees; you're crazy to worry," he'd said over the summer. "Honey, I'm just driving people up from the border," he'd said when he started transporting, a federal crime carrying a $2,000 fine and five years of imprisonment for every illegal alien involved. And now he was openly, publicly, throwing down the gauntlet to the government, in effect sticking his chin out and inviting officials to retaliate. It was a lot to ask of any family, and Marianne told John Fife that it was too much; she wasn't sure she could handle any more. Not surprisingly, the Fifes that winter were under a great deal of stress.

A gathering of churches and Salvadoran relief agencies at El Centro the previous fall had generated a mailing list of eighty to ninety organizations, and Tim Nonn, working nonstop for weeks, tried to bring other churches on board. He called people he knew in San Francisco and Los Angeles, but initially he couldn't find a congregation or a refugee that would go along with a public declaration. Finally he just started calling people in cities around the country, asking which was the most liberal church in town. He then called those churches cold, and within weeks he had pulled it all together. Sanctuary was going to be declared by five churches around the country, each with a refugee ready to tell his or her story at a press conference.[19]

The other sanctuaries included the University Lutheran Chapel in Berkeley, California, whose pastor, Gustav Schultz, had been a pioneer of the concept. Schultz had already helped form the East Bay Sanctuary Covenant Congregations in the fall of 1981, and he was able to persuade seven churches in the group to coordinate their declarations with Southside's. The other churches joining Southside were the First Unitarian Universalist Church in Los Angeles, the Community Bible Church in Lawrence, New York, on Long Island, and the Luther Place Memorial Church in Washington, D.C., which had worked with the homeless in the nation's capital. It wasn't an overwhelming response, but it was better than going out in the cold completely naked.

The final decision was the date of the announcement. March 24, the anniversary of Archbishop Romero's death, was imminent, and several churches in Tucson were planning memorial services and masses on that day. It seemed an ideal time, for attention would already be focused on human rights abuses in El Salvador.

Nonn sent out a packet of information to the participating churches and set to work on the media. He called the local papers and television stations, and they all said they would come. One TV reporter asked if the Phoenix stations would attend, so Nonn called Phoenix and said, "You'll want to see this; all of the Tucson stations will be there."[20] Then he called the West Coast, New York, Canada, and the networks, and to his surprise, he seemed to be generating national coverage. He and John Fife began to think that this thing might make a bigger splash than they had expected.

Three or four days before the twenty-fourth, one of John Fife's parishioners came over to his house and showed him a copy of a letter. "I just got this; have you seen it?" he asked. Fife glanced down. It was a copy of a letter to the FBI, dated the day after the sanctuary vote at Southside. In it a member of the congregation who had spoken against the motion informed the bureau of Southside's activities in aiding undocumented aliens and revealed the upcoming announcement. Fife felt dazed. I've been beating my brains out for two months not to let anyone know what we're doing, he thought, and *they've* known the entire time.[21]

There were other last-minute crises as the D day of the public declaration approached. Three days before March 24 the church was still uncertain whether Southside would have a refugee family willing to be embraced into sanctuary amid a fanfare of publicity. A couple of months earlier Fife had brought up from Nogales a family that had seemed perfect, an attractive upper-middle-class couple with two children. The husband had been an official in the Salvadoran land reform program, and, Fife suspected, had gotten too enthusiastic about his work. He had translated aerial photographs into topographical maps and perhaps aroused concerns that that kind of information in the wrong hands could make life uncomfortable for the armed forces. In any event, "Alfredo," as the man was called, had been imprisoned for five days, and although he hadn't been tortured, he had lain awake all night listening to the sound of screaming. As soon as he was released, he gathered up his family and fled the country.

Fife had arranged for the family to be put up temporarily in a parishioner's home, and after consulting with Corbett, he asked them if they would be willing to become the first public sanctuary refugees. They hesitated, unsure whether they wanted to run the risk of exposure, and as March 24 drew near, they still hadn't made up their minds. Finally, just before the scheduled announcement, the man called Fife. "We'll do it," he said.

The declaration was scheduled for a Wednesday. On the preceding Friday the conspirators picked up their afternoon paper, the *Tucson Citizen*, and read all about it. It turned out that the reporter, Randal Udall, the son of Arizona Congressman Morris Udall, had been planning a piece on sanctuary to coincide with the public announcement. The *Washington Post* had gotten wind of the story, and Randy Udall had asked and received permission from Corbett's group to go ahead with his article. Fife was in San Francisco for a national meeting, and on Friday, March 19, Corbett called to tell him that the news about the upcoming declaration of sanctuary was out.

Fife's first reaction was that the jig was up. The thing is jinxed; we're never going to get to make that announcement, he thought. But he told Corbett that they had to go ahead, and as it turned out, the premature publicity attracted far more coverage than the simple announcement itself ever would have.

In Udall's lead paragraph Fife was described as a paragon of western morality, a pastor "who smokes Pall Malls, wears cowboy boots, and has just returned from a ski vacation to the White Mountains."[22] Next week, the article continued, he "will publicly defy the U.S. government to arrest him as a felon in violation of immigration laws." After operating an underground railroad for months, Fife was now planning to "up the ante," in his own words.

"Fife and his church will dare the government to stop their work," the article declared. " 'This church can no longer cooperate with or defy the law covertly as we have done,' Fife said. 'When the law of the land is in conflict with the law of God, a Christian's first duty is clear. . . .' "

Fife's charismatic challenge did not go unnoticed. Forty reporters, including a man from Canadian broadcasting and several Europeans, attended the announcement and press conference at Southside on March 24. To Tim Nonn, it looked as if there were probably more media people there than ministers or supporters.

Chapter
Eight

T HE MORNING OF the public declaration was a typical Tucson spring day, sunny and clear. Two giant banners had been hung down to frame the entrance of the church. One read LA MIGRA NO PROFANA EL SANCTUARIO ("Immigration, don't profane sanctuary"). The other proclaimed: ESTE ES EL SANCTUARIO DE DIOS PARA LOS OPRIMIDOS DE CENTRO AMERICA ("This is the sanctuary of God for the oppressed of Central America"). Long tables had been set up in front of the chapel, and in the center sat the Reverend Mr. Fife in a headband, flanked by "Alfredo," the refugee, and Father Ricardo on his right and by Margo Cowan, Gary MacEoin, and Jim Corbett on his left. Immediately behind Fife stood Ken Kennon and Dave Sholin. At ten in the morning on March 24, as eight television cameras rolled, Fife introduced "Alfredo," who immediately became "one of the most publicized undocumented aliens here ever," as the *Tucson Citizen* reporter put it.[1]

A lengthy discussion had pondered the question of how to protect the identity of the refugees, and the decision was finally made to have Alfredo wear a cowboy hat and a bandanna over most of his face.

Although some thought the guise made the victim of repression look like a masked bandit, no one had a better idea, so the masked refugee became a staple of sanctuary declarations thereafter.

The short dark refugee outlined conditions in Central America, and Corbett followed with some brief remarks on the tradition of sanctuary and the history of the Underground Railroad. He estimated that some 200 Salvadorans and Guatemalans had been helped to avoid capture by the railroad, and several hundred more "ransomed" from the INS. These efforts were insignificant, Corbett pointed out, compared with the multitudes being caught and returned to their countries, but "fellowship and compassion" required them.

John Fife then explained how the decision to declare sanctuary had been made and estimated that some 100 churches around the country were indirectly supporting the underground railroad and the legal effort either by providing donations or by receiving refugees for resettlement.

That night Fife and almost a dozen other clergymen led 230 people in a one-and-a-quarter-mile procession from downtown Tucson to Southside Presbyterian Church for an ecumenical service "in solidarity with undocumented refugees in Central America." G. Daniel Little, executive director of the United Presbyterian Church U.S.A., gave a sermon urging support of the sanctuary movement, and among those who participated were Monsignor Arsenio Carrillo of St. Augustine's, the Catholic cathedral in Tucson, and Rabbi Joseph Weizenbaum of Temple Emanu-El, the city's largest Reform synagogue.

"CBS Evening News" that night carried a fiery statement by Corbett branding the deportations as "clear violation[s] of international law and of the most fundamental standards of human decency. Yet the U.S. government is telling us that it is the victims who are the illegals. Abduction, torture, and murder pose as law and authority, while the victims and those who try to help them are driven underground," he declared.

"Today, in this church," Corbett concluded, "human solidarity is out in the open, and oppression is in hiding, waiting for another time without witnesses. What is happening to the Salvadorans has already happened so many times and so many places during this century. But we are not going to stand by while it happens here in Tucson."

On the day before the public declaration a letter from John Fife was delivered to Attorney General William French Smith:

We are writing to inform you that Southside United Presbyterian Church will publicly violate the Immigration and Nationality Act, Section 274 (A). . . . *

We take this action because we believe the current policy and practice of the United States Government with regard to Central American refugees is illegal and immoral. We believe our government is in violation of the 1980 Refugee Act and international law by continuing to arrest, detain, and forcibly return refugees to the terror, persecution, and murder in El Salvador and Guatemala.

We believe that justice and mercy require that people of conscience actively assert our God-given right to aid anyone fleeing from persecution and murder. The current administration of United States law prohibits us from sheltering these refugees from Central America. Therefore, we believe that administration of the law is immoral as well as illegal.

We beg of you, in the name of God, to do justice and love mercy in the administration of your office. We ask that "extended voluntary departure" be granted to refugees from Central America and that current deportation proceedings against these victims be stopped.

Until such time, we will not cease to extend the sanctuary of the church to undocumented people from Central America. Obedience to God requires this of us all.

Copies of the letter were sent to A. Melvin McDonald, U.S. attorney, Arizona; William Johnston, Immigration Service, Tucson; and Leon Ring, Border Patrol, Tucson.

*According to Section 274 (a) of the Immigration and Nationality Act, "Any person . . . who . . . willfully or knowingly conceals, harbors, or shields from detection, or attempts to conceal, harbor, or shield from detection, in any place, including any building or any means of transportation . . . any alien . . . not duly admitted by an immigration officer . . . shall be guilty of a felony, and upon conviction thereof shall be punished by a fine not exceeding $2000 or by imprisonment for a term not exceeding five years, or both, for each alien in respect to whom any violation of this subsection occurs: Provided, however, that for the purposes of this section, employment (including the usual and normal practices incident to employment) shall not be deemed to constitute harboring)." Under the law at the time it was illegal to drive an undocumented alien to the doctor or to give him or her a bed for the night, but it was not illegal to put one to work. Not surprisingly, sanctuary workers and INS officials alike found the distinction absurd. New sanctions against employing illegal aliens were adopted in the Immigration Reform and Control Act of 1986.

As the activists were setting up for the press conference, Lupe Castillo suddenly noticed a plainclothesman across the street from the church taking pictures. "That guy over there in that car is an undercover Border Patrol agent," she told Fife.[2] The minister thereupon invited the man to get out of his car and come on over to the church, as all the television cameras swung around to photograph him. He refused to tell the reporters who he was, but Fife insisted he was with the Border Patrol.

"We're glad to know of their interest, and we hope he will accurately report exactly what our position is," the pastor told the crowd, adding that in his opinion it was remarkable that immigration authorities, who had been informed in advance of the protest, had chosen to come and watch in an undercover capacity.

. . .

That night the INS had a second intelligence agent surveilling the march and the ecumenical church service. In a memo to his superiors, he described his impressions:

Aside from the old people, most of them looked like the anti-Vietnam war protestors of the early 70's. In other words, political misfits.

Nothing derogatory toward the Border Patrol or tending to incite anyone to violate any law was said, either by the two speakers previously mentioned or by the people on the march.

I attended the "service" to see what they were going to do. . . . The service appeared to be purely a political show with all the ministers, priests, etc., at the altar area. . . . Various times during the first part of the "service" while cameras were going good, the "Frito Bandito" appeared in the front doorway instead of Mr. Udall. I refer to an alleged El Salvadorian [sic] wearing a black mask, who has been used in various photos. . . . There was nothing really inflammatory or inciting said, it was rather bland. It seemed like this "service" was a political event meant to reassure those still not firmly committed to the overt violation of Federal law. That everything was alright [sic] and "God is on our side." . . .

It seems that this movement is more political than religious but that a ploy is going to be Border Patrol "baiting" by that group in order to demonstrate to the public that the U.S. government via it's [sic] jack-booted gestapo Border Patrol Agents think [sic] nothing

*of breaking down the doors of their churches to drag Jesus Christ
out to be tortured and murdered. I believe that all political implications should be considered before any further action is taken toward
this group.* [3]

Leon Ring, the chief Border Patrol agent in Tucson and recipient of
this memo, was already less than enthusiastic about acting against the
ministers. He had been aware of their activities for several months, but
he was hesitant to arrest them; as a twenty-five-year veteran of the
Border Patrol he was well aware that the public found that sort of thing
very distasteful.

Years before, an outcry had erupted after the Border Patrol arrested
several undocumented maids when they were leaving church on a
Sunday morning. After that incident it became an unwritten rule that
the patrol would stay away from churches, and Ring was loath to
violate the tradition. Besides, he calculated that the underground railroad was an amateurish operation. He believed that his officers and
informants, with just a little dumb luck, would have run into the
smugglers if they were at all widespread, and they never had. The
Border Patrol had antismuggling units in Tucson, Phoenix, and Yuma,
with agents all over southern Arizona, plus a network of paid informants—maybe thirty or forty in all. None of these men had ever seen
a TEC "border worker." [4]

Bill Johnston was no more eager than Leon Ring to respond to the
ministers' public provocation. Just before the announcement he told
Randy Udall that he doubted that the immigration service would
openly confront John Fife and his congregation. Asked for his comments after the press conference, the district director for the INS in
Phoenix said that his office had "no knowledge" of undocumented
aliens living at Southside. Should he learn otherwise, he said, "appropriate action" would be taken. INS officials suspected that the churches
were not actually transporting anyone into the country, but were only
feeding and sheltering the illegal aliens. Although that was technically
illegal, the agency had lived with such activity in the past, and could
continue to live with it.

As the months went by, however, the Immigration Service in Arizona began to feel more pressure to act. Among other things, District
Director Ernest Gustafson had a letter from Senator Barry Goldwater's
office wondering why he wasn't doing anything about prosecuting the

defiant ministers. He had had to assure the senator that "an appropriate investigation will be conducted into the matter to which you refer."

Even worse, the media were beginning to make heroes out of the lawbreakers. In its issue of August 9, 1982, *People* magazine ran a six-page piece on Jim Corbett and his smuggling of a desperate Salvadoran couple and three of their children. The article practically canonized Corbett, leading with a royal purple paragraph: "The gaunt-faced man followed the shimmering desert highway south to the Mexican border. His hands, painfully swollen by arthritis, rested lightly on the steering wheel of the ancient Chevy pickup, but no pain or weakness or uncertainty showed on his face. The fact that he was about to commit a federal crime troubled Jim Corbett not at all."

The worshipful tone infuriated federal officials, who felt that they were being cast as villains opposite the daring and saintly smugglers. Gustafson, who attended the fundamentalist Church of Christ and taught a Sunday school class, resented it. So did Mel McDonald, the United States attorney in Phoenix. *He* was a practicing Mormon who neither smoked nor drank, and for two years as a young man he had been a missionary in Canada, going from door to door, proselytizing the faith. In McDonald's opinion, these people had no right to throw out the criminal code just because they were wearing clerical collars. Religious motives granted them no immunity. If they were taking crime into the sanctuary, he would take law enforcement right in after them.

McDonald, Gustafson, and the latter's boss, the INS regional commissioner in California, all recognized, however, that any move against the churches would be controversial. They agreed that any decision to pursue a case against the underground railroad had to be made at a higher level, in Washington. McDonald flew to the capital and met with top Justice Department officials, who told him to hold off. This was no ordinary antismuggling case, McDonald was warned; a lot of people who vote are Presbyterians and Lutherans and Catholics, and they might not take kindly to the hauling of their clergy into court.[5]

The commissioner of the INS, Alan C. Nelson, typified this cautious attitude. Nelson, a San Francisco lawyer and a good friend of White House counsel Edwin Meese, was by nature a careful man. He thought that the United States had a fair and thorough asylum system that certainly did not discriminate against Salvadorans. As a nationality, Salvadorans were fourth in the numbers legally admitted into the United States, and unsuccessful asylum applicants could turn to an exhaustive appeal system. If a claim was denied, an applicant could appeal to an independent Board of Immigration Appeals and, beyond that, all the way through the federal courts.[6] Nelson couldn't understand why John Fife and others were calling press conferences and denouncing the government. The commissioner did not doubt the correctness of the administration's policy, but he wanted to keep talking to the dissident clergy. He told his associates at INS headquarters that the underground railroad was a classic case of political dissent and civil disobedience and that the worst thing in the world would be to go out and start arresting church people. "Don't let them get our goat; don't let's make martyrs out of them," he told his colleagues.[7]

Nelson instructed his troops in Arizona to be sure that someone in the INS was always available to go out on the hustings to debate the movement. He seemed to hope that like wayward but not incorrigible children, the sanctuary workers could eventually be shown the error of their ways.

Meanwhile, the members of the Tucson Ecumenical Council hadn't planned much beyond the public declaration. Fife and Corbett had had a few quiet conversations about what they would do if and when they were arrested, but neither man was prepared for the deluge of calls and mail they soon received, both from refugees and their families and from congregations offering to help.

Most of the letters went unanswered. The Tucson task force was overwhelmed with the needs of the refugees it had already assisted, and it was now alone in dealing with the newcomers showing up almost daily. Manzo, following the sanctuary declaration, had decided that it had to devote more attention to its traditional Mexican clientele and announced that it could not take on any new Central American cases. As Margo Cowan and Lupe Castillo saw it, sanctuary was primarily a tactic to educate middle- and upper-class American churchgoers on the Central American refugee issue. In their view, most refugees didn't need gringos helping them across the border; anyone could make it except perhaps for families with small children. They needed more help in the tedious and unglamorous work of fighting their cases through the courts.

The legal challenges to the INS were already beginning to pay off. On April 30, 1982, Federal Judge David Kenyon issued an order in the Orantes case enjoining the INS from returning any Salvadorans without fully informing them of their options available under the immigration law. The injunction in effect told the INS to "Mirandaize" its treatment of Salvadorans at the border, and despite initial foot-dragging, the agency did begin to provide Central Americans with information on their legal rights, in Spanish as well as English, at least at the major ports of entry and detention centers.

In the next few months the order had a significant impact. According to statistics gathered by a church group in California, there was a 70 percent drop in the numbers of people signing voluntary departure statements after the restraining order. The number of Salvadorans who applied for political asylum jumped by 56.6 percent during the first four months of fiscal year (FY) 1983 in comparison with the same period in FY 1982 (asylum applications from all other nationalities fell 11.4 percent in the same period).[8]

But for most of 1982 the restraining order had little impact at the border and brought no change at all in the government's refusal to grant the Salvadorans' asylum requests. And as the abuses continued, an underground railroad of sanctuary churches spontaneously began to form, from southern Mexico up to the border, from California and Seattle to Chicago and points as far east as New England. (The only region where this modern underground railroad failed to stir consciences seemed to be the South, which by the end of 1982 had produced no sanctuary churches.)

The southern terminus of the railroad had been put in place by Jim Corbett in late 1981. Toward the end of that year the rancher made a trip to Chiapas and Guatemala in an effort to establish contact with sympathetic churches. (His total expenses for the five-week trip came to $388, and when a friend asked him what he had eaten, the frugal Quaker replied, "Tortillas and bananas.") One of Corbett's major findings was that Guatemalans were now swelling the refugee flow. Unlike the urbanized Salvadorans, many of whom had relatives or friends already in the United States, these new migrants, like the young couple featured in the film El Norte, were for the most part simple Indian peasants, uprooted from their villages by a brutal antiguerrilla campaign by the army.

Their country, the largest in Central America, had been under uninterrupted military rule since 1954, when a U.S.-backed coup had toppled the leftist, reformist government of Jacobo Arbenz Guzmán. Since the early 1960s the army had been allied with paramilitary death squads that ruthlessly exterminated guerrillas, critics of the government, and even common criminals. In Guatemala, the saying went, "there are no political prisoners, just political murders."

The early 1980s brought even more savage repression. By the last six months of 1981 political murders had reached a level of more than 400 a *month,* according to Amnesty International.[9]

The terror was nightmarish and random. Unmarked Cherokee station wagons and black-windowed bulletproof Broncos filled with armed men patrolled the streets, firing at victims on street corners or dragging them out of their beds at night. Fresh corpses appeared every morning along roadsides, in storm drains, under viaducts, or piled high in ravines. For sheer barbarity, the Guatemalan situation had no equal.

Human rights organizations monitoring events believed that the level of violence actually became worse than anything previously seen in Central America under the new military leader and president Efraín Ríos Montt, who came to power in another coup in March 1982, shortly after Corbett's first visit. The new government launched a bloody counterinsurgency campaign to root out rebels in the countryside, in a Central American version of the old Southeast Asian tactic of "draining the pond so the fish can't swim." The army wiped out entire villages suspected of supporting the guerrillas. Indians who cooperated in hunting down rebels were rewarded with *fusiles y frijoles* ("guns and beans"), and those who declined to participate were often massacred by newly formed "civil patrols."[10]

In April 1982 the Guatemalan Conference of Bishops estimated that 1 million people, mostly Indian campesinos, or 1 out of every 7 Guatemalans, had been displaced by the rural war. More than 100,000 of them sought refuge in Mexico. In March 1983 the number of Guatemalan Indians in southern Mexico was put at between 70,000 and 100,000 by an Americas Watch team.

At the time of Jim Corbett's visit this tragic bloodbath was just becoming apparent. Tapachula, in southern Chiapas, was teeming with some 30,000 to 40,000 undocumented Central Americans. The freight-yards were crowded with migrating men, and in the *zona de tolerancia,* the city's red-light district, Central American women sold their bodies in order to stay alive.

In one southern Mexican village, in the coffee-growing country around Cacahoatán and Unión Hidalgo, a farmer surprised Corbett by asking him whether he was from Guatemala. When the gringo said he wasn't, the man looked knowingly doubtful. "Near here, where I live, there's one of your class who came from Guatemala to avoid being killed," he confided.[11]

The encounter convinced Corbett that he had better leave his little maroon imprimatured Spanish Bible behind in Mexico along with his other subversive documents. He wasn't reassured by other reactions to his plans to travel on to Guatemala. One priest told him that six people had been killed on the other side of the river a couple of days earlier but that they had, after all, been involved in the upcoming elections.

Guatemala was, as expected, a beautiful country grim with signs of death and violence. One Guatemala City newspaper he saw in the town of Malacatán carried six stories about eleven disappearances and three stories about seven recovered corpses—"tortured," "strangled," or "intercepted by various unknown men." Many of these notices were tucked away on the back pages among the ads, like fillers.

On December 5, while he was sitting in the plaza in Malacatán watching the evening promenade, there was a sudden burst of pistol fire from the police station about fifty yards away. Everyone scurried for cover, and shopkeepers quickly shut their doors and turned off their lights. Corbett walked over to a crowd peering from the corner of a building. Everyone was talking about a guerrilla attack, but no one really knew what had happened. He hurried across the small plaza in front of the police station to get back to his hotel and banged on the locked door to get in.

Soon the Guardia de la Hacienda, in green uniforms, and the Guardia Nacional, in blue uniforms, and the secret police were out in force, and the hotel owner warned Corbett to stay indoors. When they opened up with their submachine guns, she said, they usually killed a few bystanders.

The next morning the cause of the uproar became clear. Two women from the cantinas had been picked up and put in jail, and a drunken man had tried to approach them. He was armed and wasn't known by the jailers, so they had shot him dead.

One of Corbett's tentative conclusions was that for many refugees, economic and social opportunities were better in Mexico, where they shared a language and culture, than in the United States. He had learned that at least 2,000 Salvadorans were working in Tapachula in construction, and one priest had told him that the migrants could always find some kind of work if they were at all capable and willing. In this man's opinion, one of the problems was that they tended to work only long enough to get some money to continue northward in search of something better.

In Chiapas Corbett found an active Christian community of some 150 people engaged in assisting the refugees. They included the wives of several local politicians. He also met one priest busily engaged in housing and feeding and finding them jobs. Like his counterparts in Tucson, the man had discovered that the Salvadorans were overly fond of hard liquor; his solution, which Corbett passed on, was holy water and exorcistic prayer.

Still, the refugees were not generally welcome in Mexico, and most were obviously exploited and destitute. Corbett spread the word among the local churches that a group in Arizona stood ready to help those who sought a safe haven in the United States. He left his name and address and phone number and the names of churches along the border that would shelter refugees.[12]

Chapter
Nine

T HE VERY FIRST sanctuary church in the United States had been
Sacred Heart in Nogales, where Corbett had arranged to meet his
first two refugees. And in the spring of 1982 the parish's new youth
director became one of the busiest conductors on the underground
railroad. The hot-tempered young priest had a run-in with the Immigration Service that convinced him that the government could go to
hell.

With his bushy mustache and dark good looks Father Anthony
("Tony") Clark looked more like a barrio priest than a midwesterner
who had attended seminary in Rome. Born in Pennsylvania and reared
in Iowa as one of six children—one brother became a state policeman
in Pennsylvania—Clark since high school had been a member of the
Brothers of the Poor of St. Francis. As its name implied, the order was
dedicated to caring for the underprivileged. After getting his B.A. at
Iowa Wesleyan College and a three-year stint at the North American
College at the Vatican in Rome, Father Tony was ordained in the
Roman Catholic diocese of Davenport, Iowa.[1]

Not long after that, in 1980, a priest from Tucson invited Clark to come down and work with young people in south Tucson. The young cleric fell in love with the Southwest and persuaded his bishop to give him a leave of absence to work with Hispanics in Arizona. He moved to Nogales, then a sleepy border town of some 35,000 souls, and became a priest at Sacred Heart, a towering landmark perched high on a hill overlooking Highway 19, the main route from Tucson down to the border.

The thirty-two-year-old priest had two passions: underprivileged boys and sports. He had been a 145-pound boxer in high school back in York, Iowa, and a three-in-one football, basketball, and baseball coach while in college. He had found that by introducing young people to sports, he could occasionally succeed in steering them away from the temptations of the streets. He hadn't been in Arizona long before he was coaching a city boxing team for Mexican and American kids called Los Guadalupanos.

Within a few months of his arrival in Nogales Clark had also opened up an old-fashioned boys' home. He discovered that the police in Nogales were routinely sending runaways and juvenile delinquents to the adult jail, where their chances of slipping further into trouble were geometrically increased. Clark launched the Casa Guadalupe School for Boys in his own home, a modest Spanish-style bungalow on one of the side streets near the church. He offered a few emergency beds, hot meals, and a tender, no-nonsense presence for kids who might otherwise have been locked up with pimps and drug pushers.

Over time the superior court judge in Nogales began to refer boys to the school rather than send them to a juvenile facility. After a stay at the Casa they were given a chance to convince the court that they were ready to become good citizens, with no criminal record.

As if that were not enough, by the spring of 1982 Father Clark had also taken on a prison ministry in Tucson, making regular clerical visits to the Pima County jail and various places of detention in the area. One of the stops on his rounds was the Santa Cruz juvenile detention center in Nogales, which the Border Patrol was using as a place to park undocumented young Central Americans under age eighteen before they were shipped off to be deported. Many of the boys opened up to the sympathetic *padrecito,* and Tony Clark had an unforgettable education on the horrors devastating the region. Gradually, as part of his regular routine, Father Clark began to refer the boys' names to the Manzo Area Council. Every week in the spring of 1982 he would discover four or five more teenagers whose stories were so compelling that he passed their names along, for whatever legal assistance Manzo could provide. Looking back, he recalled that almost all the kids had frightening stories to tell. He couldn't remember one who told him, "I've come up here for a job and got caught." It was difficult work. Clark routinely saw boys with marks on their bodies and their minds, and he had to be a buffer who absorbed some of the trauma of their ordeal.

Then, something happened that was more than the priest could accept. Manzo staffers told him that they could no longer deal with Central Americans. From now on, they said, he should coordinate with the Tucson Ecumenical Council and try to arrange legal representation for each refugee himself.

Almost at once Father Tony met two Salvadoran boys of about sixteen or seventeen. They both had bullet wounds, and they were terrified of being sent back to El Salvador. The priest filled out two G-28 forms, establishing that they had legal counsel, and gave them to the jailers to pass on to Immigration. The staff at the county jail seemed cooperative. But the next day, when the priest returned, everyone *except* the two boys he had referred to the INS was still in the detention center. Their sudden departure was highly unusual, for normally the INS waited until there were enough prisoners to make up a busload before they emptied the jail. Clark asked what had happened to the two Salvadoran refugees.

"Last night when the Border Patrol brought in some more, they saw those papers, made a call, and took them away," the jailer told him.

"Where are the papers?" asked the priest.

"Here, Father. They said to give them back to you," the man replied.

Clark was dumbfounded, angry, and frustrated. He finally decided that he probably hadn't filled the forms out correctly. He called Joseph R. McKinney, a young lawyer he knew in private practice in Nogales, and told him the story. McKinney, who later became the city attorney, was equally surprised. He suggested that the next time Clark ran into candidates for political asylum McKinney would undertake to represent them and fill the forms out himself. The two men agreed that with a lawyer's name on them the applications would be more persuasive.

Two days later the opportunity to find out arose. Father Tony saw a young man in the detention center and asked how he might be of help. The boy poured out a pathetic story. He had been in the Salvadoran military and had deserted because of the brutality. He said the government would kill him as a traitor if it found him and that the guerrillas would kill him if they found out he'd been in the army. One or the other side—Clark wasn't sure which—had already gotten to him, and he bore obvious marks of torture. His mother had told him to get out of the country, so he had left and headed north.

Clark called McKinney. The two men immediately went down to the jail, and the boy repeated his story to the lawyer. The attorney filled out the G-28 form, signed it, and assured the youth that he would now at least have a hearing before he could be deported. He and the priest would see to it, McKinney said, that a lawyer would help him make his case for political asylum. They left the jail feeling good. This was a legitimate case, and this boy would have a chance to tell his story. They were sure that they had done everything by the book.[2]

The next morning McKinney returned to the jail to see his client. The boy was gone. The jailer told him that the government had taken him, although no other prisoners had been moved. McKinney jumped into his car and drove to Tucson to file the asylum papers and try to intercept the boy before he was spirited out of the country. At the INS office an official, after a futile search in his computer for a sign of the boy, told McKinney, "You may as well forget it; he's not here.

"Why are you involved anyway?" he asked the lawyer.

"I'm his lawyer," McKinney replied. "Why was he taken out of the jail?" There was no answer.

The lawyer returned to Nogales and told Father Clark what had happened. It was the last straw for the priest.*

Clark said to himself, That's it. That's the last form I'm filling out. As he later described his reaction, "That was when I determined that this business about following due process was just not possible. The refugees just couldn't apply for asylum at the border. The INS was breaking the law, and I resolved not to mess with them anymore."[3]

Soon Clark, with the blessing of Monsignor John Oliver of Sacred Heart, was part of Corbett's arrangement to offer refugees a temporary resting place at the Catholic church, before they were driven on to Tucson.

For a few months the Tucson activists simply put the sanctuary

---

*Some three years after the incident Tony Clark's attorney traced the case and found out that the boy had been deported. "They had gotten rid of him fast," McKinney commented in 1987.

refugees on planes to their appointed churches. It soon became apparent, however, that the new underground railroad would have to figure out how to operate more economically and somewhat closer to the ground.

In midsummer Fife and Corbett sat down with a large map of the United States. First they marked the places where there were churches that had expressed an interest in sanctuary, and then they marked the spots where Fife knew Presbyterians and Corbett knew Quakers. When they were finished, they looked at the pattern. A highway relay system seemed feasible.[4]

The two men got on the phone and began calling. Slowly each mark on the map became a place where a fleeing refugee could hide, a place where someone was willing to drive that refugee on to his or her next destination. The new underground railroad was, more than anything, housewife chauffeurs driving station wagons and compact cars, carrying their charges from McDonald's and Roy Rogers to overnight stops in church basements. The final destination was often a garage apartment near a small church in a university community. Such was the stuff of this civil disobedience movement or, as Corbett later preferred to call it, civil initiative.

Typically the refugees aided by the clandestine network were in their late teens to late twenties. In the beginning they tended to be middle-class, educated individuals: teachers and students, labor union leaders, health and social workers; even the former Salvadoran national chess champion had briefly sought refuge at Southside. By late 1981 and 1982, however, the churches began to see an influx of simple campesinos, displaced by search-and-destroy campaigns in both El Salvador and Guatemala or uprooted by the Salvadoran crackdown on peasants who had tried to claim land in an abortive land reform program.

Many, if not most, of these hapless people had psychological problems and were prone to depression and alcoholism. A couple of men in sanctuary in Tucson attempted suicide, and one night a group of drunken refugees driving a van hit a telephone pole and vanished into the darkness, forcing Corbett and Fife to spend half the night looking for them and trying to line up medical help for the injured. "Nobody ever said we are dealing with angels unawares," Corbett reminded people who complained about the refugees' behavior.

The job of coping with the refugees' personal problems and matching them to sanctuary churches elsewhere was staggering. Corbett and Fife soon realized that they could never build a truly national movement unless somehow, someone would take the organizational burden off Tucson.

One of the groups that had contacted the TEC was the Chicago Religious Task Force on Central America (CRTFCA), a coalition of religious and social action groups, including the American Friends Service Committee, Clergy and Laity Concerned, and the National Coalition of American Nuns. The group had been organized in response to the killing of the four church workers in El Salvador and had focused on ending American support for the regime there. They had gotten a copy of Fife's first letter announcing Southside's declaration of sanctuary and had endorsed the action.

The CRTFCA realized that sanctuary work might be a good way to persuade the Chicago church communities to become more active in the campaign against American military involvement in Central America. The group approached the Wellington Avenue United Church of Christ and asked if it was willing to become a sanctuary. The church, a liberal middle-class congregation on the North Side of the city, agreed. The CRTFCA steering committee then called the TEC to ask if Tucson could send someone up to explain how sanctuary worked. Fife went to Chicago and talked with CRTFCA, and, as a member of the steering committee later put it, "We said we need a refugee who has a story to tell."[5]

Before Tucson had a chance to respond, the CRTFCA located and brought in a refugee from another part of the country. It arranged a procession of about ten cars, with coffins on the tops of the vehicles and marchers carrying signs reading 30,000 DEAD IN EL SALVADOR. The demonstration began by circling the downtown Federal Building and continued for several blocks to the Wellington Avenue Church, where the refugee remained for about two weeks. The steering committee of the task force concluded that the procession had had a powerful impact, and it was eager to receive more refugees.[6]

Fife and Corbett decided to explore whether the Chicago group might not become the national coordinator that the sanctuary movement needed: to send out brochures and information; to match the churches with individual refugees; and to handle communications between the sanctuary congregations around the country and the volunteers at the border. Toward the end of the summer Corbett conducted a refugee family up to the Wellington Avenue Church in Chicago and put the proposal to the members of the Chicago task force. For forty hours they debated what to do. The CRTFCA finally told Corbett that it was reluctant to take on a project for which it had so little preparation, but it promised that it would try to find a more appropriate group. After a month of fruitless checking, it concluded that no one had any experience with the type of operation Corbett had in mind, and it agreed to take the responsibility.[7]

As the Chicago Religious Task Force saw it, sanctuary could become a powerful means to awaken the churches of the entire country to the persecution of the church and the poor in Central America. Some of the task force's members had been missionaries in Guatemala, where they had witnessed the massacre of Indian villagers and clergy, and others had worked in Nicaragua. The group was sympathetic to the Nicaraguan revolution and opposed to American efforts to topple the Sandinista government. In 1981 one priest member had gone to work in the Zelaya Mountain region of Nicaragua, and thirty of his parishioners' throats had been cut by contras. Like the religious activists in Tucson, the Chicago task force had direct access to information through the churches about what was going on in Central America, and its set of facts was more detailed, and more disturbing, than the information that reached the average American.

Unlike the activists on the border, however, who were trying to address the immediate needs of the refugees, the Chicago task force was interested in consciousness-raising. Its members believed that they faced the same task that had confronted those opposed to the Vietnam War in the mid-1960s: how to mobilize resistance to U.S. involvement in a dirty regional war.[8]

For some months before Corbett's arrival the group had conducted massive letter-writing campaigns, held meetings in congressional offices, and even led a sit-in of more than 100 seminarians, ministers, and other demonstrators in the Chicago office of Illinois Republican Senator Charles Percy, then chairman of the Senate Foreign Relations Committee. They felt that none of these efforts had been successful; the Reagan administration, supported by an ambivalent Congress, was clearly stepping up its involvement in Central America. In the midst of an unprecedented attack on antipoverty programs in the United States, the federal government was spending more and more money to send arms to El Salvador, Guatemala, Honduras, and the Nicaraguan contras.

Corbett's proposal offered Chicago a new means of arousing the American public about the situation. The group's steering committee thought that the personal testimony of refugees who had lived through oppression and persecution would be the best conceivable way to call attention to the atrocities taking place.

"Juan," the refugee Corbett had escorted to Chicago, had provided a moving example of the power of an individual's story. He had been introduced at the Sunday service of the Wellington Avenue Church wearing a bandanna and a sombrero that covered all of his face except for his large dark eyes. Still bearing the marks of torture and blinking back tears, he had whispered his gratitude through an interpreter and finished by raising his left fist in the traditional Latin gesture of solidarity and resistance. The congregation had exploded with applause and answered his salute with hundreds of raised fists. It was an extremely powerful moment, and it all had been recorded by local television.[9]

Chicago signed up, and within two years the CRTFCA had helped open up more than 200 sanctuaries in churches, synagogues, and Quaker meetings from coast to coast. It had published and mailed more than 30,000 copies of sanctuary manuals and booklets, and had refined the concept of public sanctuary, in which church-sponsored refugees agreed to tell their story to the public over and over again.

Though the political views of the Chicago and the Tucson activists weren't all that different—both groups saw the regimes in El Salvador and Guatemala as vicious suppressors of human rights, and both opposed American support of those regimes—their different approaches to the refugees themselves contained the seeds of future trouble. It wasn't long before the conflict surfaced.

Toward the end of October 1982 border workers in Tucson got a call from a woman on a ranch in southern Arizona. She explained that a young Guatemalan couple had shown up at her place, and she wanted the sanctuary people to come out and deal with them. Fife went out and found a pair of frightened Indian adolescents—he was no more than fifteen and she was about thirteen—with pure Mayan faces and absolutely no experience outside their mountain village. They didn't even speak Spanish. Through an interpreter they explained that their village had been bombed and the local priest had raised enough money to send them away to safety. When they were questioned about what had happened, they said that the guerrillas had bombed their village. They knew this, they said, because the planes that had come had dropped pamphlets saying that the bombs were the work of the guerrillas.[10]

On the day the couple showed up, Fife had been preparing for his first trip to Central America, and he was concerned about leaving another refugee, René Hurtado, in the church during his absence. The man said that he was a deserter from the Treasury Police in El Salvador and feared for his life. Fife had arranged for him to receive sanctuary at St. Luke's Presbyterian Church in Wayzata, Minnesota, and formed a plan to send him up through the underground railroad from Phoenix.

Now Fife decided to have René escort the young couple up as far as Chicago, and he notified the CRTFCA that the latter would be arriving and would need a sanctuary.

Two weeks later, on his return from Central America, Fife had a letter from Chicago. It informed him that the two young Indians had been put on a bus back to Arizona. They had no understanding of the political conflict in Central America and were therefore not useful, the letter explained.

Reading this, Fife felt sick. We've got a big problem, he thought.

The couple was never heard from again, and Fife assumed that somewhere along the way they had been arrested and deported.

Chapter
Ten

JOHN FIFE INSISTED that he never applied a political test to the refugees who stayed at Southside Church. "We assist people from the whole political spectrum. We don't ask which side they're on," he told one journalist.[1] But Fife decided not to allow the incident with the two Indians to rupture budding relations with the Chicago Religious Task Force. Tucson was simply too overwhelmed by incoming refugees to turn away offers of help, however imperfect they might be. He and Corbett took steps to see that such an incident never happened again, and it never did, partly because Tucson avoided sending refugees directly through Chicago again.

By the end of its first year sanctuary had in effect become two movements, living in an uneasy alliance. It was a national grass-roots refugee resettlement effort, initiated by a group of individuals and churches in the Southwest and spread to congregations all over the country, from California to Colorado Springs to Milwaukee to Long Island in New York. Sanctuary was also a national network of antiwar activists, who had found a popular handle on which to hang their political cause. The two aspects of the movement were intertwined—no neat division existed between "Tucson" and "Chicago"—but one approached the refugees from a human rights perspective, and the other from a political one.*

The nuances were subtle, but that didn't prevent both opponents and supporters of the complex movement from portraying it in stark black-and-white terms. To the government, sanctuary advocates were radical wolves in sheep's clothing; to themselves, they were lambs of God, living the logic of their faith.

The Reverend Richard Lundy's congregation in Wayzata typified the inextricable mixture of religion and politics that produced the sanctuary protest. John Fife had visited the prosperous community near Minneapolis in May to explain Southside's stand, and St. Luke's Presbyterian had voted a resolution of support. For months thereafter the congregation debated whether to go further; it had long been active in peace and social justice issues, and several members—ordinary housewives and businesspeople—had even journeyed to Central America to see for themselves what was happening there. They had returned appalled by the effects of American military involvement in the area.

But when Fife called in November and asked Reverend Lundy whether he could shelter René Hurtado the debate shifted from an abstract discussion of civil disobedience to whether the congregation could say no to an individual and still remain faithful to its calling.

The following Sunday Dick Lundy devoted his sermon to the issue. It was Reformation Sunday, commemorating All Souls' Day in 1517, when Martin Luther nailed his ninety-five theses to the door of the church in Wittenberg, Germany. On the same day, sixteen years later, a young law student in Paris named John Calvin fled the city after writing a Protestant speech delivered by the chancellor of the University of Paris.

---

*To complicate matters further, an active sanctuary movement also sprang up in 1983 near the border in South Texas at the Casa Oscar Romero, a Catholic halfway house and refugee shelter in San Benito. Jack Elder, the director from 1983 to 1985, espoused a politics similar to that of the CRTFCA. Nicaraguans, for example, were not turned away, but neither were they welcomed. "If a priest called saying he had a Nicaraguan family, could he bring them over, I would say no," Elder told a reporter in 1987.[2] The Casa's facilities were limited, and Elder, who, like many sanctuary activists, sympathized with the Nicaraguan revolution, considered helping Nicaraguans a low priority. They had a better chance of acceptance into the United States than Salvadorans or Guatemalans, and the government they were fleeing was seen as far less brutal.

Lundy reminded his flock that Calvin, a refugee, had found sanctuary in Geneva, where he became pastor of a refugee Protestant church. He then discussed the proposal put before his church session that St. Luke's declare itself a sanctuary:

"Even though the offering of sanctuary has a long history, it has no standing in our legal system. . . . So we need to talk together not only about offering sanctuary as an expression of the hospitality which is asked of us by the Gospel, but we need to talk together about breaking the law as an act of obedience to the Lord who asks us to do justice.

"Should we choose to do so, to disobey the civil authority, we would be standing in a very long line of faithful folks. It all began way back there with the first of the Ten Commandments, 'You shall have no other God before me' (that is, no one, nothing is to be obeyed before or above God). It continued with the earliest Christian creed, 'Christ is Lord,' meaning 'Caesar is not Lord.' People were martyred for that confession of faith. It is the first disciples who when ordered to remain silent chose to defy the law of the state and keep on speaking, saying to the state, 'We must obey God rather than men.' And the tradition continued . . . to the Reformers in the sixteenth century . . . to Thoreau and Gandhi and Martin Luther King . . . and countless others in between. It is a noble tradition, the decision to break the law and pay the penalty if necessary. Thus far churches which have offered sanctuary have not yet been prosecuted, but the act is illegal and subject to prosecution. I suspect that's what makes the offer so powerful . . . the willingness to risk penalty in the hope that the policies of our government might be changed. The willingness to assume some risk with and for those who have experienced such great injustice in the hope that justice might be done. The opportunity not only to help those who are in need but also to make a public statement which might have some impact upon policy. The opportunity to resist evil even if we cannot change it. All of that is involved, or so it seems to me, in a decision to break the law in the name of greater justice. . . . [When Martin Luther was on trial in 1522] he was asked to recant what he had written. He decided that he could not and replied, 'Here I stand. I can do no other. So help me God.' Perhaps we too have come to such a time in our faith journey."[3]

Shortly after that address St. Luke's voted to become a sanctuary. The congregation sent a letter to Attorney General Smith informing him of the decision and declaring its belief that the administration was in violation of U.S. law. René Hurtado was welcomed to the church in December and began an active career of public speaking.*

John Fife personally had much to do with the spread of sanctuary as he explained the concept to churches and religious leaders in constant travels around the country. The minister also remained involved in the kind of corporate campaign he loved. The Immigration Service had been arranging, through a travel agent in Beverly Hills, to fly deported Central Americans to Mexico City on Western Airlines. In late 1981 Fife had had the Tucson Ecumenical Council buy five shares of Western, and the TEC had then proposed a shareholder resolution calling on management to refuse the INS's business. The resolution was on the ballot at Western's annual meeting in the spring of 1982. A woman in Denver had also been picketing Western's headquarters in that city, denouncing the company's "death flights," and she had prepared a packet for distribution at the meeting calling for a boycott of the financially troubled airline unless it stopped flying the deportees.

Fife attended the meeting and with two colleagues made a presentation on behalf of the resolution. In the end it was supported by 9 percent of the shareholders, an unusually high percentage for a dissident shareholder resolution. After the vote was announced, the minister approached the chairman of Western and asked for a meeting to discuss the issue. They agreed to get together in Los Angeles.

Fife flew to the Coast and met with Western executives along with Peter A. Schey of the National Center for Immigrants Rights and a representative of the Southern California Ecumenical Council. A top official of the airline came in a few minutes after the delegation had settled themselves in a spacious conference room and made it clear that the airline had decided to stop accepting aliens in custody on Western flights. A demonstration against the flights was currently under way at a Western ticket counter in Honolulu, and the Western executive asked

---

*The story he told to more than 150 groups around the country grew progressively more lurid and did little to commend his character. A stocky twenty-four-year-old, Hurtado had apparently resigned after a couple of years in the Treasury Police and then been drafted into the Salvadoran army. He said that he had committed rape and frequently witnessed the torture and murder of unarmed men who were suspected of being guerrillas. Once, he said, a colleague had cut the head off a guerrilla who had been shot dead on the road. On another occasion, after a gun battle in a bus station, his military companion had hacked a finger off of a man he had killed in order to steal a ring. Finally, after a history of fights with his superiors, he had deserted the military and fled to the United States.

his visitors to get the protesters on the phone "and tell them it's all over." Fife and Schey complied, and the meeting was over in twenty minutes. Before someone on Western's staff had gotten back in the room with the coffee orders, everyone was standing up, shaking hands, and saying good-bye.[4]

The churches' victory was largely symbolic, however, for TACA, the Salvadoran airline, subsequently agreed to fly the controversial passengers out of the United States all the way to El Salvador.

While Fife played his role on the national stage, Jim Corbett remained consumed with the border work. Since his return from Mexico and Guatemala word of his services had spread throughout southern Mexico, and his telephone rang at all hours of the day and night with appeals for help. Pat's only request for a birthday present that year was a night with the telephone off the hook. The Quaker coyote worked nonstop, making as many as five or six trips a week to Nogales, sometimes driving the 140-mile round-trip twice in one day, and sometimes managing "relays" of refugees for days at a time. A visiting BBC film crew dubbed him the "Scarlet Pimpernel" of the border.

Corbett soon realized that he was becoming too well known to immigration authorities to continue these exploits himself. As he explained in one of his regular letters to Quakers around the country, just being caught with him would identify his passengers as Central Americans rather than Mexican illegals. The prison work in Nogales also clearly required more than a once-a-week visit. As much as he detested organizations, Corbett realized that he needed more help.

Help did arrive, largely in the form of two lay workers with the Methodist Church. In mid-1982 a young woman named Margaret ("Peggy") J. Hutchison, who worked with a local social service agency of the United Methodist Church, offered to assist with the prison visits. Hutchison was a slender, intense young woman of twenty-seven with tight brown curls and big brown eyes hidden behind round granny glasses that gave her the look of a prim librarian. But when she spoke, her voice often trembled with passion, revealing an abundance of righteous anger underneath the composed exterior. Hutchison had grown up in Palo Alto, California, and after graduation from the California State University in Chico and in Sacramento she had spent two years as a U.S. 2 volunteer for the Methodist Church in Tucson. The U.S. 2 program was essentially domestic missionary work. Living in one of the poorest parts of the city, she had counseled abused women, people who had been evicted from their homes, and the victims of police brutality. Similar programs were offered by other Protestant denominations, including the Presbyterians, Lutherans, Baptists, and Mennonites. These U.S. mission programs had been among the models for the federal government's Vista program, a domestic Peace Corps.

In the course of her work Peggy Hutchison had become involved in all the local justice issues, from the Tucson boycott of Nestlé to conditions in the county jail, and met other local activists like John Fife and Ricardo Elford. As she later put it, "All of the people in refugee work now were doing all that then."[5]

Among other things, Hutchison's job with the Tucson Metropolitan Ministry involved setting up a border ministry for undocumented Mexicans and Central Americans, serving as an advocate and community organizer for the migrant population. She saw Corbett's Nogales prison visits as a natural part of that work.

By August 1982 a friend of Peggy's named Philip Conger had also started filling in for Jim Corbett on the prison visits. Conger was a slender, attractive young man with shining blond hair, an open, trusting manner, and a quick humor that tempered the trace of evangelism that accompanied his deep religious convictions. He had been Peggy's successor at the Tucson Metropolitan Ministry and, at twenty-five was already an old hand at social work. Working in a low-income Hispanic neighborhood, he had administered emergency rent relief and traveler's aid for the itinerant new poor; he had helped people find jobs and wend their way through the social service bureaucracies; and he had started a neighborhood association that, among other things, brought a parks and recreation program into the area and placed stop signs at dangerous intersections.

When an exhausted Tim Nonn finally left the TEC Task Force on Central America to attend seminary in San Francisco, Phil Conger, who spoke Spanish, could work with churches, knew the social service system in town, and was already committed to the refugees, was obviously the choice to replace him.

In June he agreed to take the job half time, for $500 a month plus a car and gasoline money.

Conger's background was tailor-made for Latin refugee work. He was the son of Methodist missionaries who had met in training, married in Peru, and returned to the United States to raise their family. He had grown up near San Diego, where his parents were teachers and active

members of the local Methodist church. As a boy he had traveled with
his family to Central and South America, and as he grew older, he, too,
became heavily involved in the Methodist Church. He had graduated
from San Diego State University with a degree in Spanish, and the
Methodist volunteer-in-mission program had been his first job.

Soon after Conger came on board, the TEC office was moved from
St. Mark's Presbyterian over to Southside Presbyterian, into a network
of cubbyhole offices attached to the chapel. The bulk of Conger's responsibilities for the TEC involved social services, and Southside became the center of the refugee work. But soon he was caught up in
Corbett's border work as well. He and Peg Hutchison visited not only
the Nogales jail but also the various detention centers around Tucson,
and the two young people were disturbed by what they saw. Peg met
one Salvadoran woman who had been told that her husband had been
sent back to El Salvador, and that she had to sign a voluntary departure
statement if she wanted to be with him again. Peg told her not to sign,
and she and Phil finally located the husband—a welder who said that
his life had been threatened in El Salvador—in the south Tucson jail.[6]

Peg and Phil arranged for such people to apply for political asylum.
But they very quickly learned that the chances of success were abysmal.
They were aware of the statistics: In fiscal year 1981 a total of 2
Salvadoran asylum petitions had been approved, while 154 had been
denied. In the year ending September 30, 1982, 61 applications were
approved, 994 were denied, and 22,314 were still awaiting decisions.[7]
The young religious workers concluded what their elders had earlier:
If a refugee really needed to avoid deportation, he or she had better stay
away from the immigration authorities altogether.

Peggy later explained her choices as she saw them at the time: "I
could lobby Congress; I could work for extended voluntary departure;
I could educate people; I could visit the jails and detention centers. That
could be my ministry. Or I could get involved on a deeper level, with
the sanctuary ministry. I studied the 1980 Refugee Act and the international refugee laws and concluded that it was the INS that was breaking
the law. If the values I had been brought up by meant anything, I had
to get involved in sanctuary."[8]

Gradually Peggy and Phil, along with the little group of Quakers
whom Corbett had recruited earlier, began helping the Quaker drive
refugees up from the border.

Their methods of bringing people in followed a system Corbett had worked out the previous winter. Refugees who showed up at certain churches or organizations in southern Mexico or Mexico City, and who had convincing tales of persecution, would be told about Corbett and the underground railroad. Many opted for the trip north, for the chances of obtaining political asylum in Mexico were no better than they were in the United States, and the chances of surviving economically were incalculably worse. Though Mexico, like other Latin countries, has a tradition of political safe haven for diplomats and ousted politicians, it grants political asylum to very few individuals. Salvadorans and Guatemalans with the time and money can apply for tourist visas in Mexico, but such papers are temporary and do not permit the bearers to work. For most refugees, Mexico meant trying to find illegal work in a country that could not provide work for millions of its own citizens.

Once a refugee in the underground railroad had made it to Hermosillo, in northwestern Mexico, he or she was usually contacted by volunteers and guided on up to the border, usually at Nogales or Agua Prieta, across from Douglas, Arizona. American sanctuary workers then interviewed the sojourners. If they seemed to qualify as genuine refugees, they were counseled on how to make it over the border and driven on up to Tucson.

If the wait for a propitious moment to cross took several days, refugees frequently stayed at Doña Socorro Aguilar's house in Nogales, Sonora, a spacious home on a hill with a long balcony overlooking the garbage-strewn streets of the Mexican town. There, only a mile from the American border, the travelers waited in one of a few tiny rooms that Socorro Aguilar had previously rented to boarders. For the actual crossing, Corbett sometimes accompanied the refugees across the port of entry if papers could be found for them. Father Quiñones had a few Mexican border-crossing cards, and they were used over and over again, the pictures doctored to resemble the latest user. Or knowing the desert as he did, Jim Corbett often steered a group through the backcountry into the States. At other times he or Quiñones or Phil Conger simply pointed the fugitives toward one of the gaping holes in the international fence and arranged to meet them at Sacred Heart on the other side.

After a few months of this Conger became concerned that his employer, the Tucson Ecumenical Council, had not officially sanctioned the actual bringing in of refugees. For a time the churches were aware of what Conger was doing, but he rationalized that he was doing it on his own. Finally the issue couldn't be avoided any longer. A special meeting of the entire TEC was called on February 28, 1983, and at that gathering the representatives of the sixty-five member churches voted two to one in favor of having their paid staff help transport refugees to sanctuary churches in the United States, counsel them on their legal options, and send them on to wherever their destination might be.[9]

The decision considerably eased Conger's conscience and made his position more secure. It also meant that a significant portion of the mainstream religious community in Tucson had voted to engage in peaceful civil disobedience. From that point on the church workers took the lead in the "evasion services" at the border.

By the end of 1982, Jim Corbett estimated, the underground railroad had helped some 350 people over the international boundary line. This was an infinitesimal one-tenth of 1 percent of the estimated number of Salvadorans who had entered the country without documents by that time. According to John Fife's estimates, 15 churches around the country—including Catholic, Lutheran, Presbyterian, Methodist, Episcopalian, Unitarian, and Quaker congregations—had publicly declared themselves sanctuaries for Central Americans, and some 150 others supported the sanctuaries with food, clothing, and money. The total number of churches involved represented roughly half of 1 percent of the 40,000 churches in the United States. Their members numbered in the tens of thousands, but only a few hundred people actually took part in the underground railroad.

By any measure, the movement was tiny. But it was beginning to irritate the colossal United States government. As Lyndon Johnson once said, apropos the insults inflicted on him by the Kennedys, "I have an elephant hide, but I can feel the pygmy darts."

Chapter
Eleven

THE CHRISTMAS SEASON of 1982 was not a jolly one for the Western Region of the Immigration Service. For months Arizona INS officials had been debating the sanctuary clergymen, while the local media and some citizens were wondering why the government wasn't doing anything more forceful. At Christmastime Leon Ring of the Border Patrol gave an interview to the *Tucson Citizen.* "Certain arrests could have taken place if we would have wanted to," he said, "but we felt the government would end up looking ridiculous, especially as far as going into church property—anything where ethics involved would be questioned. These church groups wanted publicity. They were baiting us to overreact. We have been deliberately low key."[1]

But as the media played it, the government was damned if it did and damned if it didn't. Another Christmas Day story in the *Arizona Daily Star* led with a taunt: "For nearly a year, they have publicly flouted the law without reprisal.

"Their contraband and their method of acquiring it have been publicized in the national media, where ringleaders detail their acts with impunity, almost daring officialdom to respond.

"So far, their activities have been met with only an uneasy silence."[2]

Bill Johnston, interviewed for that story, had to bob and weave. "There's been no policy or any suggestions that churches need to be hit, or need to be left alone," he explained. ". . . [S]ince we have such a limited staff, we try to concentrate investigative efforts where they do the most good." The paper pointed out that Johnston's investigative staff at the time was one man.

One Immigration Service official, seeing the story, penciled a note in the margin to the INS district director in Phoenix. "Mr. Gustafson, . . . Will there be a refresher course in 'How to Deal with the Media?' "

But the most galling incident occurred on December 12, when "60 Minutes," one of the nation's most popular television shows, introduced the country to a new celebrity. Jim Corbett had already been sympathetically chronicled in *People* magazine, and his exploits had been described in the *Washington Post*, the *Christian Science Monitor*, the *Times of London, Newsweek*, and the *Chicago Tribune*, not to mention extensively covered in the local Arizona papers. Now he had some twenty minutes of prime Sunday night airtime to tell his and the Salvadoran refugees' story to the American people. It was the kind of exposure major politicians only dreamed of and INS officials never dared imagine.

For openers, Corbett was asked how many people he had personally "helped smuggle into this country." After pleading that he hadn't kept count, Corbett offered a "ballpark" figure of 250 or 300.

The film focused on the plight of the Central Americans, with interviews with several refugees, with Corbett and his wife, and with Peter Schey of the National Center for Immigrants Rights, in Los Angeles. The "other side" was represented by Harry Malone, the director of El Centro, and Elliott Abrams of the State Department, who had declined to be interviewed for the show but who was shown in an earlier interview with correspondent Mike Wallace.

The show amounted to a powerful critique of American treatment of the Central Americans. The CBS narrator explained that in Los Angeles alone there were as many as 200,000 Salvadorans "seeking sanctuary from a civil war that is estimated to have cost at least 34,000 civilian lives." Schey pointed out that while hundreds of thousands of people from countries not friendly to the United States had been granted asylum, the Salvadorans and others from countries supported by the Reagan administration were denied political asylum across the board.

Abrams, assistant secretary of state for human rights, appeared on the screen at that point to say, "They come here for a very good reason. They come here for a better life. They come here for better jobs, but that doesn't entitle them to asylum. Asylum is a very special thing which we give to people who can prove that they have a well-founded fear of persecution."

> CBS: *And you think that Salvadoran refugees do not have, by and large, a well-founded fear of persecution?*
>
> ABRAMS: *That's right.*
>
> CBS: *It was fear of persecution that drove Alicia Rivera to leave her home in El Salvador, where she taught people to read and write. Two years ago she entered the United States illegally and came to live in Los Angeles.*
>
> RIVERA: *My priest was killed, his co-worker was tortured; then I went to my village where I was born, and the students had been taken out of the schools almost every day, and the teachers and a lot of bodies in the streets of the village that we would find every day in the garbage cans.*
>
> CBS: *Bodies?*
>
> RIVERA: *Bodies. I remember that if one of your relatives had disappeared, you go to a big garbage can that was in the village and there was more than twenty-five bodies there every day.*
>
> CBS: *Did you always want to come to the United States?*
>
> RIVERA: *No. I never wanted to come to the United States. I knew this country was too many people, too much noise, very difficult life, irritated life. But this looked like the only choice you have. Because you can't stay in Guatemala right now, you can't stay in Mexico right now, there are too many refugees from El Salvador already, the economy there is difficult, and sometimes you have one relative here in the United States that you can join, is the one person that can help you, so that's why most of us come here.*
>
> CBS: *What would happen to you if you were deported?*
>
> RIVERA: *I am more than sure I'll be killed. I don't want to go back to El Salvador right now.*

Later Malone was quoted saying that the reason the Salvadorans were here was "strictly economic" and that he saw no difference between deporting people to Mexico and deporting them to El Salvador. Abrams's last words were: "We just can't have a policy that says that anybody who comes from a country that has poverty, or oppression, or violence, can stay in the U.S. if he can just manage to get here illegally. Because if we did, we have—what? Five hundred million, two billion people eligible to come here and live here. That's the problem."

In a revealing final comment, Jim Corbett seemed to be almost looking forward to the possibility of arrest. "In some ways jail would be a relief," he admitted. "Because it is a treadmill, you know. It's rough, and just living with the tension all the time is not a way I want to live. Life just becomes too one-dimensional, but there aren't too many choices."

The program set off a flurry of communication within the INS. The western region office in San Pedro, California, dashed off a wire to the district director in Phoenix. It read:

> *Please conduct an investigation into alien smuggling activities of James W. Corbett and consult with the United States Attorney's office regarding Mr. Corbett's amenability to prosecution under the appropriate sections of law. Phoenix anti-smuggling unit is designated as control office in this matter and Tucson anti-smuggling unit will provide available data, intelligence and support to the control office as requested. Please provide this office with a report of investigation no later than February 16, 1983.*

The federal behemoth was finally moving against the pygmies.

The man in the Phoenix antismuggling unit who was assigned the case was James A. Rayburn, a forty-one-year-old veteran of the Border Patrol. For several months Rayburn had maintained a file of newspaper clippings on the underground railroad, like a reporter saving "string" on a topic to be explored at some later date.

After the "60 Minutes" broadcast Rayburn sent out a call for information to investigators throughout Arizona. Dean Thatcher, an intelligence agent in Yuma, dispatched an article written by Renny Golden, the former nun and free-lance journalist on the executive committee of the Chicago Religious Task Force, and sent with it his own assessment of the underground railroad. He wrote:

> *The sanctuary movement does not appear to be a serious threat to enforcement efforts by the Service when viewed in its overall context. . . . At this point, it appears that some churches are using the*

sanctuary concept to rally congregations, and create cohesiveness in hispanic parishes. This type of movement is particularly attractive to pastors with a political bent that are seeking a cause. Those who are normally satisfied to vent their ill humors in the Sojourners* *would consider sanctuary as de rigor [sic]. Risks would be minimal, considering the reluctance of the state to incur the wrath of the church. Whatever liability that is incurred from sanctuary can be written off by the relative merits of gaining martyrdom.*

Although Thatcher thought the sanctuary movement was probably insignificant, the INS was not really sure about that. The Golden article claimed that Southside Church had harbored as many as 1,600 Salvadorans and that the movement had spread to Seattle, Evanston, Illinois, Minneapolis, and Milwaukee, where Catholic Archbishop Rembert G. Weakland had expressed support for the sanctuary churches in his diocese.

Every time a new sanctuary was declared, an article appeared in the press, and reporters would call up the local INS office to ask why the agency wasn't doing anything to stop the obvious lawbreaking. Embarrassed officials would then have to pooh-pooh the whole thing. Thatcher's report reflected worry that all the publicity about a spreading underground railroad might damage the service's image as a law enforcement agency. The movement might be small potatoes, but it was also a very hot one.

No one in the INS knew more about hot potatoes than criminal investigator Jim Rayburn. Rayburn was a Texan, born in a little town in the southern part of the state exactly five weeks before Pearl Harbor. He had grown up in an oil camp west of Falfurrias and after high school had become a real, honest-to-goodness cowboy, riding herd for the King Ranch down near the Mexican border.

As the Vietnam War heated up, like thousands of other poor boys from all over the country, Rayburn shipped to Vietnam, and though he didn't like to talk about his experiences there, acquaintances told a hair-raising story of capture and imprisonment by the Vietcong before he escaped with a companion and walked through the jungle back to an American unit. Somewhere along the way he had picked up a

---

*Sojourners *is a politically liberal Christian magazine based in Washington, D.C. It is sometimes described as part of the "evangelical left."

burning hatred of communism and of those he considered its sympathizers in the United States. He was a zealot and a bit of a Lone Ranger, and there was something of the resentful underdog in his manner, an attitude that the powers that be were in some vague way against him. But when he decided to do something, he didn't play it safe or go halfway; several of his friends noted that when Jim Rayburn had a tiger by the tail, the last thing he would do was let go.

In more ways than one, he was a little like Jim Corbett.

After Vietnam and a brief stint as a car salesman in Kingsville, Texas, in 1968 and 1969, Rayburn joined the Border Patrol. Law enforcement along the southwestern border suited his temperament, and for nine years he was with the patrol in Tucson. Then, in 1978, he became an antismuggling agent, a job involving investigations of illegal alien smuggling. He was part of the investigation of the Manzo Area Council and was completely disgusted when the case was dropped by the new Democratic administration in Washington. He vowed that he would never get involved in that kind of political case again. He told one acquaintance that "all I did was create heroes out there."[3]

Although disenchanted by the Manzo case, Rayburn hadn't succumbed to burnout, an occupational hazard in the Border Patrol. He had developed the antismuggling program in Tucson and Phoenix, building a network of informants who could penetrate virtually any smuggling ring. He didn't look like a tough outdoorsman or even a cop. He was not a big man, and with his reddish skin and sandy, slightly oily hair he could have been mistaken for a clerk in a small southern insurance company. But he loved to be where the action was, and he had established a reputation as a crack field investigator—one of the best in the entire agency.

He had earned a measure of celebrity within the INS for his work on the so-called Chevron shoe case, an investigation that the service had wanted to drop but which Jim Rayburn had insisted on pursuing to the end.

In the Chevron case Rayburn had followed the tracks of several groups of illegal aliens up from Mexico to a point along the border where they were met by smugglers who led them across. At that spot he noticed a different footprint—bigger and with a distinct, chevron-shaped pattern. He assumed that the print belonged to the smuggler, whom he nicknamed Chevron.

By further analyzing the tracks, he deduced that "Chevron" led the group on a thirty-two-mile trip at night—this from traces of the tracks of certain nocturnal insects and reptiles over the human tracks. He could tell when the group had had to sit down and rest by noticing where the grass had been pressed down and bits of debris left behind. Other calculations gave him an educated guess about when the smugglers got their group to the pickup point along the road. On the basis of this information two border patrolmen stationed themselves near the probable spot, and sure enough, a pickup truck with a camper shell came and went at the exact time Rayburn had predicted. The officers stopped the truck, which was loaded with illegal aliens, and lo and behold, out stepped a smuggler wearing shoes with the "chevron" soles.

The smugglers were convicted but appealed all the way to the Supreme Court, on the ground that the Border Patrol had not had adequate cause to make the stop, therefore making it unconstitutional. In January 1981 the justices ruled unanimously for the government, and in his opinion Chief Justice Warren Burger wrote that "we see here the kind of police work often suggested by judges and scholars as examples of appropriate and reasonable means of law enforcement."[4]

After Chevron Rayburn became involved in a major sting operation that, like Manzo, put him in the center of a controversy. Operation Greenway netted a busload of illegal farm workers and resulted in the convictions of two big-time smugglers named Saldivar, Florida labor contractors who were supplying illegal Mexican aliens to the Florida citrus industry.

Although the operation had busted one of the biggest alien-smuggling rings in the United States, predictably it brought the roof down over the INS's head. Hundreds of Florida growers, with considerable political clout, had lobbied the Justice Department through their trade association to halt the prosecution. Some Florida congressmen had gotten involved, and once again Jim Rayburn was the man on the spot. As the men in the service put it, it all flows downhill. As a result, as one of his colleagues later said, "Jim was never given his due"[5] for his part in a successful case.

It was about this time that, thanks to "60 Minutes," Jim Rayburn was asked to revive the investigation of the underground railroad.

The official was determined not to stick his neck out on what was obviously a highly political case. He wanted to be sure that the entire INS hierarchy was on board, and in writing.

At the same time he was intrigued. Here was a smuggling operation that claimed to be really big, involving hundreds of aliens and a growing national network. The INS was also beginning to accumulate evidence that these assertions were at least partially true, and not just braggadocio on the part of a few publicity-seeking, leftover hippie preachers.

In early 1983 Rayburn received a copy of a letter that had been sent to the Albuquerque office of the INS by a man who had found it while cleaning out an office in the St. James Episcopal Church in Taos, New Mexico. The note, from a man in Tucson, mentioned a group of thirteen people who had been "handled in 2 groups—part went through on the relay. The rest were driven straight through to Chicago by a priest."

The letter went on to explain the legal situation of churches providing sanctuary:

> *[C]hurches have no legal status as sanctuarys [sic]. They have, however, a great deal of moral force which the Immigration authorities will not challenge, or at least have not anywhere at present. Also, to date, no one who has been harboring, transporting, or otherwise aiding Central American refugees for* humanitarian purposes *has been arrested. Smugglers, called "coyotes" who cross "wet backs" in return for money—are being arrested. We have scrupulously avoided all contact with "coyotes" and also have made sure of the origin of those we help as Central American as best as possible. In fact, because of streached [sic] resources, we have considered the very difficult task of trying to make a distinction between those who are high risk (most certainly face death if returned) and those who are "merely" fleeing a dangerous situation, in order to concentrate on the needs of the former.*
>
> *There are many contacts in Chicago (see the enclosed booklet) and also in San Francisco. The enclosed newspaper clipping will be of interest.*

In Rayburn's mind, this conspiracy posed a much greater threat to the nation than did ordinary smugglers, who were just trying to make a living. In his view, the leaders of the movement were Marxists, and the people they were bringing into the country could well be Communist spies.

In the first place, Fife and Corbett and their followers had been outspokenly critical of American foreign policy in Central America, and the liberation theology they espoused was clearly revolutionary. The material that the Immigration Service had obtained from the Chicago Religious Task Force was even more extreme. As part of its role as national coordinator of the sanctuary movement, the Chicago group had put out two publications: *Sanctuary: A Justice Ministry*, explaining the sanctuary movement, and *Organizer's Nuts and Bolts*, on how to organize a sanctuary congregation. In order to help spread the word, Chicago also put out periodic mailings describing the sanctuary projects across the country and explaining the theology and politics of the movement.

As Rayburn read this material, he was sure that he was dealing with a political, not a religious or humanitarian, cause. In his view, all Central Americans came to the United States to find jobs. The sanctuary movement's efforts to help politically persecuted individuals—those they called "high-risk" refugees—were simply a way of identifying people who were against the government of their country and who considered the United States responsible for the problems in their homeland. The sanctuary movement then used these people to try to sway American opinion against U.S. policy in Central America and against the American system altogether.[6]

In the *Nuts and Bolts* manual, for example, Philip E. Wheaton, head of the Washington, D.C., Sanctuary Committee, declared that "the history of El Salvador has been scarred and torn asunder by American businessmen exploiting those people; by US Marines and the CIA intervening [in] those lands and taking away their freedoms and democracies; and by US military aid today which is the only prop that allows those despots to remain upon their thrones." As Rayburn read it, any alien who shared these views was definitely excludable from the United States under the Immigration and Nationality Act of 1952,* a statute passed at the height of the McCarthy period.

In January 1983 Rayburn launched a surveillance of the sanctuary movement. He called in a man named Salomon Graham and asked him

---

*The so-called McCarran-Walter Act allowed the Immigration Service to bar individuals from entering the United States on ideological grounds. Those who could be excluded included advocates of world communism, anyone prejudicial to the national interest of the United States, and anyone who was a threat to national security. Under these sweeping provisions, the act has been used to keep out dozens of distinguished writers, intellectuals, and politicians, including Nobel Prize-winning authors Graham Greene and Gabriel García Márquez, playwright Dario Fo, Bishop Muzorewa of Zimbabwe, and Pierre Trudeau, who found himself briefly on the list because he had made a trip to the Soviet Union. Trudeau got himself off the blacklist and later went on to become prime minister of Canada. In late 1987 Congress repealed this controversial ideological part of the statute.

to start attending seminars and public meetings in support of the underground railroad. He told Graham to report back with names of participants, topics discussed, and whatever handout materials he could gather.

Rayburn had met Graham during Operation Greenway and had been using him as an informant for almost a year on other cases. The man was an illegal alien, a Mexican, and had a criminal record. But the INS had to take what it could get in the way of undercover informants, and Rayburn and Graham had become friends of a sort.

According to Graham's "A" file, his record with the Immigration Service, he had been arrested twice for illegal entry into the United States, in 1970 and 1971, and granted voluntary departure both times. On March 28, 1974, he had been arrested for transporting illegal aliens. He had pleaded guilty to illegal entry, had received a 180-day sentence, which was suspended for two years, and had been granted voluntary departure again. A year later, on April 28, 1976, he was arrested again for transporting illegal aliens and presented for prosecution in Yuma, Arizona, on a felony charge. (The second offense made the crime a felony.) Again he pleaded guilty to illegal entry, received a six-month sentence, served a little more than three months, and was granted voluntary departure. In 1977 he was arrested again for illegal entry, and in 1978 he was deported on foot at Calexico, California.

According to his file, Graham had made several false claims to U.S. citizenship and had used the aliases "Henry Graham" and "Henry Perea Smith." This was the man whom the government chose to start watching the sanctuary movement.

Within a couple of weeks the short, slender, dark-haired Mexican briefed Rayburn on what he had discovered. He had attended meetings cosponsored by CAUSA (Coalition Against U.S. Intervention in Central America) and CISPES (Coalition in Solidarity with the People of El Salvador). Handouts at the meetings included newspaper clippings on "sanctuary," some material that looked to Rayburn like socialist propaganda, including pamphlets on the Sandinistas and the Farabundo Martí National Liberation Front (FMLN), the principal guerrilla group in El Salvador. Graham also reported that socialist organizations had been present and had spoken at the rallies. The groups included the Arizona Socialist party, the San Diego Socialist party, and other solidarity groups that appeared to be socialist.

Rayburn paid Graham $200 for his work. If these people are not

Communists, the Texan thought, they are being manipulated by social-ists and Communists. At best, they are Communist dupes.[7]

Graham's other major contribution to the investigation was to obtain Jim Corbett's address and telephone number. Both were listed in the Tucson telephone book, but the INS did it the hard way. While the rancher was speaking at a rally at the Central United Presbyterian Church in Tucson, Graham followed him to his car and got his license number. Through that, the INS obtained his address, his telephone number, and his picture (from his driver's license). The agency then checked his house for "surveillability," as Rayburn put it in a memo. For providing this information, the United States government paid Graham another $200.

Still, Rayburn was reluctant to go too far out on what could be a precarious limb. In a memo to his district director on June 30, 1983, he summarized his findings in a manner that, if anything, downplayed the importance of pressing the case. On the basis of his findings from an intelligence-gathering trip to Hermosillo, Rayburn concluded that "a very low number is being handled" by the underground railroad. In conclusion, he wrote: "Due to a heavy work load and priorities set within the anti-smuggling program, I strongly recommend that for the present the 'El Salvadorean Underground Railroad' be assigned to a centralized intelligence office."

The silence from Washington was deafening, and for the rest of the year the underground railroad case sat on the back burner again. Jim Rayburn wanted to be certain that there were some signatures over his own before he went any further.[8]*

Rayburn had become convinced, however, that the case was not going to go away. In Hermosillo a group of coyotes had told him that the railroad was active out of that city and was linked up with a Catholic priest in Nogales named Quiñones. Rayburn was sure that eventually, the movement would have to be investigated. With that in mind, he began to discuss the possibility of a full-fledged undercover operation with a spy he thought would be just right for the job.

---

*"In sensitive cases, when push comes to shove, there is only one bad guy, and that is the lead case agent," the investigator explained in an interview in his tiny Phoenix office several years later. "He's going to be responsible for every mistake made during the course of the investigation, and if anyone in the Immigration Service decides that we shouldn't be involved, it's going to be forgotten how the case got assigned, and it will be his fault that we are involved."

Chapter
Twelve

JIM RAYBURN HAD first met Jesus Cruz during the sting operation against the Saldivars. Cruz was an old coyote who had worked for the smugglers as a driver, and the INS had turned him into an undercover informant against his employers. He had taped conversations and testified in court against his former colleagues. That collaboration had led to a long-standing relationship between the INS in Phoenix and Jesus Cruz, who had been put to good use in other smuggling cases.

Rayburn had thought all along that if he could pursue the sanctuary case, Cruz would be the perfect undercover agent. He was a plump, pleasant-faced man in his mid-fifties with more than a passing resemblance to Santa Claus. He was the kind of older man whom little Hispanic children instinctively call *tío* ("uncle"). Rayburn figured that Cruz's harmless demeanor would disarm the sanctuary activists, who would probably have been immediately suspicious of someone who looked like Salomon Graham, with his slick hair, pencil-thin mustache, and sleazy Psst-you-wanna-meet-my-sister appearance.

Cruz's history was typical of many INS informants. He had been born in central Mexico in 1927, one of six children of a small shop-keeper. After some six years of school he had drifted toward the border and worked for a time as a maintenance man in a movie theater in Juárez, across from the Texas town of El Paso. He had first entered the United States in the late 1940s as a legal migrant worker, working in the beet fields of Colorado and then in Arizona in the cotton fields. Eventually he returned to Mexico, but in 1954 he emigrated to the United States for good. Except for two years in Los Angeles in the early 1960s he had lived in Phoenix for almost thirty years. He had become a permanent legal resident of the United States, although he never really learned to speak English. He had been married for a time but later divorced and lost track of both his wife and his three children, although he thought they lived in Phoenix.

For some twenty years Cruz had worked in laundries in Phoenix. He then had a brief stint as a roofer, but that ended when business got slow. Finally, in 1978, the now middle-aged immigrant became an alien smuggler.[1]

Cruz's first venture into crime was a bust. According to his government "A" file, he was picked up in Tipton, Iowa, in July 1978 for transporting four illegal aliens to Chicago. The Mexican farm workers involved were deported, but no charges were ever filed against Cruz, who turned government informer. He agreed to expose his employers, who were in league with the Saldivars in Florida. Over the next eighteen months or so Cruz made twenty-two to twenty-four trips between Arizona and Florida in a mobile home full of human cargo, with a tape recorder concealed on his body. He eventually became the principal government witness at both trials of the case and was granted immunity for his testimony.

After that, from mid-1982 on, both Jesus Cruz and Salomon Graham worked for Rayburn and other antismuggling agents on an almost daily basis. Cruz was an informant in approximately eight other alien-smuggling conspiracies between 1982 and 1984. In all of them, he introduced himself to the suspected smugglers, offered his services, and then tried to bring an INS undercover agent in on the conspiracy as well. He used a little body bug to record conversations with the principal suspects and delivered the tapes to Rayburn at the INS office in Phoenix to be kept for evidence.

Rayburn thought that Cruz might be able to ingratiate himself with Father Quiñones in Nogales and from there infiltrate the movement in

Tucson. In the spring of 1983, Rayburn approached Cruz with his idea. At about the same time Rayburn briefed the other investigative agents in the Phoenix office about the underground railroad and asked them to provide him with any information on the movement they might come across. He explained that a number of churches were engaged in organized smuggling and asked, if they encountered anyone who said he or she had come into the United States through the church, that they keep him informed.[2]

At Rayburn's suggestion John Lafayette Nixon, Jr., a trim, curly-haired agent in his early forties, began preparing an undercover identity, to be ready if and when he was called upon to enter the case. On Halloween, October 31, 1983, Nixon obtained a driver's license in the name of John Powers, and he began to develop a profile for his alias. He rang up a church in the Phoenix area and asked to be put on its mailing list under the name John Powers. Rayburn began subscribing to materials that would help develop Powers's identity and persuaded a neighbor to give Powers cover with his firm, a company called Southwestern Vector. Nixon had fake business cards made up with the company's name on them, and if anyone called to check, a secretary told the caller that Powers was a mechanic with Southwestern Vector.

Nixon assumed his disguise easily, for he had impersonated various kinds of smugglers fifteen times in the previous two years. He liked the work and thought of it as a form of acting; his hero, in fact, was Clint Eastwood, and a huge blown-up photograph of the cinematic gunslinger later covered one whole wall of the agent's small office.[3]

Finally, in December 1983 the Immigration Service launched a full-scale investigation of the underground refugee railroad. The final impetus, ironically, came from a devout churchgoer, a Christian crusader who thought that the misguided ministers in Arizona were abusing the name of religion and ought to be behind bars. And he had the authority to try to put them there, for he was the western regional commissioner for the INS.

Harold Ezell was a plump, outspoken businessman from Orange County in Southern California, one of the most conservative areas in the country. The son of an Assemblies of God minister, he had dropped out of college but risen to become a vice-president of Wienerschnitzel International, a California chain of fast-food hot dog restaurants. He had been active in Ronald Reagan's gubernatorial and presidential campaigns in California and finally been rewarded, in March 1983, with a job as one of the INS's four regional commissioners.

The regional commissioners were the top INS officers in the field, and they were traditionally career agency people. But the Reagan administration wanted to fill the middle echelons of government with its ideological allies, and Ezell became the first political appointee in charge of the INS's largest and most important region.

The new man brought the enthusiasm of a can-do entrepreneur to his $68,000-a-year post. With messianic fervor Reverend Hal, as some colleagues called him, was soon leading groups of officials and television cameramen on after-dark "border tours," showing them firsthand the hundreds of Mexicans trying to sneak across the border south of San Diego every night. The "Lord of Border Order" became one of the most vociferous lobbyists for a tough new immigration bill and managed to pump up morale in the Border Patrol while attracting passionate detractors on Capitol Hill. (Legislators were not charmed when he bragged that his approach to illegal immigration was "catch 'em, clean 'em, and fry 'em," meaning process and deport aliens as fast as possible.) In no time Harold Ezell became the most visible and controversial regional commissioner the INS had ever had.

He was also strikingly similar to his adversaries. Like them, he spoke his mind with refreshing candor, often to his own detriment. Like them, he was impatient with the traditional methods of achieving his aims. Like them, he knew how to use the media to get his message across. And like them, he was sure of the righteousness of his cause, a position that left little room for compromise.

Ezell was almost personally offended by the sanctuary workers' invocation of religion to justify their actions. His parents had taught him that the Bible said you obey the laws of the land. To him, the entire movement appeared to be a bunch of radicals who were hiding behind religion to push their political goals and undermine the immigration laws.[4]

Toward the end of 1983 Ezell saw a rerun of the "60 Minutes" show. He hit the roof. Who the hell do these arrogant lawbreakers think they are? he thought. Corbett is holding himself up like some kind of guru. When every man takes it upon himself to do whatever he thinks is right, it's *anarchy.*[5]

The sanctuary movement had been getting increasing publicity in the Los Angeles area, where several churches had declared their participation, and the INS office was getting frequent calls from people demanding to know what it was doing to enforce the law. INS officials felt they were being challenged or pushed into a posture in which they had to take some sort of action.[6] Moreover, immigration officials were beginning to think that maybe the railroad wasn't such an amateur operation after all. In January Tucson police had picked up a Salvadoran who was carrying detailed notes on how to make his way up to the United States from Tapachula, in Chiapas, Mexico, and a notebook containing the names of sanctuary organizers in Arizona, Colorado, Nebraska, Iowa, and Illinois. The man's bond had been set at an unusually high $25,000, and the bond had been posted by a woman from Evanston, Illinois.

At a regular weekly staff meeting in late January or early February 1984 at his office in San Pedro, south of Los Angeles, Commissioner Ezell announced that an aggressive investigation of sanctuary was essential. It was agreed that an undercover operation was the only way the government could generate enough evidence against the sanctuary activists to bring a prosecution.

On Ezell's orders, Mark Reed from the regional antismuggling unit, which coordinated antismuggling for the entire Western Region, called Phoenix to confirm the decision to go ahead. Reed talked to Robert S. ("Scott") Coffin, the newly arrived supervisor of criminal investigation for the antismuggling unit there, and after he hung up, Coffin informed Rayburn, who reported to him, that a stepped-up investigation had been ordered. Rayburn told Coffin that he already had lined up someone who could probably get inside the movement and find out what was going on.

Coffin told Rayburn "to go ahead and see if he could get Mr. Cruz next to some of the people, get down and find out what he could about what was going on. . . ."[7] Coffin got back to Reed and told him that Rayburn had an informant who could probably infiltrate the sanctuary movement through a priest in Nogales, Sonora. Reed told the Phoenix office to proceed. To the best of the two men's memory, this conversation took place in early February 1984. According to Coffin, Reed wanted the Phoenix office to get started. Commissioner Ezell was concerned and was "apparently getting some kind of pressure" to act.[8]

Coffin was authorized to have Rayburn direct Cruz to make contact with the sanctuary activists in Nogales, Sonora. But the INS in Washington did place some restrictions on the investigation.[9] Cruz was not to transport any illegal aliens into the United States, he was not to engage in any other illegal acts, and he was not to begin any covert taping of conversations. Before Cruz could engage in transporting or secret taping, approval would have to be obtained from a new Undercover Guidelines Review Committee in the Justice Department as well as from the INS antismuggling unit in Washington.

In this chain of events there had never been any discussion of alternatives to an undercover investigation. No one had suggested a direct official warning to the activists, by letter or in person, that they should stop what they were doing. No one discussed the possibility of a civil injunction. Least of all did anyone within the INS, in Tucson or Phoenix or San Pedro or at the highest levels in Washington, consider modifying the government's harsh asylum policies.

Chapter
Thirteen

W ITH TIME, THE Arizona "evasion services," like every other human enterprise, had become more complicated. In Phoenix, a Catholic nun named Darlene Nicgorski had begun to locate sanctuary refugees for the Chicago Religious Task Force and had established a working relationship with Tucson. Sister Darlene, a stocky, pleasant-faced woman of about forty, had briefly served in Guatemala in the early 1980s until her parish priest, an Italian Franciscan, was murdered, shot twice in the head by unknown assailants. Sister Nicgorski and her fellow nuns, who had been running a preschool, fled the country, and after spending several months working in Guatemalan refugee camps in Mexico, she had returned to the United States still burning to do something for the people of Central America.

She had gravitated toward the sanctuary movement and was receiving a small stipend from Chicago to identify refugees who were suitable to send to sanctuary churches and to prepare them for the experience of speaking publicly.

In the beginning Jim Corbett hadn't really screened the refugees whom he helped into the country. He had assisted every Central American who seemed to be fleeing a dangerous situation, whether that meant personal persecution or civil strife. He was not interested in hair-splitting distinctions between the two.

Corbett's open-door policy became harder for the movement to sustain, however, as time went on and word of the underground railroad spread. The TEC was inundated with far more calls for help than it could respond to. Moreover, the Tucson people recognized that if and when they were arrested, they would have a much stronger defense if they could argue that they were assisting only those with individual fears of persecution, thus qualifying them for political asylum under U.S. law.

So during 1983 an informal, two-tier screening process developed.[1] The first cut occurred at the border and occasionally in Hermosillo or even Mexico City. Sanctuary workers interviewed people as they arrived and then brought their stories back to be discussed in Tucson. Unless the candidates were "high-risk"—that is, faced a high risk of personal danger if they had to return to their countries—the group would usually decide that the sanctuary movement could not help them.

Once they were safely in the country, most refugees headed for anonymity in the big cities, but approximately one in twenty out of Tucson was referred on to Darlene as a possible candidate for public sanctuary. Occasionally the sanctuary churches sent representatives directly into Mexico to recruit their own refugees, but the Tucson border workers discouraged such "free-lancing" because of its coercive potential. A desperate and vulnerable refugee might obviously agree to anything in return for help into and support within the United States.

Sister Nicgorski coached the refugees to tell their stories in a clear, consistent, and concise manner and had them practice by speaking to groups in Phoenix and in simulated press conferences. If all went well, she prepared a short biography of each refugee for the Chicago task force, which then located a suitable congregation. As soon as a match was made, Chicago arranged transportation relays, and the refugee was sent off, often with a press conference. (Another woman, a former missionary, performed the same role in Los Angeles that Darlene Nicgorski performed in Phoenix, locating refugees within the growing Central American community in Southern California for sanctuary churches.)

The movement had learned that screening for public sanctuary was essential. Jim Corbett had warned churches that the refugees they received were not the Holy Family, but some had been too much for even the most saintly Samaritan. There had been alcoholics; there had been some who beat their wives; there had been young men who made advances toward friendly parishioners. On the other side, Darlene never ceased to be amazed at the requests made by congregations, some of whom "ordered" refugees the way they might select a new pet dog. One congregation wanted an Indian family with three children, none over the age of ten; another wanted a Salvadoran family with no children under ten. One church wanted a vegetarian, nonsmoking Central American; another, after the wrenching decision to declare itself a sanctuary, in defiance of the United States government, requested a refugee with carpentry skills.

The refugees headed for public sanctuary not only had to be fairly stable and adaptable but had to be able to speak effectively before an audience and with the press. They needed to learn the basics about refugee law and INS practices. Above all, they had to have a "good story," one that described the horrors of life in their country in a politically sophisticated, persuasive way. The whole point of public sanctuary was to get the story of what was happening in Central America out to grass-roots Americans. Darlene didn't tell the refugees what to say, but she didn't want to send out anyone whose experience contradicted what she and the movement believed to be true: that the Salvadoran and Guatemalan regimes were brutalizing their people.

In many ways, then, the screening of refugees for public sanctuary— as distinct from the prior screening for assistance into the United States—became a mirror image of the government's screening of aliens for admission into the United States. For forty years the official welcome mat had been out only for those fleeing life under Communist regimes. Finally that policy was being turned upside down by American protesters, who welcomed only those fleeing the horrors of extreme anticommunist violence.

Political screening inevitably produced tensions within the movement. The farther one was from the border, the easier it was to be theoretical about those one wanted to help. The closer one was to individuals in trouble, the harder it was to apply a political litmus test to their problems.

At Sacred Heart in Nogales, where fleeing Central Americans were turning up almost daily, the sheer human desperation demanded an immediate personal response. It got so bad, as Tony Clark put it, that "whenever I turned a corner near the church, I'd see someone leaning against a wall and I'd know it was another one. I'd hear the whisper, 'Padrecito,' and think *Oh, no.* Then they'd come inside and start crying. Pretty soon they'd be camped in the place, burning their food, staring at you from the corner of the room, stinking—the odor comes with them—and we would be trying to go about our business."[2]

Father Clark found it difficult to inform pitiful, penniless Central Americans that they were not "high-risk" and send them out on the street. Phil Conger and others tried to persuade Tony to do his own screening, but in his opinion that was like Monday morning quarterbacking. The play was already over, and the refugees were *there,* in his church. "All those decisions were made in Mecca, and we were here; we had to deal with them," Clark recalled later. "In the beginning it was beautiful; we were all helping these poor refugees. Then they wouldn't come get 'em when they came in. I'd scream at Phil, '*You* come tell them they're low-risk. What do you *mean,* we can't help 'em?' We'd have to give 'em six dollars to take the bus to Tucson. Good luck."

Once Father Clark was so upset with Tucson's obdurateness that he piled a bunch of Central Americans into the monsignor's Cadillac and drove them straight up I-19 on a Friday afternoon in broad daylight, dumping them at Southside Church. Conger was horrified, for weekends were the most likely time for the Border Patrol to set up roadblocks.

On another occasion Conger ran afoul of Doña Socorro Aguilar's humanitarian instincts when a Central American he had declined to help and who was staying with her told her that Conger had told him to hike up the riverbed. It was midsummer, and a stroll through the low desert could have killed a man. She flew up to Tucson in a rage, and Conger had to explain that what he had said was: "You have several options. You can go back to Mexico; Father Quiñones can help you find a job in Nogales. You can take a bus up to Tucson, but you'll probably get picked up. Or you could try to walk in along the riverbed, and take plenty of water. None of them are really good options."[3]

Corbett came up with a compromise to help this particular man's group. If we can't transport them ourselves, why don't we provide them with bicycles and maybe helmets and biking gear? he suggested. They could look really authentic and we could give them maps and they could just ride right past the checkpoints and on up to Tucson. The

TEC checked out the scheme, but in the meantime, the group disappeared, presumably following a plan of its own.

The border workers never really developed a good way of dealing with people who just showed up asking for help. Father Quiñones, in particular, came to believe that only extremely endangered political refugees should go to the United States; others, he believed, would be doubly oppressed in the North. They would lose their cultural identity, and they would be economically exploited and always on the run from the INS. Going to the United States, in his mind, was a little like going to Babylon, where one's children would grow up strangers in a materialistic culture. He thought Corbett was "filled with a special fervor" on the matter of bringing Central Americans into the United States.[4]

These differences led to numerous disagreements between the Mexican priest and the *norteamericanos*. Once a man named Raúl arrived at Our Lady of Guadalupe with his "wife," looking for help. He said that they had just been married and that they were political refugees from El Salvador. Quiñones remembered them well, because the woman didn't want to get up in the morning and wanted all of her meals in bed. Panchita, Quiñones's housekeeper, had observed these pretensions with disapproval and reported them to the priest.[5]

With some reluctance Quiñones finally helped the couple make their way across the border because their refugee credentials had been vouched for by the sanctuary people in Tucson. Off they went, but ten months later Raúl returned, with another "wife." He had left the United States, returned to El Salvador, met a lay church worker, and made his way up to Nogales again with her. She had contacted Corbett and was probably a real refugee, but Quiñones insisted this time that he wanted no part of the couple, that he wasn't in the business of helping coyotes. Corbett told him that it was better to help one person by mistake than to let someone die. Quiñones still refused to help, and the couple left, for Raúl knew well how to make his way.

To some extent all the border workers shared Quiñones's concerns. They realized that the answer to Central America's problems wasn't bringing everyone into the United States, particularly when that meant a drain of some of the best and brightest people from the region. It was important, most agreed, to help only people who had no alternative.

Playing God by making that determination, deciding people's fate in a few hours, many times on the basis of very fragmentary information, was difficult. Father Elford, who did a lot of screening, compared it

with triage. On one occasion he had to go to Nogales, Sonora, to talk
with the brother of a man who had been freed in the big bailout at El
Centro. It turned out the brother had taken out a loan in El Salvador
and wanted to come to the United States to make enough money to pay
it off. The priest had to refuse help, but he felt sick about sending the
man away.[6]

Sometimes the counselors spent a whole day or more with a refugee,
relying on their instincts to judge the person's sincerity. Few of those
fleeing ever carried any documentation, and sometimes the most
traumatized individuals did not have enough trust to tell much of their
story. Not until they were safely in the United States would their
horrifying tales come tumbling out, like water from a dammed-up
stream.

As one way of testing their genuineness, Peg Hutchison or Phil
Conger would often ask refugees if they were willing to spend as much
as a year in jail if they were picked up. Hutchison would explain that
if they were caught, they would be put in prison indefinitely, until
their—no doubt futile—asylum hearing. Or they could opt to sign
voluntary departure statements and be free to leave the country.

Many said that they would rather take their chances on returning
home and would try to enter the United States again later. That was
not the right answer. Only those who unhesitatingly chose jail would
be offered help. The sanctuary workers felt pretty sure that anyone who
preferred detention to his or her own country was a legitimate refugee.

The group realized they often made mistakes. One of the worst
involved twenty-three Guatemalan Indians. More than a dozen of
them, mostly children, were brought to Socorro Aguilar's house one
night with no warning. In no time the unwashed villagers, who had
never lived in a house with indoor plumbing, were dipping their tin cups
in the toilet for drinking water, while the children, sick with diarrhea,
defecated all over the floor.

The meticulous Mexican housewife was appalled, and Quiñones was
furious. Among other things, a Guatemalan car-stealing ring was loose
in Nogales, and the police had decided to crack down on Central
Americans in the city. The two Mexicans were terrified that people
would notice the crowd at Socorro Aguilar's house and report them.
Quiñones had already been troubled by rumors that the North American sanctuary movement was using the refugees to gain publicity and
donations. He warned Conger and Elford that if they crossed the

Guatemalan group and paraded them in front of the press as high-risk political refugees in order to get money, he would denounce the two of them himself.

After more checking on the Indians' background, the Americans decided that Quiñones was right and that the group was not "high-risk." Conger and Elford put those who were already in the United States on a bus back to Mexico.[7]

Working on the border as often as they did, Phil and Peggy often had close calls. In September 1983 Phil traveled safely to Mexico City to guide a group of five Guatemalans across the border near Douglas, Arizona. But crossing the frontier with a group of frightened foreigners was never easy, and at times the two young church workers had some hair-raising experiences.

On one occasion Peggy picked up a group of nine or ten women and children immediately after they had crawled through a hole in the international fence near the airport at Douglas. As the family all rushed to get into Hutchison's little Toyota Corona, one hefty woman got stuck between the two front bucket seats, and it seemed like hours before she wiggled into the back seat. After they all got in, and Peggy headed down a dirt road toward town, she suddenly saw the headlights of a Border Patrol Bronco coming straight toward her. She waved as she drove by and kept going until she hit the pavement, wondering why the patrol didn't come after her. She got to the main street and saw another Border Patrol car at a fast-food restaurant, and again she drove right past.

Back at the safe house in Douglas, Phil and the others, who had been warned that the patrol car had been seen heading straight toward the crossing point, were hiding behind the curtains and looking out the window when the Toyota pulled in the driveway and into the garage. All they could see was Peg, but as soon as the car was in the garage, more than half a dozen heads popped up. The only explanation they could think of for her escape was that the breath of all the passengers had fogged up the car's windows.

In February 1984 the nerves of the "border breakers" were rattled when two women involved in similar refugee work were arrested in Texas. One of the women was a nun, and the other, Stacey Lynn Merkt, twenty-nine, had been on the border, working as a volunteer for Casa Romero, for only two and a half weeks. They had been taking three refugees north out of the Rio Grande Valley past the Border Patrol checkpoints when they were stopped.

Shortly thereafter, at the beginning of March, Phil got a call from a rancher friend in Patagonia, northeast of Nogales. A couple of Central Americans there needed a ride, and Phil agreed to go get them. He hadn't heard their story; it was just a Point A to Point B lift to help out a friend. En route back, he suddenly saw a reflector in the dark at the side of the road: the Border Patrol. As Conger drove past, the car flashed its lights on for a second or two. It was a routine check to look at a passing vehicle, to see if it was riding low, to see how many people were in the car, and so on. Conger could feel a numbness starting in his hands and going up his arms; he didn't want to get caught with these strangers. But the patrol car didn't come after him.

The next week he wasn't so lucky.

On March 7, 1984—Ash Wednesday—Phil went down to Nogales for his regular visit to the prison. With him that day was a pretty, brown-haired, blue-eyed woman named Katherine Flaherty, who had just moved to Tucson specifically to help the sanctuary movement.[8] A native of Wilmington, Delaware, and a graduate of George Washington University, in Washington, D.C., Flaherty had worked in the Peace Corps in El Salvador from 1977 to 1979. The experience had convinced her that revolution was coming, and shortly after she left, the relatively conservative family she had stayed with received threats from a guerrilla group that two of the daughters would be killed unless the family paid up. One daughter fled to the United States, and eventually the whole family left the country, partly with Flaherty's help.

After she left Central America, Flaherty started a religious task force in Washington that was trying to educate Catholic priests and nuns about conditions in El Salvador. Eventually frustrated by the growing American involvement in the war there, she read one of Jim Corbett's articles and decided that doing something directly for the victims of the violence would be more satisfying. She had been left a small trust fund by her grandmother and didn't need to worry about income, so in 1983 she began working with the sanctuary committee in Washington.

That work proved equally frustrating. Although a handful of Unitarian, Quaker, and Mennonite congregations in the capital area had joined the movement, after ten or eleven months of effort the committee had still not persuaded any mainstream Washington churches to declare sanctuary. Flaherty decided to go to Tucson and become more personally involved. The trip to Nogales was her first border run.

Kathy and Phil first went to the prison with Father Quiñones. After several hours the group went back to Quiñones's church for lunch and to talk to a small group of refugees. One of them was a man in his mid-twenties who had been doing political organizing in El Salvador and had fled after his name appeared on a death list. It turned out that Flaherty already knew him; he had been in Washington and had worked with the Central American political organizations there. He had subsequently returned to El Salvador, but his friends there had told him that he would surely be killed if he stayed. He was traveling with three sisters, one of whom had worked with Maryknoll priests in El Salvador and had seen her aunt raped and her father dragged away and "disappeared."

Phil explained to the group how to cross the international fence, through a hole about half a mile from the port of entry, how to proceed to Sacred Heart Church and there to wait for his arrival.

At about five-thirty or six in the afternoon, Kathy and Phil arrived at Sacred Heart.[9] A rock-climbing buddy of Phil's arrived a couple of hours later to be the scout car. He took off down the road and after driving past the usual sites for roadblocks with no sign of the Border Patrol, he pulled off at a phone in Sonoita and rang the church. "Everything's fine," he reported. "It's a fine night for a drive."

Phil was a little concerned. It was now dark, and it wasn't smart to do a run late at night. Real smugglers operated at that hour, and he was driving an old 1976 Ford station wagon with tinted windows—exactly the kind of vehicle that smugglers used. If there were any Border Patrol officers on the road, that car was sure to arouse suspicion.

They set off at about 11:00 P.M., with Phil driving and Kathy in front, dressed in a preppy little blue blouse and matching slacks. The young man and woman and her two young teenaged sisters were in the back. The car had gotten about seven miles outside Nogales on Highway 82 just past the airport, and Phil was explaining how the Border Patrol cars waited by the side of the road and, when they saw a suspicious car, suddenly flashed their lights. "Like that," he said, and turned around and pointed at the patrol car that had just flashed its lights.

The officers moved out onto the highway behind Conger's car and read his license plate. "Who's it registered to?" Kathy asked.

"Southside Presbyterian Church," Phil replied.

The patrol car dropped back while the border patrolmen tried unsuccessfully by radiophone to check the registration of the plates with Tucson. The officers thought that the plates were not of local origin. They were suspicious of the large, low-riding vehicle and suspicious, too, of the fact that the driver had hit his taillights when the patrol car's lights had flashed.[10] One of them, an eight-year veteran named Chase, thought that that was a nervous reflex, not the normal reaction; in his experience most people just drive on by. The speed of the station wagon seemed suspicious, too; in an area where speeding was a way of life, the station wagon was traveling at forty-five to fifty miles an hour, as if to avoid attracting the attention of the law. Then Baca, the other Border Patrol officer, thought he saw a third person in the middle seat of the wagon, and the patrolmen decided to make a red-light stop.

The officers came up again on Phil and pulled him off to the side of the road. Conger immediately got out of the car and went back to talk to the officers. Chase was already getting out of the patrol car, and as he saw the driver coming over, he thought, that has happened to me maybe six or eight times in all my years in the patrol, and every time the guy has had something to hide.[11] Chase was in his mid-forties and looked like a burly, crew-cut ex-marine, while Baca was a younger Hispanic-looking man. They climbed out and ordered Phil back in his car. Chase came up to the window and before he could say anything, Phil asked, "Is there a problem, Officer?"[12]

"I don't know for sure, sir," Chase replied, and then he asked if everyone in the car was a U.S. citizen. He shone his flashlight on Oscar and on María Antonia, who by prearrangement in the event of such a situation were stretched out on the second seat "sleeping." The two little teenaged sisters were slumped down on the third seat of the station wagon.

Oscar "woke up" and said that he was a Mexican. He had no papers. Phil was ordered out and made to lean against the car, patted down, and then ordered into the back seat of the patrol car. "I think we've got ourselves a load," Chase told Baca, as he walked Phil back to the patrol car and explained his Miranda rights. Kathy was then told she was under arrest and ordered into the back seat with Phil. With Baca driving the station wagon with the refugees, they all went back to the Border Patrol station in Nogales.

Phil felt fairly calm, although Kathy was getting more and more nervous. He tried to make small talk with Chase, but the officer's gruff Marine Corps demeanor had only slightly softened by the time they got to the station. He sat his prisoners down at some tables in the middle of a large room with little side rooms and corridors running off it. Phil told him his name and address, but refused to give his Social Security number or any other information. "If you don't cooperate, it will be worse for you in front of a judge," Chase warned. "I can get it off your driver's license anyway." Phil asked if he had to surrender his wallet, and Chase said, "Damn right." He rummaged through the wallet and found Conger's Social Security card.

During their exchange Conger kept implying that he was in no way sorry for what he had done, and finally Chase said, "Are you crazy? Are you one of those church people?" Phil smiled, and Chase caught on. It seemed to Phil that the officers were much nicer after they found out whom they had in custody. They had first thought that they had some regular coyotes, a breed they did not respect. Only a week earlier they had arrested a smuggler who jumped out of a moving car full of undocumented Mexicans, leaving it to turn over at the side of the road.

Baca asked Kathy if there was anything she needed from the car, and she went out with him and picked up two backpacks that were lying in the front seat. The officer asked permission to go through them, and began looking through the packs. There was Jim Corbett's typed sheet on "Pre-crossing Counseling," explaining how "border breakers" should interview and advise refugees on how to slip into the United States. There were some clips on the arrest in Texas and a Salvadoran passport belonging to Oscar. Confronted with it, the refugee admitted his nationality. "Can I make my phone call now?" Phil asked. The Border Patrol officers, who had denied his first request to make a call, laughed and said yes.

Conger called Fife collect. By then it was about 11:30 P.M., and the minister hadn't even known that they were out on a run. Phil told him what had happened and said he would need a lawyer. Fife agreed to make the necessary calls. When Phil hung up, the patrol was still pulling things out of the packs. "There's enough evidence here to put you guys away forever," one of the officers joked.

The sanctuary workers told refugees who were crossing alone to act like Mexicans if they were caught, so they would not be sent back to Central America. But those traveling with sanctuary workers themselves were told to tell the truth, so that the activists could claim that they were not smuggling ordinary aliens but were assisting legitimate refugees. After some coaxing Conger finally persuaded the Salvadoran women to admit their nationality, and the whole party was finger-printed and photographed. Finally the officers left Phil and Kathy pretty much alone, and Phil, who was beginning to feel shaky, asked if he could eat something. He had apples, oranges, and raisins in his pack, and the Border Patrol had been telling them that they had a hard night ahead of them. "Go ahead," said Chase. "You're not going to get anything in the Santa Cruz county jail for a long time."

Phil started munching, and as he did, his eye glanced at the papers in front of him. There were the lists of their contacts along the border; a map to the house of Mary K. Espinosa, who worked at Sacred Heart; a whole page of a letter with an address from a woman in Alamosa, Colorado, who had received a large group of Guatemalans. Slowly Phil folded up the 8½- by 11-inch sheet of paper, and after looking around, he started to chew. He kept taking bites of his apple, and finally he got the thing down. He looked around again. Still no one was looking, so he scanned the pile to see what was the most important material to destroy. He ate half a page on the movement's contacts in the Douglas area and was just beginning to nibble on another document when an agent came over and picked up the whole mass of paper and carted it off to the photocopy room.

At the next table, in front of Katherine, was Conger's wallet and a big pile of business cards. He was just wondering how to reach them when another agent picked them up and said, "Is this yours?" and dropped them in front of him. Conger managed to swallow three more business cards.

Finally, at about 3:00 A.M., the patrol officers said that they had been told to release the two North Americans, although the Latins had to remain in custody. Phil and Kathy asked to stay overnight in the cell with their charges but were refused. Chase offered to give them a ride to a nearby Denny's, and on the way he commented that he had been a little concerned about running into "you church people," because he had mixed feelings on the issue. John Fife soon arrived at Denny's with Peggy and Ellen Willis, Phil's fiancée, and as the sun began coming up over the fresh spring desert, the five headed back to Tucson.

Chapter
Fourteen

WHEN THE PHONE rang with news of Conger's arrest, Jim Rayburn was sitting at his desk on the second floor of the old Post Office Building in downtown Phoenix. The historic landmark, a once-elegant Spanish colonial-style structure, was now surrounded by a sleazy neighborhood of thrift shops, bars, and parking lots. The directory in the main lobby didn't even list the Immigration Service, and the unmarked door at the end of a long corridor gave no clue that an INS office was behind it. The ambiance was more that of a down-at-the-heels private detective agency than an arm of the federal government.

Rayburn was pleased about the Border Patrol's action, but he immediately recognized that the government would have trouble justifying the stop and search of Conger's car.[1] When he saw the photocopied documents found in it, he could hardly believe what they revealed.

The find was a gold mine. There were addresses and telephone numbers of key members of the sanctuary network all around the country. There was information about Conger's regular Thursday visits to the Nogales jail. But what excited the INS officer most of all was a document entitled "Some Proposals for Integrating Smuggling, Refuge, Relay, Sanctuary, and Bailbond Networks," written in January–February 1984 by Jim Corbett. There, in plain English, was a virtual road map of the underground railroad, drawn by the master engineer himself and complete with references to "safe houses" and "border breakers."

If the INS had ever doubted that the sanctuary movement was anything more than an exaggerated invention of the media, Corbett's memo put those doubts to rest. Here was a detailed description of the "religious communities' refugee defense activities" from southern Mexico to Canada.

The paper addressed the problem of the increasing influx of Central Americans at the border, which it attributed primarily to the famous "magnet effect": efforts on the part of those already in the United States to bring in their friends and relatives. In order to adapt, Corbett recommended that the Tucson groups must either bring in many more volunteers or else dramatically reduce their caseload. Among other things, he suggested that "personal guidance and transportation for border crossings by those who have made more than 100 runs will be limited, collectively, to 10 refugees per month." (How many people are making a hundred runs a month? Corbett's fascinated readers at the INS wondered.)

The paper made clear that the Tucson Ecumenical Council and the Chicago Religious Task Force on Central America were part of the underground railroad. It said that Tucson volunteers would be developing additional routes into the United States with congregations along the border. Volunteers would be traveling the routes in northern Mexico regularly "in order to maintain coverage of the situation from Tijuana to Matamoros on a quarterly cycle. . . ." It noted that Tucson volunteers were preparing maps and instruction sheets on the major south–north routes up through Mexico, "to be available to travellers on request."

Organizations in each center of refugee settlement, such as Los Angeles, San Francisco, Houston, Washington, D.C., New York, and Chicago, should establish "their own chains of contacts, safe houses, counselors, and smugglers from Mexico City to the U.S. side of the border," Corbett wrote. The Tucson refugee support groups, he added, were willing to "train border breakers and pre-crossing counselors who are selected by sanctuary congregations and other refugee defense groups."

On March 19, 1984, only days after Rayburn reviewed the papers found in Conger's backpack, the new undercover guidelines from the INS became effective. On or about March 22 Scott Coffin briefed Rayburn on them generally, and Mark Reed in the regional office in San Pedro, California, gave him permission to proceed with the informant Cruz and with "consensual monitoring," the secret taping of conversations and recording of telephone calls.[2]

The undercover investigation of the sanctuary movement was to be called Operation Sojourner.

Rayburn asked Cruz, who officially become Agent PHO-I-98, to begin by contacting Father Ramón Dagoberto Quiñones at the Santuario de Guadalupe Church in Nogales, Mexico. Rayburn told I-98 to introduce himself as a person who was sympathetic to sanctuary and willing to smuggle aliens for free. He was told to find out all he could about who was involved in the smuggling operation and about where the smuggled aliens were entering the United States.

Cruz had a suggestion of his own about how to proceed. He knew that a group of nine Guatemalans in Nogales, Sonora, were planning to enter the United States illegally in a few days. Why not use them as a means of luring Father Quiñones into a smuggling operation that Cruz could secretly record?

Rayburn liked the idea. And on March 26 Jesus Cruz called Father Quiñones to propose a meeting the following day at the church. Quiñones agreed.

No limit was placed on Cruz's freedom to engage in conversations with the priest in Mexico or with any members of the sanctuary movement in or on church properties. No limit was placed on secret tape recordings in private homes or churches, other than during religious services. Rayburn told Cruz that the government was interested only in criminal violations of the immigration laws, not in the religious part, and the informant was instructed not to tape "at masses, church services, things of that nature."[3] What constituted a religious service was left to Cruz's discretion, although Cruz hadn't attended a religious service in years. And Cruz was not told to forget the nine Guatemalans, even though Paragraph G of the new undercover guidelines stated that entrapment was to be avoided and that if there was to be even a potential entrapment situation, there had to be specific written authorization from the Undercover Guidelines Review Committee in Washington.

The man Cruz was going to meet was, despite his disinterest in liberation theology, remarkably similar to the priests who were being hunted down in El Salvador and Guatemala. Father Ramón Dagoberto Quiñones had never forgotten his origins. He had been born in a small town in southern Sonora, the youngest of four children in a very poor family. His mother, a widowed schoolteacher, had sent him off at the age of thirteen to the seminary at the state capital of Hermosillo, and there, in 1960, at the age of twenty-four, he was ordained a priest.

He was immediately chosen to fill several important posts within the diocese of Hermosillo. At various times he was spiritual director of the seminary; a teacher of philosophy and theology; coordinator of instruction for catechism, sports, and cultural events for all youths in the diocese; and one of three judges of the Ecclesiastical Court, a marriage tribunal. Later, at his own request, he was assigned as the parish priest in the poorest neighborhood of Hermosillo, a barrio known as Colonia Olivares that until then had had no church.

After eleven years in Hermosillo, Father Quiñones was transferred to Cananea, a copper mining town about thirty miles directly south of the United States border, near Bisbee, Arizona. One of the things he initiated there was a food basket program, raising food in various ways to help those in need. At the high school, on potato day, every student would bring a potato, and 1,500 potatoes would be donated to Father Quiñones's food program. He instituted rules for the annual Christmas procession, requiring that everyone who attended bring food. He began serving a noon meal every day at the jail.

In 1978 the priest was transferred to Our Lady of Guadalupe, the largest Catholic church in Nogales, Sonora, a city of 180,000 to 200,000 people, most of whom were living at the margin. One of his first moves was to institute a food program. Among other things, he launched a Reina de los Pobres ("Queen of the Poor") contest, in which people voted for candidates by donating food.[4]

Quiñones's first encounter with Central American refugees occurred in 1979, when during one of his visits to the Nogales prison he discovered a large group of Salvadorans who told a story about being forced off their land by the military, and for the first time Quiñones learned about the increasingly violent conditions in their country.

The priest decided to form a special ministry for the detained Central Americans. He organized a group of people to help, including Doña María Socorro Aguilar, and they scrounged up blankets and mattresses for the prisoners. They brought in a large hot meal three days a week, and Socorro Aguilar helped with catechism and other religious services. Even after he had been joined by Jim Corbett, and later by Phil Conger and Peg Hutchison, all the funds for the ministry continued to come from Quiñones's own parish of about 50,000 people. He felt that his work, to be legitimate, had to be sustained by his church.

"This ministry," Quiñones later commented wryly, "brought consequences."[5]

As Father Quiñones's name spread along the refugee grapevine, more and more Central Americans on their way north came to El Santuario de Nuestra Señora de Guadalupe as their last stop before trying to enter the United States. At times there were more than a dozen in the church at once, camping in the dormitories and living quarters behind the white stucco chapel.

Some were so traumatized that it took no special questioning to determine that they were fleeing truly horrible situations. Quiñones met women who had been raped by death squads and men who had fresh bullet wounds. Once he received a large number of Salvadorans, who went on into the United States in small groups until only a couple and a young woman were left. The night before they were supposed to leave, the priest was in his bedroom at about eleven o'clock at night when he heard a knock at his door. He opened the door, and it was the young woman. He asked what she wanted, and she said that she was going to give herself to him.

The priest laughed nervously and said, "What are you talking about?" She replied, "You've done so much for us, and I have nothing to pay you with except my body. I'm used to it; in my country everybody wants my body." Quiñones told her, "My dear, if I accepted what you propose, all of our work would be destroyed. We don't do what we do for profit but for faith."[6]

The priest never made any secret of what he was doing, and he probably couldn't have even if he had tried. One day in 1983 he ran into the chief of Mexican immigration at a store in Tucson, and just to say something, he asked the policeman if he had many Central Americans in the jail at the moment. "No," replied the official, "you have them all at the church."

Partly because his work was done so openly, Father Quiñones didn't suspect anything out of the ordinary when the man named Jesus Cruz called him from Nogales, Arizona, and said he wanted to come see him.

They made an appointment, and the next day, March 27, 1984, Cruz showed up at the whitewashed Mexican church.

It was a bright spring day, and Cruz had brought along a load of fresh grapefruit to donate to the priest's food bank. He got out of his pickup and inquired at the church office for Father Quiñones. He was a bit early, and the priest wasn't there, so Cruz wandered through the court-yard for a while. The grounds of the church were flanked by four stories of apartments and dominated by a tall, square bell tower topped by a large white cross. Behind the main sanctuary and along one side of the courtyard were several one-story buildings housing the feeding pro-gram, a center for the elderly, a milk bank, and a medical dispensary. Just before noon Quiñones arrived and invited Cruz into his office.

The small room, furnished with a desk, a sofa, and several chairs, was crowded with books, religious pictures, and a large image of the Virgin. Cruz sat down by the one window, which looked out on a nearby wall, and explained that he had been put in touch with eight or nine Guatemalans who needed immediate assistance in getting into the United States. They were in a hotel near the bus depot, he said, and had children with them who needed medical attention right away.[7]

According to Father Quiñones, Cruz asked the priest if he could help guide the group across the border. Quiñones, who prided himself on his reading of people, didn't suspect anything, but he was not about to tell this stranger that he was a smuggler. So he told Cruz: "You are mis-taken; I have nothing to do with crossing people."

The informant persisted. "But I've been told that you would help," he said.

"You've been misled," the priest repeated.

At that point Cruz apologized and asked if he could come back occasionally and perhaps be of help to the priest. He explained that he was retired and had some time and would like to volunteer to help with the Central American work. Quiñones told him that he was welcome to return.[8]

Cruz did not tape his first conversation with Father Quiñones be-cause "Mr. Jim," as he called Rayburn, had instructed him never to tape in Mexico. Rayburn was concerned that taping might be a viola-tion of Mexican law. Cruz's only other guidelines regarding taping were not to record religious services, to try to leave a tape on once it was turned on, and to return completed tapes as soon as possible.

On April 8 Cruz returned to Our Lady of Guadalupe, again bringing gifts of food and sacks of grapefruit. He spent most of the day looking around the church and visiting with Father Quiñones as the latter went about his duties. He saw no Central Americans that day. When he reported back to Rayburn, the investigator noted in his file on the case that "all efforts of church were being directed toward helping Central Americans being held in Mexican jails. I-98 was asked to return."

On April 16, at Father Quiñones's invitation, Cruz accompanied the priest and a small group of parishioners, including Doña María Socorro Aguilar, to the jail. Quiñones introduced Cruz as his "movement" helper from Phoenix. At the jail, the informer later reported meticulously to Rayburn, they visited thirty-two men, including twenty-six from El Salvador and four from Honduras, and twelve women, from El Salvador, Honduras, and Nicaragua. Father Quiñones and a second priest "told the aliens that they were going to be deported to their country by the Mexican government, but if their relatives sent money the Fathers could get them out of jail and out of being deported. The fathers would pay the Mexican Immigration."[9]

After the jail visit Cruz asked for and received the names and telephone numbers of the church's parishioners. That day he also met María Socorro Aguilar for the first time. A woman of medium height, with a plump, rounded figure, short, curly gray hair, and a warm smile, she was fifty-seven years old and had been a widow for eight months. She lived alone; her five children, a daughter living in Tucson, another daughter in Hermosillo, and three sons living in Mexico, were all grown and gone. Beginning that day, Jesus Cruz, or Don Jesús, as she called him, made it his business to become her very good friend.

Doña Socorro Aguilar's life had been absorbed by her family and her church, although at one point she had also run a small shop. She was what is called in Mexico a *cucarachita* (literally, little roach), or what would be called in English a church mouse, devoted to her priest and her church work. Her house, a rambling four-bedroom structure, was perched high on a hill off a small lane called Calle Fenocio, about a mile from her church and a mile, in a different direction, from the U.S. border. The grimy street, with its ramshackle houses and aged autos, reflected the pervasive poverty of Mexico, and the steep slope leading up to Doña María's home was frequently littered with garbage, soiled diapers, and debris. But inside was an island of middle-class cleanliness and comfort. The living room was filled with heavy Spanish colonial-style furniture, and a large crucifix hung on the wall. At the other end of a long veranda a series of tiny bedrooms had been added to the house, and the widow occasionally rented them out to supplement her income.

Gradually, as she had become more involved in Father Quiñones's Central American work, she had allowed the overflow from the church to stay in those rooms for a night or two. Her house had become a safe house in Nogales, where sanctuary workers could meet incoming refugees, interview them, and decide whether to help them cross the border. If the refugees passed the screening, Socorro Aguilar occasionally became involved in counseling the women, in particular, on how to cross. While most of the men tended to slip through holes in the international fence, many women went straight through the port of entry, using false documents. Socorro Aguilar sometimes helped obtain these papers and counseled women on how to change their Central American appearance into a more Mexican look, by altering their clothing, hairstyles, or makeup. Before she quite realized what was happening, the good Catholic widow had become an integral part of the sanctuary movement's border breaking.

Chapter
Fifteen

L ESS THAN A week after Cruz met Socorro Aguilar, she turned to
him for help. On April 22 the telephone rang at about nine in the
morning at the cheap motel in Phoenix where the older man was living
with Salomon Graham. Graham answered the phone, and a woman
named Bertha Benavidez asked for his roommate. When Graham said
that Cruz was not in, she explained that she had been trying to bring
her children into the country from El Salvador and that they had been
captured and deported. She wanted Cruz's help in bringing the children
back up.

Benavidez called back at about six o'clock in the evening, and this
time she talked to Cruz. She explained that Doña Socorro Aguilar and
Father Quiñones had told her that he might be able to help bring her
family to Phoenix if they made it as far as Nogales. She said that she
would call back when they arrived. Doña María was planning to fly to
Mexico City to meet the two children and fly back with them to
Hermosillo. From there, she would accompany them on up to Nogales,
Sonora.

Cruz hung up. Even though he wasn't supposed to begin clandestine taping on the sanctuary case yet, because of his earlier work with the INS, his telephone was already equipped to record calls. The Benavidez call had been recorded.

Two days later, on April 24, Jim Rayburn officially requested authorization to begin an undercover investigation of sanctuary. He had submitted his first formal request for permission to begin an undercover operation almost a month earlier, on March 29, but the request had been rejected. The official who reviewed it had called Scott Coffin, Rayburn's supervisor, and told him that the request did not contain adequate information and another draft would have to be prepared.[1]

Washington's action had not stopped Rayburn and Coffin from proceeding, however; both men reasoned that the undercover operation had already been approved verbally by the Western Region, and they assumed that the INS central office would swiftly authorize an investigation when it saw a more detailed request. So, after more consultations, Coffin and Rayburn drew up a second request and submitted it on April 24, roughly a month after Operation Sojourner had actually begun.

The request from Phoenix was the first that the new Undercover Guidelines Review Committee had ever received. The committee's mandate was to take a careful look at sensitive investigations, such as those involving foreign governments as targets, those that might intrude on the attorney-client privilege, or those involving religious organizations, as this one did—in short, to prevent serious and possibly embarrassing abuses. Any case involving "sensitive techniques"—i.e., eavesdropping—for more than six months also had to be approved beyond the regional level.

Rayburn's lengthy second request was important, for it provided Washington with its first comprehensive overview of the sanctuary movement. It was the document that initially formed Washington's perception of this unprecedented civil protest along the Arizona border.

Rayburn's analysis of the size of the movement echoed the previous government estimates. Although the Arizona investigator stressed sanctuary's national scope, his intelligence showed that its smuggling activity was in fact minuscule.

Rayburn noted that the movement claimed that there were "presently over 45 public sanctuary sites, with the public endorsement and support of over 600 'co-conspiring' congregations and religious organizations. An additional 50 sanctuary organizing committees in cities, towns, and rural communities stretch across the entire length and breadth of the USA. . . ."[2]

Statistics on how many "aliens" this network actually moved, however, were elusive. Rayburn ventured that "a realistic figure for TEC would average less then [*sic*] ten aliens a month. The figure of ten is based upon intelligence gleaned from a myriad of sources including undercover operatives, and an internal analysis of their operation." Among other things, Rayburn noted, the movement did not have the resources to move several groups simultaneously, and the average size of a group rarely exceeded six, including children. Since it took one to two months to move a group up through Mexico to its U.S. destination, the numbers involved had to be modest, perhaps as few as *120 people a year.*

Rayburn did not remind his superiors in Washington that the average coyote smuggling people into the United States for money might bring in as many as *forty or fifty people every few weeks*. Nor did he cite the memo from Arizona Border Patrol agent Dean Thatcher in January 1983, stating that the sanctuary movement did not appear to be a serious threat to law enforcement efforts by the INS. Unlike many people in the Immigration Service in Arizona, Rayburn did not think that the sanctuary movement's bark was bigger than its bite. The reason, at least in part, was that the anti-Communist investigator saw "red."

What he described to his superiors in the Immigration Service and the Justice Department was a highly political antiwar movement engaged in smuggling aliens who could be used for propaganda purposes in a campaign against U.S. policies in Central America. He did note in the overview attached to his request that the sanctuary activists believed:

[G]iving sanctuary to political refugees is a just act covered by accord, law, and treaty, specifically: United Nations Treaty number 2545, dated August 28, 1951 (ratified by the United States Senate and signed by the President in 1968), which states in part: ". . . No contracting party shall expel or forcibly return a refugee in any manner whatsoever to the frontiers of territories where his life or freedom would be threatened on account of his race, religion, nationality or membership in a particular social group or political opinion. . . ."

But, Rayburn's overview went on, "The movement, which may have initially expressed humanitarian motives, has slowly evolved to sanction a more lawless and political stance."[3]

To support this interpretation, Rayburn relied heavily on the pronouncements of the Chicago Religious Task Force. Quotations from *Basta!*, the CRTFCA newsletter, decorated Rayburn's request like little red balls on a Christmas tree:

Sanctuary offers a concrete and direct way to challenge the inhuman policy of the United States government in Central America and the Immigration & Naturalization Service. . . .

. . . We think a mass movement of resistance in the United States using direct action is best. . . .

If we allow the court of law or lawyers to direct the sanctuary movement, we will be letting United States law dictate the parameters of our work and the limits of our conscience. . . .

Excerpts from Corbett's voluminous writings also made their way into Rayburn's brief. They included one oft-quoted line to the effect that "Law abiding protest only helps us live with atrocity."

As further support for his view of sanctuary, Rayburn quoted from an article appearing in the *Portland Oregonian* on April 23, 1984. "Many groups offering protection for illegal aliens are for the most part using their safe harbor activities as a way of protesting the administration's policy in Central America," it stated. "They use the aliens for propaganda speeches, for rebuttals against the administration's policies in Central America they oppose. . . ."

Rayburn also cited the movement's own "Counseling Guidelines," describing the screening process by which refugees going into public sanctuary were selected. It reminded counselors to "Make sure sanctuary is presented as an opportunity for the refugees to serve their people by the conscientizing [*sic*] of large numbers of North Americans and encourage them to work to change United States Policy."

Rayburn's report went on to say: "Although those chosen for sanctuary cannot be stereotyped, they do seem to possess certain basic characteristics, i.e., young, middle class, well-educated, well-spoken, with values/beliefs inclined toward the 'left.' Aside from those recruited by the sanctuary movement, the 'railroad' does process a large number of candidates, many of whom are rejected. Those not selected are given minimal assistance, if any at all."

Under "Description of Criminal Enterprise," Rayburn summed up:

"Operation Sojourner" is an investigation of a movement which calls itself "The Central American Refugee Underground Railroad." Their recruiting starts at Tapachula, Chiapas, Mexico on the Guatemalan border and continues north through Mexico to Hermosillo, Sonora. From Hermosillo, Sonora—after circumventing Mexican immigration check points—aliens are taken through Santuario de Guadelupe [sic] to Father Dagoberto QUINONES. *Philip* CONGER *and other Tucson based members of the organization closely screen and brief aliens being moved through the pipeline. Aliens are instructed to obtain clothing with U.S. labels. If arrested, they are told to minimize conversations with officials in order to hide their Central American accents. Guides are assigned to lead the aliens across the border. The organization refers to these guides as "border breakers."*

After illegal entries are effected, aliens are transported primarily under the control of members of the "Underground Railroad." Routes of travel are dictated by final destinations. Use of Interstate highways is discouraged in favor of secondary highways. Safe-houses are assigned along the selected routes of travel and safe-house operators are alerted that a particular load is enroute.

The Reverend John Fife headed Rayburn's list of the "criminal participants involved." His description of the pastor, in its entirety, was:

Reverend John M. FIFE *of The Southside United Presbyterian Church, Tucson, Arizona states publicly that he was an anti-Vietnam War activist. He claims the "Underground Railroad" wants the United States Government to take them to court so they can challenge United States policy in Central America. Reverend* FIFE *is a United States citizen.* FIFE *is the self proclaimed founder of the "Sanctuary and Underground Movement," now called "Tucson Ecumenical Council Task Force on Central Americans' [sic] of which* FIFE *is a member of high voice and rank.*

Corbett, a "self-styled activist," he wrote, "claims to be a Quaker, a retired rancher, and a Harvard-educated philosopher." Duly noted

were the rancher's appearances on "60 Minutes" and in *People* magazine, showing him "in the act" of transporting illegal aliens.*

Describing his confidential informant PHO-I-98 as a "highly reliable
and credible informant," Rayburn argued that he had no alternative to
sending undercover operatives into the sanctuary movement. "Evidence needed for prosecution cannot be obtained by traditional means.
Witnesses won't testify against church members and church members
won't testify against group leaders. Members of the conspiracy are not
motivated by financial considerations. They are motivated by a strong
political philosophy under the guise of religious beliefs."

Rayburn requested up to $10,000 in expenses for an undercover
operation of six months. He noted that the undercover operation had
already been approved by Special Assistant U.S. Attorney Don Reno,
who "has agreed to aggressively prosecute a meritorious case," and
U.S. Attorney Mel McDonald, District of Arizona. The two, Rayburn
wrote, were "appraised [*sic*]" daily about the investigation and "are
aware of the sensitive circumstances involved." The infiltration would
be conducted with the "minimal intrusion which is consistent with the
need [to] collect evidence in an effective manner."

Underneath "invasion of personal privacy or significant risk of violence (if yes, explain:)," Rayburn wrote: "Yes. It is believed that *most*
members of the movement would not resort to violence to accomplish
their goal, however, information has been received that indicates some
of the persons they have moved are terrorists."**

The bureaucracy in Washington moved relatively quickly on the
second request from Phoenix, which was marked "Urgent" on the
grounds that the nine Guatemalans were "available to use as means
of initial contact . . . Group entering into U.S. illegally March 27,
1984." (This was a month *before* the request reached Washington.)
On May 2, 1984, Maurice Inman's office sent a telex to the INS district office in Phoenix indicating that temporary approval for the undercover operation had been granted by Associate Attorney General

*Rayburn told the author in November 1986 in Phoenix that in his candid opinion,
"Mr. Corbett" was "so educated intellectually he's probably taken himself out of the
real world. But he is sincere. He's not comfortable with some of the things the others
were doing."

**There was no mention of possible invasion of privacy in the entire document or
in Rayburn's subsequent requests for extensions of the undercover operation, although
Cruz routinely taped telephone calls and wore a body bug in private conversations in
private homes and churches. Nor was any evidence presented to support the allegations
about terrorism.

Stephen S. Trott, head of the Criminal Division of the Department of Justice.

The day after the telex went out the Undercover Guidelines Review Committee met for the first time and reviewed the request. The committee members were Lawrence Lippe, from the Criminal Division of the Justice Department; William Landers, special counsel to Associate Attorney General Trott; Humberto E. Moreno, the head of the INS's antismuggling unit; David Klein of the Justice Department; and Roger Cubbage, a career INS bureaucrat.

After looking at the proposal, several members of the committee recognized at once that the case would be controversial. The proposal was accordingly again brought to the attention of Trott, the third ranking official in the Justice Department. He gave the green light, and on the next day, May 24, 1984, the review committee approved Operation Sojourner for three months.

The approval was subject to the following limitations:

(1) Except for meetings with possible conspirators and illegal aliens, the role of the undercover operatives should be limited to transporting aliens within the United States.

(2) The undercover operatives should not engage in any activity in Mexico, except for meetings or interviews with aliens when such meetings or interviews are necessary for the continuance of the operatives' undercover roles. No consensual electronic surveillance should be performed in Mexico.

(3) Absent an emergency, any changes in the undercover operatives' roles should receive prior approval from the Undercover Operations Review Committee.

(4) Pursuant to paragraph VI of the Attorney General's Guidelines on INS Undercover Operations, the operatives should be informed that they are not to participate in acts of violence, initiate or instigate plans to commit criminal acts, use unlawful investigative techniques to obtain information or evidence, or engage in conduct that would violate restrictions on investigations or INS conduct contained in Department of Justice policy. . . .

(5) Since Philip Conger is expected to be indicted for the March 8, 1984 transporting incident, and since he is represented by counsel, the operatives should be directed not *to initiate discussions with him concerning the pending case.*

(6) Finally, the operation is approved for a period of three months. [4]

Stephen S. Trott, the man who had signed off on the operation, was by temperament and history a prosecutor. The forty-three-year-old lawyer was a former member of the Highwaymen, a folk music group popular in the early 1960s that had a gold record to its credit ("Michael Row the Boat Ashore"). He had gone on to become chief deputy district attorney in Los Angeles County, and for almost two decades he had pursued criminals with a happily uncomplicated fervor before being tapped by Attorney General William French Smith to come into the Justice Department.

As chief of the Criminal Division Trott had already established himself as a bright, aggressive prosecutor who didn't spend too much time worrying about what civil liberties groups might think of his approach. He liked to boast that the number of wiretaps had doubled under the Reagan administration. He believed that the exclusionary rule against improperly obtained evidence was "a monstrosity that creates a lot of trouble."[5]

Trott had compiled a 100-page memorandum on "The Successful Use of Snitches, Informants, Co-Conspirators and Accomplices," which offered such insights as: "Jurors are likely to despise criminal informants and to resent prosecutors 'for making deals with such scum,'" and "Never say anything to a witness, or for that matter to anybody . . . that you would not repeat yourself in open court or want to see on the front page of the *New York Times.* Assume at all times— especially when you are on the telephone—that you are being taped."

If Trott was zealous in enforcing the law as he saw it, Jim Rayburn was one of the most gung ho investigators he could hope to find in the Immigration Service. The INS, a backwater agency within the Justice Department, was chronically starved for funds, and investigations were not one of its top priorities. In 1984 the number of INS investigations was declining, and there was no formal training program to prepare agents for undercover operations. Many of those coming into investigations were from the Border Patrol, whose paramilitary, intensely physical training program resembled the preparation given military commandos.

Rayburn had been through the seventeen-week training course at the Border Patrol Academy at Glynco, Georgia. He had had some additional journeyman training, and had taken a two-week course in 1982 in advanced antismuggling at Glynco, including instruction in conspiracy law, violations of 8 U.S. Code No. 1324, and investigation techniques. Some Justice Department veterans, with experiences in both the INS and the FBI, thought that this kind of background was woefully inadequate as preparation for a sensitive undercover operation. Moreover, officials in Washington were aware that Rayburn had initiated his investigation before anyone in the INS central office had approved it. Still, no one in authority questioned Rayburn's qualifications at the time.

The central office of the INS did take pains to surround its approval of the "consensual monitoring"—wiretapping and secret tape recording—in Operation Sojourner with a thicket of restrictions. Monitoring could continue for no more than thirty days. If the period was to be extended, a written request would have to be submitted at least ten days before the expiration of the approval. That request would have to contain the dates of each conversation monitored, the names of the persons, or "targets," monitored, an indication of whether corroborating evidence of the crime was obtained by the monitoring, and the specific reasons why the monitoring had to be prolonged.

The field office in Phoenix was also supposed to advise Washington every Monday morning of the current status of the case, especially of the undercover aspects.

On paper the bureaucracy wanted to watch this one closely.

In fact, it did not.

Jim Rayburn, by his own account, ran Operation Sojourner as he saw fit, with virtually no supervision or restraints.[6] His requests for extensions of the undercover operation were regularly renewed by the undercover review committee. For more than four months no one in Washington asked any hard questions about the investigation or seemed to have an inkling of what they had unleashed.*

---

*In a convoluted attempt to explain the INS oversight of Operation Sojourner, during a telephone interview, Victor Rostow said:

"It was fairly tightly monitored all along by Washington, though we didn't always know what was going on, and we were fooled on occasion." In the end, Rostow confessed, "I was naïve. I had only a little idea of what was involved in an investigation [and] this was the first undercover operation monitored by the INS undercover review committee."[7]

Rostow stated that he only became aware of the extent of the covert taping of the church workers when at the end of the investigation Don Reno sent him the huge multiple volumes of tape transcripts.

In Phoenix Rayburn's nominal supervisor was Scott Coffin, the deputy district director. Coffin's recent appointment to that job had deeply offended Rayburn, John Nixon, and another member of the Phoenix office, all of whom believed that they were at least as experienced as their new superior. The appointment had confirmed their belief that District Director Ernie Gustafson failed to appreciate aggressive enforcement officers. The three men had even filed an equal employment opportunity (EEO) complaint against Gustafson, charging that he had failed to offer them an opportunity to apply for the deputy's job. There was no love lost in the offices of the INS in Phoenix in 1984.[8]

Rayburn kept Coffin up-to-date roughly once a week on what was going on in the sanctuary investigation, and the two men prepared the reports that were sent back to Washington. But the man he really reported to on Operation Sojourner was Donald M. Reno, Jr., the new special assistant U.S. attorney.

Don Reno, a small, intense man, had been hired by U.S. Attorney Mel McDonald in January 1984 to become the first special assistant U.S. attorney in the country designated to handle only interstate alien-smuggling cases. His salary was paid by the Justice Department but funded through the INS, for which he worked full-time. The job had appealed to Reno because it wasn't the typical assistant U.S. attorney's job, which to him meant sitting in an office waiting for the FBI, the Treasury, or other agencies to bring in cases. He wanted to play a more active, aggressive role.

Almost as soon as Reno had unpacked his books, Jim Rayburn had come over and introduced himself. The antismuggling agent assured Reno that he was going to have an "interesting, exciting job, with a lot of traveling." Over the next few months the two worked together on several major multistate alien-smuggling conspiracies. They were able to indict one of the biggest farmers in Idaho on twenty counts of labor violations and obtained a conviction, and they brought an anti-smuggling case in Florida that involved more than four undercover agents.

At their first meeting Rayburn told Reno about the underground railroad and the publicity that its organizers had received. "One of these days we'll have to allocate some resources to that case," Rayburn had remarked.[9] But the discovery of the materials in Phil Conger's car, laying out in exhaustive detail how the railroad operated, was what finally threw the undercover operation into high gear. Reno had the impression that the Conger material gave Washington the security of knowing that sanctuary was not just a loose-knit band of malcontents at the border but a nationwide movement that was "flagrantly violating the law."[10]

The documents also persuaded Don Reno that there was precious little religious motivation behind the movement. With Jim Rayburn, he believed that religion was just a facade for building a network aimed at violating the law and bringing in people who would speak publicly for the cause. The people whom sanctuary brought in were, in Reno's opinion, "real hard-core Marxists, liberation theologists, an amalgamation, however you want to call it."[11]

Reno shared Harold Ezell's and Mel McDonald's distaste for that kind of religion. Like his superiors, the new prosecutor and his wife were conservative Christians, who had recently joined a fundamentalist nondenominational church in Tempe, where they lived in a large, new Spanish-style house in an affluent lakeside development. To Reno and the others, the last thing in the world one would do in the name of religion was stir up opposition to the law of the land.

Chapter
Sixteen

IN LESS THAN a month Jesus Cruz had solidly penetrated the sanctuary network in Nogales and Tucson. Doña Socorro Aguilar told him that if he wanted to become really involved, he would have to meet Phil Conger, and she invited him to go along on one of the weekly visits to the Mexican prison. On May 3 Cruz showed up at Socorro Aguilar's house, bearing gifts of fruits and vegetables for the detainees. He and Conger had a brief conversation in Spanish on their way back to the widow's house, and Conger accepted Cruz's offer to drive people within the United States.

Cruz also ingratiated himself at Sacred Heart. He walked into the church offices one day and introduced himself to Tony Clark, who had already heard about him from Father Quiñones. Clark thought he was a remarkably kindly old man. Here was someone who could just relax and go fishing, and he was offering his truck and his time to help desperate people, not because he'd studied the issue or read some article, but because he was joyous and loving. What a model person![1]

Cruz also met Mary K. Espinosa, the coordinator for religious education at Sacred Heart and the daughter of a former longtime mayor of

Nogales, Arizona. (She had been christened Mary Katherine, but everyone called her Mary K.) Mary K., a pretty, outspoken woman of about thirty, was, like Father Tony, a warm, emotional being whose heart often led her head.

The mother of four children, she had offered to help Phil Conger one day after he had come into the church with two small children whose mother was expected to arrive at any moment after crossing the border. But she really decided to become involved in sanctuary on the day, shortly thereafter, when a Salvadoran woman about thirty-five years old showed up at the church with two children. She said that her husband, a doctor, had been killed because he had been working in refugee camps, and as the two women talked, the woman suddenly broke down and, sobbing, poured out a heart-stopping story.

One day, she said, the school had called and asked her to come get one of her children, a daughter. Thinking that the girl had misbehaved and angrily pondering how she would chastise her, the woman had arrived at the school. There, in the playground, she saw a heap of children's bodies, shot when armed men had come in, looking for the children of a guerrilla. She had had to pull her dead daughter out from the bottom of the pile.[2]

After that encounter Espinosa vowed to help the refugees in any way she could. Tony Clark tried to talk her out of her decision, and the two even fought over the issue. "Don't get mixed up in this," the priest told her. "You have four kids and a husband; let me take care of this." Her husband, a Mexican truck driver, said the same thing. But Mary K. would not be moved. She thought that having kids of her own partly explained her decision, as did her father's example. He had always treated everyone equally and with respect, and she remembered Mexican citizens calling him in the middle of the night, protesting some insult or slight that had occurred at the port of entry. Her father would mutter that the INS would never dare treat an American that way.

She told Monsignor Oliver that she wanted to help the refugees, and he gave her his blessing. In effect, she and Father Tony became Father Quiñones and Doña Socorro Aguilar's counterparts on the American side of the border.

Mary K. and Cruz soon worked together on a complicated operation to bring in a family of seven Salvadorans, a husband and wife, four children, and the wife's seventy-year-old mother. The man, a political activist, had been arrested and tortured and marked for death after his release. They took the underground railroad up to Socorro Aguilar's house, and with Jesus Cruz along, Phil Conger pointed out to the couple how to get through the international fence and find Sacred Heart.

On the next day the elderly mother-in-law was waved through the port of entry in a taxi after showing a border-crossing card and an appointment slip from a doctor on the Arizona side, provided by Mary K. The next day Mary K. pulled up to Doña Socorro Aguilar's house in a church van filled with laughing and chattering children from the American Catholic parochial school. With help from Kathy Flaherty, she dressed the family's two young boys in the school uniforms and then ordered the whole family to pile in the van. She dropped the couple and the two older children, both girls, off at a hole in the fence and drove the rest of the children straight through an international port of entry known as the "truck gate," west of the American city of Nogales.

Cruz's first opportunity to participate in a crossing came several days later. Ever since that first telephone call from Bertha Benavidez, he had assiduously cultivated the friendship of the thirty-five-year-old woman and her husband, Julio, who both were illegal aliens in the United States. They were clearly economic migrants and had no contact at all with the sanctuary movement. But Socorro Aguilar had befriended their two children during her visits to the Nogales prison, where the teenagers—Julio, fifteen, and Ana, fourteen—had been sent after an unsuccessful attempt to make it through Mexico on their way to join their parents.

The children were planning another attempt, and Cruz saw an opportunity to implicate both Socorro Aguilar and Father Quiñones in the process.

On May 11, 1984, using Cruz as a courier, Bertha Benavidez sent Socorro Aguilar $400 for airfare to Mexico City. Doña María agreed to meet the children at the airport there and bring them back up north. The three flew together to Hermosillo and from there traveled by road to Nogales.[3]

The children stayed briefly at Socorro Aguilar's home, and she and the priest helped them slip into the United States. Early on the morning of the crossing, Ana put rollers in her hair and a scarf over her head as a disguise, and with a fake identity card provided by Father Quiñones, she walked through the port of entry about ten yards behind Socorro Aguilar, who had coached her to memorize the names and addresses on the card. The immigration officer barely glanced at the documents.[4]

Immediately after they were across the border, Cruz, who had driven the two women to the international boundary and then gone to wait for them on the American side, walked up to them and told them that he had watched the whole thing and wanted to take pictures. He then drove them to Sacred Heart, where Julio and another Salvadoran were waiting after walking through the fence. Cruz then took the brother and sister on to Phoenix.

Along the way he arranged to introduce INS undercover agent John Nixon into the investigation, one of his principal objectives. At a prearranged point en route, Nixon was waiting at an Exxon station. Faking car trouble, Cruz drove into the station, and Nixon introduced himself as the mechanic, John Powers. Together they took the two Benavidez children to be reunited with their parents, whom they hadn't seen in five years. The reunion, on the evening of May 24, was secretly taped by Cruz.

Nixon slid into sanctuary like a seal into water. Cruz told Kathy Flaherty that he had a friend who spoke a little Spanish and had an air-conditioned car he was driving to California to pick up some machinery. It just so happened two young boys needed a ride to Los Angeles to join their parents, and Nixon immediately had the job.

The Chávez boys, sons of a Salvadoran union leader who had been seized by the National Guard and tortured, were a typical family reunification case, involving the relatives of refugees already in the United States. The underground railroad was besieged with requests to aid such people, but it never formulated any hard-and-fast rules about them. Usually the TEC agreed to bring in spouses and minor children of refugees, but it drew the line at in-laws, nephews, "cousins," and other able-bodied adults.

Nixon almost blew his cover on the very first day of his first assignment. As he and Cruz drove away from the house where Mervin and Edwin Chávez had been staying, he leaned out the car window and gave a clenched-fist salute. The gentle Quaker who had put up the boys quickly got on the telephone and called Jim Corbett. "These guys are either nuts or government agents," he warned. "At the least they don't know what they're doing."[5]

The next day Cruz and Nixon arrived at the parents' apartment in Los Angeles, where Nixon, wearing a body bug, tape-recorded the family reunion. After everyone had exchanged hugs and kisses and stories of their arduous journey, the father, Lucio Chávez, tried to give the two undercover men some money for their expenses.

Nixon demurred. "We bought the food, but the gasoline didn't cost me anything. The company buys the gas."

"But the trip and the bother—" protested Chávez.

"I had to make this trip," replied Nixon.

"We are going to do this, see. Take this. Take it," Chávez insisted.

"Maybe you will have to give some to the church or something," Cruz volunteered.

"Yes, because I thought that maybe you'll take it to the church," Chávez said.

"Well then, if it's like that," said Cruz.

Unlike his accommodating colleague, Nixon steadfastly refused to take the money. "They pay me to make the trip," he told Lucio Chávez. "That's why, you have two kids to—to . . . You can spend it on the kids for medicine, clothes, you know. It costs a lot. . . . It's better that you use that money for your family."

"What you have done for us . . . we will never, never will ever," said Chávez, "pay what you have done for us. Only God will."

Chávez then told the informants a little about his background, and the conversation turned to the atrocities taking place in El Salvador. "A little while ago, on the road to San Miguel," said Chávez's newly arrived brother-in-law, ". . . about thirty-two men from the army . . . they captured three guerrillas, one of them a woman. They roped the woman with all . . . they tied her up and they put fire on her and they burned her alive. When the buses were passing—"

"They were watching?" Mrs. Chávez asked.

"The people could see the woman, who was yelling as she was burning up. One friend of mine that goes to sell at San Miguel saw that. When he returned, he said that she was already burned and they still had the body burning there."

Finally Nixon spoke. "Well, your country is very pretty, but you can have it at this time." Everyone laughed.[6]

By late July 1984 the undercover operators had become a virtual taxi service for the underground railroad. By this time there were four informants: Cruz, Graham, Nixon, and a friend and fellow agent of Nixon's named Lee Morgan, a dark-haired ex-cowboy in his late thirties. Morgan, who used the alias "Lou LeBeau," was a buddy of Jim

Rayburn's as well, and the three INS men liked to dress like cowboys and ride into the mountains near Phoenix together and talk about the good old days before the *Miranda* ruling. They all agreed that while Jim Corbett seemed sincere, John Fife was a throwback to the sixties, a rebel looking for a cause who had jumped on board the only thing he could find.[7]

Together "John Powers" and "Lou LeBeau" hauled some twenty people to various destinations, including one trip to central California that ended in a comedy of errors. When the agents delivered their passengers, a family of seven undocumented Salvadorans, to the appointed address in Wasco, the person who came to the door said he couldn't help. The group then went to a neighboring house, but the residents they were seeking had apparently moved. The expedition finally ended up at the home of a Reverend Allan Doyle, who was obviously surprised to find an expectant little band of Central Americans on his doorstep in the early morning.

One of the minister's first comments was: "Are these people legal?" After making a phone call, Doyle admitted the family, named Carrillo, into his home. As he later told government investigators, unknowingly echoing the sentiments of countless members of the sanctuary movement, "What could I do, turn them away?"

The incident confirmed John Nixon's suspicions that the sanctuary workers were hopelessly naïve and ill equipped to take it upon themselves to decide who should be admitted into the United States. As the fifteen-year veteran of the Immigration Service saw it, the ministers and their helpers were assisting people they knew nothing about, who were using them in order to get into the country free of charge. Nixon himself had been lied to so often by Hispanics that he knew he had grown callous, but still, he marveled at the gullibility of Conger and company.

One of the Carrillos, for example, had admitted to Nixon that he had been a coyote for a while, smuggling into the United States Salvadorans he met in parks and hotels in Mexicali. And several members of the family had been arrested for illegal entry and deported before they sought the help of the underground railroad. Moreover, the family was not in the least political. In one taped conversation Ramón Carrillo told Cruz that "in my country, one, even if he wants to be neutral, he can't. . . . Do you understand me? If one is with the guerrillas, the government breaks you. And if one is with the government, the guerrillas break you." Both sides, he went on, "commit massacres" and "rob."[8]

What Nixon didn't know was that the Carrillos, who were probably typical of the great majority of Salvadorans who were pouring into the United States, had neither been crossed nor screened by the underground railroad. They had shown up at Southside one day asking for help, and Conger, anxious to move them out of the church, had accepted Nixon's offer to take them to California.

What really disturbed Nixon and the other participants in the investigation, however, were the political refugees that sanctuary knowingly helped. To Don Reno and the others, sanctuary was at bottom a conspiracy to smuggle "real hard-core Marxists" into the country.[9] Where the sanctuary workers saw persecuted individuals, the INS men saw dangerous radicals.*

Nixon's and Morgan's suspicions that sanctuary was transporting potential subversives were aroused most keenly by a family they were asked to drive from Phoenix to Albuquerque. The Nieto Núñezes—two brothers, a wife, and two children—were upper middle class and obviously well educated. According to Nixon's case notes, the two men "were well dressed, appeared very physically fit (well fed), had soft well-kept hands. All in all appeared to be intelligent and well off."[10] The Nieto Núñezes were definitely not *mojados* ("wetbacks"), crossing the Rio Grande on their way to better jobs.

In the early morning of July 26, 1984, Nixon and Morgan pulled

---

*John Nixon explained his point of view during a long interview in Philadelphia in November 1986, in his office behind an unmarked door in the Federal Courthouse, just across the street from the building where the Declaration of Independence and the Constitution were written. As he saw it, the church workers "had a nationwide network to undermine national security. They had no control over who they were bringing in, didn't know whether they were Communists, had no idea who these people were. They had no capability of determining who they were, of determining if they were radical and therefore excludable.

"We can't permit people who are Communists and revolutionaries to enter the United States," Nixon continued. "Some of these people had a history of arrests, of pro-unionism. That translates into Marxism. If that's true, they would bear scrutiny because of their political inclinations. Marxists don't fit into the United States. They are antidemocratic. They are enemies of their government in El Salvador. The government is pro-democratic now, according to our government, and that's all we have to go by. Why don't these people get an exit visa from their own government? The Salvadoran government wouldn't give visas to its enemies, so these people could be enemies of their government. I'd call that a potential Communist spy."

Nixon agreed that his reasoning reflected the thinking within the INS in Phoenix. "These are some of the things we consider. As government agents we have to be more sensitive than others about national security. We have to ask who are these people they are smuggling. What does their cargo consist of and where is their destination . . . ?"

their two cars, one a Trans Am, up to a trailer at the end of Thirty-fifth Avenue in Phoenix, where the Nieto Núñez family was staying. The drivers were met by Darlene Nicgorski, who had a short conversation with John Nixon before the little caravan departed. Nixon wanted to be sure that there wouldn't be a repetition of the misunderstandings that occurred with the Carrillos.

Darlene reassured him. "See, this is different," she explained (as Nixon's body bug recorded her words). "That is not sanctuary," she went on, referring to the Carrillos. "This time there is a sister there, a Catholic sister . . . you call when you get into Albuquerque, and they'll give you directions from there."

"OK," Nixon said. "No one had talked to the other group, the last group, at all."

Then, from opposite ends of the political spectrum, Nixon and Nicgorski shared their distrust of the Carrillos.

"I've gotten into that so many times it's hardly worth the headache," Darlene volunteered. "It's those kinds of people—because you don't know what they're gonna say and what they're not going to say."

"Well, I felt this gentleman might have duped Philip on that one," Nixon responded, "because I had a feeling the group leader on that sold him a bill of goods. I really do."

"Yeah, and those kind you don't know, there's a . . . sometimes my experience is they're the kind that if something would happen—"

"Exactly."

"They're gonna turn against you."

"Exactly, that's what scared me more than anything."[11]

Darlene took a few pictures of the group, and everyone settled into the two cars Nixon and Morgan were driving. The two brothers, Francisco and José Antonio Nieto, and one child rode with Lee Morgan, and Francisco's wife, Sandra, and another small child traveled with Nixon and Cruz. Morgan, a.k.a. "Lou LeBeau," recorded his conversation with the "illegal aliens," as he referred to them on the tape.

In response to steady questioning, his passengers told him that they were students, one of business administration, the other a fifth-year medical student. They were neither in the army nor with the guerrillas, they said, but they had been working with refugees. As one explained, "They [the displaced people] have been taken out of the so-called conflict zones and taken to refugee camps, but they are not refugee camps, but places where they have been lodged, to give them services.

We worked with the people that arrive, giving them educational services, or teaching them crafts. Or health services.*

"My country's situation is very difficult," he explained. "There's a lot of confusion, already four years, almost five years of war. The people no longer understand what is happening, and the people are the ones who are suffering. Neither the army ends [quits] nor the guerrillas ends [*sic*], and this can go on . . . who knows for how many more years, and it is never going to end. . . ."

"Why did you leave El Salvador?" Morgan asked.

"What has happened is that the church has started, well . . . it has been about five years, has been persecuted, after some priests . . . joined the guerrillas. And many priests were killed . . . of course, none of them fighting, but they went looking for them at the parish. Then the government said the church was collaborating with the guerrillas. . . . Since they don't ask, do not pay attention or investigate if you are Catholic, Protestant, or evangelical, or another faith . . . what is important to them is that you are a member of some church and that you are helping the displaced people. And since many of the displaced people are guerrillas' relatives . . . the army—the government—believes that in those places where these people are located are the places where the guerrillas come to bring medicine, to bring food, to bring information. That's why the army is fighting those people's refuges.

"And since we worked with them, we were under threat. . . . They started sending me anonymous communications, and then persecution, and things like that. Then these are the first indications that they are about to capture or kill you. You are not to wait for them to get to that. It is best to leave the country. It is difficult for someone who has his job, his responsibilities, who has his home, the little things that one has accomplished. It is painful to leave the country because no matter what state it is in, your country is your country."

"Weren't you having problems with the army yet—you?" Morgan asked the other, younger man.

---

*According to a detailed study published in 1986 by the School of Advanced International Studies of the Johns Hopkins University, an estimated 400,000 to 500,000 people were displaced in El Salvador at the end of 1983. Many of the refugees were in government-run camps, but many others were in church camps. According to Dale S. De Haan, director of the Immigration and Refugee Program for the Church World Service, some workers in these camps have been tortured and killed by death squads, and many others have been the recipients of death threats.[12]

"With the army itself, maybe no, but with the government, yes, because the policy that it has for dealing with religious people is basically the same that they have accorded other people who they consider are collaborating. No, many times they don't come to you and say, 'Are you a guerrilla?' But they do say, 'You collaborate with the guerrillas.'"

"Uh-huh, but until you left, you didn't have problems?" Morgan persisted. "You are healthy."

"Yes, you could say so."

"You weren't wounded or—"

"No, no, no, no."

"Not that kind of problem."

"No."

"Good."

"Because we also have relatives inside the armed forces." The older man, who was in his early thirties, spoke up again. "Those relatives recommended that rather than having [sic] serious problems, it would be best to leave the country for a while."

"Uh-huh. Are you students of a college?"

"At the university."

"In San Salvador?"

"Yes. What happened is, we left our studies when the National University was closed, because, for example, the career I was pursuing, which was medicine, only the National University offers that career. . . . There are about ten private universities, but they are mediocre, and—"

"Are they very expensive?"

"No, no, but the teaching is very bad, it is of low quality. Even so, if there had been a medical faculty . . . perhaps I would have continued studying, but they did not have a school of medicine. Only the National University had the school of medicine."

"Are you going to continue your studies here?"

"Yes."

"That's what we hope—to continue with our studies and work."

"To study and work here is better than it is in El Salvador, no?" Morgan suggested.

"Sure. Yes."[13]

Later Morgan pressed for information on how the family got across the border. They told him it was through Agua Prieta, but they said they didn't remember the names of anyone who helped them.

"Very secret, no?" said Morgan.

"Yes."[14]

When the two cars arrived at a church on Wyoming Street in Albuquerque, the government agents and the nuns greeting the Nieto family exchanged pleasantries. When one nun said that she was from Douglas, Arizona, Morgan mentioned that he had worked on all the ranches between Rodeo and McNeal and up to Willcox, in southern Arizona.

Nixon asked another woman if she was the one accepting "this beautiful family" and jokingly asked her to "figure out a way to get at least two of these children for me." In the meantime, Morgan muttered, "New Mexico license plate number GKT two-eight-one, two-eight-one," into his recording device. After a round of "it's very nice meeting you," "thank you," "take care of them," and Nixon saying, "You have precious cargo there," the two agents had a couple of words together.

"The women—we put them in CRR-seven-three-oh, New Mexico plates. The Lupita from Douglas is taking the rest in her green Turino, which we already have the plate number," said Morgan.

The two undercover agents then prepared to get into their separate cars. They called "bye-bye" to the refugees again, and Morgan invited them to "Come see us sometime. Maybe I'll get back up to see you." He started up his motor and dictated into the recorder: "This is Investigator Morgan. That ends the delivery of the illegals from El Salvador to the church on Wyoming Street in Albuquerque. I am going to deactivate this tape at this time. Time now is five-oh-seven P.M. Arizona time. I believe there is an hour difference between them and us."[15]

Chapter
Seventeen

IF JOHN NIXON and his colleagues were suspicious of the refugees, Darlene Nicgorski was equally suspicious of all four of the government infiltrators. Unlike most of her colleagues in the sanctuary movement, the nun was not a particularly open or trusting person. Her manner could often be cold and distant, and she appeared to have an edge of barely suppressed anger. Whatever its origins, it seemed to have two immediate sources: resentment at the strictures of her male-dominated church and outrage over the atrocities occurring in Central America. Sister Darlene was one of the few sanctuary activists in Arizona who had actually lived and worked in Central America, and her near-traumatic experience there had left her consumed with the cause of the refugees.

A native of Milwaukee, where she was born in 1943 into a devout Catholic family, Nicgorski had joined the Congregation of the School Sisters of St. Francis shortly after college. The order was an international community of nuns founded in the mid-nineteenth century to serve the needs of the new immigrants in the United States. The sisters originally worked in schools and hospitals serving the country's Irish,

German, and Polish newcomers. By the mid-twentieth century the order was still deeply involved in education, but with the new needy, including southern blacks and the poor of Central America.[1]

After taking a master's degree in preschool education Darlene spent a decade teaching, running a federally financed day-care center for poor black children in Holly Springs, Mississippi, and working in a low-income housing project in Omaha, Nebraska. But she had a long-standing dream of working abroad, and in January 1981 she finally arranged to set up an early-childhood program in a small Guatemalan village some thirty miles north of Guatemala City.

A summer in Guatemala had already made the nun aware of the mounting violence in the country, particularly against the Catholic clergy. But her project, run with several Guatemalan nuns, seemed safely nonpolitical. By the spring the sisters had a new preschool for forty-five children, offering them, along with classes, two good meals a day. But on July 1, 1981, after an evening mass, the local priest, an Italian Franciscan who had been in the country for twenty-two years, and his driver were found shot dead in their car.

Darlene's little community was terrified. They were afraid that Padre Tulio's murder was the beginning of a campaign to drive the Catholic Church from the area, and the day after the murders most of the Guatemalan sisters left by truck for Honduras. The day after that Darlene was instructed to close the school and destroy all records and photographs of the children. She took them into the yard and burned them. She then went to the bank in the village to withdraw the school money and was followed all the way by a man with a gun, who stood and looked over her shoulder as she signed the withdrawal slip. She walked back to the convent house, packed her suitcase, got a ride on a truck to the next village, and boarded a bus to Guatemala City.

For the next year Sister Darlene remained in Central America, working in Guatemalan refugee camps in southern Mexico and Honduras. At the request of various human rights organizations, she tape-recorded stories of atrocities. Finally, in the fall of 1982, she returned to Phoenix, Arizona, where her parents had retired. Recuperating from a gallbladder operation, she began to read about Central America and to try to make sense of her experience. Among other things, she read *Bitter Fruit,* an account of the CIA-backed coup in Guatemala in 1954, and she became angry at what she saw as the misrepresentation of the situation in the region by the North American press.[2]

"I read all of this stuff about Communists, and I kept thinking about the people I knew who had never even heard of a Communist," she said later. "They just wanted teachers, health care, some land to grow crops. Are those things Communist or subversive? That's what they were called in Guatemala, but it's not what I thought."[3]

While she recovered, Darlene contacted the Valley Religious Task Force on Central America, a group of eleven denominations headed by James A. Oines, the pastor of Alzona Evangelical Lutheran Church. Oines, whose congregation was located in a poor, predominantly Hispanic section of Phoenix, had been through a process similar to that undergone by the refugee workers in Tucson. For a couple of years he and a small group of colleagues had bailed Central Americans out of detention, finally offering sanctuary to undocumented people when they realized that Salvadorans and Guatemalans were not being granted asylum, no matter how strong their case. As Oines put it, people of faith have a right and a duty to show love to human beings in distress.

By early 1983 the Valley task force had a legal services office, a social service committee, and some seventy locations where Central American refugees could safely stay in Phoenix.[4] Darlene began helping with these services and speaking to churches about events in Guatemala. A few weeks after she began she even ran into fifteen Indians from the same tribe she had worked with in Guatemala, living in a run-down forty-six-dollar-a-week motel room in Chandler, Arizona, and working as migrant field hands. She also soon met another nun, Mary Malherek, who had been sent to Arizona by the Chicago Religious Task Force to find refugees suitable for sanctuary.

The two women had spent almost two weeks together, and the encounter became a turning point for Darlene. She was intrigued by the idea of public sanctuary. As she later described it, she had often wondered how people in the United States could ever understand why so many Central Americans were coming north. The Indians in particular were so intimidated by anyone in uniform that they never explained why they had fled; many told even the nun that they were simply looking for jobs. Not until they trusted her would their frightful stories pour out. If a few refugees were willing to speak publicly about their experiences, that silence, she thought, might be broken.

She helped Sister Mary locate an Indian family that was willing to resettle, and their subsequent trip to a convent near Concordia, Kansas, was filmed and eventually shown on PBS's show "Front Line" in July

1983. Out of that came an offer from Chicago, asking Darlene to locate and prepare more refugees for sanctuary churches, in return for a stipend of some $3,000 for six months.

By the time she met "John Powers" Darlene had been working for almost a year and a half as the link between the Chicago Religious Task Force and the national network of sanctuary churches and the Arizona activists. Dozens of refugees had passed through her apartment, and though she never participated in any so-called border runs, she did meet and resettle many of the truly political refugees assisted by the border breakers.

Darlene had thought there was something fishy about Jesus Cruz from the beginning. She first met him on July 5, 1984, at her small two-bedroom apartment in Phoenix when he came to introduce himself as someone in town who sympathized with the plight of the Central Americans. Since Phoenix had had an active movement to help the refugees for three years, Darlene asked him if he knew several of the people associated with that network. He had recognized none of the names. Moreover, Phil Conger had asked her to check out Cruz in Phoenix, and none of the people she had spoken to had ever heard of him.

Cruz didn't fit the profile of most of the other volunteers she worked with, who were usually middle-class, well-educated people connected with churches or Central American solidarity groups. His persona—a semiretired roofer who was always available on twenty-four hours' notice and who never seemed to need money to pay for his driving and errand running—was a bit unlikely. But Darlene often had to beg and cajole people to do the work that needed to be done, and Cruz was always around, volunteering his services. She tried to put aside her suspicions.

But she couldn't ignore the alarm bells that went off on the morning when he showed up to pick up the Nieto Núñezes and introduced Nixon and Morgan. One thing the sanctuary movement almost totally lacked was good-looking middle-aged American men who drove Trans Ams, acted like macho television cops, and were eager to take days off work to transport refugees around the country.

That morning Nixon did most of the talking, while Morgan stayed in the background. Darlene, staring at him through her aviator glasses, didn't like what she saw or heard. Nixon claimed that he and John Fife were good buddies, but he seemed hard and controlled, speaking to her in English and to the refugees in Spanish. Before the Nietos left, she confided to them that she didn't trust their "helpers." After the group had arrived in Albuquerque, she got a call from the sister who had received them to say that everyone had arrived safely. Then came a second call, telling her that the refugees had reported that they were suspicious, too. The drivers had asked a few too many strange questions about who had helped them into the country, questions that Sister Darlene had never asked them. And the drivers had stopped often on the way to Albuquerque to make telephone calls.

Darlene had mentioned her concerns in TEC meetings, where the subject of the odd "volunteers" was discussed several times.

Peggy Hutchison also distrusted Cruz, and she had asked the group not to firm up the travel plans of any refugees in his presence. Peggy made it a point never to work with the Mexican, but it never really occurred to her that Cruz was a full-fledged informant, complete with code name and body bug.

John Fife tended to pooh-pooh the women's suspicions and even told Darlene that she was being paranoid. He assured his colleagues that Cruz was just an old man who wanted to be accepted. And Cruz did do all the right things: He was always saying "God bless you" and bringing presents of food to people, and once he even knelt and said the rosary with Socorro Aguilar, who had become a constant companion.

Jim Corbett was characteristically unperturbed as well. Even if Cruz was a spy, he reasoned, could they act against him without evidence? "We could probably end up converting ten percent of undercover agents anyway," he commented at one TEC meeting.

So despite her sense that Cruz and his friends were *orejas* ("ears"), as spies for the government were called in Guatemala, Darlene rationalized that she could use them to help with local activities and keep them away from the political refugees who were passing through the underground railroad. She warned refugees not to let Cruz get near them, but it was difficult. He particularly befriended Joel and Gabriela Morelos, political refugees from Guatemala, and admired and petted their little daughter Lucy. After they left Arizona for a sanctuary church in Philadelphia, they put a picture of their special friend Jesus Cruz on the wall of their new apartment.

Salomon Graham, Cruz's "cousin Jose Morales," was even more unbelievable, with his open shirts, gold chains, and annoying habit of sidling up to all the women in the movement. And relatively soon everyone, including the easygoing Fife, agreed that the quartet of overeager helpers was to be avoided. The problem was how to convey the message to stay away.

Phil began to tell the Phoenix "volunteers" that they didn't have to attend TEC meetings in Tucson. On September 10 he told Nixon, who was calling from Jim Rayburn's office in Phoenix, with Rayburn listening in, that there would be a meeting that night but that it was not worth driving down for.

"We were talking about it last week, and we were thinking that maybe it would be good to save people's energy and stuff if Darlene, who usually comes anyway, if she kind of acted as the information spreader, and if you needed to find out what was going on, you could contact her," he suggested.[5] That night Nixon still showed up at the church.

On another occasion, after a meeting during which it was decided that Cruz and the others would not be used if possible, Conger walked into the office and overheard Kathy Flaherty arranging for one of the agents to transport someone to Phoenix. "What are you doing that for?" he asked her. She explained that they were always available, and she got tired of spending hours on the telephone trying to find people who were bilingual, had cars, and were available to help.[6]

Later that summer the group again had the matter of the Phoenix volunteers written in bold letters on the agenda of the Monday night meeting. But Cruz drove up just as the meeting began, and Phil quickly had to tear off the bottom part of the agenda so the Mexican couldn't see the words, in letters several inches high, "Jesus Cruz and what should we do about him."[7]

Despite his misgivings, Phil had casually invited Cruz to his wedding that fall to Ellen Willis, a pretty, outgoing Catholic girl who had worked in refugee camps in Honduras before coming to Tucson the previous year. The ceremony was held at St. Francis in the Foothills, a lovely Spanish-style church at the edge of the desert, and Fife and Ricardo Elford performed the service. It was a warm autumn afternoon on October 13, and some 250 people danced and drank champagne at the reception. Afterward the couple held a private dinner for their families and close friends, and Cruz, who escorted Doña María Socorro Aguilar, insisted over her protests that they attend the more intimate gathering. He sat next to Phil's parents, who chatted with him in Spanish for much of the evening. He was wearing his body bug, but he told his government handlers that he did not activate it that night.[8]*

Nixon knew that Darlene distrusted him and that there had been at least a couple of close calls on Operation Sojourner. On August 6 Lee Morgan had called Phil Conger and after an exchange of greetings, Phil had asked, "Who am I speaking with?"

"This is Lou," Morgan replied. "Lou LeBeau. John Nixon's friend."

"Huh, Lou LeBeau, John Nixon's friend."

"John Powers," Morgan quickly corrected himself.

"Help me a little more," said Phil. "Where did I meet you? I am sorry, I just meet so many people."

Morgan then reminded him that he and "Powers" had been working with Mr. Cruz and had delivered the people to California. "Uh, yes, of course," said Phil.[10]

A few weeks later, on August 29, Nixon went over to Nicgorski's apartment with Salomon Graham to develop information about a man who had offered to work for the movement. The volunteer claimed to have been an undercover agent in Mexico for the U.S. Treasury Department and had told Darlene that he could set up a "professional" pipeline for refugees from Central America up to the United States— something he said the movement would need if Reagan got reelected and put more heat on the region and on critics of his policies.

Fife had suggested that Darlene investigate the individual through his church affiliations, the only method that the church workers had for investigating volunteers. But Nixon, not having much faith in that process, wanted to do a little investigating of his own. He was concerned that the man might be a mole from some other government

---

*For a very brief period the government placed a third paid informant into the church movement. In late July or early August a Hispanic woman about thirty years old walked into the TEC office at Southside and offered her services. "Gina Sanchez" said that she had worked in San Diego for sanctuary and for CISPES, the Central American solidarity group opposed to U.S. intervention in Central America.

Phil contacted San Diego, and the sanctuary people there confirmed that "Sanchez" had been involved with them. So she began to help in the office at Southside, despite widespread misgivings about her and her habit of arriving at the spartan church offices in open blouses, shorts, and heavy makeup.

Her downfall came swiftly. She told Kathy Flaherty that she was going to "stay with her aunt" in Nogales, and wanted to visit the prison there. Socorro Aguilar invited her to come along on a regular visit the next day, and "Sanchez" showed up in tight little shorts. Father Quiñones and Socorro Aguilar informed her that she was not going into the prison looking like that. That was the end of her undercover career in the sanctuary movement. Jim Rayburn, disgusted with her lack of performance, took her off the case.[9]

agency, also spying on the movement, and he didn't want the feds to be tripping all over one another.

He pressed Darlene for any information she might have dug up and urged her to get the man's full name and date and place of birth, which would enable him to obtain whatever information there was on him in the government's computers.[11] But then Darlene began asking questions of Nixon, revealing her doubts about *him*.

"So, how did you guys get involved?" she inquired, referring both to Nixon and to Salomon Graham, who was with him.

"Well, I don't know . . . I think . . ." Nixon began. "Don Jesus . . . I used to work with him and he worked at—"

"Yeah, he used to work . . . [unintelligible word] he got fired," Graham added.[12]

They chatted some more about the importance of not helping purely economic migrants. Darlene mentioned a man the group wouldn't help who "really wanted . . . a job, a car, and a woman, and I'm not sure in what order."[13]

She commented that the group at TEC had also agreed not to drive people just for the purpose of family reunification, "but it's a constant battle and we all agree on it and all of a sudden another case comes up. . . ."[14] She hesitated. "Do you belong to any particular church?" she asked Nixon.

"Well, yeah, I do, yeah, I've been baptized Lutheran, been baptized Baptist and then been baptized Presbyterian," the agent replied, truthfully.

"Tri-baptized. I thought you [Protestants] only had to do it once."

"Well, you probably do, but they told me I could do it," Nixon said. ". . . my wife is a Catholic; my children have been baptized Catholic, which was something we agreed upon when we got married."

"I'm Catholic," Graham said. "What are you?"

"I'm a Catholic Christian," Darlene responded.[15]

Darlene then told the agents something of her background in Guatemala and how she became involved in sanctuary. She explained that the reason why people "are becoming a little more cautious" is that there had been three arrests that year.

The first, she said, was Stacey Merkt. The twenty-nine-year-old refugee worker had been arrested with a nun who had pleaded guilty and had got off with a year's probation. Merkt had subsequently been tried and convicted, by a Chicano judge and Chicano jury, of conspiracy to transport and transporting illegal aliens. To Darlene, the incident illustrated the importance of having dedicated drivers and refugees, people who would act out "of moral and religious principles . . . [who would be] willing to stand up and take the consequences," she explained, into Nixon's secret tape recorder.[16]

The second incident was Phil Conger's arrest. On May 15, 1984, Phil had finally been indicted on four counts of transporting illegal aliens. Kathy Flaherty, his companion, had not been indicted. The government had described the indictment as a routine alien-smuggling case, but Don Reno, the prosecutor, had offered Conger a deal: If the church worker would sign a letter of contrition and pledge not to cross or transport anyone again, the government would drop the case.[17]

Conger declined the offer, and in July Federal District Court Judge Alfredo C. Marquez had thrown the case out on the ground that the Border Patrol had made an illegal stop and search.

The third arrest that took place that year was of Jack Elder, a forty-year-old former Peace Corps volunteer, Vietnam veteran, and father of four who ran Casa Romero, the shelter for Central American refugees near Brownsville, Texas. Elder had been arrested on April 13 on charges of having transported Salvadorans from the Casa to the nearest bus station, about seven miles away. His apprehension was the result not of a Border Patrol stop but of a grand jury's hearing of testimony about his actions. Federal officers had then gone onto church property to arrest him.

Darlene and others in the Arizona sanctuary movement feared that Elder's arrest was the beginning of a government crackdown, and they were on the alert for the calling of a grand jury in Tucson or Phoenix. They believed that if Ronald Reagan were reelected in November, the chances of more arrests were very great.

Nixon listened while Darlene, her short brown hair framing her face, spelled out her concerns. She won't act on her suspicions, he thought; she needs to use us too much. That's how most criminals get caught.[18]

Chapter
Eighteen

B Y THE END of the summer of 1984 the government realized that
its agents, if not actively exposed, were at least being shut out of the
inner councils of the sanctuary movement. That in itself was not too
serious, for Operation Sojourner had already acquired enough evidence
to indict dozens of people. But the government still lacked a strong case
against the two people it most wanted to prosecute: Jim Corbett and
John Fife. Until enough evidence to convict the two ringleaders was in
hand, the investigating team in Phoenix wanted to keep the undercover
operation running.

Corbett was especially elusive. Since the "60 Minutes" broadcast he
had become a national figure, a symbol of conscientious objection to the
growing American involvement in Central America. Between 1981 and
1984 he averaged about five trips a year to Mexico City, Chiapas, and
Guatemala, and during much of the government investigation he had
been on the road, speaking to sympathetic groups and returning to
Latin America to monitor the fluid refugee situation.

Even when he was in Tucson, Corbett did not spend much time at
the TEC office, as did the generally younger group of sanctuary sup-

porters. He was rarely around when one of the undercover agents or informers dropped in at Southside Church to chat and to record conversations secretly. The iconoclastic rancher had always been a loner, and even as a leader of one of the most significant grass-roots movements in twenty years, he remained one.

As a result, the government had precious little hard evidence against him. His home was under constant surveillance, and the license numbers of his visitors were dutifully taken down and traced. But the only information in Don Reno's possession that seriously implicated Corbett was a newspaper series about one of his exploits. Ironically, press coverage of Corbett had drawn the government into its investigation of sanctuary in the first place, and after months of undercover work all the authorities really had on him was more press coverage.

In July 1984 the retired rancher had gone down to Mexico City to bring back a thirty-two-year-old Guatemalan woman named Juana Beatriz Álvarez. A reporter and photographer from the *Arizona Daily Star* had accompanied him on his journey north and written a seven-part series about the trip.[1]

The woman told a nightmarish story, like so many from her ravaged homeland. Early in 1982 her husband, a factory worker who had been active in a union, had been dragged out of their house by four men and kidnapped at four in the morning. Three days later their apartment was broken into and searched while she was out. Whoever it was, she guessed, was looking for a folder that her husband had taken with him to union meetings.

She reported the disappearance but never heard a word about his fate. And within months the short, dark-skinned woman noticed that men were watching her house and following her in the street. She moved out of her house, leaving her three children with her mother, and lived with various relatives. She was near nervous collapse, and a sister finally advised her to leave the country for a while.

Juana made her way to Mexico City, where, with the help of a priest, she started classes to become a seamstress. Three days after the classes began, she told Corbett, she was kidnapped on the street by four men in dark blue suits who took her to an empty house and raped her repeatedly for three days. On the fourth day she was given another pair of pants and a blouse, and she turned her own torn clothing into a sanitary napkin to stanch her heavy bleeding. The men took her into the Ministry of Interior building and left her, one of them warning her that if she said anything about the incident, he would kill her.

She was questioned about her nationality, and when she admitted that she was Guatemalan, she was taken to a prison to await deportation. She lay there for days, bleeding and in severe pain. Finally, when there were enough Guatemalans to fill a bus, she and several others were taken to the border and dumped.

After about a month near the border, working and trying to recover, Juana sent a telegram to her mother asking if it was safe to return home. The answer was no, two men were still watching the house.

The woman returned to Mexico City, this time determined to continue all the way north to the United States. She contacted a refugee organization that promised to put her in touch with a man who might help her, a North American named Jim Corbett.

Not long thereafter Juana Álvarez met Corbett in his modest second-story hotel room. Outside the door two men, whom Corbett suspected were with the Mexican secret police, watched everyone who entered and left the room. Mexican officials in Chiapas had already threatened the Quaker with death if they caught him helping refugees there again.

Corbett had heard dozens of stories like Juana's, of female refugees abused by Mexican officials, and he told Juana that he would help her. He explained how they would travel: by plane, taking separate seats, to Hermosillo, then by car to Nogales, and across the border to Tucson.

Two other refugees made the journey on the same flight, and in Hermosillo all three met Corbett and another volunteer by prearrangement at a hotel. They were then driven to Socorro Aguilar's house in Nogales.

Because of Juana's distressed state, the members of the underground railroad decided that she did not have the presence of mind to walk across the port of entry with false papers. She would have to cross in an isolated area. On the morning of her eighth day in Nogales, she dressed in pants, a T-shirt, sturdy tennis shoes, and a baseball cap with a Colorado State University logo, and set off into the desert with Jim Corbett and the two journalists. After several hours of hiking the party reached the border, and as Corbett helped her, the *Star* photographer, Ron Medvescek, took a picture of Juana climbing over the barbed-wire fence separating the United States and Mexico.

That picture, and reporter Carmen Duarte's series, was the government's strongest evidence against Jim Corbett, the mastermind of the underground railroad and the man the INS had vowed to put behind bars.

The investigation had a similar problem with John Fife, who by 1984 had become a national figure, a compelling spokesman for the sanctuary movement and an articulate critic of the government's refugee policy. Like his Quaker colleague, the Presbyterian minister frequently traveled throughout the country in his efforts to build a national community of sanctuary congregations.

John Nixon had managed to wrangle a few friendly conversations with Fife; once they even joked about the minister's philanthropic smuggling service. Fife mentioned that the coyotes' going rate from El Salvador was $2,500.

"Hey, we're in the wrong business," Nixon exclaimed.

"Yeah, if we'd have been charging the going rate for this, I wouldn't be living here today driving this old pick-up truck."

"At the very minimum you'd have a brand-new church uptown," Nixon responded, to laughs all around.

On another occasion the two men had a discussion about Fife's silver belt buckle, which bore an Indian design resembling a maze.

"There's no way out of it," Nixon observed.

"Oh, yes, there is," said Fife.

But in its dozens of hours of taping at his church, the INS had been able to record only a few incriminating comments by the minister. Fife almost never said anything that linked him personally to a specific violation of the alien-smuggling laws. Don Reno wanted more. He felt that he could not issue indictments in Arizona and omit the two main targets of the investigation.

The INS men had been intrigued by a conversation taped during a TEC meeting on August 27, 1984, indicating that another big group of refugees would be moving up through the underground railroad in a few weeks. During that meeting Corbett had spoken on behalf of five Salvadorans who were still in Mexico City. There was a woman of about thirty, Elba Teresa López, and four children—two of her own and two of her sister's, a woman named Pilar, who was in sanctuary at the University Baptist Church in Seattle, Washington. Elba Teresa was on her way to Seattle, and Corbett suggested that someone go to Mexico City to meet her group and bring them as far as Arizona.

Corbett told his colleagues that Pilar had been held in prison and tortured and raped repeatedly in the presence of a four-year-old daughter. According to Corbett, the child, who was with Pilar in Seattle, was now mentally and emotionally disturbed as a result of the traumatic experience.

According to Corbett, Elba Teresa had lost her husband, a union organizer, about a year earlier and had been in hiding ever since. Now, with the help of the Reverend Donovan Cook in Seattle, who was sheltering Pilar, she was on her way to join her sister with the rest of the family.

"It is a question of getting someone down simply to do the basic counseling," Corbett explained. "The church [in Seattle] is prepared to pay the expenses of at least one person, perhaps both. . . . [W]e would need, if this is done, to provide a pickup in one of the Sonoran places that they might fly out to, and they would probably be arriving in about a week. . . ."

"Is there a rush?" asked Fife.

"There is a rush in this sense, that they may still have a valid visa [for Mexico] which gives them extra leverage if anything goes wrong. They probably do still have a valid visa that's going to expire very shortly. There is a second problem in that the woman is apparently feeling pretty depressed and discouraged. The folks in the seminary who might have helped won't, because she does not want to go into public sanctuary."

"Oh, we got to right that wrong!" Fife exclaimed.

"No, there's no way we can, we can convert people," Corbett answered. "We just want to do instrumentally valuable things . . . but anyway, that's what I gather from Donovan is the situation. Apparently it's a situation where you have the kind of survivor's guilt coming out, and then you're put down for, you know, being afraid to do something . . . so that there's a question of her feeling depressed enough that she might almost just say, 'Well, go back,' or whatever."[2]

The group then began to discuss how to handle the Elba Teresa matter, but just as the details of the operation began to be discussed, the informer's tape suddenly ran out. The only evidence of the remainder of the conversation was John Nixon's notes. According to Nixon, the group discussed, among other things, how to dispose of the vehicles being used by the church to transport refugees, including a white Volkswagen, a red van, a pickup, and a 1971 station wagon. John Fife suggested that the cars and the station wagon be traded or sold, because they had been "burned"—recognized or identified by the Border Patrol.[3]

The government next heard of the Elba Teresa group on September 4, when Cruz attended a meeting of the TEC in Tucson. He failed to record it, but Jim Rayburn's notes of the following day state that Phil Conger said that the Elba Teresa party should be arriving at the border that coming weekend. He asked Corbett to explain more about them.

Corbett, according to Cruz, said that he had talked to Pilar in Seattle and to another Salvadoran woman living in Arizona who knew the family and that he now knew that they would have a "good story." He said that Peggy Hutchison and Ellen Willis would go to Nogales that weekend to meet them if they arrived. The two women complained that occasionally Father Quiñones put too much pressure on newly arrived aliens during his interviews to determine whether they were political or economic migrants. The pressure often caused the aliens to change their stories, they argued. According to Cruz, as summarized in Jim Rayburn's notes, Corbett told them, "That's the way it is and he told Ellen and Peggy not to pressure the aliens for any story as it may change from the original stories received at interviews in Mexico City. He said all he wants them to do is show the aliens how to cross."[4]

A few days later, in a bid to transport the group, Nixon called Phil Conger and asked if there was anything he could do. He had a trip coming up, he said, to the state of Washington. "Anything . . . along those lines up to Washington you might want to—"

"Are you flying to Washington?" asked Conger.

"No, I'm driving up."

"OK."

The young church worker didn't take the bait. Finally Nixon told him to "stick that in the back of your mind," and asked if there was a meeting that night. Conger told him again that it was "probably nothing that would be worth [his] while driving all the way down for."[5]

After weeks of delay the Elba Teresa group finally made it through. No government agent was anywhere near the crossing. But on October 22 Cruz and Graham attended and taped another Southside meeting at which the evidence they had been waiting for so long finally surfaced. When the investigators listened to that tape, they thought that at last they had the hammer that would nail John Fife to the wall.

Cruz had recorded the following conversation between Father Ricardo Elford and John Fife:

> ELFORD: *I found out that you made it OK, but I didn't get any details.*
> FIFE: *Yeah, we made it fine . . . they are doing fine. They were great!*

ELFORD: *Really?*

FIFE: *Yeah. Yeah, they're real troopers [*sic*], did just fine . . . no problems at all. . . . There was one Border Patrol car sitting alongside of the road there. . . . There wasn't anything out in the desert. . . .*

ELFORD: *Nothing at all?*

FIFE: *Well, it's such a lousy day, you know . . . just raining off and on. . . .*

ELFORD: *Oh, yeah. Oh, OK. Very good. I understand.*

FIFE: *We arrive over here at nine o'clock.*

ELFORD: *How are they?*

FIFE: *They're doing great . . . it was really nice. We got, we were back here by four o'clock in the afternoon. And they called their mother, and see, you know, they hadn't seen her in [unintelligible word] years.* [6]

During the same meeting Ken Kennon and Fife also discussed their efforts to support Senator Dennis DeConcini's reintroduction of a bill calling for extended voluntary departure for Salvadorans.[7] (Such a bill had first been introduced by Congressman Joseph Moakley of Massachusetts in 1983, but it had died, and in the meantime, between October 1, 1982, and September 30, 1984, 8,692 persons had been returned to El Salvador. During the same period roughly 3 percent of Salvadorans and an even smaller percentage of Guatemalans who applied for asylum were granted it.) The sanctuary workers commented that the outlook for the refugees was still as grim as ever.

John Fife also told the group that he had reason to believe that a grand jury was going to be convened in Austin, Texas, to investigate the sanctuary movement nationwide, probably after the reelection of Ronald Reagan in November.[8]* Fife suggested that everyone present should think about refusing to cooperate with a grand jury. ". . . the question that you're gonna have to deal with is 'are you prepared to go to prison, ah, and fight the religious conscience issue from there rather than testify before a grand jury?' And everybody is going to have to make their own decision about that." If that happened on a large scale, Fife went on, and large numbers of church people were "willing to keep their mouths shut and go to jail, the response of the church [nationally] is going to be extraordinary. . . . It would be overwhelming support for

*Fife later told Agent Nixon that the rumor about a grand jury was a "false alarm."

us." He added that he was "hopeful that they [the government] are that stupid at this point, but I don't think so. I mean I'd love it if they were."[9]

On October 29 Cruz and Graham went to Darlene Nicgorski's apartment to pick up Elba Teresa and her two children, Carlos, ten, and Elizabeth, who was almost eight, as well as Pilar's two children. Darlene had asked the two Mexicans to drive the group, including "Jennifer," a woman from Seattle who had flown down to escort them, as far as the Los Angeles area. On that morning they all piled into a truck and started out on their long journey west.

En route Jennifer told the spies that Darlene had given her some money for expenses on the trip, and Cruz pumped Elba Teresa for information on who had smuggled her into the country. She told him that she had had to spend twelve days in Hermosillo and twelve days in Agua Prieta on her journey north. "Who went?" he asked. "Peggy?"

"No," she replied. "It was a couple . . . American."

"But you did walk a lot when you crossed, right?"

"For eight days I couldn't even sit down," Elba Teresa answered. "It's because everything was like a rocky mountain. Horrible!"

"Who was there? Peggy?" Cruz persisted.

"Peggy and another lady."

"Yes," said Graham.

"Well, thank God you are fine now," Cruz said.[10]

On November 1, trying to sweep up a few last crumbs of evidence against Fife, Nixon and Graham paid a visit to the minister at his home. Graham volunteered that he had taken the four children and Elba Teresa to Los Angeles. "They're pretty good kids," he offered.

"Nice kids," he replied. "They were really good when we crossed them."

"Yeah?" Graham responded.

"Yeah. 'Kids,' you know we told them, 'you just can't say anything. Can't make a sound, you just gotta—no playing around, no hollering, no nothing. You just gotta be cool.' "

"They said you walked them to death, though," said Nixon.

"They did? They did great. They're better than most adults."

Fife then explained that the kids were headed for Seattle to meet their mother, whom they hadn't seen in two years. She had had to leave El Salvador, he explained, because she had been picked up and tortured.

"Oh," said Graham.

"I didn't know that," said Nixon. "The ones that you just brought in?"

"Yeah," Fife replied.

"Oh. Fantastic. I imagine she's happy."[11]

When Don Reno heard the tape of this conversation, he knew that he finally had his "haymaker," the crucial evidence he needed on Peggy Hutchison and John Fife.[12]

Chapter
Nineteen

IN CENTRAL AMERICA the liberation clergy used Scripture to instill a renewed spirit and awareness among a dispirited peasantry. As the liberation theologians and their lay interpreters read the Bible, economic and social equality and the dignity of all people were the message of the Gospel. Yet to the governments of the region, those ideals were the stuff of revolution. As John Fife put it, "The issue of what the government considers political and what the church considers its mission was played out in spades in Central America. All the clergy and lay workers did was give poor people the Bible, let it percolate, and then say, 'You go live it out.' "[1]

In the United States liberation themes and ideas had become popular in the late 1960s and early 1970s in the upper levels of many mainline Protestant denominations as well as among religious social activists like John Fife. The minister visited Central America for the first time in December 1982 and became fascinated with the possibility of putting liberation theology into practice in his own country. In this he resembled many of his spiritual and political colleagues, who saw in the new theology a way to reach and enliven the dispossessed, including the refugees, in North as well as South and Central America.

But to the Reagan administration, as well as to the governments of El Salvador and Guatemala, this new theology was radical politics in religious guise. And as Operation Sojourner ground on, the American government allowed spies to enter churches and to monitor meetings conducted by clergy. The ministers involved described these gatherings as religious; the INS said they were political. The government's investigation of the sanctuary movement drifted, in short, into the no-man's-land between church and state, into the minefield separating a criminal investigation from an intrusion by the secular authority into the practice of worship.

The first eavesdropping of this sort occurred at Alzona Evangelical Lutheran Church in Phoenix. In late September 1983 Pastor Jim Oines, an attractive midwesterner in his late thirties with a sincere, boyish manner and a shock of red-brown hair, started a regular Sunday evening Bible study group for Central American refugees.

The meetings, which were conducted in Spanish and English in the main sanctuary of the little Phoenix church, typically began with a prayer, and then a portion of the Book of Exodus was read. The Old Testament book, describing the exile of the Hebrews in Egypt, was a favorite text of liberation theologians, who gave it much the same meaning it had had for the early settlers in North America. Both the eighteenth-century colonists and the twentieth-century reformers saw themselves as emerging from the thrall of an oppressive empire, which they identified with "Egypt" or "Babylon." Both groups identified with the early Israelites' search for freedom in a Promised Land.[2] The Central American refugees in Phoenix also readily identified with the plight of the Israelites in Egypt, and the biblical reading served as a stimulus for them to tell their own stories and to share their problems. To an outsider the meetings worked somewhat like group therapy sessions, bringing the refugees out of their isolation and depression, but the classes most closely resembled the base community gatherings organized around the reading of Exodus by liberation church workers in Latin America. Oines and Darlene Nicgorski, who had helped launch the study group, hoped that the refugees, by relating their experiences to those described in the Bible, would gain emotional strength and find a new sense of community and power in their lives, just as the base communities had sought to empower the people of Latin America.[3]

Oines thought that the classes were a success. Occasionally only a few people would show up, but generally twenty to twenty-five Central Americans came, along with a few North Americans who worked with refugees. These included Sister Nicgorski, two other nuns, Ana Priester and Mary Waddell, and a young woman named Wendy LeWin, who had worked in refugee camps as a translator. Every so often a potluck dinner was held, or a birthday celebrated, but by and large, the Central Americans simply sat in a circle or around one or two tables set up in the sanctuary and talked. They described their week and how things were going for them, sang a few songs, and discussed a passage from the Bible. The group went through almost the entire Book of Exodus, and some people whose emotions had been buried for months or even years were finally able to talk about their traumatic experiences and to cry.

Oines thought the process resembled confession in the Catholic Church, with the difference that Protestants confess to their faith community instead of to a priest.

Into this community, based on trust, came Jesus Cruz. In July 1984 the government spy started regularly attending the meetings at Alzona and befriending the refugees there. He drove them to and from the meetings and volunteered to take them on other errands. He learned their names and addresses, what had happened to them in Central America, and how they had made their way to the United States— information that the government could use as evidence for criminal charges against them.

Cruz originally tried to tape the Bible study meetings, but there was too much background noise for the conversations to be intelligible. He reported his problem to his boss, "Mr. Jim," and Rayburn double-checked with Don Reno about whether tape recording should be pursued. The two men were mindful of INS Commissioner Alan Nelson's decision that no taping would be done in religious services. Reno asked Rayburn what Cruz was doing at Alzona and if he really needed to be there.

Jim Rayburn believed that the meetings provided excellent access to the illegal alien community in Phoenix. Reno checked with Victor Rostow in the INS's central office in Washington, with whom he touched base if he had to make any quick decisions on what the spies were doing. Rostow reiterated the policy that there was to be no taping of religious services, but he raised no objections to the informant's presence at the Bible study class.

Accordingly Reno agreed to Cruz's continued attendance at the Alzona gatherings but vetoed the idea of taping. He had other good evidence against Darlene Nicgorski, and he wasn't that interested in indicting anyone else attending the meetings.[4] Cruz was allowed to remain a quiet government fly on the church's wall.

Both Rayburn and Reno thought that the Bible study meetings were political gatherings. As Cruz described them, the refugees sang "revolutionary" songs, attacked American policy in Central America, and criticized governments supported by the United States in the region. They talked about how to get jobs, how to avoid being picked up by the immigration authorities, how to bring the rest of their families into the country, and a host of other very worldly matters. To Cruz, and those he reported to in the INS, the fact that such meetings were held in a Lutheran church was incidental.

It was at one of the Bible study meetings at Alzona that Cruz learned about a special service to be held at Camelback Presbyterian Church, a small congregation in the affluent neighborhood of Paradise Valley, just north of Phoenix. The church shared a modern chapel and building on East Lincoln Drive with Sunrise Presbyterian Church, and both congregations planned a special ecumenical service for a Salvadoran refugee family that was passing through Phoenix on the way to a sanctuary in the north.

The Reverend Gerald Roseberry, the pastor of Camelback, prepared what he described as a traditional liturgical service, along the lines of his regular Sunday morning service, with an invocation, some religious songs in both Spanish and English, and readings from the Scriptures. He even typed the program up himself.[5]

The night before the service Salomon Graham stopped in at Alzona and got directions to Camelback from Jim Oines, who also invited him to a supper before the service at the Franciscan Renewal Center, a house operated by the Catholic order of Franciscans. Cruz offered to give some of the refugees a ride to the dinner.[6]

The following morning Graham called a nun named Sister Dottie to get more information on that evening's activities and the refugees' means of transport and route out of Phoenix. She told him that a caravan would be leaving the next morning for Flagstaff and then on to Albuquerque.

Ever since Phil Conger's arrest the previous spring, the sanctuary movement had tried to transport refugees on their way to public sanctuary in as public a manner as possible, both as a show of defiance to the government and a means of generating publicity before the possible silencing of the leaders of the movement by more arrests. Often a press conference was held in each major city the refugees passed through, and a car caravan escorted them at least partially down the road to their next destination.

Sister Dottie told the spy that it was "great" and "marvelous" that he wanted to join in the cavalcade. He should get some signs for the outside of his car, saying things like "Caravan for Peace," she told him, and reminded him to be sure to come to the dinner and the ecumenical service that night.

"It's just like everybody come and they'll probably ask for a donation . . . and tonight at the prayer service they will, too," she told Graham. "Oh."

"But I don't think . . . they won't charge you to get in or anything." "Oh."

"What they ask is that you bring something. It's like, you know, a dish of some kind."

"Oh."

"You know, whatever you want to bring. Like if, you know, you want to stop and get some rolls or something and take that along. Whatever." "Oh, I see."

"You know, whatever you feel like bringing. I am going to stop by and get some fruit. You know, stuff like that. You know. . . . Then they all put it together. It's a potluck."

"Uh-huh."

Graham took down all the addresses again, and the nun said, "I'll be forward [*sic*] to meeting you. Tell me your name again."

"Jose Morales."

"OK. See you tonight, Jose."[7]

The service, which began at 7:30 P.M., was long. After prayers and readings the Reverend Ray Manker spoke. "We believe in a God that delivers," he began. "A God who is liberator. The prophet Isaiah wrote: 'The sovereign Lord has filled me with the Spirit. The Lord has chosen me and sent me to bring good news to the poor, to heal the broken-hearted, to announce release to the captives, and freedom to those in prison. The Lord has sent me to proclaim: The time has come when the Lord will save the people and defeat their enemies. The Lord has sent me to comfort all who mourn, to give to those who mourn joy and gladness instead of grief. A song of praise instead of sorrow. They will be like trees that the Lord has planted. They will all do what is right and the Lord will be praised for what has been done.' "[8]

After Manker's words had been translated into Spanish, a dialogue began between Darlene Nicgorski and one of the refugees, who called himself "José Sánchez":

J.: Now we have awakened. We have come to recognize that many are rich because we are poor. Before we were passive; now we can't remain silent. It's not enough to speak of love; our people are dying.

D.: We hear you. What you are saying matters very much to us. We will call upon our people to share your sorrow. Protest our government's part in your pain and try to get the killing stopped.

J.: A lot of us are disappearing. Many are dying horribly. We have to return to the sense of indignation over the destruction of the image of God.

D.: We will seek to change all warlike policies. To work together ecumenically, to change all unjust laws. To open our church buildings as sanctuaries for refugees. And to raise our voices in protest against injustice and violence.

J.: We must maintain our hope. We have to see hope where blind eyes don't see it. We have a reason to wait. There's strength in Central America. The power of faith. The grass-root communities exist, and they are the people.

D.: We seek to share your hope. Part of the reality that must be transformed is our country—the USA. We must find courage to transform the situation before us. Awakening our people to the crisis in the world.

J.: These are days of glory for our churches. Our church grows out of the seeds of pain, of torture, of death. Our martyrs are our witnesses; the poor are our gospel preachers.

D.: We believe you, and we believe in you, sisters and brothers in Central America. And we join in solidarity and action. [9]

Long before this point in the service a little five-year-old girl in the audience started to fidget and to demand to go outside to play. Her mother thought the child would be safe if she stayed near the side door leading to the church parking lot, so she let her go outside.[10]

The service continued with songs, accompanied by a guitar, and Scripture readings, and then "José," with Sister Nicgorski translating, told a little of his story. He said that he and his family had left their country on March 20, 1981. He had worked for a government agency and been a member of a labor organization. After the assassination of Archbishop Romero, the offices of his union had been broken into and the membership lists stolen. A few days later two of the directors of the organization were killed in their homes, along with their families.

"José" then was informed that the government was looking for everyone in the union, and he decided to flee with his wife and two daughters. They first went to Mexico City, where they lived for three years, but because of the difficulties in surviving there, they were on the verge of returning to El Salvador when they met some church people from the United States who had helped them into the United States three months earlier.

"We haven't come here for the purpose of taking away work from any of you, as the government of the United States portrays us," the man continued. "We come here because we have been forced to leave our country and because of that fear of being assassinated, imprisoned, and tortured. . . . We have had to live with ten companions in one apartment of five square meters and earn less than minimum wages because of being illegal. And above all, have had to hide from immigration. That is why I have decided of my own will and with my family to enter sanctuary.

"So that on behalf of the six hundred thousand Salvadorans who find themselves in American land we can tell you that we don't want any more military aid for El Salvador. And for the people to make it known to your government that that military aid only serves to continue the oppression of the people. That having placed a president in our country has only served to continue the violation of human rights.

"I am also asking on behalf of those who have no voice, for those people who, even if they shout in the mountains, are not heard; for those farming people that have to flee and live in caves, to defend themselves from five-hundred-pound bombs; to defend themselves from the white phosphorus that is being thrown on those people; and also to request that the three planes that they have on Salvadoran soil not be used. With which they intend to do away with the nonconformist people of our country.

"I would like you would stop to think for a moment, What are the taxes that you pay used for? A great part of those taxes are used to manufacture weapons. I am sure that not one of you would give one dollar to manufacture a bullet and kill a human being. However, unconsciously, you are collaborating in that. But . . . you are still in time to do something to prevent greater killing. Because Central America is being invaded by American troops.

"It's impossible for me to tell you of so many killings that I have seen. But to prove to you the kind of people that are in the government, I will tell you that the majority of the soldiers that are being sent to fight in the front are young men between the ages of fourteen and sixteen. And in order to take away their fear of confronting other people, they are drugged and gotten drunk before going out on the street.

"We are tired of seeing so much innocent blood shed. And believe me that what we desire with all our hearts is to again see our parents, brothers, and friends, and I think and am sure that a big part of this wish, a great part of the destiny of our Central American countries, is in the hands of you all—the North Americans. Thank you."[11]

Father John Fitzgerald, a Catholic priest, spoke next:

"I would just like to preface what I'm about to read to you with the point that I work in the county jails and for the last couple of years I've had mass each Wednesday afternoon for women who are getting ready to be shipped back to El Salvador, to Equador, to Colombia, Guatemala, and have them crying during mass about what they fear would happen when they get off the plane and on Friday afternoons another mass for those men who are being shipped back. And I mentioned often to people that I felt kind of like I have a funeral mass each Wednesday and Friday. . . . I saw those who did not get a chance to join the sanctuary and wonder which ones of them will not be alive a week later.

"Down through the centuries the church has recognized that the power to govern was entrusted by God to the legitimate authorities, in order to nurture and protect human life. However, when governmental power is used to threaten or destroy human life, it loses its moral authority and must be opposed. Instead of using its powers to protect life, the United States government continues to put human lives in jeopardy, by deporting persons back to possible death and torture in El Salvador and Guatemala. The duty of believers in such situations is indicated in the Scriptures as follows: 'When a stranger sojourns with you in your land, you shall do him no wrong. The stranger who sojourns with you shall be to you as the native among you, and you shall love him as yourself; for you were strangers in the land of Egypt; I am the Lord your God.'

"It is the duty of people's faith to promote ways of showing love to fellow human beings. One acknowledges God as Lord by loving the stranger in one's midst. The situation of persecuted Salvadorans and Guatemalans in our midst is a clear example of the need to show love to those not of our own country."

In conclusion, one of the several ministers present appealed to the congregation: "We thank God that there is a natural illumination inspired by God that captures such an emotional experience as we've had tonight. We find ourselves asking, 'What can I do? What should we do?' And some things that we can do are . . . give offerings as have been extended tonight to continue the support for the sanctuary movement; that provides gas money for people who are transported through Phoenix and beyond, going on regularly, you know; coming through here and transported on to different parts of the country. And occasionally it's publicized . . . a demonstration of solidarity is happening all the time. So funds are needed for gas money, funds are needed for publicizing. . . ."[12]

At that point two members of the audience quietly slipped out of the church. Jesus Cruz and Salomon Graham went into the parking lot, and Graham's body bug, which had picked up virtually all of the preceding service, continued to record as he began to dictate the license plate numbers of the cars in the church parking lot: "BRC six-one-nine Arizona plate. Looks like another van . . . was used to transport from California to here . . . BAH nine-oh-two . . . CEJ, Asix-seven, CAV as in Victor nine-oh-four, another small van. . . . Temporary plate is eight-one-seven, four-two-oh nine/twenty-six/eighty-four, registered to Jeep. . . ."[13]

A few feet away the little girl was playing. Several months later her mother, a lawyer named Sara Baird, learned that the informants had infiltrated her church and must have been in the parking lot at the very moment when the child was nearby. Sara Baird didn't hesitate. She organized a group of ministers, churches, and national denominations, including the Presbyterian Church (U.S.A.) and the American Lutheran Church, and they all filed suit against the United States government, the Department of Justice, the Immigration and Naturalization Service, and several individuals, including Jim Rayburn, John Nixon, Jesus Cruz, and Salomon Graham.

Mrs. Baird, the wife of a prominent local attorney, was no stranger to litigation. When she was graduated from law school in the late 1960s, she had been shocked to discover that every applicant to the bar in all fifty states in the United States had to sign a loyalty oath to the United States government. She had refused and sued to have the oath dropped. The case went all the way to the Supreme Court, and in February 1971 the Court had ruled that the loyalty oath was unconstitutional.[14]

"We can't have the free exercise of religion in this country as long as this kind of thing is going on," Sara Baird told acquaintances. "We've got to stop it."[15]

When Jim Rayburn and Don Reno heard the tapes from Camelback, they didn't see any problem. The gathering was clearly a public political rally, with the purpose of criticizing American foreign policy. "José Sánchez" had even suggested that Americans not pay their income taxes. Reno fully approved of Cruz's and Graham's taping; any meeting covered by reporters and television cameras, as the October 1 service at Camelback had been, was not a sacrosanct religious service in his mind.[16]

Victor Rostow, who had flown down to Phoenix that weekend to check on the progress of the investigation, had not even been aware that the spies were going to the church.[17]

Chapter
Twenty

WASHINGTON HAD BEEN worried that Don Reno was not in control of the investigation, for Operation Sojourner was not producing the kind of evidence that it should have. And in fact, the assistant U.S. attorney left the day-to-day running of the undercover operation to Jim Rayburn. Don Reno could not speak Spanish, let alone monitor Hispanic informants, so for the most part he just listened when Rayburn called to tell him about some of the more bizarre things that happened.

The INS officials in Phoenix were particularly fascinated by John Fife's language and irreverent sense of humor, which they considered uncharacteristic of a minister. The undercover agents had been startled by Fife's occasional "goddamn" and by his suggestion on one occasion that someone buy "booze" for a TEC retreat. Another time the minister had mentioned to "John Powers" that a man from Los Angeles who was writing a movie script was in town and might want to talk to him "about all this bullshit."[1] Nixon took the remark to mean that the minister didn't take sanctuary seriously and had an unseemly interest in the publicity it generated.

The government officials were most titillated by a comment Fife
made on August 27, 1984, as the Southside group discussed an upcoming retreat. On that occasion Fife remarked, waving at Ellen Willis,
"Who's going to keep those warm?" in a kidding reference to her
breasts.[2]

Despite these distractions provided by a fraternity brother (Fife and
Reno were both members of Phi Gamma Delta), for most of the summer of 1984 Don Reno was preoccupied with clearing out his other
outstanding cases. He knew that the sanctuary case was a locomotive
coming down the tracks and that when the prosecution of the movement's leaders began, it would be one of the most controversial cases
the INS had ever undertaken.

On September 13, shortly after the crucial August 27 meeting at
Southside, Reno began drafting his indictment. A few weeks later, at
a meeting in the U.S. attorney's office in Phoenix, he presented a list
of sixty-three people to be charged with federal crimes.

The lengthy "hit list" set off a storm of discussion. Reno's colleagues
warned him that he was not just going for a little canter around the
park; he was going to be in for a wild, wild ride. The defendants would
attract extensive—and sympathetic—media coverage, he was reminded, and a few people present even suggested that the government
should drop the case, with the argument that if we ignore them, they'll
wither away. Everyone agreed that the number of people indicted had
to be reduced, perhaps to around thirty. In late October the Justice
Department sent a man from the Criminal Division to Phoenix to
reinforce the suggestion, and Reno agreed to reduce his indictment to
fewer than twenty-five people.

A number of officials within the Justice Department in particular did
not share the INS's enthusiasm for the sanctuary case. Justice had
continually questioned the value of the Immigration Service's undercover operation and why it was continuing so long. And as it gained
experience the undercover review committee itself grew increasingly
leery about extending the clandestine monitoring.

In the late summer, Victor Rostow had turned down Reno's request
for permission to allow undercover agents to infiltrate the Chicago
Religious Task Force. Reno had wanted to show the grand scale of the
conspiracy, but Washington feared that an expansion to Chicago would
bring in the more controversial political aspects of the case.

Nevertheless Operation Sojourner continued to be approved, partly because the Arizona investigators held out the tantalizing possibility that the sanctuary workers, far from being the neon saints depicted by the media, were in fact smuggling drugs and even children across the border. If evidence of such activities could be obtained, the indictment of church workers would be infinitely more palatable politically.

As it was, Washington was steadfastly opposed to bringing the indictments before the presidential elections in November. Mel McDonald, who was anxious to move ahead on the case, was told in effect to "cool his jets" and sit on the runway for a while.[3]

The stalling infuriated the U.S. attorney for Arizona, who told his superiors in the Justice Department that if they scuttled the case at that late date, after spending all that time and resources, he would try to make sure that they could never bring another sanctuary case in Arizona. In several heated telephone conversations with the second-ranking official in the Justice Department, Associate Attorney General D. Lowell Jensen, McDonald warned that if the department didn't authorize him to proceed with the indictments by January 21, 1985, when he planned to leave the government to go into private practice, it would be giving the sanctuary movement "a green light to proceed forever." McDonald said that he would instruct his successor to "forget the whole thing. And you just try to get this office on board anything like it again," he added. "We're five yards from the end zone, and you can't throw us a block now."[4]

On November 6, 1984, Ronald Reagan was reelected president. Almost immediately McDonald was authorized to proceed with the criminal indictments. Less than a week later Don Reno and Jim Rayburn were on a plane to Washington to discuss the prosecution with top INS and Justice Department officials.

Reno was flabbergasted by the tone of his first meeting with INS Commissioner Nelson, Maurice Inman, Victor Rostow, and others.* He thought he would have to talk about the details of the alleged conspiracy and the nuts and bolts of the prosecution. Instead, after more than two years of investigation and almost eight months of undercover operations, he found his superiors still wavering over whether the government should prosecute sanctuary workers at all.

Alan Nelson was typically cautious and expressed serious reserva-

*In reviewing this passage, Don Reno denied that he had been "flabbergasted," but that is the word he used in an interview with the author, according to notes of the conversation.

tions about criminal charges. He asked Reno if there wasn't any other way to proceed, possibly through an injunctive procedure or a civil proceeding. Nelson indicated that he would like to talk to Stephen Trott about the latter possibility. Reno, who believed that he had come up with overwhelming evidence of a major smuggling conspiracy, thought, If they've got cold feet on the criminal indictment, why didn't we pull the plug on the criminal investigation a long time ago? Aloud, he wondered about the consequences of not acting. What impression would be created if the Justice Department went this far and failed to proceed? he asked.

On the following day Reno and Rayburn, who had accompanied him in case detailed questions about the investigation arose, met at the Justice Department with Steve Trott's special counsel and a deputy assistant attorney general. As he had the day before, Reno vigorously argued for issuing search warrants on the churches involved, particularly Southside, in order to strengthen the case.

Again the federal officials were skeptical. After all the months of investigation Rayburn had turned up no criminal activity other than alien smuggling, and now he wanted the government to take the potentially embarrassing step of searching churches. "Do you really need what you think may be in there in order to meet your burden of proof?" Victoria Toensing asked Reno. "You'd better think real hard about whether we need to go into a church."[5]

Reno and Rayburn talked about the question on the flight back to Phoenix, and several days later the assistant U.S. attorney called back to say that he didn't need to search Southside. But he did persuade Washington that he should see what he could find in Darlene Nicgorski's apartment; she was, after all, the link with the political radicals in Chicago.

Reno's next task was the rebuttal of any suggestion that the sanctuary case could be handled civilly; for example, by having the government file a civil injunction, asking a court to preclude the activists from violating the law. In a lengthy memo to the Justice Department Reno argued that there was no precedent for taking such an action against criminals and that if it were taken, every alien smuggler along the border would ask for the same treatment. A civil proceeding, he added, would be a circus; the defense would take depositions from the White House on down, file endless motions, and probably succeed in having the complaint dismissed.

On November 21 the U.S. attorney's office in Phoenix had a final indictment review. Some of the most experienced prosecutors in that office were still dragging their feet, and they insisted that Reno cut his indictment even more, down to roughly fifteen people. Their arguments were mainly practical: Any more defendants would necessitate two trials and place a horrendous work load on the U.S. attorney's office and on Reno. "You'd be embracing a tar baby," one prosecutor told him, and Reno interpreted the advice to limit the prosecutions "almost as a condition of presenting the indictment to a grand jury."

Reno complied and cut his indictment down again. But he was still unsure whether that would suffice to persuade the U.S. government, in the end, to prosecute the founders of the sanctuary movement. The issue wasn't fully decided until one day in December, when at the close of a long trial Mel McDonald walked into his office and addressed all the higher-ranking members of the Justice Department in Phoenix and Tucson.

"I've heard all of the arguments as to why we should and why we shouldn't prosecute this case," he told them. "I've always run this office as a democracy. Now let's have a vote."

The majority, including the United States attorney in Tucson, voted against an indictment. As McDonald remembered it, only he and Don Reno were in favor of prosecuting the sanctuary workers.

McDonald surveyed the room.

"The only thing I didn't tell you," he said, "is that I have the most votes. I just wanted to get your feelings. We're going with this case."

In December McDonald made his last official trip back to Washington before retiring from his post. He shook hands with President Reagan during a brief formal visit and talked again with top INS officials, making sure that his ducks were still in a row. Sure, these sanctuary people will have political support, he told them, but if we don't act, they'll never stop this illegal activity.[6]

On Thursday, January 10, 1985, almost three years after the sanctuary movement had publicly begun, a federal grand jury in Phoenix secretly returned indictments of sixteen people, including a Protestant minister, John M. Fife; two Roman Catholic priests, Father Ramón Dagoberto Quiñones and Father Anthony Clark; and three nuns, Sisters Darlene Nicgorski, Ana Priester, and Mary Waddell. The others indicted were María Socorro Aguilar, Philip M. Conger, James A. Corbett, Mary K. Espinosa, Katherine M. Flaherty, Peggy Hutchison,

Wendy LeWin, and Nena MacDonald, a Quaker visiting from Texas who had been working at Southside for only a few weeks. Rounding out the list were two Latin women from Phoenix, Bertha Martel-Benavidez and Cecilia del Carmen Juarez de Emery, who had used Jesus Cruz and the Mexicans in Nogales to help bring family members into the United States.

The list revealed the enormous discretion in the hands of the prosecutor. The government had had to decide whether to investigate sanctuary, whom and where to investigate, the methods of investigation, and how long to continue investigating. It then debated whether to prosecute and, if so, whom and how many to prosecute. Subjective judgments and the pleasure of officials had intervened at every step, and the fate of dozens of individuals hung on every choice made. The law may be the law, but law enforcement is far less cut-and-dried.

Don Reno, for example, had decided to weight the list of those indicted heavily toward Phoenix, rather than Tucson, so that the trial would be held in the more conservative city. This meant that several of the key participants in the underground railroad, like Ricardo Elford, Ken Kennon, and Kay Kelly, a parishioner at Southside whose activities had been thoroughly monitored by the government, were allowed to slip out of the noose. On the other hand, it meant that people whose participation was only peripheral, like Wendy LeWin, Ana Priester, and Mary Waddell, were part of the roundup in Phoenix.

Reno had included these women and Nena MacDonald also in order to send a strong signal to the religious community. "A conspiracy doesn't function without the gofers," he said later. "This prosecution was really for deterrence; it was not for punishment."[7]

Reno had deliberately not indicted Ellen Willis-Conger, for she and her husband (who had taken joint surnames after their marriage) made such an attractive couple that he feared their presence in the dock would stir a troublesome degree of sympathy from the jury. Like Kelly and more than sixty others, Ellen was named an unindicted coconspirator.

In the next few days the INS also rounded up and arrested many of the aliens whom the sanctuary movement had helped, and who were among those named by the grand jury as unindicted coconspirators.

On Friday, January 18, 1985, Mel McDonald held his farewell banquet. "After what I've done to Christianity this week, I wonder whether I should open this thing with a prayer," he joked to the assembled audience. Among them were all the previous U.S. attorneys in Arizona save one, a man named A. Bates Butler III, who had been McDonald's immediate predecessor for a brief period.

After the indictments had been announced, Butler had called and canceled his tickets to the dinner. He was a dedicated supporter of the sanctuary movement, and since the previous April he had been representing Phil Willis-Conger.

The Reverend John M. Fife greets a member of his congregation at Southside United Presbyterian Church.

James A. Corbett rests for a moment in the desert while escorting a refugee across the Arizona-Mexico border.

(Left to right) The Reverend Richard Sinner, Father Ricardo Elford, and the Reverend Ken Kennon conduct religious services for Salvadorans released from El Centro detention center in Southern California.

Southside United Presbyterian Church declares itself the first public sanctuary for Central American refugees in the United States on March 24, 1982. In the center at the table is the Reverend John Fife. To his left, seated, are Gary MacEoin and Jim Corbett; to his right at the table are a Salvadoran refugee called "Alfredo" and Father Ricardo Elford.

Father Ricardo Elford embraces a Central American refugee child during his weekly church service in Tucson.

Father Ramón Dagoberto Quiñones of Our Lady of Guadalupe in Nogales, Sonora, Mexico, greeting a parishioner at the parish's home for the aged.

Philip and Ellen Willis-Conger in the legal office of the Arizona Sanctuary Defense Fund, Tucson.

Sister Darlene Nicgorski at a convent in Tucson where she resided during 1985–86.

James A. Rayburn, INS investigator, outside the Federal Courthouse in Tucson. Rayburn directed the undercover investigation of the sanctuary movement.

The Reverend Anthony Clark of Sacred Heart Church in Nogales, Arizona.

María Socorro Aguilar in the living room of her home in Nogales, Sonora, Mexico, where Central American refugees stayed on their trip north to the United States.

Jesus Cruz (right) and the Reverend James Oines (left) at Alzona Evangelical Lutheran Church in Phoenix. Cruz, an undercover informant for the Immigration Service, spied on a weekly Bible study class conducted by Oines.

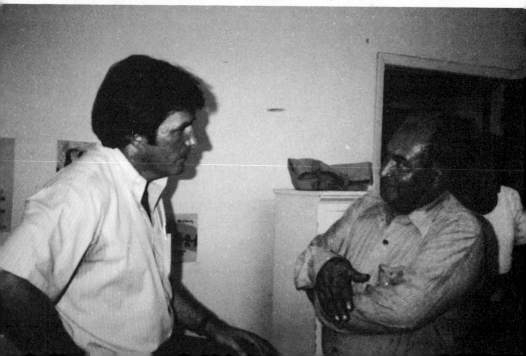

Guatemalan refugee Joel Morelos and his daughter Lucy.

Jim Corbett assists Guatemalan refugee Juana Beatriz Álvarez over the fence between the United States and Mexico.

Special Assistant U.S. Attorney Donald M. Reno, Jr., prosecutor at the sanctuary trial, in Phoenix.

Defense attorney James J. Brosnahan in Tucson.

Robert J. Hirsh, counsel for the Reverend John Fife.

A. Bates Butler III, lawyer for Philip Willis-Conger.

Demonstrators against U.S. policy in Central America in front of the Federal Building in Tucson. By 1986 this weekly protest and prayer vigil had become the longest-running public demonstration in the United States.

Judge Earl H. Carroll, Tucson.

The Reverend John Fife addressing an
ecumenical service in support of sanctuary
at St. Augustine Catholic Church, Tucson.

Nena MacDonald, a Quaker volunteer
in the sanctuary movement, in a
moment of play with her daughter
in Tucson. The prosecution called
MacDonald, who was indicted despite only peripheral involvement in
the movement, a "throwaway."

(Left to right) Sanctuary defendants Mary K. Espinosa, Tony Clark, Wendy LeWin, Katherine Flaherty, Jim Corbett, and Darlene Nicgorski in Phoenix, while pretrial hearings were under way.

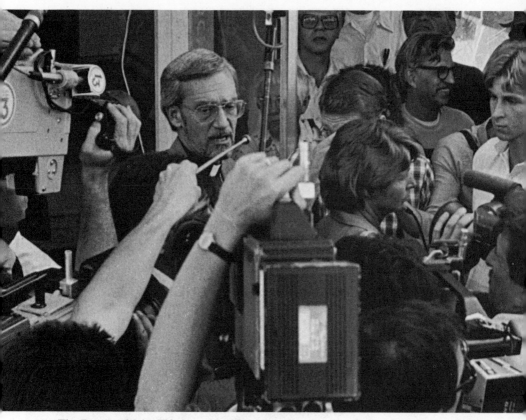

The Reverend John Fife is mobbed by reporters after the verdicts in the sanctuary trial, May 1986.

Mary K. Espinosa and the Reverend Ken Kennon at a posttrial demonstration in Nogales in solidarity with sanctuary and the Central American refugees.

Ken Kennon gives hundreds of declarations of support for sanctuary to INS official
William Johnston outside the Federal Building in Tucson, May 1986.

Chapter
Twenty-one

WHEN GOVERNMENT AGENTS came to deliver the indictment against Jim Corbett, they stopped in bewilderment for a minute and surveyed the scene. There were three different addresses on the property, a scraggly one-and-a-half-acre lot at the end of a dirt road in northeast Tucson. Scattered in apparent disorder were assorted vehicles, goats, geese, debris, trailers, and two houses. Which one was 3331 Flanwell Drive? The men, one of them in cowboy boots, finally approached the most likely-looking structure, a tiny white house with azure blue trim. A dog started barking, and a tall woman in a bathrobe, her long graying hair pulled back in a bun, appeared out of one of the trailers. The agents showed Pat Corbett the papers for her husband.

"Do you have a warrant to be here?" she demanded. "You were on private property as soon as you turned down that road." The men retreated.[1]

At eight on the same morning, January 14, 1985, Phil and Ellen Willis-Conger's telephone rang. Ellen answered, and it was Kay Kelly on the other end of the line. Kelly, a grandmotherly woman in her early sixties, had been sheltering the refugee Juana in her home for several months.

195

"There's a government car outside my house, and Juana didn't come home last night from a birthday party she went to," said Kelly. "I'm really worried they're here to pick her up. Can you try to find out where she is and tell her to stay away?"

The Willis-Congers located Juana at the home of another refugee family and told her that someone was on his way to pick her up. Then they called Kay Kelly back.

"They're inside now, going through everything," said Kay, her voice shaking. "They have a search warrant for her."[2] The Willis-Congers decided that Kelly, a widow who lived alone, shouldn't be on her own, and they called Jim Corbett.

The rancher answered the phone. "I can't leave right now," he said. "My house is surrounded by immigration. They went next door. They had the wrong address, and now they're looking all around here for me."[3]

Next Ellen called John Fife and got no answer. That's strange, she thought; he never leaves the telephone or his coffee before nine-thirty. She asked a friend who lived near Southside to drive out and check the church. The woman drove past and returned with a report that she had seen Border Patrol cars outside the building. Then John Fife called.

The minister had been in bed enjoying his Monday morning when he'd heard a heavy pounding on his door. "To hell with them, I'm sleeping in this morning," he thought. The banging continued, and after fifteen minutes or so he got up, pulled on a pair of pants, and started toward the door. On his way through the living room he glanced out the window and saw the Border Patrol standing on his porch. Four or five refugees were staying at Southside on that day, and Fife's first thought was, my God, they've raided the church! Half-dressed, he invited the INS men in, offered them coffee, and slowly started reading the indictment, trying to stall in hopes that someone might spot their car and help the refugees get out. But they were only interested in him that day, and as soon as they left he called Phil.

Willis-Conger answered the phone. "It's an indictment," Fife said.

Phil's first reaction was: "I don't want to be left out," and as Fife read off the list, he learned that he wasn't.[4]

That morning, when Jim Oines heard about the indictments and about Cruz's infiltration of his church, he immediately realized that the spy knew where many of the refugees in his Bible study class lived. The minister raced out to his car and began driving around to their homes to warn them. About half of them had already been picked up and arrested.

The Bible study class never met again; those refugees who had escaped arrest were too afraid to return. One of them, a Salvadoran woman, told Oines that now she realized that "this country is not really different; it is just like my country."[5]

Jim Rayburn delivered the indictments personally to the Sacred Heart Church in Nogales. "If I were you, I'd say Tucson was using you," he suggested to Mary K. Espinosa, after settling himself in her office at the church. "You really don't want to get involved in this," he continued, in what she immediately interpreted as a bid to turn her into a government witness.

"I've got a lot of work to do," she told Rayburn. "Will you please do what you have to do and get out of my office?" He served her and left, and she cried for the rest of the day.

Her young son, trying to console her, said, "It's OK, Mommy, what you did was the right thing. If you have to go to jail, I'll tell everyone that you went away to school."[6]

Tony Clark was at Casa Guadalupe when a reporter from the *Star* came around and said, "Hey, you just got indicted." Then the monsignor called and told him that Rayburn was at the church and wanted to serve him.

Father Clark went over with the reporter. As soon as Rayburn saw him, he said, "No pictures." He served Clark with what looked to the priest like a three-inch-thick document and asked him to sign a receipt. Rayburn left quickly, leaving his hat.[7]

The investigator had already contacted José Rivera Cortés, the Mexican consul in Nogales, Arizona, with the news that the U.S. government was indicting two Mexican citizens for alien smuggling. The consul informed Quiñones and, by prearrangement, accompanied Rayburn to the priest's office at Our Lady of Guadalupe. As the two men walked in, Father Quiñones quietly and surreptitiously activated a tape recorder in his desk drawer.[8]

"Come in," Quiñones greeted his visitors.

"Hello, Father, how are you?" said Rivera Cortés. "These are the men whom—"

"Whom you talked to me about by phone, right? How are you? Sit down, please. Mrs. Aguilar is around here."

Quiñones called in Doña María Socorro Aguilar, and Rayburn began speaking, in Spanish: "Well, to me, Father Quiñones, Socorro Aguilar, in my opinion, the thing is you were used by the people in Tucson. Ah, I did this investigation; I started out around in May, well, in April or in May like that, and immediately it's clear to me that the people in Tucson are using you, and also you [alluding to Socorro Aguilar]. Your opinion and their opinion is [*sic*] not the same. For me, your reason is more honest. For me they are liars. . . . You should know that what I am going to give to you is an order to report to court, but you aren't in the United States; you aren't a citizen, nor do you live in the United States, and you don't have to do it, but the government of the United States wants your cooperation and also wants to cooperate with you.

"By word of the attorney general of the United States, I am able to state to you, in exchange for your testimony, you could be let go from this case without being punished and everything would be over with up to the date that you did this with the government. . . . But the government of the United States is going to want your testimony and just the truth."

"Is that all?" asked Quiñones.

"Have I explained well?" Rayburn asked.

"Everything is clear, very clear, everything very clear."

"If you want, you could think it over and afterward answer him," the consul suggested. "You don't necessarily have to—Right now if you want to think things over and decide afterward, right, you don't have to say yes or no."

"No, no, you don't have to say anything," Rayburn agreed.

"But . . . I think this is the opportunity for stating a principle," Quiñones replied. "We were surprised that the government of the United States has brought charges against Mexican citizens for acts carried out in Mexico. By what legal precedent, what right, where is it contained that the United States can accuse us for acts carried out in Mexico, assuming the case? Supposing without admitting it that we had carried out those acts?"

"Well, it is very clear in the papers that I have here, but it's going to be better that a lawyer explain to you that the violations are for conspira—"

"Conspiracy," finished the consul.

"Conspiracy to, ah, to bring people over the line," said Rayburn, "over the border, smuggling people, keeping people from the law, from officials."

"Hiding people," said the consul. ". . . They accused you and Mrs.

Socorro Aguilar on some occasion of having received money as payment for having crossed over a person. In another even of having
dressed a person as a priest in order to cross him over to that side and
on another occasion to have said to a person, 'There's the hole, cross
over through there.' . . . But I would like you to see the accusations that
there are, so that you could read all of it and might find a way to answer
so that everything turns out clean, proper."

"Yes, yes," Quiñones replied, "undoubtedly I think, Mr. Consul,
that it's very clear for the community of Nogales what is being done
on the part of the priest, on the part of the Catholic Church in Nogales.
Very clear the ministry which we have in jail with the Central Americans. Very clear the ministry that we have in our church with all sorts
of persons, including Central Americans . . . openly helping all types
of people without asking them their nationality. . . . We are doing it;
it is the avocation of the Catholic Church, and this lady, well liked by
us, simply supports what her clergy here in Nogales . . . we do. She puts
people up when we are unable to give them lodging. She gives them
lodging because she feels sorry for them in spite of the fact that she must
make a living in some fashion on the rooms for rent which she has in
her house. . . . The motives that United States citizens may have with
respect to the attitude of the government of the United States in Central
America, these are totally personal motives belonging to them. Our
motives are religious motives, absolutely religious. On the level of the
charges that we dressed one of these people up, that is totally false. On
the level that we, in a certain way, are urging them, pushing them, that
is totally false. . . . We [just] came from the prison in which we gave
food to twenty-four Central Americans who are being detained . . . and
not because we were sent over there by any United States movement.
Nor much less are we calling on anyone to do something, but because
they have the desire, for whatever reason, political reasons or economic
reasons, the desire to get into the United States. They all have that
purpose. . . ."

Quiñones agreed to accept the indictment. It was agreed that he and
Doña Socorro Aguilar would appear in Phoenix later that month in
response to the summons, and they were assured that they would have
no problems in continuing to enter the United States. (For both, this
last was an important consideration. The priest had had at least two
heart attacks, and his doctor, and several members of Socorro Aguilar's
immediate family, lived across the border.)

After more discussion of who would represent them, Doña Socorro

Aguilar commented sadly, "I feel really bad about being seen as a criminal."

Rivera Cortés reminded her that "in the United States everybody is innocent until things are proven."[9]

The widow, who had been the closest of all those indicted to the spy Jesus Cruz, went home and threw out the chair that the informant had habitually used when he visited her home.[10]

Just before the indictments were handed down, Darlene Nicgorski had left Phoenix for a workshop for returning missionaries in Adrian, Michigan. On January 14 she returned to her room after a long walk in the cold and found a stack of telephone messages. One was from a friend and fellow sister who had just gone by Darlene's apartment to check on a refugee who was staying there. Opening the door with her own key, she had stumbled upon several government agents going through Darlene's papers and personal belongings.[11]

The government videotaped the search of the nun's modest two-bedroom apartment, to forestall any charges that they had ransacked the place. The film showed a frightened refugee, a Salvadoran woman named Margarite, opening the door to Agent Lee Morgan and several companions. They arrested the twenty-two-year-old woman, who had told Darlene that two of her brothers had been killed by death squads and her husband shot by a drunken national guardsman. For the next four hours the agents went through the nun's voluminous files on the underground railroad and sanctuary network, her address files, and her personal diaries and letters. As Morgan went through the apartment, sorting through the nun's papers, the camera kept swinging back, as if fascinated, to a large poster in her living room. "Dump Reagan in 1984," it read, under a cartoon of the president.

The agents took forty-nine items out of the apartment, including a notebook on liberation theology, plus forty-four photographs, including one of Darlene with Tomás Borge, the interior minister of Nicaragua, whom she had met while on a tour of the country with a group of nuns. (Later, referring to this photograph, Don Reno told the press that the government had found a picture showing Nicgorski with "Communist guerrillas down in Central America.") None of the material revealed any connections to any political organization or foreign government or betrayed Sister Darlene to be anything other than what she said she was: an activist nun who firmly believed that God was on the side of the poor. Yet the seizure reinforced the INS investigators' conviction that they were dealing with a tough, dedicated Marxist. For their part, the break-in convinced the nun from Milwaukee and her colleagues that the government would stop at nothing, even the most egregious invasion of personal privacy, to destroy the sanctuary movement. Their first reaction was to show the government that it could do no such thing.

Two days after the indictment one of the unindicted coconspirators led a family of four Guatemalans, a man and wife and their two children, ages seven and ten, over the border, after an overnight walk across the desert. The family told the sanctuary workers that about a year earlier the mother had taken two older daughters to visit their grandfather. When she returned to pick up the two girls, plainclothesmen were hosing out her father's garage. When she asked where her family was, she was told that they didn't live there anymore. Five people were missing and never heard of again—the grandparents, the two children, and an aunt.[12]

For months a national sanctuary conference had been scheduled to be held in Tucson on January 24–25, 1985. Only a few hundred people had been registered for the meetings, but after the indictments were announced, conference organizers suddenly couldn't find enough tickets for all the people who wanted to attend. Twelve hundred people showed up on the first day. The government's tactics were condemned, and support for the sanctuary movement was expressed by the governing bodies of the American Lutheran Church, the Presbyterian Church (U.S.A.), the United Methodist Church, the National Council of Churches, the U.S. Catholic Mission Association, the United Church of Christ, Disciples of Christ, the Rabbinical Assembly, the American Baptist Churches, and the American Friends Service Committee, among other religious institutions.

Conspicuously missing from the list was the Catholic Church, although five of the eleven defendants were Catholic, numerous priests and nuns were active in the movement, and the overwhelming majority of Salvadoran refugees were of that faith. The U.S. Catholic Conference, made up of the American bishops, was loath to endorse anything resembling civil disobedience and for years remained silent on the sanctuary issue, even after the indictments. The bishops did consistently support legislative efforts to establish a safe haven in the United States for the Salvadorans, however, and a few individual bishops, including the bishop of Milwaukee, went further and endorsed the sanctuary work.[13] Immediately after the indictments the Arizona Catholic Conference sent a letter to President Reagan, signed by Bishop Thomas J. O'Brien of Phoenix, Bishop Manuel Moreno of Tucson, and Bishop Jerome Hastrich of Gallup, New Mexico, stating that "sanctuary is consistent with our national history and biblical values," and urged the administration to offer Salvadorans extended voluntary departure. Gerald O'Keefe, Father Tony Clark's bishop in Davenport, Iowa, sent him $250 out of his own pocket for defense money.

More typical of the clergy who supported sanctuary was the Reverend William Sloane Coffin, a veteran of the anti-Vietnam War movement and a social activist for decades. Coffin, pastor of Riverside Church in New York City, attended the conference and told supporters, "There's only two things that increase in value when they're stepped on: Persian rugs and the Church."[14]

On the evening preceding the opening of the symposium Elie Wiesel spoke and invoked the lessons of the Holocaust. "From the ethical perspective, it is impossible for human beings today, especially for my contemporaries, who have seen what people can do to themselves and to one another, not to be involved. We must be with those who have suffered, and we must be with those who have tried to prevent others from suffering."

Wiesel recounted the following story:

"A few months ago we had a conference in Washington, which we called Faith in Humankind, a conference of rescuers of Jews during the war. It was devoted to what we called the righteous Gentiles. The idea came to us because I wanted to understand what made some people care and secondly, why there were so few. We brought seventy-five righteous Gentiles to Washington; we brought scholars and philosophers and moralists, and we met together and we tried to understand what it was.

"One of the great surprises for me was to realize that those people who cared—or, as we put it, who had the courage to care—were not people of high stature. They were not generals, ministers, university professors, or industrialists. Most of them were simple people who didn't even know that what they were doing was courageous; they didn't even know that their acts were heroic.

"They did it because it was the thing to do. And I felt then, woe to our society if to be human becomes a heroic act."[15]

Despite the brave words, however, the sanctuary movement was threatened by divisions within its ranks as well as by the government assault from without. The January symposium had been billed as the "shoot-out in Tucson," for the split within the movement had been widening ever since the incident of the two young Guatemalans two years earlier.

The members of the Chicago Religious Task Force on Central America were angry that Tucson was referring only some 5 percent of the Central Americans it assisted on to public sanctuary. In December 1983 the CRTFCA had sent a letter to the TEC insisting that only refugees who were going into public sanctuary should be helped through the underground railroad. Chicago argued that since the railroad could assist only a small proportion of all Central American refugees, it was no more than a "humanitarian Band-Aid" unless it was used for a broader political purpose. This should be to supply churches around the country with refugees who could help Americans understand the underlying situation: that Central America needed economic and political change and that the United States must stop supporting the forces that opposed such change.

The Tucson activists flatly disagreed, and Corbett took up the debate with passion. The refugees' "needs, rather than their roles in what we see as the overall political situation, must continue to determine our priorities," he wrote, in a discussion guide prepared for the Arizona border workers. Sanctuary, he declared, "is for the persecuted, whatever the political origin of the persecution."

The two camps also differed over the related question of whether the movement needed a more centralized organization. The Chicago school felt this was essential to set policies and to speak with one voice; to coordinate its opposition to American intervention in Central America; and, since the arrests of sanctuary workers in 1984, to raise money for legal defense. Chicago seemed to be proposing itself for such a dominant role.

Corbett and the others felt strongly that if sanctuary was to retain its vitality and broad-based appeal, it had to remain a local grass-roots initiative, fueled by the energies of individual volunteers, congregations, and communities. On a more purely practical level, the "rhetoric coming out of Chicago," as Phil Willis-Conger referred to it (Corbett called it the "rhetoric of rage"), was already creating problems. The government and critics of the sanctuary movement inevitably picked hard, radical quotes from Chicago's newsletter *Basta!* in their attempts to demonstrate that the movement was not humanitarian but was "using" Central Americans in a cynical political game. If Chicago had its way, the Arizona group thought, it would turn sanctuary into the very thing that the Reagan administration was accusing it of being: a purely political left-wing pressure group.

Underlying these differences lay the deeper issue of what the sanctuary movement really was: a political protest against the Reagan administration's war in Central America or a humanitarian effort to assist the victims of the war. It was in truth both, and by 1984, even as the number of sanctuary churches, caravans, and demonstrations proliferated, its two sides were having a hard time coexisting.

Corbett took the dispute public in 1984 in a series of letters called "A View from the Border" sent to various sanctuary churches and Quaker communities. In them he posed a question: Why had sanctuary thrived in places like Champaign-Urbana and Elgin, Illinois; Pasadena, California; Colorado Springs, Colorado; Douglas, Arizona; Santa Fe, New Mexico; Tulsa, Oklahoma; and Kalamazoo, Michigan, but had only one church in liberal New York City—the Reverend William Sloane Coffin's Riverside Church? He wrote:

> *The explanation is sure to be complex, but we can reasonably suspect that if the availability of professional activists, organization headquarters and left-wing political traditions is relevant to the vitality of the Sanctuary movement, the relation may be inverse. From what I've seen, Sanctuary almost never grows out of political platforms and theories . . . people in this country who would never rally to shout slogans or engage in symbolic acts of civil disobedience are coming forward to risk being blacklisted and imprisoned. . . .* [16]

The clash came to a head in October 1984, when the Chicago group refused to send Tucson a copy of its mailing list of the network. The TEC had repeatedly requested the list, both to resettle refugees directly and to invite interested parties to the symposium scheduled for January. But the Chicago group was afraid, after Corbett's "diatribes" that year, that he would use the list to send his epistles to a wider audience, thereby spreading even more confusion and dissension within the ranks. [17]

The Tucson group interpreted the refusal to share the list as an attempt to take over the movement from the very people who had started the underground railroad and built it across a continent. It was an outrage, and it was absurd: Chicago was a tail that was trying to walk off without the dog.

As 1985 rang in, the dispute was on the verge of tearing the movement apart. At a TEC meeting on January 7 John Fife suggested that six people be delegated to sit down and have a dialogue with Chicago at the coming symposium. Kathy Flaherty asked someone to please explain to her what the problem was.

"Well, I can give you a stack of letters," said Tim Nonn.

"Is it like a power struggle or what?" Kathy persisted.

"Yes, ideology," replied Fife.[18]

As another example of Washington's inability to monitor the undercover operation properly, this conversation was taped weeks after Victor Rostow had ordered the INS in Phoenix to stop the secret monitoring.

Three days after that conversation the government handed down its indictments in Arizona. Two weeks later the sanctuary symposium was held as scheduled. Ninety percent of the members of the steering committee of the Chicago Religious Task Force came to Tucson, determined to try to heal the split. They stayed over two extra days to talk over their differences. The majority of the conferees sided with Tucson, but feeling was unanimous that for the moment all divisions must be put aside in the face of the government challenge.*

*In 1984, the year before the indictments, 328 Salvadorans were granted asylum while 13,045 were denied it, according to INS figures.

Chapter
Twenty-two

THE JUSTICE DEPARTMENT chose to indict not in Tucson but in Phoenix, in an obvious attempt to secure a law-and-order jury that would be more sympathetic to the state's case. But at least one lawyer for the accused was certain that the choice of venue was part of an elaborate scheme on the part of the prosecution to have Federal District Judge Earl Hamblin Carroll try the case.*

Carroll was not known as a friend of the dissident, the poor, or the oppressed. An Arizona native and a graduate of the University of Arizona College of Law, the short, white-haired judge qualified as a member of the so-called Phoenix 40, the handful of corporate executives, lawyers, and developers who called many of the shots in the city. His neighbors in Encanto Park, an area of exclusive old homes, had included William Rehnquist before the latter left for Washington, and among his acquaintances at the Phoenix Country Club were John and Sandra Day O'Connor, before they, too, were called to the capital.

---

*In Phoenix, right after the grand jury returns an indictment, a clerk reaches into a drawer full of envelopes with judges' names on them and pulls one out. That judge hears the case. Only four judges were in the criminal draw in Phoenix at the time of the sanctuary indictment, so the chances of getting Carroll were 25 percent.

Prior to his appointment to the bench by President Jimmy Carter in 1980, Carroll, a registered Democrat, had practiced corporate civil and administrative law with a prominent Phoenix firm, and his clients included many of the major corporations in the area. As a lawyer he had never tried a criminal case, and some lawyers who had tried cases before him thought he was almost naïve about the way the world worked.

One story told about Carroll involved a case brought against several Phoenix firemen for conspiracy to possess and distribute cocaine. As one fireman witness was testifying, it came out that they were playing poker in the firehouse. Carroll reportedly leaned over the bench and exclaimed, "You were *gambling* in the firehouse?" The man stammered something about no money being on the table.

During his closing argument in that same case Larry Debus, a well-known Phoenix defense lawyer, talked about how common the use of cocaine had become. Doctors, lawyers, even some *judges* used it, Debus orated. Carroll became so outraged that he almost held Debus in contempt, and the story spread around the courthouse that two other judges painstakingly had to talk him out of it.[1]

Debus, a bright, irreverent, and aggressive criminal lawyer, thought that defense lawyers in general seemed to rub Carroll the wrong way. During one trial a defense attorney had to review two rooms full of some 250,000 corporate documents, stacked on the floors, on tables, and up the walls. Judge Carroll issued an order that an FBI agent had to watch the man while he went through the papers, implying that he didn't trust the defense counsel, a well-known local lawyer who had helped set up the public defender system for the Ninth Circuit in Arizona. When it became clear that the lawyer planned to spend night after night, often until midnight, poring over the documents, Carroll tried to rescind the order. The attorney objected. "You wanted him, and there he'll stay, as long as I'm in there," he reportedly informed the court.

"I knew Carroll's proclivities," Debus later joked. "I told the sanctuary defense attorneys, and they didn't believe me. Later they questioned whether I'd been completely honest with them."

The prosecution was initially just as anxious not to have Carroll on the case. A constant topic of conversation in the U.S. attorney's office was whether it would draw Carroll. As some prosecutors saw it, although he was a warm and gracious man off the bench, in court Carroll was a pompous, overbearing, rude, and generally obnoxious judge.

On the day of the draw Don Reno went downstairs at about 5:00 P.M. He asked the clerk about the draw, and she told him that she had already drawn the judge's name.

"Who is it?" he asked.

"It's Judge Carroll," the clerk replied.

Reno remembers clasping his head and muttering something like "Oh, shit." The clerk took about two steps backward and exclaimed, "Mr. Reno, Mr. Reno!" in such shocked tones that he was afraid that she would run upstairs and tell the judge that he had had a fit. He went back upstairs, and when he walked into his office, everyone could tell from his face that it was Carroll.[2]

Reno soon realized that Carroll was not going to be the liability that some in his office had thought. Carroll, like the prosecutor, was a workaholic. One story about the judge held that he had more billable hours in one year at his old firm than any three other attorneys. Once, when William Rehnquist was in Phoenix for a judicial conference, he was overheard teasing Carroll about working seven days a week.[3]

Reno knew that Carroll believed that most U.S. attorneys were generally ill prepared, and he figured that the judge might recognize how hard he was working on the case and appreciate it. For the assistant U.S. attorney was planning a personal test of strength. It was his first case as a prosecutor, and he was approaching it as the "ultimate in a competitive event," as he put it.

Don Reno was a fiercely competitive person, a trait most apparent in his athletic regimen. He worked out daily, lifted weights, ran forty-five miles a week, and had acquired an impressive array of muscles on his rather small frame. (One female colleague compared him to a "banty rooster.")

A descendant of Huguenots, he had grown up in Illinois.[4] At the age of fifteen he won numerous national speed-skating competitions, and he thought he might have made it to the Olympics if he hadn't dropped skating for football, a tougher challenge for a youth who weighed little more than 150 pounds. When he got to college, at Illinois Wesleyan, he was told that he was too small for the sport, so he gained 45 pounds and became a center for the team.

After law school at John Marshall in Chicago, Reno became a criminal defense attorney in his father's law office in Champaign, Illinois. During his seven years in private practice he earned a reputation for defending pornographers, including a movie exhibitor who was indicted for showing *Deep Throat*. In 1975 he moved to Phoenix and with partners built up a wide range of investments, from fast-food franchises to restaurants to nightclubs. At one time his enterprises employed 500 people in Arizona, and Dooley's, one of his clubs, booked name acts like B. B. King and was the highest-grossing nightclub in Arizona for a while before he sold it in 1982.

Reno married in 1981 and decided to liquidate most of his holdings; he later said that he didn't want to raise a family and be involved in "all that," implying life in the fast lane. He put the cover on his black Porsche 928, rented a motor home, and set off from Tempe on a long vacation. After about forty-five days the newlyweds returned to Phoenix. Reno took the Arizona bar exam and went to work as a prosecutor.

The career shift was compatible with Reno's political views; he was a conservative Republican and had tough go-get-'em attitudes toward law enforcement. This first case perfectly suited his view of life as a struggle. On one side was the dedicated, hard-driving prosecutor, single-handedly trying the biggest case the INS had ever taken on, and on the other was a veritable platoon of defense attorneys, much more experienced than he in trying criminal cases. Don Reno loved the challenge and was ready for sheer sacrifice. In his mind, the trial would be "a test of whether energy, punishment, and preparation could outdo superior numbers and superior ability."

The nucleus of the defense team had already been formed back in March 1984. On the night of Phil Conger's first arrest the telephone had rung at around midnight at the home of A. Bates Butler III, in Tucson. John Fife was on the other end of the line. "Phil's been arrested," he said. "Can you defend him?"[5]

Although the slender, bespectacled attorney had never defended or tried a criminal case before, he immediately agreed, for he was one of the stoutest supporters of the sanctuary movement in the Presbyterian Church.

Like his father, who had been a special agent of the FBI for almost two dozen years, A. Bates Butler III was as straight as a bullet from a gun. He had never been to Nicaragua. He was no friend of the Sandinistas, no connoisseur of revolution, no enthusiast of liberation. Forty years old, he had spent a dozen years as a federal prosecutor, including a stint as U.S. attorney for the state of Arizona.

He was also an active layman in the Presbyterian Church and had

first had to face the sanctuary issue when Southside declared itself a
haven for undocumented Central Americans. Some members of Butler's own Trinity Presbyterian Church wanted their governing body, or
session, to declare support for Southside and its pastor, John Fife, but
Butler and his father, both of whom were members of the session,
agreed, while driving to church on the night of the debate, that however
moral Southside's stand might be, civil disobedience was going too far.
They voted against a sanctuary resolution and brought the other members of the session around to their point of view.[6]

Butler was a conscientious man, however, and after that night he felt
obligated to learn a little more about the situation. He wrote letters to
the State Department requesting information but got no meaningful
response. The statistics he saw on asylum troubled him. He studied the
relevant law and reports by representatives of the Presbyterian Church
on their trips to El Salvador. After two years both he and his father
changed their minds and came to believe that the sanctuary ministers
were right, that the lawbreaker was the U.S. government itself, not the
church workers.

Butler deeply regretted the confrontation between the churches and
the state. But he believed that as a Christian he was not supposed to
file into line just because the government said he should. That had
happened before, in Europe in the 1930s and 1940s, and millions of
Jews had lost their lives. He didn't relish civil disobedience. But as a
Christian he believed he had a higher responsibility: to see that his
government followed the law. And no worldly authority could take
away his right to help his fellowman.

Bates Butler had not come to this place easily; by inclination and by
background, he was a conservative man. In his office in La Placita
Village in downtown Tucson he had a framed letter from J. Edgar
Hoover, written in 1957, when he was in seventh grade. The boy had
sent Hoover a picture of himself, and the venerable director had replied.

"Dear Bates," the letter read, "Your father has just been in to see
me and has given me the autographed photograph of yourself and I
want to tell you how much I appreciate it. I understand that you are
looking forward some day to following in your father's footsteps and
becoming an FBI agent. That certainly is a worthwhile ambition. With
every good wish, I am sincerely, J. Edgar Hoover."

Butler never became an FBI agent, but he did become a lawman: first
a deputy Pima County attorney handling criminal prosecutions, then

an assistant U.S. attorney in Tucson, and in 1980 and 1981, U.S. attorney for the District of Arizona. He still thought working in the U.S. attorney's office was the best job he had ever had. As he talked to John Fife that night, he wondered what his old colleagues, and J. Edgar Hoover, would think of him now.

Butler told the minister that they would need another attorney to defend Kathy Flaherty. "Do you mind if we call Bob Hirsh?" asked Fife. And so began the collaboration of one of the oddest couples in the courtroom.

Robert J. Hirsh was another story. One of the best defense lawyers in Arizona, and possibly in the country, he was as moody, flamboyant, and outrageous as Butler was calm and methodical. If Butler looked like a banker or insurance man, the blue-eyed, blow-dried, string-tied Hirsh could have passed for a riverboat gambler. A long and lanky Jew who had just turned fifty, the twice-divorced lawyer drove a Mercedes, dated voluptuous-looking women, and trailed a sensuous air of bemused cynicism behind him like musk. He specialized in getting ax murderers acquitted and bottomless dancers set free.

Hirsh was the terror of local prosecutors. According to one oft-told tale, during a trial he repeatedly referred to a state's witness as the "great detective." When the prosecutor finally complained, Hirsh jumped to his feet and told the jury that he certainly was willing to withdraw the description. "All right, I'll agree with the prosecution," he said. "He is not a great detective." Hirsh sat down and smiled. His client, who had been charged with a double murder, was acquitted.[7]

The celebrated advocate was also not above joking about the mental acuity of some of his clients. He told the story of two of them, drug dealers, who were having a telephone conversation. "Be careful what you say, the line may be tapped," one warned. "What do you mean?" the other inquired. "You know, the IBF," the other cautioned. Two others were chatting over the wires, using *umbrella* to mean a lid of dope. "How many umbrellas do you need?" the seller asked. "Oh, about two and a half," the other replied.[8]

Hirsh was a master of the I-shot-him-but-he-was-a-bad-man defense. It was usually, however, a "bad" woman. In one month in 1982 juries acquitted two of his clients on the ground of temporary insanity, one who had butchered his wife with a kitchen knife and the other who had blown away his ex-wife and her lover with a shotgun. Later, in 1984, he almost did it again, winning a verdict of second-degree murder for a deranged young man who had stabbed an unconscious seventeen-year-old girl sixty-seven times and sexually mutilated her. Hirsh convinced the jury that the accused had had a very bad mother.[9]

Butler was one of Hirsh's old opponents, and after the two joined together on behalf of Phil Conger and Kathy Flaherty, one of Hirsh's former law clerks told Butler, "I can't believe you two are on the same case—he *hates* you. You should hear the things he says about you!"

"He should hear what's been said about him," replied Bates's wife, who knew that many of her husband's former colleagues in the government had often talked about investigating the man who helped so many drug dealers and mafiosi get off scot-free.[10]

These awesome talents were never put to their full use on the Conger case because the government dropped the charges before the case ever came to trial. But when the sweeping sanctuary indictments came down several months later, it was to Bob Hirsh that John Fife turned. Some people even saw similarities between the tall, silver-haired, witty, and charismatic lawyer and the tall, silver-haired, witty, and charismatic preacher. At least there was agreement that John Fife, the most visible spokesman for the sanctuary movement, would need all the skills of the so-called cocaine lawyer if he wanted to walk away from the charges against him.

Hirsh and Butler had felt personally affronted by the sweeping indictments because Don Reno had assured them for months that the sanctuary workers had to fear arrest only if the Border Patrol caught them out on the highway transporting refugees. The defense lawyers had asked Reno directly whether the government had any investigation of sanctuary under way, and the prosecutor had assured the two attorneys that the INS had no real interest in the movement and would do nothing further to investigate it, at least in Arizona. After the indictments Butler talked with a number of reporters who had gone back and checked their notes and found that the exact same thing had been said to them. "I was naïve enough to think that, at least as a former prosecutor and as a former United States attorney, I would not be lied to," the deeply moral Butler told acquaintances after the indictments were announced. "But I was." (When asked about this, Don Reno acknowledged that he had not been candid with the attorneys, adding, "What was I supposed to say, 'I've been to Washington and we've got a full-scale investigation of the movement under way'? I was under oath as a prosecutor and as a member of the Arizona bar not to reveal confidences. . . . I would have been fired and disciplined by the state bar for such a disclosure."[11])

It was Bob Hirsh's plan to assemble a team of the best criminal defense attorneys in Arizona to represent the other sanctuary defendants. Hirsh reasoned that if worse came to worst, the defense would at least have more than a dozen superb closing arguments.

Peggy Hutchison had already hired Tucson attorney Michael Piccareta to represent her, and Michael Altman, a professor of criminal and immigration law at Arizona State University, was cocounsel for one of the nuns. Hirsh asked William G. Walker of Tucson to join the case and recruited five other aggressive litigators from Phoenix, including Larry Debus, who, like Hirsh, was listed in *Best Lawyers in America*.

As Hirsh saw it, the trial should be played like a straight criminal case. To him that meant, as he explained it, "if you have anything going for you emotionally, which we did in this case, that the jury would latch on to that. They would reward us for putting on a good show, and even though we might be a little bit guilty, it really wasn't a very, very bad thing that we did and we could be forgiven for putting on a good show. And that's how it works. I've been doing that for twenty-one years. You make the points, and they think, didn't the government do the wrong thing here, and isn't this kind of bad, and isn't it inappropriate for the government to do this? And that was our thinking, because we knew we were going to have a lot of problems with the judge and a lot of problems in being able to really get to the truth of what this case was all about."[12]

But problems developed with Hirsh's scheme almost immediately. Friction soon sprang up between some of the women defendants and the tough-talking attorneys. The latter took a no-nonsense, take-charge approach: This is a criminal trial, we're the best there is, sit back, and we'll get you off. Do you have a habit? Wear it in the courtroom and you'll never get convicted. And so on.

Darlene Nicgorski, especially, resented the macho, arrogant style. As she saw it, she was not a criminal, and she didn't need to be protected, especially by abrasive men who didn't know anything about sanctuary or Central America or female clergy. The nuns in her order hadn't worn habits in years; how were they supposed to live and work among the poor in headdresses and cumbersome robes that set them apart like relics from the Middle Ages? Darlene didn't want to pose as a meek and pious nun. She didn't want to be a client at all: she wanted to be her own advocate and openly declare her motives for her actions. She dropped the lawyer who had been assigned to her.[13]

Shortly after the indictments it became known that another of the nuns, Ana Priester, was seriously ill. Reno was already reconsidering the wisdom of including Priester and Mary Waddell in the indictments. They were bit players; some of the evidence he had cited against them was turning out to be false; and they were, after all, members of the order of the Sisters of Charity of the Blessed Virgin Mary, whose very charter was to help refugees. Reno dropped the charges against the two nuns. The two Hispanic women had already pleaded guilty in plea bargains, so, gradually, some of the local criminal lawyers dropped out of the case.

They were replaced by more politically sympathetic advocates. Altman, who was interested in the constitutional issues in the case, had impressed Darlene at meetings as being one of the few lawyers who laid out options for the defendants rather than tell them what was good for them. A supporter of the sanctuary movement, he had also made clear that he wanted to bring out the moral as well as the legal justification for sanctuary. She asked him to represent her.

Others volunteered to join the case. The National Lawyers Guild, a liberal/left organization, in 1984 had set up a network of members to help in sanctuary cases, and after the indictments several of its members contacted Hirsh and Butler and told them that they wanted to join the case. Hirsh was wary of the guild and its predilection for showcase political trials. He resisted, and by the time Ellen Yaroshefsky, the lawyer sent by the guild, had arrived from New York, all the defendants had been assigned lawyers. For a time Yaroshefsky, a smart, outspokenly radical woman in her late thirties, helped with pretrial motions, and eventually she replaced one of the local attorneys as Wendy LeWin's lawyer. As she put it, some of the defendants "wanted a woman on the case with a political perspective."[14]

Another guild lawyer with a political perspective was Nancy Grey Postero, an attractive young Tucson attorney who specialized in peace and justice work, including a case involving anti-cruise-missile protesters. Postero came to represent Mary K. Espinosa. William J. Risner, a veteran defender of radicals who, like Postero, spoke fluent Spanish, was asked by the Mexican consul, whom he represented, to defend Father Quiñones.

Jim Corbett ended up with another "cause lawyer," Stephen W.

Cooper, who had won an acquittal for Jack Elder in Corpus Christi, Texas, and a split decision in the Elder/Merkt trial in Houston. Cooper was based in St. Paul, Minnesota, where he headed the Neighborhood Justice Center, a nonprofit organization providing legal assistance for minorities.

The most experienced of the volunteers was James J. Brosnahan, a former assistant U.S. attorney and president of the Bar Association of San Francisco, who was head of litigation for the prestigious San Francisco firm of Morrison & Foerster. A tall, imposing man in his early fifties, Brosnahan was the son of a Boston Irishman who had worked for the Immigration Service in Maine and Galveston, Texas. The lawyer had tried more than 100 civil and criminal cases for his firm, including a successful defense of NBC, with Floyd Abrams of New York City, against a plaintiff who claimed that she had been brutally raped right after an NBC television show had depicted a similar attack. Brosnahan had a nationwide reputation as a topflight First Amendment lawyer.

A young associate of Brosnahan's, and a member of the National Lawyers Guild, Karen Snell, had assisted in the appeal in the Fifth Circuit of the Merkt conviction and had alerted her senior colleague to the issues involved in the sanctuary affair. When the indictments came down in Phoenix, he was outraged and told Snell that if the defense team needed any more help, he would be glad to talk to its members. The next thing he knew, he was in Tucson meeting with the attorneys, and shortly thereafter he found himself representing Doña María Socorro Aguilar. She took him to the jail in Nogales and introduced him to the inmates as the "great *abogado* [lawyer]" who was going to save her. He was moved.

Brosnahan and Snell, whose parents were neighbors of Judge Carroll's, were a major addition to the defense, for they brought with them the vast resources of Morrison & Foerster. The firm provided backup staff, prepared the dozens of motions introduced during the course of the trial, and enabled the defense to utilize the latest in courtroom techniques, including the staging of a mock trial and an expensive jury selection analysis. At one point in the pretrial period Brosnahan commented that "some people work on the side of money, and some on the side of the poor; you make your choice." His involvement made sure that the church workers, all people of modest means, had the best legal defense that money could buy.

Money was still clearly going to be a problem for the defense, however. None of the defendants, save Kathy Flaherty, had enough income to pay for his or her own defense. They qualified for court-appointed counsel, and Tom Hoidal of the Federal Public Defenders Office in Phoenix took the case of Nena MacDonald. The others would have to have attorneys who were on the list of public defenders, but one of Judge Carroll's first moves was to rule that none of their attorneys could be put on the panel. Only Postero and Walker were already qualified, so that left nine lawyers who somehow had to be paid. They all had agreed to work for the public defender rates of $40 for hours out of court and $60 for hours spent in court. This represented an enormous financial sacrifice for most of them; lawyers like Brosnahan normally charged $250 an hour.

A National Sanctuary Defense Fund had been established to raise money for the Texas trials. After the multiple indictments in Arizona the organization began to gear up for the task of raising what might amount to more than $1 million to defend the latest charges. And it did, from churches, foundations, and small individual contributors.[15]

The prosecution, of course, had the printing presses of the U.S. Treasury and American taxpayers to draw upon. In a speech before the Presbytery de Cristo, the governing body of the church for southern Arizona and southwestern New Mexico, shortly after the indictments were handed down, Bates Butler challenged that particular choice of expenditures.

"Whether you agree or disagree with the sanctuary movement, whether you are a liberal or a conservative, a Democrat or a Republican, you've got to wonder, especially with the budget crisis that we have in this country, whether destroying the sanctuary movement is how we want our tax dollars spent," he said. "To mount a ten-month undercover operation, as was mounted here, costs hundreds of thousands of dollars. And the two thousand to three thousand people who have been assisted by the sanctuary movement are so few compared to the numbers of people who cross our southern borders every week."[16]

Butler said that he, for one, had never believed that the government would use undercover agents in churches unless those organizations were engaged in violence, such as blowing up buildings in the name of religion. The government itself had consistently said that the sanctuary movement was a low priority, that it had better things to do with its time and money. Like everyone else involved in the case, Butler asked himself again and again why the authorities had decided to eradicate the movement.

Later, as more evidence about the government's motives came out, he decided that the "real reason" behind the prosecution was clear. "It was to silence the churches," he told the 197th General Assembly of the Presbyterian Church. "It was to stop criticism of U.S. actions in Central America by Christians."[17]

Chapter
Twenty-three

DON RENO HAD a strategy about how to prosecute the sanctuary activists. As a former criminal defense attorney facing almost a dozen of his own kind across the courtroom, he thought he knew what his opponents would try to do. He would just have to prevent them from doing it.

In defending anyone, whether a pornographer or an alien smuggler, a good attorney will constantly try to get before the jury collateral matters that have nothing to do with the criminal conduct itself but that cast the accused in a sympathetic light. This might be called the "Forget I shot him, and think about what a good guy I am" approach.

A good defense will also divert attention from the specifics of the alleged criminal action to the broader societal issues involved. Thus, when defending the exhibitor of a porno film, Reno would try to steer the jury away from the sexually explicit material toward the question of whether the public has a right to walk into a theater and see what it wants to see. In his obscenity cases he always tried to make the issue the right of an individual to read or see anything he or she chooses and the right to purchase those materials. The more he could get the jury to focus on those basic rights, the better chance he had of an acquittal.

Reno saw no difference in the sanctuary case. He well knew that the underlying issue was the history of the United States as a last haven for the oppressed, the powerful tradition of the Pilgrims, the Statue of Liberty, and Ellis Island, and the right of Americans to uphold that tradition as part of their faith. He well knew that if the trial got into discussions of refugee policy and definitions of what a refugee was or what religious freedom was, he'd be a certified loser.[1]

His first task, then, as he saw it, was to convince the judge to see the case at its simplest level: Did these people engage in a conspiracy to smuggle aliens into the country? He had to curtail seriously what the defense could say in the courtroom or, he feared, he would have a fiasco on his hands.

The same day the indictments were made public, Reno filed a motion *in limine,* a motion to preclude the defense from introducing certain issues and evidence into the trial. In the motion, he listed everything he could that might exonerate the sanctuary workers—everything that he would want to talk about if he were defending them.

Specifically Reno asked the judge to preclude the following arguments as defenses:

> *1. That the Refugee Act of 1980, or any international document or organization (e.g., Geneva Convention, Helsinki Accords, the United Nations), confers asylum/refugee status upon any of the illegal aliens/unindicted co-conspirators named in the indictment.*
>
> *2. That the defendants' conduct was justified as a result of their religious beliefs.*
>
> *3. That the defendants had good motives and beliefs which negated any criminal intent to violate the laws as charged in the indictment.*
>
> *4. That the defendants were compelled to violate the law out of necessity.* [2]

Reno's motion *in limine* further asked the judge to bar any mention or evidence in the courtroom of the following issues or subjects:

> *1. That the aliens whom the defendants have (at any time) unlawfully transported, harbored, or brought into the United States are "refugees" or "asylees."*

2. That any past or present policy of the United States and/or the current Administration regarding its foreign policy of financial or military aid (or lack thereof) to any Central American countries, and particularly El Salvador, is immoral or violates some international law. Included within this restriction would be any reference to the Department of State, Central Intelligence Agency, Department of Defense, or any other federal agencies or international organizations associated therewith.

3. Any alleged episodes, stories, or tales of civil strife, war, or terrorism that may have occurred or are occurring in Central American countries, and particularly El Salvador. . . .

4. The number of aliens from Central America who have applied for, and have been granted or denied, asylum status. . . .

5. Past or present policies regarding the granting or denying of refugee/asylum status to aliens from any countries seeking to enter the United States, either communist-dominated governments or countries undergoing a socialist or communistic revolution.

6. The impact that a guilty verdict involving the defendants in this indictment would have upon . . . Central Americans applying for immigration status under the Immigration [and] Nationality Act.

7. Amnesty or extended voluntary departure regarding El Salvadorans and/or the illegal aliens-unindicted co-conspirators in the indictment. [3]

Reno didn't think that the judge would go along with all these restrictions—they were his ultimate wish list—but he did believe that he had a shot at narrowing the issues that would be discussed. Just to reinforce his argument, he attached to his motion a copy of *Basta!*, containing articles about the indictments. In that issue the Chicago group declared its intention to turn the upcoming trial into a political event, an opportunity to make a political statement and educate the country about the abuses taking place in Central America. The judge and the defense attorneys won't control the proceedings; we will, the *Basta!* writers promised.

We'll see, thought Reno. Not if I know Judge Earl Carroll.

Reno's sweeping motion *in limine* had stunned the defense. The lawyers realized that if it were successful, it would rob the sanctuary workers of any possibility of explaining and justifying their actions in court. Within a matter of weeks the defense team countered with a barrage of major motions—fifteen in all—challenging Reno's motion and seeking to have the case dismissed altogether.

A central line of defense was the sanctuary workers' claim that the Central Americans they were accused of smuggling, transporting, harboring, and concealing qualified as political refugees under the Refugee Act of 1980 and the 1967 United Nations Protocol Relating to the Status of Refugees, which the United States had signed. By that argument, the sanctuary workers were acting in accord with U.S. and international law, and the INS, by trying to deport those people, was not.

One of the defense's first moves, then, was to file a motion to dismiss the indictments on the ground that the acts named in the indictment were in fact legal. The motion argued that the international law is the "law of the land," directly incorporated into U.S. law. "Customary international law norms" prohibit forced repatriation of people fleeing armed conflict, argued the motion, written by Paul Hoffman of the ACLU in Los Angeles, and international refugee law prohibits the forced return of refugees to their countries of origin if they face danger of persecution. Because the defendants all knew and believed that there was civil war and gross violation of human rights in El Salvador and in Guatemala, and that the people they were assisting were fleeing such circumstances, the Geneva conventions and international law required them to act as they did.

In a related motion the defendants argued that they had believed that all the Central Americans they assisted were refugees under the definition of the 1980 Refugee Act—the well-founded fear of persecution definition—and that therefore, they believed that their actions were legal.

In other early motions the defense took a different tack, arguing that the defendants' acts were "justified" and were therefore not illegal, even if committed. Under the legal concept of justification, acts committed out of self-defense, duress, or necessity are not illegal. The defendants argued that their acts had been necessary to prevent greater harm to the refugees assisted. This defense required the court to weigh the harm caused by the criminal act against the harm sought to be prevented. The defendants maintained that they had pursued every reasonable alternative to their actions and found that they were necessary in order to prevent serious danger to the refugees.

The sanctuary workers also claimed to have been implementing the principles laid down at the Nuremberg trials. Since World War II various legal scholars had developed a theory of civilian resistance, or civilian initiative, by which citizens were legally obligated to disobey government officials rather than collaborate in official crimes. Jim Corbett had written extensively in favor of this principle of "civilian human rights initiative." The defendants were justified, their lawyers maintained, by a recognized humanitarian exception to the criminal statutes under which they had been charged.

Finally, the defense attorneys presented a motion to dismiss based on their First Amendment right to free exercise of religion. In this argument the defendants maintained that they were motivated by their sincerely held religious belief that it was their duty to help the stranger. Hundreds of ministers in countless sermons had quoted the verse from Matthew: "For I was hungry, and you gave me meat. I was thirsty and you gave me drink. I was a stranger and you took me in." The defendants had followed that biblical injunction as part of their faith, and their acts, they claimed, were protected by their constitutional right to practice their religion. (In practice the courts have ruled that the individual's religious rights must be balanced against the government's compelling interest in prosecuting particular individuals. Thus the defense motion argued that in this case the defendants' First Amendment rights outweighed the government's interest in prosecuting the sanctuary workers.)

Meanwhile, while the judge pondered this first flurry of motions, the defense team went to work on what it knew would be one of its most critical tasks: undermining the credibility of the men who would be the state's key witnesses, Jesus Cruz and Salomon Graham. A massive search began for information that would throw into question the character and truthfulness of the two Mexicans. The digging yielded pay dirt beyond the lawyers' wildest dreams and gave Don Reno, who admittedly had asked too few questions about the informants' past, a series of very unpleasant surprises.

Salomon Graham, it appeared, had engaged in activities that looked suspiciously like pimping. The defense produced numerous affidavits from farm workers stating that since the late 1970s, while he was working for the government, Graham had brought women out to the orchards to have sex with the field hands for money.

The most descriptive affidavit was from a woman named Eva Campbell, who said she had been a bartender at the El Sombrero Bar in El

Mirage, Arizona, near the citrus groves. From about mid-August through November 1979, Campbell swore, Graham sometimes gave her and two other girls rides to various places where farm workers were staying "so that we could work as prostitutes to earn extra money to support ourselves." She went on:

> He would say things to us like "If you girls need a ride, I can give you one"; "If you girls need some money, I know where you can make some"; and "If I bring some guys over, will you girls still be here?" There might have been times when he took three of us at one time; sometimes two of us. We all got in the car. The guys out at the ranches wanted a girl. If they lived in the trees, Delgado took us to the trees. If they lived in a house, he took us to a house. At various times Delgado took us to be with the men at Arrowhead Ranch, Martori Ranch, and Tal Wi Wi, where they grow Sunkist Oranges. . . .
>
> Although I didn't give Delgado any money for taking us to the various places, sometimes I would buy him some gas or buy the beer. There would be anywhere from thirty to ten guys each time and I would usually charge them anywhere from $15 to $20 each.
>
> Delgado seemed like an alright [sic] guy. He drank with everyone and seemed like just one of the guys. He has a medium build, dark hair, brown eyes and he had a mustache. He dressed mostly in work clothes and wore boots and a cowboy hat. I believe he was in his late thirties or early forties. He always drank a lot but he doesn't dance very good.
>
> At the end of November of 1979 I was sent to prison for a drug-related charge. At that time, I quit my job at the bar and moved away from El Mirage. After my release from prison, I went to Superior, Arizona, until about three years ago when I returned to El Mirage. I now have a baby and spend most of my time working and taking care of my child so I do not go to the bar and party much any more. [4]

Don Reno called Graham in for a little chat about this aspect of his private life. Graham assured him that he had only done the girls a favor but denied having acted "in the capacity of a broker," as Reno put it. Jim Rayburn went out to the migrant workers' camp to check out the story and was told, he said later, that Graham was not a full-fledged pimp but had given women he had met in bars rides out to the camp, waited while they went about their business, and driven them back.[5]

After hearing that, it didn't take Don Reno long to decide that he would be wise not to put Salomon Graham on the witness stand.

The next revelations had to do with Reno's star witness, Jesus Cruz. The prosecutor had spent hundreds of hours with Cruz preparing for the trial, and he had painstakingly reconstructed much of the man's past from the interviews. He had concluded that Cruz was "the cleanest and most holy of a rather unholy set" and was so sure that Cruz was relatively innocuous that when Victor Rostow, during a visit to Phoenix, had asked about his criminal record, Reno had assured him that the informant had none. Shortly thereafter, Reno called Rostow and corrected himself, explaining that Rayburn had just informed him that Cruz had a history of arrests for alien smuggling (all of which were clearly spelled out on Cruz's "A" file).

Nor was Reno aware, as the defense charged with much fanfare in the courtroom, that while on the government payroll, Jesus Cruz had apparently been violating federal gun laws. On numerous occasions after he had become a government informant, the attorneys claimed, Cruz had taken money from farm workers to drive them from the fields near Glendale, Arizona, to the Jewel Box, a gun and pawnshop in Phoenix. Cruz then served as an interpreter to help them buy guns.

Judge Carroll quickly ruled that this explosive allegation was not to reach the jurors' ears, forcing the defense to bury it in an offer of proof.*

As if that were not enough bad news about its witnesses, the government also had a problem with its chief investigator. In lengthy pretrial testimony Jim Rayburn had seemed to have an ideological ax to grind, and Reno was afraid that his obvious distaste for the defendants would crucify him.

In one exchange Rayburn had said that Cruz described the songs sung at the Alzona Bible study classes as "revolutionary" or "protest" songs, prompting Judge Carroll to remark that the man "would have thought the Battle Hymn of the Republic was a protest song."

The chief investigator had also made it clear that unlike his superiors in Washington, he fully expected and wanted the defendants' political

---

*An offer of proof is a statement made for the appellate court of the evidence that the jury would have heard if the judge had ruled it admissable. The implication is that if the judge had not made a mistake of law in excluding it, this evidence might have changed the course of the trial.

views and motives to become an issue in the trial.[6] This was a view he shared, ironically, only with Sister Nicgorski, who was eager for a full-scale political trial. The defense attorneys recoiled at the prospect, for fear of muddying the defendants' purely good Samaritan image, while the government was anxious to avoid any appearance that it was prosecuting dissenters for political purposes. The defense was already seeking to prove that the sanctuary workers had been singled out for prosecution by the conservative Reagan administration, and Rayburn's anticommunism would only make it look even more as if the government were out to "get" them.

During his pretrial testimony Rayburn had also been forced to concede a number of irregularities in the investigation. The government had technically violated its own undercover guidelines by taping a telephone conversation between Cruz and Bertha Benavidez and sending Cruz to Mexico to meet Quiñones before the undercover review committee had even met. The guidelines provided that "undercover operations involving sensitive circumstances *must receive prior approval* of the Commissioner of the I.N.S. . . . ." "Sensitive circumstances" were expressly stated to include "activities of a religious or political organization." In pretrial testimony Rayburn admitted that he had not received that necessary authorization.[7] (Don Reno later dismissed these transgressions by noting that the guidelines were not codified and didn't have the force of law.)

Then there was a question of entrapment, involving the nine Guatemalans Rayburn had allowed Cruz to mention to Quiñones, in an effort to lure the priest into smuggling them into the United States. Entrapment was expressly prohibited by the guidelines. The defense argued that these transgressions in toto gave rise to violations of due process and invasions of privacy. Taken all together, these problems led Reno to conclude that it would probably be wise not to put Jim Rayburn on the stand.

Operation Sojourner was not the first time that the U.S. government used paid informers to infiltrate churches. In the 1960s the FBI had sent informants into services conducted by Dr. Martin Luther King. But the sanctuary case was the first in which such infiltration was litigated in federal court.

Both the government and the defense agreed that since there were no precedents, there were no cases directly on point of whether surreptitious monitoring of church services was lawful or unlawful. From the standpoint of the constitutional separation of church and state, the heart of the matter was what authority is to determine when a meeting in a church is a protected worship service or a political gathering.

The prosecution held that the meetings the informants had attended were not religious. In pretrial testimony Jim Rayburn said that he had told Cruz not to tape "church services or prayer services, things like that. And I briefly discussed what type of services I was talking about."

Judge Carroll then asked: "What services did you tell him not to tape record?"

A. Masses, any church service. That type of thing. . . .

Q. You knew that Mr. Cruz was going to Alzona Bible Studies at the Alzona Lutheran Church?

A. The way that was described to me, it was not described to me as a Bible study. . . .

Q. But Mr. Cruz in fact went in Alzona church on those meetings with a body bug on him, didn't he?

A. On one occasion. We discussed it beforehand and I approved it. [8]

Don Reno supported this flat denial that anything religious had been monitored. He argued that neither the First nor the Fourth Amendment prohibits the "utilization of informants to 'infiltrate' criminal activity, regardless of the nature or the locus of the illicit enterprise." He maintained that only one of the ninety-one tapes recorded by the government "remotely" suggested that a religious event was under way. And that tape "relates to the October 1, 1984 'presentment' of an illegal alien espousing his socio-political opinions. . . ."

In his reply to defense motions to dismiss, Reno wrote: "Parenthetically, it should be noted that this event was part of a highly publicized 'sanctuary caravan' that was to depart Phoenix the following day with illegal aliens from Central America. The 'presentment' of the alien at this 'religious service' was intended to draw media attention to the forthcoming caravan and the political issues advanced by the 'sanctuary' movement."[9]

When religious adherents gather in a public setting, where members of the public can listen and attend, that activity is not protected by the First Amendment, he maintained.

The problem with this line, wrote Ellen Yaroshefsky, arguing the defense position, "is that it assumes that the state has the power to determine what is religious. That is not the law. The law is that if a minister says 'We are having a worship service,' and the assumption of the pastor is that this is a religious activity, then . . . the state cannot come in and say this is not a protected activity."[10]

If religious adherents cannot seek confidential counseling or gather together in mutual trust without fear of government monitoring, the defense argued, the very heart of religion has been violated by the state.

There was no doubt that the government's tactics had indeed had a chilling effect on the practice of worship in the churches that had been investigated. The Reverend Oines testified in pretrial hearings that the Alzona Bible study class had been destroyed. In welcoming Cruz into the circle, Oines ruefully noted "we were as gentle as doves but maybe not as wise as serpents."[11] The minister was referring to Jesus' injunction to the early Christian missionaries. They were told to "unite the wisdom of the serpent with the innocence of the dove" (Matthew 10:16).

Later, during a conversation in his small office at Alzona Lutheran, Oines reiterated that the Bible study meetings were "one of the most authentic expressions of 'church' I've ever seen, and the government has completely destroyed it. Religion is not to be a tool of the government. The government can't say if religion doesn't do what we want it to do, then we'll try to control it."[12]

Eugene LeFebvre, the pastor of Sunrise Presbyterian Church, which shared facilities with Camelback and participated in the October 1 prayer service, testified in pretrial hearings that his parishioners too were shocked, outraged, and intimidated by the government's actions. One woman who had taken part in the service, but who was not involved in the sanctuary movement, told LeFebvre that she was a schoolteacher and was now worried that her name might be on file with the FBI. She was afraid that at some point, when she looked for another job, her record might affect her chances for employment.

LeFebvre also told the court that another woman, whom the pastor counseled occasionally on the telephone, had recently told him that she did not want to talk to him on the phone anymore because the line might be tapped.[13]

According to Gerald Roseberry, the pastor of Camelback, one of the worst consequences of the infiltration was the effect it had had on the ministers themselves and their ability to embrace the newcomer. Since they had learned about the infiltrations, Roseberry and several ministers in Tucson noticed a new wariness and suspicion within themselves toward members of their own congregations.

"We had a young adult come in, a man, and my first reaction was, What is he doing here?" Roseberry said during an interview a year later. "We have another—a woman—and I'm as suspicious as hell of her. She's from an evangelical background and asks funny questions.

"You know, freedom of religion wasn't something that just happened, that arrived gift-wrapped," Roseberry continued. "It was hard won; people had to struggle for it. We don't want the government to say you can worship in this way but not that way; you can't include certain people or address certain themes. Yet that is what happened. The government sent untrained, uneducated, uninformed agents into churches and put them in the position of defining what religion is. Cruz and Graham reported to Jim Rayburn that we were conducting a political rally."[14]

This was one of the means by which the governments of Czechoslovakia and the Soviet Union, and of Nazi Germany undermined the open practice of religion in those countries, Dean Philip Wogaman, a professor of Christian ethics at the Wesley Theological Seminary in Washington, D.C., pointed out. "Such conduct simply cannot be sanctioned in this country. Our Constitution and our people demand more of our government than this," declared the Methodist theologian.[15]*

These were powerful arguments, and Reno took them head-on:

It is truly unfortunate that the defendants have sullied the historical respect that the government and our society has [sic] had for churches as an American institution, free from association from criminal behavior. However, the government's historical sensitivity to purposely avoiding any semblance of an interest in monitoring church activity does not mean that criminal enterprises become sacrosanct when they operate in churches. Our Constitution does not protect criminal activity performed in the name of religion. [16]

On May 23, at the conclusion of the pretrial hearing on the defense's motion to dismiss the case on the ground of outrageous government

---

*Wogaman was planning to testify a second day on the infiltration, but Judge Carroll refused to allow it. "What could he add that he hasn't already said?" Carroll commented. "What could he say that the average person off the street couldn't say?" Wogaman found Carroll's attitude, implying that a court need not take into cognizance the views of theologians on matters of religious liberty, "an outrage."

conduct, Judge Carroll volunteered his response to what he had heard and read:

Let me just say, regardless of how I rule . . . as a matter of personal observation, and I am sure that there is no one here or generally that is comfortable with the concept of the government going into many places and many associations . . . there should be little occasion or reason or opportunity for the government to send people, let's say, paid to do it, and wired to do it, into places of religious interest or concern, no more than they should feel compelled, as a general practice, to do it in a judge's office, or a senator's office, or any other citizen of this state—of this country. That is what the Constitution really tells us.

In deciding in this particular instance whether or not it is outrageous or sufficiently outrageous to dismiss the action, because after all when you dismiss the action you not only favor, in a sense, particular people who benefit by that ruling, but you also take actions which affect the public, generally, regarding what they have a right to expect of the courts or the government or our system of justice.

. . . I would think it clear to me, that what has occurred here, without having read all the tapes, but heard some of the discussion, that undoubtedly everything that was learned through that effort could have been otherwise determined, would have been otherwise determined.

It was inevitable, based upon the history of these defendants, that I think, almost without exception, they want to be discovered. They want to be known. They want to be identified. They wanted to be leaders.

And it is truly unfortunate that the whole process is sullied, in a sense, by the informers and the recordings.

So that is at least my general feelings on the subject and how I rule, of course, necessarily depends upon the additional information I get, but I would not encourage the government to regard this, however I rule, as any kind of approbation to them for having done it. [17]

A month later Judge Carroll denied the defense motions to dismiss on the grounds of the government's conduct.

Chapter
Twenty-four

B Y LATE JUNE the judge had ruled against all of the defense's most important motions. He denied that the state's tactics violated the First Amendment guarantee of the free exercise of religion. He denied they violated the Fourth Amendment, against unreasonable search and seizure, because no law requires a search warrant for clandestine monitoring in a criminal investigation. He found the government's conduct "unacceptable but not outrageous" and therefore not a violation of the due process clause of the Fifth Amendment. He refused to dismiss on the ground of international law. And he ruled that the defense could not introduce details of the violence in Central America in evidence.

The prosecution might have been having witness problems, but the sanctuary workers were slowly being denied a defense at all.

Then, on June 25, the court heard arguments on whether "necessity" could be a defense, the rather practical question of whether there had been a reasonable legal alternative to the defendants' actions. The defense wanted the jury to hear evidence on whether the available alternatives were reasonable or not.

For example, why hadn't the defendants encouraged Central American refugees in Mexico to apply for asylum en masse at the border?

The defense lawyers wanted to answer that question with an affidavit from a refugee and asylum expert at Harvard Law School. Her statement asserted inter alia that "applying for asylum at the Mexican border is not a reasonable legal alternative, given the practice of adjudication without interviewing, exclusion without a hearing, the institutional prejudgment of such claims apparent from the available statistics and the credibility problems which appear to be insurmountable, particularly given the lack of availability of trained U.S. counsel in the border areas, let alone inside Mexico itself compounded by the reported dangers to a Central American of safely remaining in Mexico during this process."[1]

Another question repeatedly put to the sanctuary activists was why they hadn't instructed their refugees to apply for asylum with the INS once they were safely in the country. Then, by law, they couldn't be deported until the lengthy appeals process had been exhausted.

In response the defense wanted to introduce evidence about the arrest and detention of applicants, the fact that families were separated and held in penal facilities with minimal access to legal assistance or opportunity to coordinate their asylum requests. They wanted to tell the jury that 97 or 98 percent of the Salvadorans and Guatemalans who did go to the INS were eventually denied asylum. And they wanted refugees to testify that they believed that if they turned themselves in to the Immigration Service, it might communicate information to their own governments that would endanger them if they were returned. (Allegations that this did indeed occur had surfaced; see Appendix II.)

Judge Carroll pressed the defense lawyers on why there hadn't been more lawsuits challenging INS procedures at the border and in the various detention centers. Paul Hoffman tried to explain that several cases of that sort had been filed but that most of them had not yet been resolved. "Every attempt has been made to try and organize and finance and bring this kind of litigation and it is very difficult," he told the court.

Carroll seemed sympathetic. "I know there is considerable complaint . . ." he lectured Reno, "and I would certainly again encourage the I.N.S., as you represent them here, to concern themselves with . . . all of those matters, because they contribute, if nothing else, to the dissatisfaction with the system and the excuse, if it be such, to avoid that system and go someplace else, go some other way. And I would— as you appear here for the I.N.S., I would certainly encourage you to look at it.

"Have you been to El Centro, for example?"

"No, Your Honor. I'm not representing the I.N.S. I am representing the Government," Reno responded.

"The I.N.S. is all a part of the Government. I don't view the Government as being different things. . . . You are here for the I.N.S., all those good folks," the judge said.

"I am here to prosecute a case, Your Honor. I have my hands full with that. And to get involved in a civil proceeding is beyond my capability," Reno replied.

"We should all try to improve the system as we go along," answered Carroll, like a schoolmaster administering a rap on the wrist with his ruler.

A few minutes after admonishing the prosecutor, Judge Carroll again ruled against the defendants.

". . . our country recognizes that there is the I.N.S. process, and to the extent that that process is disinterested, perfunctory, badly handled, failing in due process characteristics, then it seems to me that that can be questioned, and can be questioned directly, and perhaps could have been and should have been long since questioned," he said.

Yet Carroll reminded his audience that there is a long appeals process available to anyone seeking refugee status. "To suggest that these defendants or any other individuals, no matter how well motivated, as a matter of necessity or dissatisfaction with that process, can set themselves up as immigration officers and determine the status of these people is, I believe, improper. . . .

"I don't find here any basis for a defense of duress, necessity, or futility. . . . So, accordingly, with respect to this issue, I will grant the Government's Motion in Limine as to this being a defense."[2]

A month later, on July 25, Carroll swung his ax against the defense again. Sanctuary, he ruled, is not a religious ministry and therefore not exempt from prosecution under the Bill of Rights. In a lone ruling favoring the defense, he did agree to permit testimony that the defendants did not have specific *intent* to violate U.S. immigration laws. He ruled that a "mistake of law" was not a defense, but that a "good faith" misunderstanding of the law was. This meant that the defense could argue that it did not intend to break the law, because, for example, it believed it could present the refugees to the INS at a reasonable later date.

Aside from that small victory, the defense by midsummer had been stripped of its central arguments. The most important part of the trial was over before the proceedings had begun. All evidence on the 1980 Refugee Act and international law had been barred. Religious and humanitarian motives were irrelevant. The government's treatment of the refugees was irrelevant, despite the fact that in the *Orontes* case, Ninth Circuit Court Judge David Kenyon had found that the INS "engages in widespread illegality, so widespread that it is not a matter of individual misconduct but a broad systematic process." Distinguished witnesses such as Aryeh Neier, the vice-chairman of Americas Watch, which monitored the human rights situation in the Western Hemisphere, had flown into Tucson to testify on conditions in Central America and been sent home before they could utter a word. Judge Earl Carroll had essentially bought the U.S. government argument that this was a simple alien-smuggling case, a cut-and-dried matter of whether the immigration laws had been violated.

If *United States of America* v. *María del Socorro Pardo de Aguilar et al.* was an ordinary criminal case, María Socorro Aguilar *et al.* were extraordinary criminals. If not martyrs, they were men and women of passionate conviction, and the series of setbacks in the courtroom, if anything, strengthened their determination. As the rulings rolled in against them, Don Reno called for a meeting with defense attorneys Butler, Hirsh, and Altman. He was prepared to offer their clients a deal, he said, approved by the Justice Department in Washington. The government would give all the defendants the opportunity to plead guilty to a misdemeanor and receive a six months' suspended sentence and probation of five years. If they refused, he said, he would ask for a three-year sentence for Jim Corbett and four to six years for Fife and Nicgorski (who had not even been charged with smuggling anyone into the United States). Reno added that because of his earlier arrest, Phil Conger would also be sure to get time from Judge Carroll if he were convicted.

The lawyers dutifully relayed the offer, and the sanctuary workers became, no doubt, the first alien smugglers on record to throw a plea bargain back in the government's face. Reno's carrot and stick drew only sarcasm and anger.

Michael Altman, Nicgorski's lawyer, dashed off an angry letter to the prosecutor:

I have discussed your plea offer with Sister Darlene. She immediately rejected your offer saying she could not possibly plead guilty: she is innocent, her actions were actions of her religious ministry and

*she has always believed her conduct was lawful under the Refugee
Act of 1980 and International Law.*

*Sister Darlene instructed me to advise you that it has been a soul
searching experience for her to come to terms with the fact that the
United States Government would ask for a five year prison sentence
for helping to save the lives of refugees.* [3]

Despite having agreed not to violate federal or state laws pending
their trial, several of the defendants were also continuing to help refugees into the country. "Our clients will need to anticipate the following question," one confidential defense memo warned. "Have you
brought anyone in since the indictment?" The lawyers worried that
some of the defendants might have to take the Fifth Amendment.

For their part, the defendants wanted to argue that far from their
having any intent to break the law, their actions actually upheld the
1980 Refugee Act. They believed that their stand was no less than that
of Henry David Thoreau regarding the Fugitive Slave Law: "They are
the lovers of law and order who uphold the law when the government
breaks it."

This was hard to claim, however, in the face of flat statements to the
contrary out of Chicago.

Despite the Arizona defendants' claim that they were defending good
laws that the Reagan administration was flouting, the publications of
the Chicago Religious Task Force on Central America persisted in
describing sanctuary as civil disobedience directed against unjust laws.
As Jim Corbett put it, that was not only false but like plea bargaining
without any bargain.

The CRTFCA was also persisting in its efforts to "nationalize" the
sanctuary movement. The task force had been instrumental in forming
something called the National Sanctuary Movement, with a National
Sanctuary Communications Council. The NSM and the NSCC were
allied with the National Sanctuary Defense Fund, an independent
board set up the previous year to raise money for the defense of indicted
sanctuary workers in Texas and later Arizona. These organizations
were now acting in the name of the "sanctuary movement."

The NSDF had sent out a fund-raising appeal to 450,000 prospective
individual donors, hired a public relations agency from the East Coast
to represent the movement, and prepared a slick press packet on sanctuary that took considerable initiative in defining what the movement

was. In fact, the packet came close to being a disaster because of an article it contained discussing sanctuary as a civil disobedience movement, written by Renny Golden and Michael McConnell. Only at the last minute was the pamphlet prevented from being sent out around the country.

The National Sanctuary Communications Council had also sent out a set of policy proposals that came to be called the Chicago Creed, which described sanctuary as a means of ending American intervention in Central America. The implication—that the national grass-roots movement was primarily political—seriously undermined the Arizona activists' legal position that they were exercising their First Amendment right to carry out their religious ministry. The INS was actually using the Chicago Creed as a way of discrediting the defendants' claim that they acted out of humanitarian motives.

In short, as Corbett and some of the defendants saw it, the hard-line ideologues in the Chicago Religious Task Force were acting like mirror images of the Reagan administration. Indeed, one sanctuary supporter even raised the question of whether Chicago might have been infiltrated by a government provocateur.

The end of the summer brought another unsettling straw in the wind. On August 17 an elaborate rehearsal of the trial was staged at the sun-baked campus of Arizona State University's College of Law in Tempe, an affluent suburb of Phoenix. More than seven defense lawyers, defendants Fife, Willis-Conger, Nicgorski, and Socorro Aguilar, and a panel of jurors randomly selected from the community attended the daylong event. Bob Hirsh played the part of the prosecutor, and Larry Debus played his old nemesis Judge Carroll.

The defense presented its side with a worst-case scenario: that it would be sharply limited in the type of evidence it could introduce. After hearing all the arguments, a majority of the jurors voted to convict.

In an analysis of the outcome of the mock trial, Mike Altman noted that on the plus side, the jury had had a hard time believing that anything as open as the sanctuary movement could really be a conspiracy or that the defendants had really induced illegals to enter the United States. Either they were planning to enter anyway or Jesus Cruz had done the inducing.

On the other hand, the jurors seemed to have been offended by the notion that anyone could be above the law, whatever his or her motives or religious convictions. They kept saying, "You have to go by the law," and, "We shouldn't be moved by emotion." Some were even put off by the defense's emotional appeals (prompting Altman, who had been moved to tears by one argument, to comment, "Phoenix jurors are apparently tough nuts").

Intent, interestingly, was not an issue. How could anyone think he was acting legally when he was showing someone a hole in the fence, one juror commented, and that ended the discussion.

The defense had been able to show, as Altman put it, that "Jesus Cruz was a slime bag." But the jury had paid no attention to that in its deliberations. Refugees had been flown in to testify and got some of their frightful stories into the record. It didn't help. The jury thought Darlene was remote and cold: sincerely religious and well intentioned, but a tough-minded person engaged in civil disobedience. Phil's sincere admissions that he had helped people across the border hurt him. Few could understand Socorro Aguilar and why she was involved, unless it was for money. And the jury didn't trust Fife; there was something about him.

"The prescription for the future is clear," Altman concluded. "All we need to win is a jury that is not a cross section of the community, a much better story from our clients and several new defenses."[4]

At the end of the summer the defense had its first good news in months. Judge Carroll agreed to a request to move the venue of the trial from Phoenix to Tucson. The change had been requested on the ground that the smaller city was more convenient; among other things, the defendants from Nogales had to commute three hours from the border to Phoenix every day.

The real significance of the shift, however, was the prospect of a friendlier jury in Tucson, and to test that hypothesis, the lawyers staged a second mock trial in September with two Tucson juries.

This time Jim Brosnahan played the part of the prosecutor, and Hirsh, Yaroshefsky, and William Walker, a balding, slightly disheveled man in his forties, acted as the defense attorneys. John Fife was put on the stand. Once again one of the juries voted to convict. A majority on the other jury voted to acquit, but several people argued strongly for conviction.

The lawyers watched the juries deliberating on closed-circuit television. To their surprise, the jurors didn't particularly like Fife; they found him too smug. And like their counterparts in Phoenix, the supposedly friendlier Tucson jurors agreed that "these are nice people, but they admitted they did it."

Brosnahan found that given Judge Carroll's rulings, playing the role of the prosecutor was frighteningly easy. All the government had to do, once a defendant was on the stand, was ask, "Is it true you helped so-and-so across the border?"; "Is it true you intended to get so-and-so into the United States?"; "Is it true you transported them here and there?" and all the witnesses could say was yes.

The lawyers concluded that they absolutely had to have jurors who already sympathized with the sanctuary movement, who needed only a good reason or two to act on their basic instincts. Thus jury selection became their immediate focus when the case of the *United States of America* v. *María del Socorro Pardo de Aguilar et al.* opened for trial on October 22, 1985, in the Federal Courthouse in downtown Tucson.

Chapter
Twenty-five

THE SQUARE YELLOW-STONE Federal Courthouse in Tucson
sits roughly between the modern office towers and airy plazas of
the new part of the city and the old downtown, with its five-and-ten-
cent stores, one-story shops, and the funky old Congress Hotel, a
historic establishment with an aging buffalo head mounted over the
front desk. A few blocks away to the north is what remains of the old
colonial city, an area of low whitewashed adobe buildings now filled
with art galleries, Mexican restaurants, government buildings, and professional offices.

Down the street from the courthouse a vegetarian café, its walls
plastered with notices of upcoming cultural events, opens at seven in
the morning, and on the morning the trial started, spectators began
what became a habit of grabbing a fresh orange juice and pastry before
the day's proceedings began. The defendants and their attorneys began
the day with a prayer breakfast, a morale-builder that became a routine
during the trial. Judge Carroll, for his part, had set up residence at the
Santa Rita Hotel, just across the street from the courthouse, where he
usually dined in lonely comfort.

By the time the trial started the sanctuary case had become celebrated, and on that first day, as on many more to come, a long line of
people formed outside the building, waiting to get seats in the small
first-floor courtroom where the proceedings were to be held. A couple
of blocks away, in a Spanish-style office plaza, the defendants had set
up a bustling media office to get their story out, and it was already busy
issuing press releases, scheduling interviews, and answering queries
from the horde of journalists and sympathizers in town for the show.
If the trial wasn't quite a circus, as some in government had feared, it
most definitely qualified as a major media event.

Few of the spectators realized, as they entered the courthouse, that
one of the federal marshals inspecting their belongings at the door was
none other than Leon Ring, the former Border Patrol officer who had
first monitored the sanctuary ministers' activities. Months later, over
a cup of coffee at the Santa Rita Hotel, Ring, a tall, handsome man who
had taken early retirement from the INS, confided his belief that "this
[the trial] never would have happened if the Democrats had been in
office."[1]

Of the original sixteen people indicted, only eleven appeared in the
dock to stand trial. Charges against four had been dropped, and two
weeks before the trial began Katherine Flaherty had decided belatedly
to accept the plea bargain offered by Reno. She had been under intense
pressure from her family to withdraw from the case and, despite her
reluctance, had finally given in to their entreaties.

The others had held firm in a united front, including several whose
connections to the sanctuary movement were tenuous at best. Reno
himself had told defense lawyers that he didn't believe that Socorro
Aguilar or Quiñones belonged in the case, and he had told Nena Mac-
Donald's lawyer, Tom Hoidal—to Hoidal's disgust—that she was a
"throwaway." MacDonald was a thirty-seven-year-old Quaker, a softly
pretty woman who had come to Tucson for only two months in the
summer of 1984 to help the movement. She had done nothing more
than drive Central Americans around the city and offer them a place
to stay. She had a husband and two young children back in Lubbock,
Texas, and standing trial probably meant months of separation from
her family. When Reno had included her in the indictment, he had
thought she was more involved than she was. But by the time of the
trial he realized that, as he put it, "she was a bit player."[2]

The prosecutor wanted to dismiss the case against MacDonald. He felt sorry for her and realized that the jury would, too. Reno talked MacDonald's case over with Stephen M. McNamee, who had succeeded Mel McDonald as U.S. attorney. The Quaker's gentle, wholesome sincerity could create compassion that would spill over to Nicgorski, he warned McNamee. No, McNamee advised him, let the jury decide. In McNamee's mind they had to keep deterrence in mind; if they let MacDonald go, people would be lining up from Phoenix to Tucson to join the movement.

The first order of business was selecting a jury. But the lawyers had scarcely begun the process of voir dire, the interrogation of prospective jurors, when Judge Carroll walked into the courtroom and reversed his July ruling that the defendants could use a good faith misunderstanding of the law as a defense.

A few days earlier Carroll had ruled that international law would be excluded from the trial. Now, with one swoop, he eliminated intent as a defense: the argument that the good Samaritans had had no intention of breaking the 1980 Refugee Act and certainly no conspiracy to do so. Their real intentions, whatever they were, were not going to be explained or made comprehensible to the jury.

Specifically Carroll's order ruled out any defense based on the defendants' good faith belief that each of the aliens assisted was also a refugee and therefore lawfully entitled to be in the United States. For such a belief to be a defense, Carroll argued, refugee status had to entitle refugees to enter or reside in the United States. He found that it did not.[3]

The effect of this order was devastating. Normally, to convict, the prosecution has to prove both criminal action and intent; now Reno had only to prove the former. Combined with the orders that had preceded it, the order on intent gave the government the depoliticized proceeding it had dreamed of; as Reno put it, "the trial had been sanitized, in conformance with my prayer."[4] Virtually none of the complex reality, the struggles, and the blood that lay behind the defendants' actions would now be admitted in the courtroom. The sanctuary case, which raised profound political and ethical issues, had been reduced to the level of a technical were-these-specific-acts-committed affair.*

---

*Another order of October 28 made clear the extent to which the defense's case had been gutted. It listed the prior rulings by the court restricting the introduction of evidence:

"1. No evidence will be received offered in support of or in opposition to the wisdom

From that moment on, the defense attorneys saw the judge as an outright enemy. "Until then we didn't appreciate to what extent he would go to convict," said Bates Butler later. "It made us recognize his viciousness."[5]

The defense team moved to adjourn the trial while it regrouped and reevaluated its entire approach. In their motion to adjourn the lawyers maintained that the only conclusion one could draw from Carroll's orders was "that the Court seeks to do the maximum damage to the defendants' case. The defendants are being denied a fair trial."

The motion to adjourn was denied.

For some time the defense lawyers had been having an intense debate among themselves on what to do about Carroll. Almost from the beginning a few had argued that he would never be an impartial arbiter, that he was an adversary and had to be removed from the case. Others had pooh-poohed these dire sentiments. Despite his frequent shows of displeasure and unfavorable rulings, they told their colleagues, Earl Carroll was still a scholar, a man who could be educated.

On October 28 that mood changed dramatically. Mike Piccareta, one of those who had been willing to give Carroll the benefit of the doubt, finally concluded that the judge was the perfect example of the axiom that the law sharpens the mind by narrowing it. Piccareta and others who had shied away from the idea of recusal, a radical step that rarely was successful anyway, changed their minds. If Judge Carroll would not permit their clients a full and fair hearing, the defense attorneys decided, they had to try to remove him from the case.[6]

On October 29, the day after Carroll's final sweeping orders, the defense introduced its first motion for recusal. They focused on an alleged conflict of interest. Prior to his appointment to the bench, Earl Carroll had been a member of the firm of Evans, Kitchel & Jenckes for twenty-eight years, and one of his primary clients had been the Phelps

---

of any government policy or regarding any political question respecting a foreign country.

"2. No evidence will be received offered to demonstrate that there was or is civil strife, lawlessness or danger to civilians in any foreign country.

"3. No evidence will be received offered to establish good or bad motive on the part of a defendant or defendants.

"4. No evidence of religious beliefs will be received as a defense to the charges in the Indictment. . . .

"5. No evidence will be received offered to prove either necessity or duress on the part of any defendant for the surreptitious entry of an alien into the United States."

Dodge Corporation, an international copper mining and smelting company. The defense had recently learned that Carroll and his wife owned stock in Phelps Dodge, 293 shares to be exact, worth between $15,000 and $50,000.

Phelps Dodge had in El Salvador a subsidiary, Conelca, that was begun as a joint venture with the Salvadoran government. The company was the major supplier of telephone cable to the national communications network, and managers of the plant had become members of the government of El Salvador. The court, the defense argued, had a direct economic interest in the productivity of the plant and therefore in the political stability of El Salvador. "A stockholder with a direct economic interest in the stability of El Salvador should not judge the exclusion of testimony about killings, torture and disappearance in that country," they argued.[7]

Moreover, one of those who could testify about conditions in El Salvador was Lucio Chávez, the refugee whose two sons had been brought to him by the underground railroad and who was named in six counts of the January indictments. Chávez had been a union organizer at the Phelps Dodge plant from 1974 to 1979 and, because of that activity, had been arrested and tortured. Citing a statute providing that a judge shall disqualify himself whenever he or his spouse has a "financial interest in the subject matter in controversy," the motion called upon Carroll to relinquish the case.[8]

The motion further argued that the judge's "deeply held bias" also disqualified him from the case. Presented as evidence were a few of Carroll's "constant quips, comments and innuendo," including a remark at the first meeting between him and the defense counsel. On that occasion Carroll had commented that "what I read in the paper, everybody says they did it and we are proud we did it."

Likewise, at the beginning of voir dire, the judge had said that because the defendants had admitted guilt on "60 Minutes," the defense could not expect jurors who had seen the show to be excluded even if they had an opinion on guilt. During the pretrial hearings on infiltration, Carroll had also asked counsel when religious people had ever before stood on the church steps and "openly defied the law."

In response to a comment by one prospective juror that "I thought sanctuary was something for birds," Carroll had quipped, "There is a comment there but I won't pick that up either."

District Chief Justice Richard M. Bilby was called in to rule on the motion to disqualify Judge Carroll. After watching the courtroom proceedings for a day, he denied the motion, retaining Carroll on the bench.

The defense still didn't give up, although increasingly, some of the attorneys felt like Laocoön caught in the coils of the snake. Every move seemed to bring a tightening of the restraints on their defense. Their next effort was an attempt to have the case thrown out on the ground of so-called selective prosecution. The essence of this argument was that the government was not just enforcing the law, plain and simple, as it claimed, but was pursuing a "unique prosecution outside the normal policies of enforcement." The defense had to prove this in two ways: first, by showing that sanctuary had been unfairly singled out for prosecution, *and* that others were not being arrested for similar acts, and secondly, by showing that the government had an *intent* to target these particular people because of their public dissent from its policies.

As if to underscore the claim of unfairness, on October 15, 1985, just as the trial was starting, most of the immediate family of José Napoleón Duarte, the president of El Salvador, was flown out of the country on a U.S. Air Force jet to safe haven in the United States. Duarte's eldest daughter had been kidnapped by guerrillas in September, and he had received threats of another kidnapping as well as death threats against other family members. All this prompted him to seek sanctuary for his three other daughters, two sons-in-law, and four grandchildren. (One of Duarte's two sons, a World Bank employee, already lived in the Washington, D.C., area.) U.S. Ambassador Edwin G. Corr had arranged for the family to board the military plane, which had previously been scheduled to fly American military officials back to the United States. The family was expected to remain in the United States indefinitely.

Seizing on the Duarte incident, the defense charged: "The news reports for October 15, 1985 read like the agent reports that led to the Indictment in this case. . . . The government's enforcement system clearly has a discriminatory effect: church workers are being prosecuted while other persons arranging for Central Americans to come to the United States and providing transportation and shelter to them once here are not." This prosecution, they concluded, not only violates the equal protection clause and the right to due process but "is fundamentally unfair and should be dismissed."[9]

In response, Carroll commented that there are "powers reserved

. . . to the political branch" that are not to be exercised by other Americans.

In an angry courtroom exchange Brosnahan retorted, "I really don't think the American people much care for a rule of law that turns upon status . . . or for the notion that the exercise of compassion is a privilege reserved to the executive branch."

Over the next two weeks, as the jury selection proceeded, the defense lawyers pursued their claim that the sanctuary workers had been singled out for prosecution. If they couldn't win a dismissal on this ground, they at least wanted an evidentiary hearing on selective prosecution, complete with discovery and government witnesses who could testify about the government's failure to prosecute prominent ranchers and growers.

The lawyers unearthed encyclopedic evidence that smuggling cases were not presented for prosecution in Arizona unless they involved economic gain for the smuggler or violence or exploitation of the illegal worker. Indeed, according to Bates Butler, the former prosecutor, the sanctuary case was the only immigration case not involving economic gain, violence, or threats to human welfare that had been brought in the state of Arizona in the previous ten years.

The defense presented evidence that the state had declined to prosecute growers that it knew were actually going into Mexico and soliciting undocumented workers. A statement provided by Leonel Castillo noted that "it is a well known fact that ranchers and growers encourage and induce the entry of undocumented aliens. It is also a well known fact that ranchers and growers send their employees to Mexico for this purpose or employ 'agricultural worker recruiting teams' to serve as their agents in procuring their workforce." Despite knowledge of these activities, the government rarely, if ever, investigated or prosecuted the companies involved.

At the time of the sanctuary trial the most publicized of these non-prosecutions involved the Whitewing Ranch southwest of Phoenix. Lupe Sanchez's struggling farm workers' union had been trying to organize the workers at Whitewing, and sixty-seven men had reported to the union that company personnel went to the park in the Mexican border town of San Luis and recruited workers. Several alleged that the ranch had hired them as guides to bring the men across fifty or sixty miles of desert to a freeway near the farm, where a company foreman picked them up and trucked them onto the property.[10]

Sanchez was interested in halting this illegal traffic, for it not only damaged his ability to organize Arizona farm workers, but was actually murderous for those migrants who failed to make it across the harsh, uninhabited desert. The union leader had documented that sixty bodies had been pulled out of the desert in the previous three years and estimated that close to 300 people had died in the area in the last five years.[11]

At the time of the trial Sanchez provided the Immigration Service with a list of sixteen witnesses to the alleged soliciting, including six or seven guides. But in the end the government decided not to prosecute. Sanchez swore that a member of the antismuggling unit in Yuma, Arizona, informed him that it would be impossible to bring a prosecution unless it could be proved that the workers paid money for the trip into the United States or that money was deducted from their wages. Otherwise, the official told Sanchez, it was not a smuggling case.[12]

Sanchez added that from mid-1979 until 1985, he had met once or twice a week with Jim Rayburn to discuss forty or fifty smuggling cases and that Rayburn had continually stressed that unless they could prove that workers were being charged a certain amount of money, there was no case. "Usually my experience with border patrol has been pretty much the same," Sanchez continued. "They are not going to go out of their way to prosecute somebody that is transporting without pay."[13]

The defense also tried to show that the government did not recommend prosecutions against family members who "bring in" other family members on a first offense. In pretrial testimony Jim Rayburn said that he had no personal knowledge of such a prosecution in the Tucson area for a first-time event. Yet more than one-third of the counts against the sanctuary defendants involved family reunifications.[14]

Next the defense turned to the task of demonstrating that the state had a reason for singling out the sanctuary movement for punishment. The great unanswered question was why the authorities had finally moved against a small band of religious workers who, by the INS's own estimates, were assisting only a tiny percentage of the illegal aliens coming across the border. Leon Ring of the Border Patrol had estimated in 1982 that the movement had helped fewer than 100 people— one-sixth of the 605 Central Americans caught by the patrol's Tucson sector that year.[15] Sanctuary might have helped 2,000 to 3,000 people in its entire existence—a fraction of the 500,000 illegal aliens who were estimated to cross into the southwestern United States from Mexico each year.[16]

Why, then, did the government, with its admittedly limited resources, focus on these people in the helping professions and charge them with serious felonies?

One answer given in the motion for selective prosecution was that their public statements criticizing the government, and the resulting publicity, had embarrassed the Immigration Service. This the prosecution acknowledged. In an interview later Don Reno stated emphatically that "without all of the media attention, there would have been no trial."[17]*

But the defense went further, arguing that publicity alone could not explain the prosecution. It cited numerous examples of local press coverage of alleged violations of immigration laws by growers. As recently as September 18, 1985, the *Arizona Republic* in Phoenix had run a front-page story on the soliciting of workers in Mexico by the foreman of the Whitewing Ranch, which was followed by articles in, among other papers, the *New York Times*. The stories did not state, however, that the ranch had offered to provide guide service into the United States, and since the hiring of aliens was not at the time against the law, it was hard to see just how the publicity had embarrassed the Immigration Service in the way that the very public underground railroad had.

That left the defense's second argument for selective prosecution: that sanctuary had been targeted because it alone, of all the known violators of the immigration laws, was a critic of the government's policies. The state wanted to silence a vocal opponent, and that, the motion of selective prosecution argued, was an "improper political motivation."

In support of this contention the defense cited the government's consistent refusal to acknowledge that the movement was a humanitarian one. It mentioned Agent Rayburn's frequent references to the defendants' "left" politics and his uncritical acceptance of Cruz's characterization of church meetings as political gatherings.

The defense quoted a letter written in 1984 by W. Tapley Bennett, Jr., assistant secretary of state for legislative and intergovernmental affairs, to California Senator Pete Wilson: "We are concerned about those activists who have a political agenda as well as humanitarian

*Maurice Inman, after he had left the Immigration Service to go into the practice of immigration law in Los Angeles, explained in a telephone interview with the author in November 1987 that the INS had been pressured by members of the public and Congress, including Senator Strom Thurmond, to take action against the sanctuary lawbreakers. "It was embarrassing!" Inman exclaimed.

goals, and who not only want to help illegal Salvadorans in this country, but also want to use them to further their campaign against U.S. support for the government of El Salvador." The defense motion charged:

> *In choosing to bring this particular case and to devote such enor-*
> *mous departmental resources to this one investigation, the U.S.*
> *government, at the highest levels, was attempting to deter the exer-*
> *cise of fundamental rights and to stifle dissent.*
>
> *The message of deterrence from this case is clear: if you break the*
> *law for economic reasons—growers, dairy operators, landscapers,*
> *etc.—you will not be prosecuted. But if you are critical of adminis-*
> *tration policies you will have the vast machinery of the government*
> *turned on you to crush the criticism.*

Judge Carroll postponed his ruling on the selective prosecution motion indefinitely, indicating that he wanted the long-delayed trial to proceed.

Meanwhile, while all these legal maneuverings were going on, a parade of some eighty prospective jurors had filed through the courtroom to be vetted by the anxious attorneys. After three full weeks the lawyers ended up with a panel of fifteen people, including three alternates, that neither side was really comfortable with.

The defense team had utilized an expensive system of attitudinal research and developed a profile of the kind of person who was most likely to be sympathetic to its clients. It was clear that they would fare best with what Bob Hirsh called the "liberal intelligentsia": well-educated people, probably Democrats, in the helping professions or active in volunteer work. On those criteria, there was general agreement about most of the jurors. The defense felt confident of the support of Sandra Johnson, thirty-seven, a college-educated Catholic nurse in a drug rehabilitation program; Lynn Cobb, thirty-nine, who worked in a bookstore and was an acquaintance of defense attorney Bill Risner; Angelina Farfan, the mother of a court reporter who knew two other defense attorneys; Irene Doherty; and Anna Browning, twenty-five, an overweight community college student who had a Mondale-Ferraro sticker on her car and made no secret of her sympathy.

The lawyers had fought particularly hard to keep Mrs. Johnson, a Democrat, on the jury. Arthur Mathieson, forty-seven, also ranked high on their scale. A building inspector, he headed a weekend bricklaying crew and had seen crews raided by the INS. There were no strong feelings about another man, David McCrea, twenty-six, who worked in an electronics firm. McCrea had told the judge that he had no particular religious convictions, although he bore a tattoo of Jesus on his right arm. "How can a guy with a tattoo like that come in against us?" joked Piccareta.

Its elaborate research had made the defense suspicious of other jurors. Lori Dorazio, thirty-six, was a college-educated, Catholic computer programmer with the Hughes Aircraft Company. Janice Estes, thirty-three, was an evangelical Christian with four children married to an army officer stationed at an army information and military intelligence base. Susan Hagerty, thirty-two, was a school crossing guard who admitted that she never read newspapers. Ethel Smathers, forty-four, was a heavyset woman who headed the salad department of the cafeteria at Hughes Aircraft. But the juror who had the defense most worried was a woman named Catherine Schaefer. Most of the jurors had already been picked when her name came up, and a lively debate developed over whether the defense should use one of its peremptory challenges to exclude her. She had few of the attributes it considered desirable: though a college graduate, she had worked for almost ten years as an administrative officer for an association of local, state, and federal government groups, implying a bias toward the government. She had recently become an evangelical Christian. Forty-seven years old, dark-haired and well groomed, she looked prim and proper and very controlled. Cooper and Risner, the radicals, violently opposed letting her on the jury.

Bob Hirsh wasn't so sure. He didn't like the idea of classifying everyone's psyche according to his or her demographic characteristics. He thought Schaefer was charming, he liked her smile, and he was impressed by one fact: She had apparently recently changed her party affiliation from Republican to Democrat. Hirsh thought, something has happened here; maybe she is against Reagan. He argued strongly for Schaefer, and he won.

After several dropouts during the trial, including defense favorites Doherty and Farfan, the actual jury of twelve who decided the fate of the sanctuary workers included nine women, four college graduates, three fundamentalist Christians, three Catholics, and seven people under the age of thirty-five. Such a group, by any measure, could be swayed in either direction.

Chapter
Twenty-six

O N THE DAY before the opening arguments were scheduled to be heard in the trial, the routine murmur of voices in the courtroom was suddenly shattered by a loud cry. "The blood of Central American martyrs is on all of our hands and heads because each of us is our brothers' and sisters' keeper," a man shouted. To the horror of the other spectators, he leaped up, poured blood—or a red liquid that looked like blood—all over his hands, and smeared a huge, dripping stain all over one wall of the wood-paneled courtroom.

After he was ejected from the courtroom, the man, a sixty-five-year-old resident of Tucson named Duncan Murphy, explained that he had been one of the liberators of the Bergen-Belsen concentration camp in Germany and had worked for two months with the recently freed prisoners. He said that they had told him stories of torture and death very much like those he had heard from people coming out of Central America. "I feel very much in a bind because I am a loyal citizen of the U.S. who fought for three years against the Nazis, but now our own government is picking up where the Nazis left off," Murphy, a tree specialist, declared. He issued a prepared statement denouncing the trial as a "kangaroo court" and Judge Carroll as a "hanging judge." He told a crowd of fascinated reporters: "I am in solidarity with anyone who is oppressed."

Whatever it was, the sanctuary trial was not going to be, as the government kept trying to claim, an ordinary alien-smuggling case.

On Friday, November 15, 1985, fully ten months after the indictments against the sanctuary dissenters had been handed down, the jury finally entered the courtroom to hear the opening statements. They knew nothing of the weeks of bitter legal wrangling that had just ended, nothing of the severe evidentiary restrictions that had been placed on the defense, and nothing of the powerful passions and outrage that the prosecution had unleashed.

Immediately in front of the jury sat Don Reno, trim in a three-piece business suit, and his assistant Joan Grabowski, an attractive INS lawyer in her late twenties. Across the room, opposite the jury, the eleven defendants and their twelve lawyers sat at a long L-shaped bench, in a show of numbers and superficial might that belied the actual weight of the forces behind each side.

Father Quiñones and Father Clark were dressed in black, with white clerical collars, and Doña María Socorro Aguilar wore a large crucifix over her black dress. Darlene Nicgorski, who had traded her habitual Guatemalan peasant blouse for a severely tailored suit, looked more like a very proper schoolmistress than the potential bomb thrower of the government's fantasies. Phil Willis-Conger, slight, blond, and the picture of wholesome youth, might have been one of her students.

Fife was himself, smiling and waving to supporters and joking with the lawyers. He was wearing a large silver cross over his dark shirt. Corbett, his partner in crime, sported a western shirt and looked like the rather fragile frontier intellectual that he was. Corbett's wife, his sister, an arthritic confined to a wheelchair, and his eighty-five-year-old mother, Gladys, were among the spectators, along with Nena Mac-Donald's husband and two well-behaved blond children, lugging toys, drawing materials, and a princess doll into the courtroom. Throughout the trial the children appeared periodically during visits from Texas and watched and drew pictures while the government halfheartedly labored to convict their mother as a felon.

The moment was a difficult one for John Fife's pretty blond wife, Marianne. She was the daughter of a corporate lawyer and the granddaughter of a Supreme Court justice in Pennsylvania. A well-groomed woman in her early forties, she looked more like the spouse of a stock-broker, or a Peter Marshall, than of a man indicted for smuggling. Her husband had not chosen an easy life, and she had had to pay much of the price.

Southside had been difficult since the first time she had come to Tucson to look at the new church John Fife wanted to accept. No one had lived in the rectory for two years, and it had been a haven for every wino in south Tucson. The roof had holes, there wasn't a door on the house, and all the windows were kicked in. Marianne had burst into tears and announced, "I cannot live here; I will not live here; if you come here, I'll divorce you."[1]

The national Presbyterian church had promised to repair the house, and she had made such a list that she was sure the work would never be done. But it was, and for fifteen years she had made a home out of the three-bedroom ranch-style cinder-block bungalow next to the church, its "lawn" a dusty corner of desert defined by a rusting chain fence. She had worried at every stage of Fife's deepening involvement in the underground railroad and had often been left alone while he traveled for the cause. And it all had led, as she had feared, to this moment in a federal courtroom.

Don Reno, for his part, was primed for the event like an athlete parading into an Olympic stadium. He was scheduled to begin the proceedings with the government's case, which he had actually written, along with his closing arguments, a year earlier, at about the same time that he drew up the original indictments. He had rehearsed his opening statement every night as he ran his regular five miles and gone through what he described as "excruciating pain" memorizing all the facts of the case and all of the federal rules of evidence that he might need. By the time the trial started, he was able to stand up and deliver the government's charge against the sanctuary workers for almost four hours without using a single note.

Reno knew that he was starting with a leg up. Judge Carroll had, in the prosecutor's phrase, "slam-dunked" the defense and given Reno everything he had asked for in his extensive pretrial motions, even barring religion from the courtroom. That gave the government an advantage not enjoyed by the prosecution in other sanctuary cases in Texas. In two of the three other sanctuary trials, all held in South Texas, evidence about religious motive and conditions in Central America had been permitted. The government had still won convictions in

two of the three proceedings, although one conviction was later overturned on appeal.*

The government, in short, had had decidedly mixed results in its
actions against the sanctuary movement, and the special U.S. attorney
thought of himself as a lonely warrior up against a phalanx of formidable and well-armed opponents. He rather liked the image of being
outnumbered and had even planned to have no assistance at all on the
case, until top INS officials in Washington had insisted that he bring
in some support. Reno had finally brought in Joan Grabowski, who
spoke fluent Spanish, but he continued to write all the major arguments
the government presented in the case.

By the time the trial began, Reno had worked himself into a controlled frenzy. For months he had gotten up at four-thirty or five every
morning, seven days a week, and worked until he dropped at ten-thirty
at night, a regimen that invariably included up to two and a half hours
of running, weight lifting, and calisthenics. He had rented an apartment
in Tucson in mid-October with the expectation that the trial would last
from six weeks to two months. In fact, it was to drag on for six months.
For almost a year the prosecutor rarely saw his wife or three-year-old
daughter and one-and-a-half-year-old son. He calculated that while the
trial was going on, he went home a total of two days for Thanksgiving,
one week for Christmas, and two other days, one of which he worked.

Don Reno believed that the 90- to 100-hour workweeks were necessary in order to keep up with more than a dozen defense attorneys. He
was determined to be the one lawyer in the room with a complete

---

*At sanctuary worker Jack Elder's first trial, for illegally transporting, the judge had
allowed pretrial testimony on Central American atrocities and on Elder's humanitarian
desire to save lives. The jury had not heard this testimony but still had acquitted him.
Some evidence on motives and conditions in Central America had been heard in Stacey
Merkt's trial in Brownsville, Texas, but she had been convicted of aiding and abetting
the unlawful transportation of undocumented persons and of conspiracy to transport.
That conviction was reversed by the Fifth Circuit Court of Appeals in New Orleans.
   Elder and Merkt had been indicted again in December 1984 on charges of illegally
transporting undocumented aliens. Merkt had been acquitted on two counts and convicted on one, while Elder had been convicted on six counts of transporting and had
been sentenced to 150 days in a halfway house. (His alleged crime was meeting a party
of Salvadorans near the Rio Grande and driving them to Casa Romero.) Elder was
released for "good behavior" after serving 133 days of his term. Both the Elder and
Merkt convictions were on appeal when the sanctuary trial in Tucson began. Those
appeals were rejected by the Fifth Circuit Court of Appeals in New Orleans, and Merkt
served time, while pregnant, in Texas. Amnesty International declared her one of its
"prisoners of conscience," one of the few ever so named in the United States.

mastery of all the facts of the staggeringly complex case. The original indictment had contained seventy-one counts, although by the time the case went to trial, that had dropped to fifty-two counts against eleven defendants. (Shortly after the beginning of testimony in November, further restrictions on the type of evidence admissible into the courtroom forced the government to drop additional counts—Reno termed this "trimming the fat"—bringing the total counts down to forty-five.)

Reno believed that doing his homework would build confidence with the judge, but it also gave him enormous satisfaction when he caught one of his better-known, more experienced opponents on a point of law. As the trial started, for example, he jumped up again and again, objecting that the defense was making a "403" argument, and he was convinced that the first time he did it none of the other attorneys knew what a 403—a highly inflammatory and irrelevant argument—was.[2]

Both sides had been confronted with the daunting prospect of mastering the nearly 100 hours of taped conversations that the government had accumulated during its lengthy undercover operation. A transcript of the tapes had been prepared, at a cost to taxpayers of more than $100,000, and it came to 40,000 pages, bound into four huge volumes. To simplify matters somewhat, Reno informed the defense team that he was planning to use only twenty-one of the ninety-one tapes made by the government.

A week before the trial started he changed his mind. The judge had scheduled a hearing on October 15 on what would be introduced into evidence from the tapes. Reno commented to his law clerk that the whole process was going to be a nightmare, with the defense arguing "If he can use this, we should be able to use that," and so on interminably. The clerk said something to the effect that the prosecution didn't really need the tapes to make its case.

A lightbulb went off in Reno's head. He had Jesus Cruz, John Nixon, and some fifteen alien unindicted coconspirators—the Central Americans who had been in contact with sanctuary—as witnesses. Why did he need anything else? And if he didn't introduce the tapes, the defense couldn't use them either, with all their conversations about refugees, conditions in Central America, and the other gritty realities that had been excluded from the trial.

On the day before the scheduled hearing on the tapes, Reno went into the courtroom and said that he didn't plan to introduce any of the tapes into evidence. None of them. The body bugs, the monitored telephone calls, the clandestine recordings of church services, the jotting down of license plates, the transcribing of tens of thousands of pages of conversations, the hundreds of hours of lawyers' time, the poring over the transcripts—all was for naught. The tapes were not going to be used. The state's case would rest, overwhelmingly, on the word of Jesus Cruz.

Reno began his opening statement by noting that the case was best described as an alien-smuggling case, "conceived and initiated by . . . Mr. Fife and Mr. Corbett." He then proceeded to sketch for the jury a picture of a tightly structured, highly regimented conspiracy that more closely resembled a corporation or an organized crime family than the disorganized, decentralized, often chaotic sanctuary movement.[3]

Pulling out a large chart, Reno noted that there were three "tiers" in "this criminal enterprise." The first tier included Fife, Corbett, Conger, and Miss Nicgorski. "Miss Nicgorski I refer to as Miss Nicgorski," he explained. "She is a nun and perhaps her attorney may refer to her as Sister Nicgorski. I certainly mean her no disrespect by referring to her as Miss Nicgorski, but for that purpose I will refer to her in that manner."[4]

The second tier, according to the prosecutor, consisted of Miss Hutchison, Miss LeWin, and Miss (*sic*) MacDonald. The third was Father Quiñones and Mrs. Aguilar, Father Clark, and Mary K. Espinosa.

As Reno explained it, the people in the first tier were the CEOs, the chief executive officers, of the conspiracy. Fife was honored as the "principal person at the top," Darlene was a sort of "travel agent" (no mention of politics in the courtroom), and Phil Willis-Conger was the "nuts and bolts organizer that put this conspiracy together and kept it coordinating through the second tier, the transporters, the smugglers, as well as . . . coordinating with the persons in the third tier." That subordinate group Reno characterized, in a particularly fanciful analogy, as the "Nogales connection," evoking images of drugs and French connections. Socorro Aguilar's house, the scene of much of the crime, Reno said, would be referred to "in alien smuggling parlance as a 'safe house' or a 'drop house.' "[5]

After this recitation of the cast of characters, the jury was dismissed for the noon recess. Out of its hearing the defense lawyers went bananas. They called for a mistrial on numerous grounds, but principally that Reno's remarks had been prejudicial and not based on any evidence. Michael Altman had a special complaint, that Reno "has referred to all the men who are clergy in this case as Reverend or Father, but he does not show Sister Darlene the respect of giving her her religious title as well. I would like him to stand up before the jury and acknowledge what her title is, call her by that name as he's called everyone else and not refer to her any differently than anyone else in this case."

After lunch the judge ruled. All the mistrial motions were denied, and Reno was admonished. The prosecutor "at least ought to be consistent with respect to all of them, whether they are priests, nun, or otherwise," Carroll suggested. As for the "argumentative" descriptions of the conspiracy, "I don't expect to hear any more of that from Mr. Reno nor anyone else during these proceedings," Carroll warned, as if talking to children.[6]

Reno then went through in detail the overt acts of the defendants and the major groups of Central Americans the government knew they had assisted. All were called illegal aliens; there was no mention of refugees. And whenever possible, Reno seemed to impugn the character or motives of both John Fife and Phil Conger, both of whom he tried to portray as cold manipulators of the Central Americans.

He also cast aspersions on the motives of Father Quiñones and "Mrs. Aguilar," implying that the Mexicans had taken money for their activities.* He described money sent to Socorro Aguilar from Bertha Benavidez for expenses as a "fee," and twice he told of occasions when Bertha Benavidez had sent a note with $100 in it to Quiñones via Cruz, who then watched while the priest read the letter, "put the money in his pocket," and told Cruz "thank you."

The defense was not entirely displeased by Reno's opening statement, as scurrilous as it was. By mentioning the motives underlying the underground railroad and a host of other subjects that Carroll had ruled were verboten, he opened doors that the lawyers were ready to hurl themselves through.

---

*Paul Hoffman, who had handled the international law aspects of the case during pretrial motions, wondered later why the government had stooped to such innuendos, "as if they were afraid to take them on their own terms."

He commented in an interview with the author in Los Angeles in April 1986, while the trial was still continuing, "If I were Reno and the government trying to be straight, I'd say you can't take the law into your own hands just because you disagree with the government. Why did the government have to challenge their motivations?"

On the following Tuesday the defense attorneys responded. The courtroom, which held only eighty-four people, was packed with sanctuary supporters, who all but cheered as the defense team rolled out its big guns one by one. Bob Hirsh led off the defense opening statements with one of his standard ploys.

Draping his lanky form over the lectern and bringing the jury into his confidence like a Times Square tout offering stolen goods, he began: "Now, lawyers are contentious people and we are argumentative and we fight about this or that, but I want to tell you at the outset of what I have to say to you that there are parts of Don Reno's argument I agree with . . . he said 'Nothing that I say to you right now is going to be fact,' and I tell you that I absolutely agree with that assessment of this case with respect to Jesus Cruz."[7]

Hirsh painted the sanctuary workers' long history of active concern for the poor in pure gold leaf, prompting cynics among the press corps to wonder who was going to propose them for sainthood. "This is not a paramilitary organization," he assured the jury. "If there is a conspiracy here, here is a conspiracy of thousands of people and hundreds of churches to help other people."[8]

Ellen Yaroshefsky, softening her usually pronounced New York accent and rapid-fire delivery, reached the heights in proclaiming the defendants' moral credentials. "There is only one leader of the sanctuary movement, and that leader is just beyond the reach of the Immigration Service," she told the jury.[9]

The integrity and character of Jesus Cruz, in contrast, came under withering examination. The defense emphasized that Cruz had been paid by the government depending upon how much information he came up with, giving him an incentive to exaggerate, to entrap, and to out and out lie about what he had observed. "Cruz has the ability to stand face to face with you, at close range, and lie," said Piccareta, provoking both the judge and the prosecutor to protest.[10] The defense estimated that the Judas-like figure it described had been paid about $18,000 for his services to the government, while Salomon Graham, the other principal informant in the case, had received some $12,000. (This was, in fact, rather modest compensation. As John Nixon put it in an interview later, "It was embarrassing, compared with what other government agencies pay their informants. An undercover operator for the DEA [Drug Enforcement Agency] can get as much as Cruz got for one stinking hit."[11])

Each of the five defense lawyers who spoke first tried to correct Reno's selective references to certain events and to counter his implications of base motives on the part of the defendants. But again and again, as they tried to respond to Reno's allegations, they ran up against Judge Carroll's restrictions on what they could say. Tempers grew hotter as the day wore on. Finally, late in the afternoon, as Bates Butler was addressing the jury, he made passing references to the money given to Socorro Aguilar and Quiñones as funds "to pay expenses." He alluded to conditions at the INS detention center at El Centro and said that the INS had a policy of summarily denying asylum applications from Central Americans.

With that, Reno objected, and Judge Carroll dismissed the jury.

Reno, calling the defense's statements "blatant" and "grossly inappropriate," charged that the attorneys were violating the judge's orders.

The judge turned to Butler. "How can you explain, Mr. Butler, your arguments with respect to the situations at El Centro, the fact of your perception that the I.N.S. is violating the law, et cetera? How are these justified under my orders?"

"Your Honor . . ." Butler replied, "if this jury is going to make a decision about whether or not my client specifically intended to violate any law, then this jury needs to know what was in my client's mind, and I have a right to argue and introduce evidence of what he knew."

"Mr. Reno—Mr. Butler, how do you have the right to argue that in view of my ruling, for instance, no evidence will be received, offered to prove either necessity or duress on the part of any defendant . . .? There is going to be no evidence admitted as to whether the I.N.S. is following the law or not in your client's perception. There is going to be no evidence offered or admitted with respect to economic gain. . . .

"Now let me tell you, Mr. Butler, what I am going to do in this instance and any succeeding instance that occurs. The lawyer will be cited for contempt."

Butler protested. He insisted that his comments were relevant because Reno had talked about what the defendants had told the Central Americans in the Nogales jail and stated that they "somehow recruited them to come into the United States.

"I submit that that is not factually correct, and it is certainly not complete. They were also told, as I told the jury, that they ought not to enter the United States," said the lawyer.

"That isn't the subject of our discussion," Carroll replied.

"Your Honor, one of the reasons . . . that they were told, by my client at least, as to why they shouldn't enter the United States, was because if they filed for political asylum, which they had a right to do, the I.N.S. was summarily denying those. . . . and what Mr. Reno said in his opening statement by him talking about what was said in that jail, . . . I have a right to complete the story.

". . . I am sure that this Court would not entertain a situation where Mr. Reno can say whatever he wishes in his opening statement, open any door he wants, and then defense counsel merely has to sit there."[12]

Hirsh put in his two cents. "Your Honor, your order, if Your Honor please, of the 28th, and I carry this with me and read it carefully a number of times, you said, 'No evidence will be received, offered to establish good or bad motive on the part of a defendant or defendants.' That applies, I would imagine, to the Government as well as defense counsel."

Continuing with the theme that Reno's insinuations had to be answered, Hirsh protested, "It is simply impossible for the Government to be able to get up—the Government told us on Friday, that these people left El Salvador with the intention of coming into the United States illegally. Now we can't say that these people were fleeing? We can't explain? We can't counter that? And say they were fleeing from injustice and oppression and torture? And—"[13]

"That's right, you can't say that," Carroll interrupted.

The lawyers and the judge wrangled on and on, with frustration, animosity, and contempt slowly poisoning the room. Steve Cooper, referring to Reno's "clumsily" opening up of issues that encroached on restricted areas of evidence, told the bench, "Now the Court has a choice to make, mistry this thing because of his blunders or let us answer."[14]

Finally court was recessed, amid a flurry of defense motions for a mistrial, which Carroll immediately denied. He did agree to read overnight several cases mentioned by Tom Hoidal, suggesting that once the government has introduced motive into a case, the defense has the right to rebut. As the session adjourned, Bill Walker repeatedly asked to be recognized, noting that he needed to be heard because he was giving his opening statement the following day. Carroll refused to acknowledge him.

Thereupon Walker exclaimed, "Could the record please reflect this is the second time that the Court has refused me to make a record, after allowing all the other attorneys to be heard? I object to it and I think you are singling me out, and I think you are prejudiced against me."

"It is regrettable that you think that, Mr. Walker," Carroll said. "Anything else, then? All right. We will be in recess then until 8:30 in the morning."[15]

On the following day the arguments over possible violations of Carroll's orders resumed. Before calling in the jury, the judge advised the attorneys that he had studied material pertaining to what could and could not be said in opening statements. Though he did not explicitly relax his rulings on the admissibility of evidence, it became clear, as the day progressed, that he was granting the defense attorneys significantly more license than he had the previous day. The defense attorneys did not significantly alter their comments, but they were not cited or even cautioned to the extent they had been on Tuesday.

Michael Altman warned the jury to "look for government distortions, exaggerations, and omissions" and at one point called Jim Rayburn an "ideologue" who had pursued the case for political reasons.[16] Tiptoeing around the restrictions on evidence, he gave jurors a glimpse of the violence that had prompted many Central Americans to flee their homes. He explained that Sister Darlene had had to leave her village in Guatemala because "suddenly, tragedy struck," and later Altman added the fact that "her pastor had been assassinated in Guatemala by the Guatemalan Army," prompting her own flight.

Describing sanctuary's efforts to help only high-risk refugees, Altman wove in references to "a Guatemalan kid who had had his ears cut off by the Guatemalan Army"; to Juana, "who was raped for days in Mexico" and "who left Guatemala because they were trying to find her. They had killed her husband."[17]

Reno objected to all this, but Carroll failed to cite Altman for contempt, despite his order excluding testimony about conditions in Central America. The door was now slightly ajar for evidence on religious motives, conditions in Central America, the definition of a refugee, and more, and the defense planned to ride through it like a thundering herd.

Reno realized what was happening and thought that Judge Carroll must have felt a little guilty about his earlier orders. Maybe he's remorseful, Reno thought, or maybe he's second-guessing whether he did the right thing.

Oh, my God, the prosecutor thought. Why did we go through hundreds of hours on that motion only to have a free-for-all now?[18]

Chapter
Twenty-seven

O N THURSDAY, NOVEMBER 21, the first government witness
took the stand. Jesus Cruz, dressed in a simple white shirt and dark
trousers and speaking in Spanish, immediately launched into a description of how he had ingratiated himself with Father Quiñones and Doña
Socorro Aguilar. Almost mechanically, in a flat, affectless voice, he
detailed their visits to the prison, how they had sheltered Central
Americans, and helped them across the border to churches in Arizona
and beyond.

Throughout this impassive recitation, Cruz avoided looking directly
at Socorro Aguilar, the woman who, of all the defendants, had the most
reason to feel betrayed by the friendly, self-effacing gentleman who had
pretended to be her friend. Cruz had gone to great lengths to win the
widow's trust, giving her gifts of a radio, carpeting, a camera, and a
lamp. He had chauffeured her in his car, done various household jobs
for her, and encouraged her to telephone him collect because she
couldn't call him frequently otherwise. He had escorted her two or
three times a week, to the prison and to occasional events like the
Willis-Conger wedding. He had knelt with her in her living room and
said the rosary beads.

"Who are the real conspirators?" Socorro Aguilar asked a visitor when she finally learned the scope of the undercover operation. "They say we broke the law, but they paid criminals like Cruz and Graham to come into my home. They violated my privacy, in my country, in my own house."[1]

No one close to her believed that the widow had actually had an affair with Cruz—she heatedly denied anything of the kind—but her rage and her pain were obvious. There was no doubt that she had been deeply wounded by his betrayal.

At noon on the day that Cruz began testifying, Doña Socorro Aguilar and Father Quiñones held a press conference. "He has disfigured the truth of works of justice for the poor, for the persecuted. He lied from the start," Quiñones declared. "He lied about his faith in God, in order to serve the government of the United States."

"It is sad to know people who, for money, are capable of anything . . ." Socorro Aguilar said. "All the bad, the false. It gives me sorrow, much sorrow."[2]

A hint of just how difficult Cruz's testimony was for Socorro Aguilar came on the following Monday, November 25, when she slipped and fell outside the courthouse after listening to Cruz's testimony the previous week. She felt unable to attend the trial the next day. Because so much of the informant's testimony dealt directly with her and because all defendants had the right to be present during the trial, the judge felt obligated to suspend the proceedings. He warned, however, that "If Mrs. Aguilar is not here [next] Tuesday, she will be severed," meaning that her trial would be separated from that of the other defendants.

Doña María returned to court to hear her erstwhile companion make the case for her and her friends' criminality. In the following days she would occasionally shake her head of gray curls in disagreement, once even speaking aloud to protest Cruz's version of what the sanctuary workers had done. After that incident Judge Carroll warned her against similar "demonstrations" in the future.[3]

Almost immediately after Cruz's testimony began, the defense attorneys started to object to many of the prosecutor's questions on the ground that they asked for hearsay statements from the witness. According to rules of evidence, hearsay testimony, or testimony by one person about what he or she heard another person say, is not admissible unless the person who originally made the statement is not available to testify. In conspiracy cases, some types of hearsay are admissible, but

Judge Carroll upheld most of the defense's objections, thereby limiting the prosecution to direct testimony.

On the following day the judge called a morning session to discuss guidelines on the admission of hearsay evidence. Reno made it clear that he wanted to have Cruz testify on what the Central Americans had told him about what they had seen and said and done. The defense strongly objected, claiming that the government had not made a good faith effort to locate those witnesses so that they could testify in person. Obviously it was to the government's advantage to filter the Central Americans' testimony through Cruz, and the defense was determined to prevent such an effort from succeeding.

The judge asked the prosecution to substantiate its claims that the Central Americans involved were indeed not available, and Reno agreed to call INS Agent Lee Morgan, a.k.a. "Lou LeBeau" of Operation Sojourner, to testify about the government's attempts to locate potential witnesses.

Morgan's appearance turned out to be highly embarrassing to the government. What he described sounded more like a Three Stooges comedy than a government operation. On one occasion, he swore, he and two other INS agents had spent six hours surveilling the wrong building in New York City, in spite of the fact that they had been given the right address. (The building was Riverside Church. Trying to explain what happened, John Nixon pointed out that the church occupies an entire city block, and "it is hard for someone unfamiliar with it to know which entrance is which."[4])

It also came out that the INS had overlooked certain basic steps in trying to locate the witnesses. No one had looked in the telephone book, contacted well-known refugee service agencies, talked with the refugees' neighbors, or utilized old electric or telephone bills. Contrary to an earlier statement by Reno, subpoenas had not even been served on several of the refugees, a fact that Reno then acknowledged. Morgan also testified that during the INS's "search" for the refugee witnesses, almost no notes had been taken, and that relying on his memory, he had prepared notes only the previous week at Reno's request.

In the face of such ineptitude, the judge ruled that he would not accept further testimony from Cruz concerning statements made by the refugees in question until their unavailability had been more firmly established by the government.

In response, the government renewed its search, and the following week Reno announced that he had been able to locate and arrest one witness whose statements he had sought to introduce as hearsay.

Carroll, however, still had not issued a definitive and comprehensive ruling on the admissibility of hearsay evidence, and in the end he granted Reno's request for a hearing on the matter. On December 10 INS agents from New York City, Los Angeles, and Albany, New York, flew into Tucson to testify about their efforts to locate the missing witnesses.

Their statements were anything but helpful to the prosecution. Charles Ferrigno, an antismuggling unit special agent in New York City, revealed that the government had made almost no effort to find the refugees in Riverside Church until the defense had challenged the government's good faith efforts. Officers from Los Angeles and Albany testified to the same effect, admitting that they had not followed up the most routine leads until after November 24.

Most damning of all, the defense attorneys came up with a memo from INS District Director Benedict J. Ferro in the Albany office indicating that the Arizona INS should send an agent to Albany for a "pro-forma visit only for the purpose of satisfying the court" as to the unavailability of the witnesses.[5]

After spending an evening reviewing the testimony, Judge Carroll ruled the next day that because the government had not made a serious effort to produce the witnesses, it would not be allowed to use Cruz's hearsay testimony in place of their statements. In delivering the decision, Carroll explained that he had been significantly influenced by the Ferro memo. "It's unfortunate," he declared, "that the person responsible for an investigation for that purpose cannot be further censured. Someone within the government organization was not undertaking to responsibly carry out the terms of our constitutional system."

Reno later acknowledged that "the defense did a good job in showing that we didn't make a good faith effort to get those people." Carroll ruled correctly, he conceded. "He could have been overturned; that alone would have been a problem on appeal."[6]

Carroll's decision had enormous consequences for Jim Corbett.

Most of the refugees were needed by the government only to establish their "alienage," in order to prove that the people the sanctuary workers had aided were, in fact, illegal aliens. But one of them, Juana Beatriz Álvarez, was a key material witness in the government's case against Corbett. Without her, the prosecution still had embarrassingly little on the very founder of the underground railroad. Under cross-examination, Cruz admitted that he had seen Corbett only once during the entire nine-month investigation. Reno did have evidence about one TEC meeting Corbett had attended, and undercover agent Nixon could testify that he heard him say something about bringing in Elba Teresa, but it wasn't much. Reno knew that without Cruz's testimony about Juana, he had a weak case on one of the main instigators of the movement.

Reno's only other hope was the incriminating newspaper series on the rancher's trip north with Juana. The articles were almost as good as having an informant, Reno thought, but he couldn't just introduce the series as evidence. Carroll pointed out that a picture of Corbett helping Juana through the international fence could have been staged "in someone's backyard." If he wanted evidence, Reno would have to have the testimony of the reporter or the photographer who had witnessed the illegal crossing.

After Carroll's decision on hearsay, Reno had opened up negotiations with the *Arizona Daily Star.* The paper had been sympathetic to the sanctuary movement editorially, and Carmen Duarte, the reporter who had written the articles about Juana, had been particularly friendly in her coverage of the movement. Ron Medvescek, the photographer for the Juana series, was married to a local journalist who had worked for the movement in its early days. It became clear rather quickly that the *Daily Star* did not intend to cooperate with the government, and Reno recognized that if he wanted one of the journalists to testify, he would have to issue a subpoena and launch a bitter public battle with the newspaper. Indeed, the paper had assured John Fife that it would fight a subpoena all the way to the Supreme Court. The *Star*'s editors believed that to allow a reporter on assignment to become a government witness would jeopardize the bond of confidentiality and trust that must exist between reporters and their sources if the press is to function independently.[7]

Moreover, any subpoena would have to be approved by the Justice Department in Washington. Reno nevertheless decided that he had to have the testimony of the photographer, who could verify that the dramatic picture had indeed been taken at the border. The prosecutor spoke to his superiors in Washington and explained that he had to have Medvescek's testimony. Washington promised to get right back to him by telex. Two weeks passed with no word. In the meantime, Judge

Carroll said to Reno one day, from the bench, "It's paradoxical that everyone in this community can read about an event and you can't get it into evidence."

"It's not as simple as that," Reno responded.

"That's your problem," snapped the judge.[8]

Reno read Carroll's remarks as a prod: "Get the needed evidence in, or we'll have a travesty of justice here." He called Washington again, and finally the Justice Department got back to him. Reno was told, in effect: "Look, if we subpoena that guy, we'll create such a media circus; it would be just what the *Star* wants. It would further sensationalize the case; they would trumpet it as a monstrous First Amendment issue and run to the Ninth Circuit and try to get the subpoena quashed. We can't do it."[9]

Reno was sure that now Corbett was home free.

The defense got another major break during Cruz's lengthy direct testimony, which continued for two weeks, until December 6. The judge required Cruz, when testifying about meetings held in English, to speak in English, without the aid of an interpreter. The defense attorneys had argued that if he heard and understood the meetings in English, he should be able, and required, to reproduce them in English. Under oath Cruz described his fluency in the English language in this way: "I can understand some things, not correctly, but, more or less I can surmise what they mean."[10] But as the informant began to describe several important sanctuary planning meetings in August and September 1984, Reno realized to his dismay that Cruz's virtually incoherent testimony was getting only about one-tenth of what had been said into the record. With the government tapes not in evidence, Reno had nothing to supplement and back up Cruz's account. The jury would have to balance the word of a spy-for-hire against the sworn testimony of eleven practicing Christians as to what had occurred at the meetings.

On Cruz's last day of testimony, Reno, calling the meetings in question "critical to the government's case," asked that Carroll allow Cruz first to testify in English and then to go back and repeat his version of the meetings in Spanish through an interpreter. Carroll initially granted the request, but the defense succeeded in halting the procedure almost immediately. They pointed out that the conspiracy charge depended primarily on conversations in English among the defendants. The accuracy of Cruz's testimony about those meetings had to be assured. As Bates Butler put it, "In a conspiracy case that depends on conversation between the defendants, we cannot rely on the hunches of the government's witness as to what was said."

Reno tried to argue that Cruz could accurately relate in Spanish what he had heard in English. But Carroll, to the prosecutor's surprise, sustained the defense's objections and agreed that the testimony in Spanish would not be necessary.

So the government's star witness proceeded to describe the key "conspiratorial" meetings in halting, barely intelligible English.* Reno went home that night and read the tape transcripts of the meetings again, comparing them with what the jury had heard. It was clear that he was losing a critical part of his testimony.

It suddenly hit Reno like a sledgehammer. He was not making his case in chief—the government's case against the sanctuary movement.[11]

Cruz's stumbling performance in English made his near-total recall of events in Spanish seem all the more suspicious to the defense team. During Reno's direct examination the government witness had displayed incredible powers of memory, recalling addresses and telephone numbers and dates, times, and detailed conversations from meetings that had occurred more than a year earlier. The attorneys said that they found it hard to believe that Cruz could turn in such a performance unless he was working from a script written by the prosecutor or from the tapes made by the informants during the undercover investigation. But much of Cruz's testimony dealt with material that was not on the tapes.

Government pay vouchers obtained by the defense indicated that Cruz had met with the INS for 100 of the 110 days immediately preceding his testimony in order to prepare his remarks. Yet Reno insisted that the government had taken no notes during those meetings that might aid the informant during his testimony. The defense lawyers were skeptical. According to the law, they had a right to any information, including notes taken by the prosecution, that might help prove their clients' innocence. In addition, the sanctuary case had been declared an open file case by the government, meaning that the defense was supposed to have access to all materials used by the government to prosecute the case.

---

*In a typical statement (December 6, 1985, on page 653 of testimony) Cruz said, "Señor Conger speak, 'Sister Darlene Nicgorski is a how long speak Elizabeth?' And Sister Nicgorski speaking is Kathy Flaherty interview this lady long time ago. And Mr. Conger is approve, okay for the help Elizabeth."

Some of the lawyers frankly thought that Reno was lying and withholding important documents or that Cruz was fabricating under oath. On December 5 Jim Brosnahan told Carroll, "I think there is some perjury going on in Your Honor's Court."[12]

Finally, on December 11, Carroll called Cruz to the stand to explain, out of the presence of the jury, what kind of coaching he had received. Although Reno had stated that he had never read Cruz's own statements back to him, Cruz swore that Reno had read his statements back "out of a book." Cruz explained that the "book" was in fact the prosecutor's own notes, and the latter were produced for Judge Carroll under seal. The judge then tabled the matter until a later date.

That afternoon Bob Hirsh began the cross-examination, displaying all the aggressive brilliance that had made his reputation. It became clear at once that Cruz's memory was significantly less acute than it had been under direct examination by the assistant U.S. attorney. When pressed by Hirsh about one occasion, Cruz responded, "I just can't remember; it was so long ago," even though the event had occurred many months after others that he had recalled in lucid detail. Cruz also claimed that he could not understand enough English even to identify courtroom exhibits that were labeled using single letters. After Hirsh reminded the Mexican that his English had been adequate when he had been asked to perform the same tasks for the government, he managed to identify the exhibits.

Hirsh focused first on the government's payments to its informer. Cruz stated that he had been paid some $18,000 for his services on Operation Sojourner. He claimed that he had been paid on a "time plus expenses" basis, although he had kept no records of time and no receipts for expenses. Jim Rayburn had told defense attorneys that he paid Cruz whatever he thought was appropriate and available. As a resident alien Cruz was required to file a form each year stating his employment. The defense produced his form for 1980, in which he stated that he was employed by "Atlas Roofing," a company that had gone out of business in late 1977.

He had, of course, been smuggling aliens between 1977 and 1980. Hirsh was able to bring out that he had, in violation of the law, made up to two dozen smuggling trips for some $5,000 to $6,000 in profit in the late 1970s and that he had begun his cooperation with the INS as an informant against the Florida smugglers only after the Border Patrol had threatened him with criminal charges and/or deportation.[13]

Cruz claimed to have no knowledge of payments made to his housemate Salomon Graham, although a pay voucher indicated that he was paid Graham's share of one paycheck and asked to pass it on to his friend. He claimed in testimony that he did not know of Graham's involvement in the case until the end of May 1984, although by then the two men had been living together and working on the case for weeks.

Defense attorney Yaroshefsky pointed out numerous discrepancies between Cruz's statements about what defendants said at certain meetings and what the government tape recordings revealed they had said. Cruz attempted to explain the discrepancies by saying that the tape recorder had been deactivated when the statements he mentioned were made. That assertion prompted Reno to submit a written statement to the defense team stating that the tape recordings covered the conversations in their entirety and that at no time had the tape recorder run out or been turned off.

On the following day the prosecutor once again had to correct his key witness. After Cruz had testified that the telephone conversation he had had with Bertha Benavidez in April 1984 had been "automatically" recorded by a machine that turned on when his number was dialed, Reno told the court that transcripts of the conversation indicated that the recorder had actually been activated manually after the conversation had begun. That admission meant that Cruz had deliberately used a secret recording device before he had been authorized to do so.

But the most devastating moment for the prosecution came when the defense entered the courtroom on December 19 and dropped its bombshell. Under cross-examination Cruz admitted that from 1980 to 1983 he had taken undocumented farm workers to a gun shop in Phoenix and then transported them back to Mexico.[14] Brandishing more than thirty documents from the Bureau of Alcohol, Firearms, and Tobacco, the defense alleged that Cruz had violated federal law against exporting firearms from the United States without disclosure, during a period when he was working for the government and had sworn to uphold the law.

According to Jim Brosnahan, the defense even had testimony that Cruz on one occasion had "personally put a pistol in each boot and walked it across the border into Mexico, which is illegal in both countries, at a time when he was transporting workers from the Martori camp in Phoenix to Mexico."[15]

Don Reno seemed stunned by the revelations, and Cruz testified that he had never told Jim Rayburn about his stops at the Jewel Box gun shop. Judge Carroll quickly ruled that because the government had had no knowledge of the alleged gunrunning, it was irrelevant to the case. As a result, the jury never heard the charges, which, if true, would have impeached (i.e., disqualified) Cruz as a witness and destroyed the government's case against the sanctuary workers.

In any event, Cruz's credibility had emerged from his six grueling weeks on the stand like paper out of a shredder. Perhaps the most telling exchange occurred when defense attorney Piccareta brought out the fact that Cruz, a permanent resident alien in the United States, hoped to remain in the country and apply for citizenship someday.

"If Immigration permits?" asked Piccareta.

"Exactly. It depends on my behaviors also," Cruz replied.[16]

Chapter
Twenty-eight

A S THE NEW year rang in, the sanctuary defense team had many
more reasons to be hopeful about the outcome of the trial than it
had had a few months earlier. The once-solid government case had been
battered by the blows to Cruz's character and veracity. Once the defense
had finished with him, it appeared that there was nothing that the man
would not do for money or to please his government handlers. He was a
duplicitous snitch who turned on his friends. He was a smuggler of
aliens. His statements under oath were riddled with contradictions. He
admitted that he had even thrown his notes from the sanctuary investigation into the garbage, after claiming that he had taken no notes.

In one particularly chilling display of perfidy he had asked for the
addresses of the refugees he had helped and befriended, on the ruse that
he wanted to send them Christmas cards and presents. He had handed
the information to the government, and a few weeks later, when the
sanctuary indictments came down, more than sixty Central Americans
were picked up and arrested by the INS, in large part because of Cruz's
betrayals.

The cross-examination of the informant had particularly weakened the government's charge of conspiracy. The defense attorneys were able to show that many of the alleged conspirators had not even met when Cruz encouraged them to get together for the first time. Cruz had admitted that he had never seen many of the defendants together during the entire ten-month investigation; he had never seen Father Quiñones or Father Tony Clark, for example, in the company of most of the other defendants. This supported many of the sanctuary workers' claims that they had never met one another until after the indictments came down. Brosnahan and Butler also had shown that it was actually Cruz, not the sanctuary defendants, who had initiated some of the immigration violations alleged in the indictments.

Moreover, despite the judge's strict ban on such evidence, the defense had continued to slip into the trial occasional references to the sanctuary workers' religious motivations and to the conditions in Central America. Michael Altman had written up a vocabulary list of the words the defense could use and those that were forbidden, like *torture* and *kill,* and his occasional revisions of Judge Carroll's "Index" showed a few, albeit pitifully small, victories.

The judge, for example, had prevented the defense from using the word *refugee* to describe the Central Americans, prompting the attorney to complain that the prosecutor should also be prohibited from calling them by his favorite term: *illegal aliens.* After heated argument Carroll had ruled in January that neither term would be used. "From now on, we will call them by name," he decreed.

Using the technique of asking Cruz about what he had heard at the Monday night TEC meetings, Piccareta squeezed a series of thought-provoking questions into the record:

> . . . *do you recall being present for discussions about what were referred to as refugees being held in the INS jails . . . ?*
>
> *And you do recall . . . that they talked about raising money to try and get—bond these, what they called refugees, out of the jail . . . ?*
>
> . . . *how the men would be put in one jail and the women and children would be kept at another location?*
>
> *And they talked about the problems that—that having the family split up caused for the families . . . ?*
>
> . . . *they talked about providing food and clothing for what they referred to as refugees or Central Americans?*

> *. . . there were discussions that there was a war going on, a civil*
> *war going on in Guatemala and El Salvador . . . ?*
> *. . . they discussed problems of people being persecuted in those*
> *countries or people being physically hurt in those countries?*

When Cruz replied that "it was confusing because sometimes I didn't understand what everything was being said," Piccareta whipped back: "I realize you had trouble understanding."

"Just proceed, Mr. Piccareta, with your question," Judge Carroll warned.[1]

In reference to some of the sanctuary meetings Cruz had attended, Michael Altman inquired: "Do you recall people discussing disappearances in El Salvador?"

"At times they said that, yes, sir."

"Do you recall a discussion that a 500 pound bomb was being dropped on people?

"Do you remember [Nicgorski] described the white phosphorus that the Salvadoran Army was throwing on people in El Salvador?"

Cruz replied that he couldn't remember "word for word."

"Do you remember her saying this: 'We hear you. What you are saying matters very much to us. We will call upon our people to share your sorrow, protest our government's part in your pain and try to get the killing stopped'?"

Not until Altman tried to ask the informer about another refugee's statement—"A lot of us are disappearing. Many are dying horribly"—did Carroll sustain an objection from Reno.[2]

The most direct challenge to Carroll's orders came when the first refugee witnesses—the unindicted coconspirators—took the stand and tried to tell the court why they had fled their countries. The first to be called was "Alejandro Rodriguez," a forty-five-year-old production manager and labor leader from El Salvador. Rodriguez's real surname was Gómez, but during the trial and the ensuing publicity he used Rodriguez to protect the family's remaining relatives in El Salvador. The Gómezes were the family of five who had been helped into the country by Phil Willis-Conger and Mary K. Espinosa, among others, and were classic political refugees. The defense attorneys were anxious to have as much of their painful story heard in the courtroom as possible. Reno objected every step of the way, calling Gómez's personal history "irrelevant and prejudicial," and Carroll backed him up. "For the purposes of this case," he reminded the defense, "we do not need to hear about the experiences of a witness or any members of his family in a foreign country."

Gómez did manage to say that he feared being sent back to his homeland "because I could be killed," and he answered another question, about whether he had told Phil Willis-Conger about his union activities, by replying that he had, and that "for that reason I had been jailed and tortured in El Salvador."[3]

But Judge Carroll barred testimony describing torture, and when Gómez's wife, Letitia, testified about why they had fled their country, Carroll ordered stricken from the record her statement that "we had no choice, we were in great danger."

The defense lawyers protested, with the jury out of the courtroom, that Carroll was dismantling their case. "You rob us of the opportunity of showing the jury what the truth is here," Altman charged. "If he was tortured, if he was psychologically abused, if he was imprisoned, the jury is entitled to hear about it."

Reno responded by arguing that such information would be "prejudicial and confusing."[4]

In the end Alejandro Gómez was allowed to tell his story, but only for the record, out of the presence of the jury.[5] He had been born in 1940 into a middle-class family in San Salvador. He was trained as an industrial electrician and took additional university courses in production and business management. The 1960s were a relatively stable and prosperous time in his country, and like many young people, Gómez believed that change was not only possible but imminent. He had become deeply involved in union and other political activities, and later, during the 1970s, he became responsible for organization and education at the National Union Federation. As its name implied, this was a federation of all the unions in the country, including construction, mechanical, food products, garment workers, transportation, and so on, and its membership numbered in the tens of thousands. As one of its top officials Gómez was one of the most prominent union leaders in El Salvador.

His position brought him a great deal of publicity; his public speeches were written up in the newspapers, and he was often sought out by the press and television. He also lived well. By the early 1980s he was earning between $600 and $800 a month as the production manager of a large factory, and he owned a bus that he used to conduct a passenger service in a part of the city, an entrepreneurial venture that brought in more income than his job.

Letitia Gómez had a position as an accountant for the subsidiary of an American company, a large firm that manufactured paints and cements. She had worked there for seventeen years, and by the early 1980s her job involved preparation and monitoring of budgets and regular financial statements, copies of which were sent up to the United States each month. The family's income was between $1,300 and $1,500 a month, not including the bus income. The couple had four children, who were cared for during the day by Mrs. Gómez's seventy-year-old mother. They were more than comfortable, with two houses and a farm, a personal automobile, and all the trappings of middle-class life. As their lawyers in the United States were later to emphasize, these were not the kind of people who would leave their country and all their ties and possessions to sneak across borders in search of a better life.

Yet that is what the Gómezes were suddenly forced to do. In June 1983 Alejandro was arrested by the Salvadoran police and jailed for more than two weeks. During that time, he stated, he was brutally tortured: slapped; punched; kicked; hit with sticks, iron rods, and towels, hung by his arms and beaten again; and given electric shocks through electrodes in his ears. He was left with a permanent loss of hearing and a constant ringing in his ears.

His tormentors accused him of being a guerrilla and a subversive, charges that were based, he said, on his involvement with the union and with an activist Christian base community that had been demanding the release of political prisoners.

His captors were uninterested in such subtleties as the distinction between violent and peaceful political protest. They told the prisoner that unless he admitted his "guilt," his children would be kidnapped and murdered. After about three weeks he was transferred to a general jail, where he finally signed a blank piece of paper. He never saw what was written in above his name.

He was next transferred to a prison where there were some 500 political detainees, the majority of whom appeared to be teenagers. As many as nine to twelve prisoners were jammed into rooms with three or four beds, and each given a cup of coffee and a tablespoon of beans on a tortilla three times a day. At all hours of the day and night members of the security forces threatened the prisoners with suggestions that they were going to be taken out and murdered. Gómez spent six months in this hell. He had never been charged with a crime and never been allowed to see a lawyer.

His wife was finally able to obtain his release by approaching one of the owners of his factory, a wealthy and politically powerful man whom Gómez had known slightly. The man spoke to the military judge who had the case, and since there was no evidence actually linking the union organizer to the guerrillas, he was finally freed.

Gómez was aware, however, that the death squads had a special practice of waiting for those who were just released from prison. Instead of going home, he went to the house of some friends, and they all agreed that he had no choice but to leave the country immediately. So that night, before his children had even seen him, he left El Salvador alone. He didn't want to take his family, he said, because that would have implied that he would be gone for a long time. He also feared that if all of them tried to leave at once, the killers would be alerted, and the entire family might be captured and murdered. As the refugee told the story, the interpreter and several spectators were crying. Let the jury hear this, the defense lawyers pleaded once again. Citing his discretion, the judge refused and Gómez continued.

He traveled to Mexico City and immediately went to the office of the high commissioner of the United Nations for refugees. The UNHCR recognized that Salvadorans had a *prima facie* case as political refugees, and unlike most people in his predicament, Gómez was carrying evidence of at least some of his political activity. Along with identification papers, he had taken out of the country a newspaper containing a story about how some members of an organization called Judicial Christian Relief, including himself, had been jailed for demanding the freedom of political prisoners.

He was interviewed at the UNHCR for an entire morning. After hearing his story, the representative certified him as a United Nations refugee and helped him obtain a visa to stay in Mexico for several months. The UN officials had warned him that Mexico was not a signatory to the 1967 UN Protocol on the Status of Refugees and allowed refugees to be in the country only temporarily, while they sought permanent asylum elsewhere. The UN suggested five countries as possibilities: the United States, Canada, the Netherlands, Belgium, and Switzerland.

Gómez decided to try the United States. An official in the UN office approached the American consulate on his behalf and began to help him collect the documentation that would be necessary for his application for political asylum.

Four months went by. Letitia and the children joined Alejandro in the winter of 1984, leaving behind them relatives and friends, their children's friends and school, and a lifetime of associations and memories.

Yet slowly the Gómezes realized that their chances of being admitted into the United States were virtually nil. First they discovered that in effect, Salvadorans could not be admitted as refugees from outside the United States. The U.S. refugee law, they learned, works in the following way: If a person is applying from abroad, he or she comes under the overseas refugee admissions program. The numbers to be admitted under the program are set each year by Congress. In fiscal 1984 the allocations were 1,000 people from Latin America, 3,000 from Africa, 6,000 from the Near East and South Asia, 11,000 from the Soviet Union and Eastern Europe, and 40,000 from East Asia.

In addition to the quotas, the American government sets criteria that refugees from each region must meet in order to be eligible to apply. In Latin America the U.S. government had decided that Cuba was "of special humanitarian concern." In practice, ex-political prisoners from Cuba were the only Latin Americans who met the necessary criteria to be admitted as refugees. Other Latins fleeing persecution, including Central Americans, Argentines, Chileans, and Nicaraguans, were overwhelmingly rejected if applying from abroad. Between 1983 and 1985 the United States even temporarily ceased to process Cubans, and in fiscal 1984, the year Gómez was trying to apply, there were only 200 refugees admitted into the United States from all Latin America.[6]

With the United States seemingly ruled out, the Gómezes then learned that it could take as long as one to two years before they would know whether they could be admitted anywhere else. In the meantime, they were not sure they could renew their temporary Mexican visas, raising the specter of deportation back to El Salvador. Their children were not in school and were showing signs of psychological stress. They decided that they had to try to get into the United States on their own.

The jurors heard almost none of this tale, which was recorded for purposes of appeal. They did hear Reno make much of the fact that the Gómezes had not actually applied for asylum at the U.S. consulate in Mexico City, although when the defense attorneys tried to explain that not a single Salvadoran asylum application was granted at the consulate in 1984, Carroll cut them off. Gómez was also silenced when he said he hadn't presented himself to the INS at the border because it was "well known" that asylum applications were not accepted at the border.

The jury heard only the next part of the story. After making their way to the border, the Gómez family, including the parents, the mother-in-law, and four children, ages thirteen, eleven, eight, and seven, stayed with Socorro Aguilar for about one week in early May 1984. After several days Phil Conger arrived and interviewed Alejandro, to determine whether he was a political refugee. Once that had been established to his satisfaction, Conger, with Cruz, took the Salvadoran to a hill overlooking the international border and pointed out the fence and Sacred Heart Church beyond it. Conger told him, he testified, that "through there was where many people would get in, and through there I also, if I wanted to do so, I could also go in."

Although Cruz offered to take him to the border in a taxi, Gómez was afraid to accept the ride; in El Salvador taxi drivers frequently doubled as government agents. So the refugee, with his wife and two older children, both girls, walked through the fence and on to Sacred Heart on their own.

". . . did you enter the United States by going through a hole in the international boundary fence?" the prosecutor asked the refugee on direct examination.

"I came in through one of them," Gómez replied.

"And did you make the entry into the United States in that way in order that you would not present yourself to the United States government?"

Gómez tried to explain. "That is a question that I would like to . . ."

"Is it a question that you cannot answer 'yes' or 'no'?"

"Yes, I would like to explain the reason why. Why maybe . . ."

"That is not the question, Mr. Rodriguez. Before you entered the United States, did you contact any members, any agencies of the United States government to enter the United States, asking permission to enter the United States?"

At this point Yaroshefsky objected. "Where, in Mexico? In the United States?" She was overruled.

"May I explain a little?" Gómez requested.

"No," Reno replied. "The question, Mr. Rodriguez, is, before you entered the United States with Letitia and your two children—Excuse me, Mr. Rodriguez, I would like to finish my question—did you ever obtain the permission of the United States Immigration Service?"

"No."[7]

The jury also heard how a woman arrived at Socorro Aguilar's with a van filled with schoolchildren, dressed the two youngest Gómez children in school uniforms, and drove them all back across the border, where the boys were reunited with their parents. When he was asked on the stand to identify the woman who brought his children back to the church, Gómez described her as tall, thin, fair, and with blondish hair, "I think." Reno asked him to look around the court and "tell us if you see that lady in the courtroom today."

"No, I do not know. I don't remember," Gómez replied.

Reno assumed that the Central American was lying. The woman was Mary K. Espinosa, and she was sitting with the other defendants right in front of the witness. But she thought the witness might be telling the truth. She had gained sixty pounds since she had seen him last.[8]

When Gómez was asked if the person who had sheltered him in Nogales was in the courtroom, Doña Socorro Aguilar stood up proudly, tears running down her cheeks. Asked to identify her, the refugee did so with emotion. "She was the only person that offered me a roof over my head when I was most in need. People told me she had a very good heart. I remember her with much love."

Reno jumped to his feet, furious that this unsolicited information had reached the jury. Carroll sustained the objection, and as one spectator observed, Socorro Aguilar's heart was stricken from the record.[9]

After passing through Tucson, where they were driven by a three-car escort, the Gómezes eventually found sanctuary at the Downtown United Presbyterian Church in Rochester, New York. There they found a lawyer and began to put together an asylum application. Gómez amassed some 300 pages of documentation on the violence and human rights abuses in El Salvador and 100 pages on his own personal history.

On the day after his testimony, the defense tried one last time to remove Judge Earl Carroll from the case. It seemed that on the previous day, after Gómez had vainly struggled to explain his actions, Carroll had remarked out of the presence of the jury, "I think that people from Latin America perhaps have a difficulty in just answering the question 'yes' and 'no' by nature of their personal attitudes, maybe they don't."[10]

The church workers declared that they were "appalled" by the "racist" remark, and Brosnahan asked Carroll to consider the motion carefully. Carroll immediately ruled against it.

From that point on it seemed to many observers that the judge dropped all pretense of impartiality. The defense's barrage of attacks on Carroll seemed to have finally taken their toll on an obviously proud and touchy man. The courtroom became a battlefield between the bench and the bar, which began to think of Carroll, even more than the prosecutor, as its real opponent. The raw hostility in the air transcended anything reflected in the official record of the trial, and at times various antagonists seemed to be almost choking as they struggled to repress the rage boiling inside.

Privately Hirsh started calling Carroll Judge Mumser, *Mumser* being a Yiddish word meaning "bastard," and both he and Brosnahan told friends that in more than twenty years of law practice they had never seen a judge display such bias from the bench.[11] The lawyers were convinced that Carroll would do anything he could to help secure a conviction for the government. A few days after the imbroglio over Carroll's insensitive remark, they thought he demonstrated this with an even greater vengeance.

In his previous testimony Jesus Cruz had sworn under oath that he had not worked on any INS investigations other than Sojourner since March 1984, that he had had no contact with Central Americans mentioned in the charges since the indictments, and that he had reported all payments made to him by the government. INS chief investigator Rayburn had been sitting in the courtroom when Cruz had given this testimony and said nothing either to the court or to the prosecutor.

Now Reno revealed that before the trial Cruz had approached one of the unindicted coconspirators—a man named José René Argueta—with a deal: The government would look favorably on Argueta's efforts to remain in the country in return for his cooperation at the trial. The defense attorneys already suspected as much. Argueta was the only Central American witness who had tried to incriminate the defendants, and the defense attorneys were sure that he expected preferential treatment from the Immigration Service in return. Argueta denied having been promised any special favors, but unlike most of the other material witnesses, he had been released on his own recognizance rather than having to post bond, and for some reason he hadn't found it necessary to retain a lawyer.

One night, while sitting in a motel room going over his upcoming testimony with Don Reno, Argueta had casually commented that Cruz had worked with him on a recent undercover operation that had taken place during the sanctuary trial.

Reno felt obligated to set the record straight, and on January 21, 1986, he stood up in court and revealed that Cruz, contrary to his previous testimony, had arranged for Argueta to set up an antismuggling operation in Los Angeles.

Argueta had apparently mentioned to Cruz that a Mexican alien-smuggling ring was bringing his wife into the United States, and Cruz suggested that he pass the information on to Jim Rayburn. Rayburn, with Cruz's help, then made arrangements for Argueta to tape a telephone conversation with the smugglers. Rayburn forwarded the evidence to the INS antismuggling unit in Los Angeles, which launched an investigation entitled the "El Salvador to Los Angeles Express." Cruz then took Argueta from Phoenix to Los Angeles, where the INS paid Cruz $300 for expenses, a payment he had not previously disclosed. According to Reno, Cruz then gave $150 of that to Argueta. A few days later, when one of the smugglers brought Mrs. Argueta to the hotel room where Cruz and her husband were staying, she and the smuggler were arrested, as were several of his colleagues in the same operation. Cruz then brought the Arguetas back to Phoenix, where Mrs. Argueta was released without bond pending her deportation hearing.[12]

When Reno revealed this in court, the defense attorneys immediately moved to have all charges against the defendants dismissed. Bill Risner called the incident "a threat to the integrity of the proceedings as a whole." The defense asked Carroll at least to disqualify Cruz as a witness and strike all his previous testimony. Reno responded by trying to disassociate himself from the whole affair. He insisted that he had known nothing about the incident and maintained that a reasonable person could argue that Cruz was not obligated to reveal it during cross-examination. Rayburn, for his part, claimed that he had told Reno that Cruz was going to take a witness to Los Angeles. But Reno did not remember being told that, and he was sure that Rayburn had never mentioned that it was a witness in the sanctuary trial or that it was Argueta.

Reno maintained that Rayburn hadn't behaved improperly but had been operating on the theory that one never volunteers information unless one is asked. Rayburn believed the defense would distort, misrepresent, and "do anything to get a win," Reno later commented, and he "always had to remind Rayburn that we couldn't play by their rules or it would blow up in our faces."[13]

Carroll agreed to grant a hearing on the imbroglio the next day, January 22, and at the request of the defense called Rayburn to the stand to explain his role in the incident. In an unusual twist, the judge required the attorneys to submit their questions to him, and then he examined the investigator himself. The attorneys protested that the procedure deprived them of the opportunity to pursue the matter through follow-up questions, and Hirsh exclaimed that he had "never seen anything like it, and I've been in this business for 21 years."

Rayburn did not inspire confidence on the stand. At first he denied that he had known that Cruz and Argueta were going to participate in the investigation, a statement that flew in the face of evidence that he himself had initiated it. Blasting Rayburn's actions as "unacceptable," Judge Carroll lectured the official: "Mr. Rayburn, the form of government we have depends on individuals, and that begins at the lowest level of government. At times I wonder what that level is."[14]

Carroll then recessed the court, indicating that he would announce a decision the following day. The courtroom had been packed for the hearing, for the first time since the beginning of Cruz's testimony, and both the press and the spectators anticipated a dramatic ruling, possibly even a dismissal of the charges themselves.

The next morning Carroll opened proceedings on a minor matter, completely ignoring the perjury issue. When the defense attorneys pressed him, he informed them that he would not take the "drastic step" of dismissing the case, primarily because the matters Cruz had lied about did not prejudice the defendants. The only thing the defense might do, he indicated, was to direct future questions to Argueta when he appeared as a witness.[15]

The defense called a noon press conference after the decision and announced to a flock of reporters that Carroll was now openly acting like a part of the prosecution. Darlene Nicgorski noted that the judge had more harshly reprimanded the defendants for chewing gum or laughing than he had chastised the prosecution for perjury. John Fife told reporters that "if Judge Carroll had been the one presiding over the Watergate hearings, the American people today would still not know that they had been lied to by Richard Nixon."[16]

A few days later the question of government impropriety rose yet again. One of the Central American witnesses, Candida Núñez de Villatoro, testified that in January 1985 Jesus Cruz had approached her at her home in Phoenix and offered to arrange a work permit for her if she would agree to be interviewed by INS agents who were preparing the sanctuary prosecution. She accepted the offer and in return received a document that she believed to be a permit, although she could not read English. In court Nancy Postero pointed out to her that, in fact, the paper was an order to appear in immigration court.[17]

The next witness, José Rubén Torres, raised an issue that had surfaced repeatedly throughout the trial: the government's failure to turn over relevant information in its files to the defense. Judge Carroll had even noted the phenomenon of "information that just keeps floating down the pipeline." Torres testified that one of his interviews with INS agents had been tape-recorded. The defense had no such tapes, despite repeated requests for all records of witness interviews by the government. Reno had even claimed that there had been no record made of the Torres interviews, and now here was testimony to the contrary.[18]

Reno looked into the matter and discovered that his records did indicate that a tape and a transcript of an interview with Torres had been made. But they were nowhere to be found.

The files had been kept in the office of chief investigator Jim Rayburn. Rayburn and the agent who had interviewed Torres were called to the stand in an attempt to clear up the matter. Rayburn swore that despite Reno's instructions to turn over to the defense all materials having to do with the case, he had never looked into the Torres file until the previous day nor had any agent reviewed the alien witnesses' files at the start of the trial to see whether they contained any material that might be useful to the defense. Rayburn added that out of a total of about ninety witness files, he had examined only "about five."[19] When asked specifically about the missing material, neither he nor the other agent could explain it.

Carroll once again ordered the government to turn over all materials having to do with the sanctuary prosecution and, after lunch, sat back to hear the arguments over what to do about the problem. The defense had moved to dismiss, and Piccareta, arguing for the motion, said that the government's disclosure violations were subjecting the church workers to a "trial by ambush." At the least, he asked, Judge Carroll should dismiss Torres as a witness.

Reno called the motion "very radical and certainly not in the interest of justice." He assured the court that there was no bad faith on the part of the government and explained that it was difficult to keep track of the "unprecedented monumental amount" of paper generated in the case. As an alternative to the defense's proposed remedies, he suggested that "the jury be advised of the situation so that it can make its own decision about the witness' credibility and the conduct of the government."

Carroll ruled. "My final analysis with respect to the government's behavior is that it was inattentive and negligent." He then denied the defense's motions. "In deciding what to do," he explained, "I'm also mindful of the amount of time that has been spent so far in this case."

Carroll offered the defense the opportunity to make a statement to the jury about the incident. The attorneys, some slouched in their chairs in resignation, listened to his ruling in uncharacteristic, stoic silence.[20]

A few days later, after they had had a chance to examine the government witness files, the defense announced that the government had lost or destroyed a total of six tapes and transcripts of witness interviews and had failed to turn over additional records of payments made to witnesses. According to the prosecutor, the tapes had been lost by a typist hired to transcribe the interviews of Torres and other Hispanics. After hearing the arguments, Judge Carroll ruled that testimony from all the witnesses in question would proceed as planned. Nothing was done either to penalize the government or to remedy the situation.

Chapter
Twenty-nine

WHILE THEIR ADVOCATES did battle in the courtroom, the accused sat in silent dignity, in an impressive united front reminiscent of the popular Latin American protest chant *"El pueblo unito, jamas sera vencido* ["The people united will never be defeated"]."

In truth, the trial had thrust the church workers into the very heart of the noisy, tumultuous publicity mill that quickly engulfs public figures. Inevitably, some were anointed stars, while others were stirred to resentment and what one unindicted coconspirator jokingly called "subpoena envy." The media had discovered an endangered species that had seemed almost extinct: the social activist, whose motives were selfless, whose deeds were compassionate, and whose capacity for outrage was undimmed. A breed so rare, and so newsworthy, had not been spotted in years.

Like his Quaker colleague, John Fife now had his story told in *People* magazine, and his smiling face appeared in a host of other publications, including *Family Circle*. Corbett, Fife, Nicgorski, and Hutchison in particular became featured speakers on the church and university circuit, keeping interested groups around the country informed about the progress of the trial and the refugee situation. Peggy Hutchison was named one of *Good Housekeeping* magazine's one hundred promising young women in 1985, and she and Mary K. Espinosa were written up by *Glamour* magazine. The BBC did a one-hour documentary on Corbett's border work, and screenwriters of all descriptions were encircling and courting various defendants.

Even Father Tony's passion for boxing was chronicled by a national magazine. An article in *Sports Illustrated* told how the priest had converted John ("the Beast") Mugabi, a middleweight contender from Uganda. Apparently Clark had seen Mugabi training in Nogales, Arizona, for a March fight with Marvin Hagler, the middleweight champion, and asked him to talk to his young boxers in Nogales, Sonora. Mugabi agreed, and the two had a pleasant session until Clark tried to drive Mugabi back into the United States. It turned out that the boxer's visa had expired. Father Clark started arguing with the immigration authorities, who recognized the notorious smuggler and refused to let Mugabi back into the country, despite the boxer's protestations. After three hours of detention and some phone calls to Mugabi's lawyers, the two were released. The incident endeared Clark to Mugabi, and not long after the twenty-five-year-old African converted to Catholicism.

On March 10, when Mugabi finally met Hagler in Las Vegas, Father Clark took a break from the sanctuary trial to be in his corner.[1]

In Mexico Father Quiñones and Doña Socorro Aguilar achieved similar prominence. Some 7,000 people showed up at a picnic honoring the priest after the indictment, and the widow was named Woman of the Year by the governor of the state of Sonora. PAN, a rightist opposition party in Mexico, had even taken her up as something of a nationalist heroine, who had defied the eternally arrogant Yankees.

Still, one flyer sent out all over Nogales, Sonora, urged Mexicans to come to the defense of Quiñones with not a mention of Socorro Aguilar.[2] And a few of the other women defendants, particularly Darlene Nicgorski, objected to the press's enduring fascination with the Anglo male defendants.* Although six of the eleven people on trial and most of the foot soldiers of the movement were women, when the national

---

*In a speech in Nogales during the trial, Sister Nicgorski vented her feelings on this issue. "In the U.S. media, the leadership of white male clerics is stressed, and receives the overwhelming attention rather than the courage of the Latin Americans themselves or the women who are the heart of the underground railroad," she declared. On one caravan from Phoenix to Chicago, making twelve stops, there were women in charge at every stop: driving, feeding, housing, and doing legal work with refugees. Yet these mainstays of the movement were rarely given their due, in the eyes of some of them.

media sought out a spokesperson for sanctuary, it always seemed to be Fife or Corbett, and it was their pictures, along with Willis-Conger's, that most frequently graced the pages of the newsmagazines. Neither Nicgorski nor Peggy Hutchison, another strong feminist, associated this relative neglect with the fact that, by and large, they disliked and distrusted the press.

Still Sister Darlene had attracted a devoted retinue of nuns, many of whom had also served in Latin America and who were in constant attendance at the trial. She as much as the other defendants had become instant folk heroes of the left, which had few enough in the Age of Reagan, as the trial became a magnet for journalists, filmmakers, and activists hoping for a replay of the great civil disobedience scenes of the 1960s. On key days spectators lined up as early as 6:00 A.M. outside the courtroom, and the local press and supporters had to compete with visiting priests and nuns and writers, including a playwright just back from Soweto, for seats. One of the journalists assigned to the trial, Gene Varn of the *Arizona Republic,* even paid a young man to stand in line for him every day.

Hollywood actors, like former "M*A*S*H" star Mike Farrell, flew in for fund-raisers, and academics arrived to study the psychology of those who would defy the most powerful government in the world. Carol Gilligan, author of *In a Different Voice,* a seminal work on how women's constructions of moral problems differ from men's, interviewed the women defendants. A professor from Humboldt State University in California who was a survivor of the Holocaust and an expert on those who had helped the Jews in Europe sent in a graduate student to interview Corbett and others for a project on the altruistic personality. The professor, Dr. Samuel Oliner, concluded, after extensive interviews with people who had come to the rescue of Jews in Nazi-occupied Europe, that altruists had three common characteristics: a value system stressing fairness and compassion; high self-esteem and a feeling of competence; and a supportive emotional network.[3]

Typically the press and the public paid far more attention to the heroes than to the victims, with their often depressing stories of torture and oppression. Yet the parade of Central American witnesses that followed Alejandro Gómez finally brought the refugees' reality into the courtroom. Their histories came out fitfully, in snippets of fact and allusions, like the jumpy, grainy images on an ancient TV set. But their testimony at last gave the spectators a sense, however truncated, of the human realities that lay behind the massive flight from Central America.

Some of the witnesses, particularly those who had come into the country through the auspices of Jesus Cruz and the "Nogales connection," had fled for a tangle of economic and political reasons. Typical of this was a twenty-one-year-old named José Noe Segovia, who had first come to the United States in 1982 from San Miguel in El Salvador after his cousin had been slain. After two years he was arrested and applied for political asylum; but his application was rejected, and he didn't appeal after an attorney told him the cost, beginning with a fifty-dollar application fee. He decided that he wouldn't bother since such appeals were rarely granted anyway, and he was deported.

The Immigration Service gave Segovia a letter saying that if he wished to reenter the United States legally, he should go to the American embassy in San Salvador and obtain a visa. He first returned to San Miguel, where he discovered that the population had been "reduced by about 50 percent," an observation that was corroborated by other witnesses. He went to the U.S. embassy, as he had been instructed, but was refused entry. A machine-gun-carrying security officer outside gave him a slip of paper which stated, he testified, that he had to have a house, a car, and a $10,000 bank account in order to be eligible for a visa.[4]

Segovia had a sister in the United States who knew a man named Jesus Cruz, and through that connection he had been put in touch with Quiñones and Socorro Aguilar in Nogales. When he arrived at the border, they gave him food and shelter and pointed out the fence and Sacred Heart Church beyond. He had crossed the line on his own and was helped by sanctuary workers once he was inside the United States.

The only refugee witness who tried to damage the defendants was, as expected, José René Argueta.* The forty-four-year-old accountant testified that Father Quiñones had given him the border pass of a deceased priest to use to get into the United States and instructed him to say that he was a Mexican if he was caught. Socorro Aguilar, he claimed, had purchased "a priest's clothing" to make the disguise complete.

---

*Apparently Argueta was not a man who inspired confidence in anyone. John Nixon told the author that if the sanctuary people thought the shifty Central American was working for the government, *he* didn't know *whom* Argueta might be working for. "There was something about him that didn't add up," Nixon commented.[5]

Under cross-examination, however, Bill Walker brought out that it was Argueta himself who had bought the clothes and that they were ordinary street clothes, not clerical garb.

Argueta also claimed that after crossing the border and being driven to Tucson by Nixon, Morgan, and Cruz, he stopped at Southside, where he met John Fife. Fife's attorney shortly advised the court that the minister was actually in Los Angeles on July 9, 1984, the date that Argueta and, earlier, Cruz swore that they saw him.[6]

Argueta tried to play down the violence in his native country. He claimed to have no knowledge of death squads, disappearances, forced military conscription, and other occurrences described by his fellow migrants. He described the situation in San Miguel, his former home, as "tranquil." When pressed about the civil war raging around the town, he elaborated. "It was a peaceful kind of war," he said.

Others of the Central American witnesses were, like Alejandro Gómez, classic political refugees. One of the most moving was Francisco Nieto Núñez, thirty-two, the former intern from El Salvador who, with his wife, a teacher, his three small children, and his younger brother, had been driven from Phoenix to Albuquerque by INS Agents John Nixon and Lee Morgan. The Nietos had proceeded on to Piscataway, New Jersey, where they found sanctuary in St. Michael's Chapel with the help of the Reverend Henry L. Atkins, Jr., Episcopal chaplain of Rutgers University.

The jury heard only the most general description of the family's ordeal. Francisco Nieto had completed his medical training and was interning at various hospitals when his education was interrupted in 1980 by a military intervention and shutdown of the National University. He had then begun working in private clinics and in clinics set up for refugees. In mid-1983 he had been arrested.

In his cross-examination Piccareta asked: "Now again without giving any details, you were arrested on the basis of your political and religious beliefs, isn't that true?"

"That's what I think."

"So the jury understands, you committed no, what people would think of as crimes to be arrested."

"Objection, Your Honor, to the form of the question and irrelevant," Reno interrupted.

"Sustained as to relevancy," Judge Carroll agreed.

"Sir, at some time after your release, you and your family left the country of El Salvador?" Piccareta went on.

"I went directly from the jail to the airport."

"And without going into the details, again the reason you left El Salvador was that you had a fear for your own physical safety?"

"Exactly."

"And, in fact, during the times of your initial jailing you suffered some type of injury to your physical well being, correct?"

"403 objection, Your Honor," said Reno.

"Well, he can answer that 'yes' or 'no'; then we will go on," said Carroll.

"It is difficult to answer 'yes' or 'no.' There has to be an explanation so that people will understand," said the witness.

"All right, Your Honor, can I ask him to explain?" Piccareta inquired.

"No," Carroll replied.

"Sir, when you were jailed, you were separated from your family, correct?"

"Correct."

"And your children were separated from your wife eventually, correct?"

"Yes, but they were in jail for eight days with my wife also."

"And then they were taken away from your wife without knowing where your children went?"

Reno: "Your Honor, I—"

"Correct," replied the witness.

Reno: "I object to this continuing line of questioning."

The Court: "Yes, I sustained the objection to that line of questioning, Mr. Piccareta, and I think I have made that clear."

"Your Honor, I am trying to—"

The Court: "If you want to discuss it we will excuse the jury."[7]

Piccareta proceeded in his frustrating task, and later, in an offer of proof delivered by Michael Altman out of the presence of the jury, the courtroom heard yet another dramatic story that those passing judgment on the sanctuary workers were not permitted to hear.*

According to the offer of proof, the Salvadoran police had come to the Nietos' home and taken the entire family away. Husband and wife were taken to separate prisons, where they were beaten and tortured, and for days they had no idea what had happened to the three children,

---

*Neither this nor any other of the refugees' stories, it should be added, was ever subjected to any kind of critical scrutiny because the court already had ruled that they were irrelevant to the case.

one of whom was still a nursing infant. When Mrs. Nieto was released after a week or so, the children were returned to her, but the police then arrived to take the infant away again. He was taken to the prison where his father was jailed, and, while Francisco Nieto watched helplessly, the several-month-old child was held underwater. The police threatened to drown him unless his father signed a paper saying that he was a "subversive." He did.

After about a year of imprisonment and after the International Red Cross had intervened on his behalf, Francisco was finally released in July 1984. He immediately gathered his family together and fled to Mexico. Shortly thereafter the family's home was stripped of its furnishings and their car disappeared.[8]

In his direct examination of the Nietos, Reno focused on the assistance they had received from the sanctuary workers. Nieto had testified that the UN high commissioner for refugees in Mexico City had told him that the United States was approving only about 2 percent of asylum applications from Salvadorans and that in some cases the forms were torn up before they were processed. But when Nieto mentioned the 2 percent rate, Reno cut him off with an objection that was sustained by Carroll, who called the statistic "irrelevant and prejudicial." Steve Cooper took issue, arguing that the 2 percent figure was not disputed. "Well, I don't know about that," Carroll replied.[9]

Nieto had been assisted by North American clergy and Salvadoran exiles in Mexico City, and through them he met Jim Corbett, to whom he told his story. But the prosecutor had no idea how the Nietos had gotten to the border or across into the United States. When Reno asked Francisco Nieto directly where on the border he had entered the United States, the refugee said, "Agua Prieta." And when Reno asked, "Would you please tell us the names of those persons [who assisted in the entry]?" Nieto clearly stated, "It was Peggy Hutchison and Elena [Ellen] Willis-Conger." He identified Hutchison in the courtroom and, in response to further questions, explained that the two women had led the group to a spot in the international fence where there were holes underneath, "and that is where we went through."[10]

Reno was pleasantly surprised. He had known that Peggy Hutchison had been working the border constantly; but he had very little hard evidence of that, and he feared that the case against her would be dismissed. Still, he couldn't understand why Nieto had just matter-of-factly pointed her out instead of saying, *"No recuerdo"* ("I don't remember"), as so many of the alien witnesses had done. Again and again they answered, *"No recuerdo,"* in response to direct questions about who had aided their entry, clearly lying, in his opinion, to shield their benefactors.

The mystery of why Nieto had not had a similar memory lapse was cleared up under cross-examination. Piccareta asked Nieto if it was at a church in Agua Prieta that he had met Ms. Hutchison and "also [if] there was a reporter and a photographer from a newspaper, an American newspaper," there, too.

"That's right," replied Nieto.[11]

As Reno then learned, the refugees' journey across the border had been chronicled by the *Sacramento Bee,* and the defense had assumed that Reno had seen the series and knew that Hutchison had been involved. "If he had said 'no recordo,' " Reno said later, "she would never have been convicted."[12]*

Shortly after Nieto's appearance in court Joel Morelos was called to testify. Morelos was one of two Guatemalan political refugees who had been met by Cruz at the border and later befriended by the spy. A slight, dark-haired man of thirty, the son of a sugarcane cutter, he was from a small village near the southern coast of Guatemala. His story was if anything even more violent, a brutal tale of the kind of primitive retaliation meted out against any peasants in that sad and beautiful country who dared to challenge the status quo.[13]

Morelos grew up on one of the country's largest plantations, and by the time he was thirteen, he had gone as far as he could in the local school. The only secondary education available was in private schools in nearby towns, which the family could not afford. So at fourteen he went to work like his father, cutting cane.

The teenager spent several years on the huge El Salto plantation in Escuintla, becoming a carpenter in the maintenance shop. He also started attending night classes and became a leader of a student association. In the mid-1970s many of the small towns of Guatemala, including Escuintla, still had no secondary schools, and groups of teachers, students, and young workers were beginning to petition the government to build more schools.

Morelos's group had actually petitioned the Ministry of Education

---

*Reno pronounced the Spanish "no recordo." The defense ridiculed the repeated mistake in pronunciation, as a sign of the prosecutor's ignorance of all things Hispanic.

for a secondary school, to no avail, and his association became part of a major struggle between Guatemalan youth and the government for better education. There were protest marches and demonstrations in the countryside and in Guatemala City, and Morelos frequently spoke at rallies, which the government labeled "subversive." After one such demonstration in 1977, as Morelos was walking away from the rally, four men in plain clothes grabbed him, shoved him into a car, blind-folded him, and drove him to a cinder-block house. For two hours they beat him, kicked him in the head, tortured him, putting out cigarettes on his body, and stabbing him in the shoulder. He was left with perma-nent scars and a total loss of hearing in his left ear.

His abductors demanded that he give them the names and addresses of the leaders of the organizations he was involved in and called him a Communist who deserved to die. In the end they let him go but warned him to stay out of politics from then on.

After his abduction Morelos continued his political activity. He be-came a leader in the national union of sugar industry workers and participated in talks with plantation owners on a new collective bar-gaining agreement. When discussions broke down in the spring of 1980, the union went out on strike, and the army was called in. Several union leaders and their lawyers were killed. In May a death list was circulated at the plantation by a group calling itself Squadron of Death. The list said at the top: "They will be assassinated soon as Communists and traitors to their country." There were some two dozen names on the list. One of them was the local mayor, and another was Joel Morelos. Within weeks several of those targeted were dead.

At this point Morelos finally went underground. Three days before the death list came out, he had been married. "That was my honey-moon," he said bitterly. He rushed his wife, Gabriela, to his parents' house and left to hide with friends. He continued working in the cane fields, but every day he took a different route to work, and he avoided going out in public. Once he eluded someone on the street who seemed to be following him, and another time a gunman shot at him in the marketplace but missed. On still another occasion the army made a sweep through his village looking for people, including him.

This nightmarish existence continued for more than two years, while a veritable bloodbath engulfed Guatemala. The Moreloses realized that they no longer had any choice but to leave the country. The local and the national sugarcane workers' union had been destroyed. The pastor of the evangelical church on Morelos's plantation had been forced to flee because of his sympathy for the union, and armed guards had been placed in front of the church. Of the eight men who had been on the union negotiating committee, seven eventually left Guatemala. Three of the twelve directors of Morelos's student association were killed, and four others to his knowledge had fled the country. Many of his teachers had been killed. And Gabriela's brother, also a union member, was abducted and disappeared.

The final straw was the appearance of a second death list with Morelos's name on it. "Sons of the South," it read. "Be it known that this is a continuation of the list of Communists and agitators that will soon be dead at whatever hour, place or in whatever form. They will be killed with knives, by beating, choking and burning. This list of Communists is a society within our progressive country that impedes the development of our democracy." It was signed ESA, for Ejército Secreto Anticomunisto ("Secret Anticommunist Army").

Penniless and with no contacts, the young couple headed for Mexico, taking back-road buses and walking through the mountains, carrying their one-year-old daughter on their backs. Three days and 200 miles later they crossed the border.

By the time they arrived in Tapachula, in Chiapas, the Mexican government had begun a campaign to turn back the hordes of Guatemalan refugees streaming into the country. The refugees were being herded into overcrowded camps along the border, and those who resisted were arrested and summarily deported. The Moreloses decided to try to pass themselves off as Mexicans and try to live as normal a life as possible. They rented a small room in a modest house, and Morelos found a job selling photo albums door to door. It paid just enough to cover the rent and provide one meal a day.

For a year and five months the family lived in this way, always in constant fear of *la migra*. They had two brushes with Mexican immigration. Once the authorities, acting on a tip that Morelos was a Central American, appeared at his house and ordered him to get in their car. They asked him where he was from. He answered in his best Mexican accent, but they made it clear they knew he was Central American. "It's OK," one of the men said, "if you could just give us a little something." Morelos had no money. When he left Guatemala, his mother had taken her watch off her wrist and said, "Take this; it might help you along the way." And his father had told him that he had no money to give him, but the old sugarcane cutter had passed on to his son a beloved straw-brimmed hat. Now, with all of them sitting in the car, the Mexican immigration officials asked Joel for the watch and the hat. He handed them over.

The Moreloses had been trying to legalize their status in Mexico but were told by the United Nations office in Chiapas that their chances of receiving asylum were slim; there was a long waiting list of Guatemalans trying to get in, and they would have to wait their turn. The UN official suggested they try Canada, where the government had declared a policy of offering safe haven for Guatemalans for the duration of the violence.

While the couple pondered this information, their constant canvassing of local churches, unions, and other organizations finally paid off. A man from a Mexican church group came to their door and said that he had information that they had been asking for help. He said that he was a member of the sanctuary movement in Mexico and explained that there were congregations in the United States that were helping Central Americans resettle. All the refugees had to do, he said, was to speak out to the local community about the reasons why they had had to flee.

If Joel and Gabriela were interested, the man went on, the churches would pay for their trip north and provide clothing and shoes for the journey, as well as all legal and medical expenses when they arrived.

The young couple seized on the offer, and in May 1984 they began the trek north. The man accompanied them by bus from Tapachula to Mexico City, showing them how to get off the bus one or two miles before an immigration checkpoint, walk over the mountains for three or four miles and then down to the road again to pick up the next bus. The trip, which normally takes a day, took them twice as long. Their guide put them up in a hotel in Mexico City, where they stayed for about ten days, and then gave them money for food and plane tickets to Hermosillo.

In Hermosillo, at the immigration checkpoint, the Moreloses were stopped and taken into an office. The authorities grilled them: Who has been helping you; how much money are you carrying; where are you going? Joel tried to persuade them he was Mexican and refused to answer their questions. They called in two airport policemen. Two pistol-wearing cops warned Morelos to tell the truth or they would get the information out of him their own way. Joel, now desperate, told them, "I can tell you where I'm from, but if you want to deport me there, it's better that you kill me right now."

"We don't want to deport you; we just want to know where you're from," replied one of the immigration officers.

"I'm from Guatemala."

"Where are you going; how much money are you carrying?" the police persisted.

Joel was carrying about 3,000 pesos with him, worth no more than a few dollars. Cheerfully the police took the money, told the Moreloses to be on their way, and wished them good luck.

The family left the airport to look for a ride to take them into town. As they were standing by the side of the road one of the same officials they had encountered in the airport came along in a van. He pulled up in front of them and asked where they were going. Before they could answer, he told them that he could give them a ride to the church. As they rode along, he reached in his pocket and handed them back about 1,000 pesos. "Here," he said, "for your child. She doesn't need to have these problems."

Very little of this travail came out at the trial, although Joel was able to slip a reference to his torture into the record. On one occasion, when Don Reno was pressing him to recall a conversation that had occurred in his presence at Southside, Morelos said that he probably didn't hear it because "I don't hear with one ear. And that is because of the torture that I was subjected to in Guatemala."[14]

What the jury heard were the dry-boned details of the illegal entry: the family's arrival in the United States through the help of the defendants, their drive to Phoenix with undercover agents and on to Santa Fe, New Mexico, with Wendy LeWin, the first stage of a journey to sanctuary in Philadelphia. Their departure from Phoenix on July 20, 1984, with Frederico Cruz and Ana Toledo, a Guatemalan couple who were going to Riverside Church in New York City, had been the occasion of a press conference. That night Channel 5 in Phoenix had shown tapes of the refugees' good friend Jesus Cruz hugging them and their small daughter, Lucy, with tears in his eyes. There their story apparently ended.

But there was more. A few months later, at Christmastime, "Uncle" Jesus called the Moreloses and told them that a good friend of his was coming to Philadelphia and wanted to drop off a present for Lucy. Morelos gave him their address, and on the morning of January 14, 1985, Gabriela Morelos went to answer a ring at the door of their apartment, located over a day-care center in the residential suburb of Germantown. She opened the door, and there stood INS Agent John

Nixon and two colleagues, who introduced themselves as friends of Jesus Cruz. She invited them in, saying that Joel was out but should be back shortly. The visitors sat down, and while they waited, Lucy brought out her books and asked them to read to her.

After a few minutes the agents dropped their ruse and told Gabriela that they were from Immigration and had a warrant for her arrest. She realized at once that their information had come from Jesus Cruz, Tío Jesus, whose last words to them in Phoenix had been: "May it go well for you. May God help you."

"It was a real kiss of Judas," said the Moreloses' lawyer later.[15]

At the time of the Moreloses' arrest their attorney, Walter Walkenhorst III, of Jenkintown, Pennsylvania, told them the Immigration Service would require their real names. Up to that point they had consistently used pseudonyms, for they had been publicly critical of the regime in Guatemala and feared that family members remaining there might suffer retribution. But Walkenhorst explained that the law required proper identification and that Joel would have to comply if he were to have any chance of winning political asylum. So on January 14, 1985, the INS learned his real name and his home address in Guatemala.

On February 2, 1985, Joel Morelos's brother in Guatemala was seized by men in a white Toyota pickup truck with smoked glass windows. He was never seen again. News of the incident appeared in a Guatemalan newspaper on February 11, and a couple of months later a memorial service for the young man was held at the First United Methodist Church of Germantown, the church that had provided sanctuary for the family.

The jury never heard this story either. Instead, they learned that when the family left Phoenix, Jesus Cruz had cried. "They had a very lovely family, yes," he explained on the stand. "Because it is true. That the child was very sweet, very cute."

Chapter
Thirty

DESPITE—OR BECAUSE—of the enormous stress they were under, the indicted church workers kept their sense of humor as the trial ground on into its fifth month.

Mary K. Espinosa relieved her tensions with a ribald wit that had previously been directed at her colleague Father Tony Clark (she had once told the handsome priest during an argument that what he needed was a good piece of ass). Now a wider audience came in for her lusty ribbing. On one occasion when the defense lawyers were huddled over some frustrating point, she walked up and announced, "Judge Carroll's wife is here. I just met her, and she told me this great story. She told him she wanted more foreplay, and he said, 'Motion overruled, let's proceed.' "[1]

Michael Piccareta, a bushy-mustachioed litigator whose hero was Clarence Darrow, was another defense comedian. Once when quizzing a refugee, Don Reno said, "I don't speak Spanish, do I?"

The witness's reply was mistakenly translated as "Yes, you don't speak English."

"Right on both counts," Piccareta quickly volunteered.

"Let's proceed," said the judge.

Even the beleaguered, much maligned Carroll showed not only that he had a sense of humor but that he miraculously hadn't lost it. After one long argument with the defense he said, "Let's bring the jury in . . . assuming they will come in."

At another point, an acrid, burning smell wafted through the courtroom. Someone thought it might be the electrical translating device, whereupon Carroll suggested to William Walker: "Why don't you go over there and grab it and see what's wrong?"[2]

The sanctuary defendants were buoyed up by the support from around the country that had been aroused by the government crackdown. In an important vote of confidence, Amnesty International, the prestigious human rights organization, decided that if the defendants were convicted and imprisoned, they would become Amnesty "prisoners of conscience"—in other words, political prisoners in the United States. Since their full story was not coming out through the heavily censored evidence presented at the trial, the defendants at least had the cold comfort of knowing that if the worst happened, they would achieve a unique distinction.

In January the city of Santa Fe, New Mexico, declared itself a "city of refuge for refugees from El Salvador and Guatemala," and Governor Toney Anaya followed up with a written statement declaring the entire state's support of the sanctuary movement. A week later Seattle, Washington, declared itself a sanctuary city in a unanimous vote by its City Council. The declaration made a total of twelve American cities that had acted in support of sanctuary, including Madison, Wisconsin; San Francisco, California; Los Angeles, California; and Cambridge, Massachusetts.[3] (The largely symbolic declarations meant, in effect, that the local city agencies, including the police, would not act as enforcers of the immigration laws by checking on residents' alien status or handing over suspected aliens to the INS.)

Conspicuously absent from the list of sanctuary cities was Tucson. Fourteen congregations in the birthplace of the movement had declared themselves sanctuaries, but the City Council had decided not to lend its official support. The influential local Catholic hierarchy had not given sanctuary official endorsement, either, so John Fife and others were pleasantly surprised when, on December 4, 1985, Roman Catholic Bishop Manuel D. Moreno of the Tucson diocese issued a strong statement acknowledging the plight of the Salvadoran refugees and calling on the U.S. government to "give them extended voluntary departure status."

The Arizona bishop referred to a recent letter to Congress from Salvadoran Archbishop Arturo Rivera y Damas, pleading for passage of the Moakley-DeConcini bill.* Rivera y Damas, the successor to Archbishop Romero, had been known as a conservative prelate before his accession to high church office, but now he wrote: "[T]he profundization [sic] of the military conflict offers a future of greater pain, uncertainty and suffering for the grand majority of Salvadorans. . . . During my visit to the United States, it was with profound concern that I was able to confirm, through numerous testimonies, that the authorities and members of the government of the United States have closed their doors and their hearts against the suffering of my people."[4]

Despite their celebrity and their claim to moral leadership, the refugees' sanctuary supporters were paying a high price for their deeds. They had become a lightning rod for the deep ideological divisions in their country; and if they were heroes and heroines to part of society, they were criminals to another, far more powerful segment. They faced the prospect of prison, and their normal lives and work were completely disrupted. Among other things, Father Clark had to close his home for juvenile offenders, prompting Bates Butler to drop notes to Mel McDonald and David Klein, a member of the INS Undercover Guidelines Review Committee and an old acquaintance, congratulating them on their contribution to law enforcement.

Even more disturbing, all the defendants and others in the sanctuary movement—and by extension everyone sympathetic to it—had to contend with ominous indications that their government, or some other entity, was trying to intimidate them by clandestine means.

A deeply troubling pattern of break-ins of sanctuary churches and of organizations supporting leftist groups in Central America had emerged, reminiscent of the bad old days of COINTELPRO, the FBI's

---

*In April 1985 in hearings on S.377, the bill to suspend deportations of Salvadorans, Elliott Abrams testified that he had had contact with Archbishop Rivera y Damas and Tutela Legal, the human rights office of the archdiocese, and that neither believed that Salvadoran deportees met up with violence upon their return. Abrams's comments prompted a letter from the archbishop to Cardinal Timothy Manning, auxiliary bishop of Los Angeles, in which the Salvadoran archbishop stated his concern "that Salvadorans have returned to this country only to meet their deaths a few days later."[5]

secret counterintelligence program to sabotage domestic political protest movements in the 1960s and early 1970s.

The numerous "black bag jobs," beginning in mid-1984, amounted to overwhelming evidence of surveillance and harassment: of individuals returning from or receiving mail from Nicaragua or Cuba; of individuals and organizations active in Central American "solidarity" work; and of people and churches working with Central American refugees. By the spring of 1986 information had been gathered on three dozen break-ins in more than twelve cities of groups opposed to the Reagan administration's policies in Central America. In most cases nothing of value was stolen, but papers and files were rifled.

The sanctuary movement was obviously a prime target of this intimidation. A project of the Center for Constitutional Rights, a New York City-based nonprofit advocacy group focusing on civil liberties issues, compiled a long list of incidents involving sanctuary that indicated a clear pattern of harassment:

- *In September 1984 the apartment in Riverside Church housing Frederico Cruz and Ana Toledo and their child was broken into twice, and a file folder on the sanctuary movement was removed.* [6]
- *In October of the same year the apartment of Joel and Gabriela Morelos in Germantown, Pennsylvania, was broken into. His wallet, with the names and addresses of the people who had helped the family travel from Phoenix to Philadelphia, was taken, along with books, tapes, money, and envelopes with the address of his wife's family in Guatemala.*
- *On the night of November 27, 1984, the office doors of three Central America solidarity organizations, housed in the Old Cambridge Baptist Church in Cambridge, Massachusetts, were broken through and the offices' file cabinets disturbed. The church had become a sanctuary for a Salvadoran refugee one week before. Nothing of value was taken. That same night an office of the First Congregational Church in Cambridge and the office of the University Christian Movement of New England, a pro-sanctuary student group, were also entered.*

  In the next year and a half the offices in the basement of the Old Cambridge church were broken into eight times. A Cambridge police detective, James Dyer, reported to the City Council that the burglars of Old Cambridge and of another church, the

Church of the Covenant in Boston, were "interested only in the organizational files and data" of the organizations. A note left behind after one break-in read: "The great I am . . . Gringoes. You're going to save my Indio-hispano friends? You?! Don't make me cry. You're so clearly being used. . . ."

The Old Cambridge Baptist Church filed a Freedom of Information Act (FOIA) request for any files on the church the government might have. After months of waiting, the pastor finally received a reply from the FBI stating that the files could not be released, for they "might reveal the identity of an individual who has furnished information to the F.B.I. under confidential circumstances."

- *In December 1984 a New York City woman active in the sanctuary movement on three occasions found that her mail from other sanctuary activists had been opened before delivery.*
- *In February 1985 the East Bay Sanctuary Covenant offices in the Trinity Methodist Church in Berkeley, California, were rifled. Envelopes filled with cash in a desk drawer were ignored.*
- *On March 24, 1985, a Denver staffer of Representative Patricia Schroeder (Democrat-Colorado) was contacted by an agent of the Defense Investigative Service and asked to identify people who had attended a prayer meeting commemorating the assassination of Salvadoran Archbishop Oscar Romero. A secretary at the Colorado Council of Churches was also contacted for the same information.*
- *On June 17, 1985, the Los Angeles office of Amnesty International discovered that a list of 1,500 celebrity donors, many of whom were active in Central American issues, was missing from the files.*
- *On July 16, 1985, the offices of the University Baptist Church in Seattle, Washington, were robbed. This was the church providing sanctuary to Pilar and Elba Teresa López and their children. The keys to the rooms housing the refugees were taken, legal and personal membership files were rifled, and several personal records of Pastor Donovan Cook, an unindicted coconspirator in the sanctuary trial, also vanished. A few months later, in December, Cook had a letter from the church's insurance company threatening to cancel the insurance unless the church ceased to offer sanctuary.*

- *On September 16, 1985, Father David A. Myers, a Jesuit priest who was also an attorney working on political asylum cases for Central Americans, discovered that his office had been burglarized. A file box of "cases on appeal" was missing. Father Myers, whom Socorro Aguilar had gone to see in efforts to free Frederico Cruz from detention, did not feel that the break-in was a matter for the local police. (Among other things, the Guadalupe, Arizona, police department was then under investigation by the Arizona Department of Public Safety for possible criminal activity.) He wrote the FBI and received a reply from the Phoenix office stating that the agency had no jurisdiction over a local burglary— "an attempt to get salable office equipment"—and that no action would be taken. [7]*
- *On October 25, 1985, the Phoenix office of another attorney working with refugees, Susan Giersbach, was raided. Desk drawers, file cabinets, and telephone logs containing information about clients were examined.*
- *On November 20, 1985, a volunteer at St. William's Catholic Church, a sanctuary church in Louisville, Kentucky, found files disturbed and scattered about. A previously filed letter from Central Americans applying for sanctuary was lying on top of a desk.*
- *On December 29, 1985, the Pico Rivera Methodist Church, a sanctuary church in Los Angeles, was broken into and its offices were searched.*
- *On April 2, 1986, two secretaries at the United Church of Santa Fe in New Mexico discovered that the door to the church's educational area had been broken and the inner offices searched. Membership lists were left on a desktop. Though the church was not a sanctuary church, many members were vocal advocates of sanctuary and had lobbied to have Santa Fe and the state of New Mexico declared sanctuaries.*

In June of 1985 Ellen Yaroshefsky sent Don Reno a letter about the burglaries of sanctuary churches and asked him to determine whether any agency of the federal government was involved.[8] Reno subsequently queried the INS offices and U.S. attorney's offices nearest the church break-ins and received replies assuring him that the Immigration Service had played no part in the incidents.[9] The defense attorneys also called for a congressional investigation of the break-ins, as had other church groups around the country, and appealed to Representative Don Edwards (Democrat-California), head of the House Judiciary Committee's Subcommittee on Civil and Constitutional Rights.

Edwards, an ex-FBI agent, told reporters that he didn't think the bureau or other federal intelligence agencies were involved. Edwards wrote the FBI, asking that the bureau investigate the "disturbing pattern," suggesting that the break-ins might possibly be the work of foreign agents.[10] The bureau considered Edwards's request, and then, on March 14, 1986, FBI Director William Webster, testifying before Edwards's subcommittee on the agency's budget, said that the FBI didn't have jurisdiction over the matter and would therefore not take any action.[11]*

The sanctuary defendants tried to focus public attention on the pattern of harassment. In early February 1986 several hundred sanctuary activists, including seventy-five in the Tucson area, and all eleven defendants in the trial, announced plans to send FOIA requests to the FBI, INS, CIA, National Security Agency, and other intelligence agencies for any files the government might have on them in relation to their sanctuary work. Several congregations and one national denomination, the Unitarian Universalist Association, joined the action, in response to a written request from the Tucson defendants. The letter urged them to release whatever information they obtained to the media "to expose the extent of government infiltration and investigation of the sanctuary movement."

Within a few weeks this dragnet brought in one small fish. It turned out that the FBI did have a file on Darlene Nicgorski. Reno and Judge Carroll were allowed to see it, but the FBI refused to release it to the nun.

*Suspicion of government involvement persists among those familiar with the break-ins. Patricia Schroeder, a member of the subcommittee and a victim of COINTELPRO harassment and break-ins in the mid-1970s, told the author that she believes that private individuals who hand their findings over to federal agencies may be responsible for the incidents, yet another example of "privatization." Under a new executive order and attorney general guidelines on United States intelligence activities, approved by the Reagan administration, so-called black bag jobs could be interpreted as legal if executed in the name of foreign counterintelligence. At the March 14, 1986, hearing on the FBI budget authorization request, Congressman Robert W. Kastenmeier, Democrat of Wisconsin, noted that $41.8 million, "about half" the increase sought by the bureau that year, was for foreign counterintelligence. "That has found a high priority, obviously," he commented.[12] (See Epilogue.)

On top of everything else the defendants and other sanctuary activists were convinced that their telephones were being monitored. Don Reno denied any knowledge, pointing out that the INS lacked the authority to engage in electronic surveillance.[13] In the meantime, strange static, dead lines, mysterious overheard conversations, and other irregularities on many lines persisted, and in February 1986 the defense attorneys filed motions requesting a formal probe into any electronic surveillance ordered against the church workers.

The prosecutor argued against these motions, on the ground that such a search could take six to eight weeks. Judge Carroll sided with the prosecution, saying that the request was too general and would be too time-consuming. Thus, as they sat silently through the long trial, the defendants had to worry not only about its outcome but about the elusive, anonymous forces that seemed to be arrayed against them.

Chapter
Thirty-one

IN FEBRUARY THE government called three North American members of the sanctuary movement to testify against their colleagues. All were unindicted coconspirators who were in a position to verify much of what Jesus Cruz had said.

One was the Reverend George Lockwood, thirty-nine, pastor of the Menlo Park Methodist Church in Tucson, the church attended by Peggy Hutchison and Phil Willis-Conger. Lockwood had flown down to Mexico City to help the Elba Teresa group of refugees up to Hermosillo.[1] A second North American witness was Kay Kelly, the sixty-two-year-old grandmother and deacon at Southside who had been active in sanctuary since the death of her husband in the spring of 1983.[2] The third North American subpoenaed to testify was Mary Ann Lundy, fifty-three, cochair of the sanctuary committee of Riverside Church in New York City and coordinator of the National Student YWCA. Lundy, an ordained elder in the Presbyterian Church, was also the wife of the Reverend Richard A. Lundy of St. Luke's Presbyterian Church in Wayzata, Minnesota.

On February 13 the three religious activists entered their motions to override the government's efforts to call them to the stand, arguing that the order violated their First Amendment right to free exercise of religion. In her affidavit to quash the subpoena, Lundy declared, "By granting me immunity the government seeks to force me to testify in order to convict my brothers and sisters. . . . How could I, who have received their trust and confidence . . . become their Judas?"

"I've never been a squealer, and I don't intend to start at age sixty-two," Kelly told friends.[3] In her affidavit she stated that she felt "guided by a Higher Power."

Lundy's lawyer, Marcia Levy of New York, injected the one note of levity when she brought up Lundy's religious influence on her own life. After working with her client for six months, Levy said, she had telephoned her Jewish mother and said, "Mother, I've finally found religion." After listening to the satisfaction on the other end of the line, she added, "It's Presbyterian."[4]

In the end Judge Carroll ruled not to quash the subpoenas, thereby compelling all three to take the stand, along with a fourth unindicted coconspirator who refused to testify, the Salvadoran Elba Teresa López. Carroll told the courtroom that these are "good caring people who have contributed much to society" and that he appreciated their religious convictions. But he recognized religion as a motivator, he said, not as an excuse. The recalcitrant witnesses had evidence necessary to the government's case, Carroll said, and the law requires that all the evidence available in a case should be heard in the courtroom.[5] That particular reminder was heard with more than a little irony by the defense.

On the following Tuesday, February 18, all three North American witnesses still refused to testify. Lundy declared: "I choose not to testify on the basis of my First Amendment right to freedom of religion and invoke my privilege as a Presbyterian Elder not to speak against my community of faith." Carroll charged Lundy and the others with contempt of court and sentenced them all to house arrest. They were ordered to remain in their homes until the case ended, leaving only to obtain medical treatment and to attend a regularly scheduled religious service once a week. A few days later Elba Teresa López, who had also refused to testify, was cited for contempt and given the same sentence of house arrest.

After Carroll's rulings, the defendants, their attorneys, and sanctuary supporters in the packed courtroom stood up as each of the three recalcitrant witnesses filed from the room. Twice the judge warned the defense lawyers that "such demonstrations are for outside the courtroom, not inside," and he threatened to hold them, too, in contempt if they continued the show of support. As the last witness left the courtroom, the attorneys remained in their seats while everyone else rose a third time.[6]

Kelly, Lundy, and Lockwood stayed confined for a month, until the defense rested its case on March 15. Carroll could have sentenced the three to jail, and Kay Kelly and Lockwood, as it turned out, were able to leave their homes on several occasions to visit hospitalized relatives. Nevertheless, the sentencing of nonviolent protesters to house arrest was an unprecedented occurrence in the United States, more evocative of South Africa than Arizona. Kelly's attorney, Mark P. Rosenbaum of the ACLU Foundation of Southern California, noticed, while saying good-bye to her after a visit one day, that all her doors and windows were covered with security bars. He was struck by the symbolism as her face peered out at him from behind her barred kitchen door.[7]

At first blush it appeared that the government case had been dealt a severe blow by the loss of the testimony. The prosecution would now have to rely even more heavily on the garbled words of its discredited informer. But Don Reno quickly realized that the incident was a blessing in disguise, providing yet another dramatic turn in the trial.

The prosecutor told the judge that he needed the unindicted coconspirators' testimony so badly that if he couldn't have it live, the next best thing would be to have it on tape.[8]

As it happened, the tape that best illustrated the "conspiracy" was one of a September 10 meeting at Southside, attended by John Fife, Peggy Hutchison, Phil Willis-Conger, Jim Corbett, George Lockwood, Ken Kennon, and others. The discussion was clearly that of a group of people organized for a common purpose. One of the purposes that night was to plan how to bring the Elba Teresa group up from Mexico City. Since Lockwood's testimony would have dealt with that plan, Reno asked Carroll to permit him to introduce selected portions of that tape, as well as several others, into evidence.

The defense countered by asking Carroll to admit all the tapes in their entirety. Carroll refused, so the next few days were filled with lengthy wrangling over the admission of particular snippets of the tapes, with tedious argument over individual pages, lines, and even words on the tape transcripts. The nit-picking reflected the fact that in some instances the government's case against a person depended on a single word or phrase.

At one point, for example, the attorneys and Judge Carroll spent at least an hour with their ears pressed to bright yellow and black headphones in an effort to discern the true meaning of the term *uh-huh,* uttered by Elba Teresa when Cruz asked if it was Peggy Hutchison who had brought her into the country. Later the headsets went on again to focus on two sentences attributed to Peggy Hutchison. According to the attorneys, two felony counts and one misdemeanor hinged on admission of the sentences as evidence.

The painstaking tape editing provided a few light moments. Once, after the roomful of lawyers had donned all the gear necessary to listen to the tapes, the player was turned on and nothing happened. After a silence Brosnahan quipped, "They've got us now!"

Not amused, Carroll frowned out from underneath his yellow headset and snapped, "What was that comment, Mr. Brosnahan?"[9]

In the end the jury heard brief portions of four of the ninety-one tapes. They now had something more than Jesus Cruz's word to link certain sanctuary workers, particularly Fife, Hutchison, and Willis-Conger, to conspiratorial acts, and they had heard concrete evidence that the defendants did meet regularly to set in motion common projects. The reintroduction of the material was a boon to the prosecutor, who was sure that the defense team thought the tapes had been banished forever.

As Reno saw it, the defense attorneys would have been better off telling the unindicted coconspirators to take the stand and say, "I don't remember."[10]

The last government witness to take the stand was undercover agent John Nixon. Wearing a conservative suit and tinted glasses, the fit, strong-jawed INS man looked and seemed to be playing a part written for his western hero, the cinematic scourge of bullies and cowards.

In a laconic monotone, the undercover agent testified about his meetings with the defendants at Southside Presbyterian, at Sacred Heart Church, and at Sister Darlene's apartment in Phoenix. In one poignant exchange Reno asked him to describe how he arrested Francisco Nieto Núñez on August 6, 1985, almost one year to the day after he had transported the refugee and his family from Phoenix to Santa Fe.

"As he was leaving the church grounds in which he was being harbored . . . when he was approximately two blocks away I—we approached him."

"What did you say to him?"

"I asked him if he remembered me."

"What did he say?"

"Yes."

"What occurred then?"

"I shook his hand and held it firmly until Agent Morgan could walk around and place him under arrest."

"What—after you placed him under arrest what did you do then?"

"Put him in the back seat of our sedan."

"Who was driving the car?"

"I was."

"Will you please tell us what occurred after Mr. Francisco Nieto was placed in the rear seat of your vehicle?"

"As Agent Morgan was reading him his Miranda rights, he suddenly and without provocation leaped toward the front passenger's window and he yelled at some people who were standing on the sidewalk."

"Do you recall what he yelled?"

"It was in Spanish, he said twice 'soy refujiado' and he said 'Ayu-dame.' "

"Do you speak Spanish fluently?"

"No sir, I do not."

"Do you understand the Spanish language well enough to converse in it?"

"Yes[,] I do."

"Do you know what that means?"

"Yes. 'I'm a refugee, I'm a refugee. Help me.' "

"After he made that statement, what occurred then?"

"Agent Morgan and Agent Rayburn restrained him, sat him back in the rear seat, and asked him to be calm."

". . . At any time . . . did you or any of these other two persons ever abuse, physically abuse Mr. Francisco Nieto Nunez in any way?"

"No, we did not."

". . . did you ever threaten him verbally?"

"No, we did not."[11]

Nixon did his best to incriminate the defendants, even at one point reporting, like a tattletale, John Fife's reference to "all this bullshit." When the minister left the courtroom during the first break after that testimony, his friends all chanted, "Na, na, na-na, na."

In its cross-examination the defense endeavored to demonstrate Nixon's lack of prowess as an investigator. The agent testified that he had given John Fife, Darlene Nicgorski, and Phil Willis-Conger his telephone number, with the suggestion that if they ever needed any help, they should call. None of them, he admitted, ever did. He also admitted that during the investigation he did not know what the Tucson Ecumenical Council was, he was not familiar with the screening process that the sanctuary movement used to identify high-risk refugees, nor was he aware of the social service activities of the Tucson Ecumenical Council, whose meetings INS agents had infiltrated. None of that was "relevant," he declared.[12]

Nixon also indicated that he had not inquired very deeply into the background of the people he had met during the sanctuary investigation. He even doubted that Darlene Nicgorski was really a nun, although he had never checked to find out. He did accept, he said, the religious credentials of Tony Clark, Ramón Quiñones, and John Fife.[13]

While Nixon was on the stand, the pent-up animosity that had been simmering in the courtroom for months finally erupted in a spectacularly nasty outburst, like a marital spat in which hostile partners, to their horror, finally say what they really think. Previously the worst clashes with the judge had involved defense attorneys Brosnahan and Walker. Both were hot-tempered men, and Brosnahan in particular was convinced that the only way to handle Carroll, who he believed would try to bully the defense, was to take the offensive and intimidate him first. (The strategy was privately criticized by some local attorneys like Larry Debus, who, as much as he detested Carroll, thought that the sanctuary defense team should have shown a sitting judge more respect.)

But the uproar that culminated on March 6 involved everyone and had less the ring of a tactic than the cry of a roomful of wronged children. On February 28 Mike Piccareta had asked the judge to listen to a tape of "the words and the tone and the manner that our objections are being overruled and compare it to the tone and the manner when the Court reprimands [Reno] and I would suggest that it is in the tone of like a father-son reprimand to Mr. Reno while our general objections . . . get more of a snappy response. . . . I think you might notice that at least the jury—I know the Court doesn't do it intentionally—might inadvertently pick up some type of partisanship by the Court."[14]

A few days later the attorneys complained again about the harsh manner in which Carroll spoke to Bob Hirsh during his cross-examination of Nixon. Brosnahan cited recent research on how the appearance of a judge's verbal and nonverbal behavior can affect the outcome of criminal trials. "When Your Honor scowls as Your Honor has this morning and many times during this trial you scowl at counsel, you scowl at the defendants . . . we would ask Your Honor not to do that because as soon as you do it you convey a message that you don't like the defendants or the defendants' case. . . ."[15]

On the following day Walker put his gloves on. "Your Honor"—he opened the proceedings—"I felt it necessary to again put on the record my objection to the Court's conduct yesterday in front of the jury. . . . When Mr. Hirsh began reading from the statement the Court with face red and scowling and giving very, very—I don't know how to characterize them except death looks to the defense . . . raised its voice and admonished Mr. Hirsh in front of the jury. It was not necessary. It clearly indicated Your Honor's animus in this case. It was at a time when there were no objections from the prosecution at all. The jury I think got the clear impression again, as it has frequently throughout this trial, of your bias and prejudice in the case.

"I also want the record to reflect that the Court's tone had gotten harsher and more cryptic in front of the jury and has gotten more angry in front of the jury as we have proceeded in this case."[16] Walker later commented that in his opinion, the only conspiracy in the courtroom was the one between the judge and the prosecutor.

Reno finally could not take it anymore. During the course of the trial he had come to have enormous respect for Carroll's intelligence and his ability to withstand what Reno thought must be the "most unprecedented judge bashing ever experienced by a sitting federal judge."[17] On the day of Walker's "rant" he stood up and addressed the bench. "Your Honor, I have been hesitant over the weeks and the—virtually the months that I have heard Mr. Walker and Mr. Brosnahan and at times Mr. Piccareta and Mr. Altman make the accusations against the Court. What concerns me is these daily diatribes that continue and that I believe are part of the defendants' trial strategy. . . . I want the record to reflect, Your Honor, that you are faced with an extremely difficult task in having to control eleven defense attorneys that persist in violating the Court's orders blatantly, notoriously. . . .

". . . when the Court took a positive stance to enforce the orders, to enforce the proper decorum and the atmosphere in this courtroom, then the defense attorneys stand up and object vigorously, make personal accusations against the Court, their accusations, Your Honor, are vindictive, they are mean, and they are an attempt to intimidate this Court. . . .

"Your Honor, several days ago we had a very brief discussion about the Court keeping perhaps a list or making comments not on the record about the conduct of the attorneys in this case. On behalf of the United States Government, on behalf of the United States Attorney, I strongly urge the Court to keep a list, Your Honor. Because as a defense pack, these gentlemen run very, very, very strong in this courtroom in attempting to intimidate this Court. . . . If Mr. Walker is out of line, if I am out of line or if Mr. Hirsh is out of line, then, Your Honor, I believe that you have an obligation to cite us at the end of this case and note any contemptuous conduct that takes place in front of this Court. . . . I hope that you are keeping a list, Your Honor. That's all I have to say."[18]

The defense attorneys all shouted to be heard. Among others, Piccareta noted that "Mr. Reno's comments drip with hypocrisy when he presents perjured testimony on the witness stand with Mr. Rayburn sitting here, realizing, does nothing. And the Court admonishes Mr. Rayburn in a quite more soothing tone than [it did] the defense lawyers. . . . That is not a criticism of the Court. . . . If Mr. Reno in good faith gets up here and makes those allegations then he should first clean up his own house if he's going to criticize trial conduct when the violations of the United States Government in this case by the agents, by the witnesses and by the prosecutor are far more serious."[19]

Yaroshefsky added: "I think it is fair to say that in the collective experience of all of the lawyers no one has ever seen a trial in which the U.S. Government attorney and the witnesses on the government stand have behaved the way that they have. . . . Beyond that I think it is time to put the matter of this list to rest. And my experience and from what I have heard from other counsel has been that if a court feels that counsel have done something inappropriate they are cited at the time, that it is incredibly intimidating for the Government to suggest or for the Court to keep a list where at the end of the case the Court will take some appropriate measures. Seems very much like a school room."[20]

Bob Hirsh arrived late at the courthouse that morning, after some of the smoke had cleared. He was immediately filled in on the exchange, including an accusation by Reno that the defense had programmed or "cued" the courtroom spectators to laugh and comment at appropriate

times. (Reno had said that he believed that many times the laughter and
bantering behind the rail where the audience was sitting were staged.)
So Hirsh, who heretofore had had a fairly decent courtroom relationship with the judge, finally let his own feelings come out.

"One does get the impression that Your Honor is against the defendants," he said to Carroll, and "if we are wrong, we are wrong. But that
is the perception that we have. You have shown disdain and dislike for
us and our clients and our position, and we, I suppose, react to that."
A little later, after Hirsh had taken up his cross-examination of Nixon
again and had been admonished by the judge again, he burst out:
"I can't understand for the life of me the way the Court is interacting
with me. When you talk to me it is either out of sarcasm or anger or
hostility. And it has gone on repeatedly. For the life of me, I don't
know what I have done that would warrant that sort of conduct by
the Court. . . . I cannot seem to interact with you the way lawyers
and judges interact. I don't know why."

"It is disconcerting to me, Mr. Hirsh," Carroll replied, "when I rule
before the jury that an objection is sustained or that we are going to do
something and you roll your eyes and shake your head and seem to give
the impression, at least as I would perceive your conduct, that somehow
I am less than a blithering idiot."[21]

Chapter
Thirty-two

ON MARCH 7, 1986, after eighteen weeks of courtroom Sturm und Drang, prosecutor Don Reno finally rested the government's case against the eleven sanctuary workers. The case was considerably less sweeping than when the trial had begun, and the prosecutor acknowledged as much in mid-March, when he moved that a number of the remaining counts against the defendants be dismissed, on the ground that the government had not presented sufficient evidence to support the charges.

In its final form the indictment listed twenty-five felony charges, six misdemeanor charges, and the conspiracy charge, also a felony. Of all the counts remaining, only two involved bringing illegal aliens into the country. Only one charge, of conspiracy, remained against Jim Corbett, the man the government had most wanted to prosecute.

Phil Willis-Conger faced the stiffest potential penalty, with seven counts against him, in addition to the conspiracy charge, and Darlene Nicgorski was a close second, with five counts. Three substantive counts and the conspiracy charge remained against John Fife. María Socorro Aguilar still faced three felony counts, and the two priests, Father Quiñones and Father Clark, faced two each. Of an original

eleven counts, only two remained against Peggy Hutchison. And only
the conspiracy charge remained against Nena MacDonald, leading to
considerable speculation that more than a year after her indictment, she
would finally be dropped from the case. According to the evidence
presented, the Quaker woman had used the telephone in John Fife's
office while an alleged conspiratorial conversation was taking place
there. The government had acknowledged that she had not taken part
in the conversation. Nevertheless, Judge Carroll refused to lift the
single count against her.[1]

The defense had listed more than 150 witnesses whom they might
call, although the lawyers had been very guarded about the strategy
they planned to employ. Jim Rayburn was slated to be the leadoff
witness, and on Friday, March 14, he was sworn in and took the witness
stand. Judge Carroll asked the defense team how they would like to
proceed, and Bob Hirsh indicated that they would go in sequence, as
with previous witnesses. Then, instead of beginning the examination of
the government investigator, he startled the courtroom with a surprise
announcement.

"Your Honor," Hirsh declared, "the defense for the Rev. John Fife
rests." One by one, as Don Reno sat rigid in his chair and Judge Carroll
stared from the bench with a look of astonishment on his face, each of
the other attorneys rose in rapid succession to rest his or her case. The
last was William Walker, who declared, "The defense for Father Tony
Clark, and the sanctuary defense, rests." In one of the most stunning
moves of the trial, the defense rested its case without calling a single
witness.

The defense attorneys subsequently told the press that they believed
that the government had not proved its case, so that any further defense
was unnecessary.[2] Privately several admitted that the lessons of the
mock trial had been well learned: Too many of the defendants would
have had to admit to their acts on the stand, without having any
opportunity to explain their reasons.

The jury had heard all the evidence that it was going to hear, but the
long and bitter trial was far from over. The next and extremely critical
step was for the attorneys and Judge Carroll to arrive at a set of
instructions for the jury, laying out for them the law that should be
applied to the evidence.

Both the prosecutor and the defense submitted a set of proposed
instructions. While these were being debated, Judge Carroll seemed
unusually polite and considerate to the defense, behavior which the

attorneys attributed to the fact that among the spectators that week were Karen Snell's parents. Snell's father was the head of Ramada Inns, and the couple were prominent members of the same Phoenix social circles in which Carroll traveled. Several of her colleagues kidded Snell that she should have had her folks sitting in on the trial earlier.[3]

When the instructions were announced, the brief truce was shattered. Carroll had accepted only 2 of the 126 instructions proposed by the defense. He had changed some of the instructions proposed by the prosecutor to make them more unfavorable to the defense. The normally calm Bates Butler told the judge during the discussion of the instructions that he was ignoring all the defense's arguments to such an extent that it seemed futile to make them.

"Mr. Butler, if you want to leave the courtroom you can leave," the judge responded. During the next recess, furious, Butler walked out of the courtroom, went home and packed, and left with his family for Mexico, where he stayed a week on a long-delayed vacation.[4]

Jim Brosnahan went even further. He angrily told Carroll that his instructions reflected his own wish to see the government win the case.

"I have not seen anything like it in all my years of practice," the tall, muscular attorney charged.

"Perhaps you're not too old to learn," the judge angrily responded.

"I'm not too old to fight, I'll tell you that," Brosnahan shot back.

"Maybe you are too weak."

"No, I'm not too weak, either."

"Maybe it's too late," Carroll finished.

Later Brosnahan confided, "He's the worst judge I've seen in twenty-six years, by a factor of ten."[5]

From the point of view of the defense the most serious problem was that Carroll had failed to include the usual instruction on intent, which both Reno and the defense team had assumed would be given. Instead, Carroll gave the jury the following instruction: "Intent ordinarily may not be proved directly, because there is no way of fathoming or scrutinizing the operations of the human mind. But you may infer the defendant's intent from the surrounding circumstances. You may consider any statement made and any act done or omitted by the defendant, and all other facts and circumstances in evidence which indicate his state of mind."

The next instruction read:

Intent and motive should never be confused. Motive is that which prompts a person to act. Intent refers to the state of mind with which the act is done.

Personal advancement, financial gain, political reason, religious beliefs, moral convictions or some adherence to a higher law even of nations are well recognized motives of human conduct. These motives may prompt the person to voluntary acts of good and another to voluntary acts of crime. Good motive is not a defense to intentional acts of crime.

So, if you find beyond a reasonable doubt that the acts constituting the crime charged were committed by the defendant with the intent to commit the unlawful act and bring about the prohibited result, then the requirement that the act be done knowingly or willfully as defined in these instructions has been satisfied even though the defendant may have believed that his conduct was politically, religiously or morally required, or that ultimate good would result from such conduct.

The judge also used a stiff "Pinkerton charge" on the alleged conspiracy, meaning that if any one of the coconspirators was found to have committed the crime, all the others under the conspiracy were also to be found guilty of conspiracy. The government had charged each individual separately, with separate crimes, and was not relying on the Pinkerton rule, which is usually reserved for judging conspiracies by organized crime.[6]

The defense was also disturbed that Carroll told the jury that the government was not required to prove guilt beyond *all* reasonable doubt, but only beyond *a* reasonable doubt. And he ignored the defense's request for an instruction to the effect that if there were material witnesses that the government could have called but didn't, the jurors should infer that their testimony would be unfavorable. Instead, he told them that "the law does not require the prosecution to call as witnesses all persons who may have been present at any time or place involved in the case. . . . However, in judging the credibility of the witnesses who have testified, and in considering the weight and effect of all evidence that has been produced, the jury may consider the prosecution's failure to call witnesses or to produce other evidence shown by the evidence in the case to be in existence and available."

One of the defense attorneys called Carroll's instructions "killers," and a reporter covering the trial told Butler that several journalists thought "you guys had a reasonable shot at winning, but now it will be fifty-fifty at best."[7]

After the instructions had been decided, the closing arguments were scheduled. The prosecution was to lead off, followed by the defense and then a rebuttal by the government, before the instructions were read to the jury. On April 1 Reno stood up, a slender, balding figure in a gray suit, and went to the lectern facing the jury. Lying on it was a small cross, placed there by Michael Altman. Ignoring the April Fool's joke, the prosecutor reiterated the judge's instructions and then launched into a lengthy, excruciatingly detailed restatement of the government's charges against the eleven defendants, apologizing at the outset. "I don't relish this task because it's going to be somewhat tedious . . . somewhat time-consuming," he told the jurors, some of whom chewed gum and looked increasingly bored as his recital of the alleged crimes ground on.[8] He presented intricate charts illustrating the charges, with neatly drawn cars, churches, and little stick figures—black for the defendants and green for the aliens. Though the judge had already decided that the defendants' motives were irrelevant to their guilt or innocence, Reno once again impugned them. There is not a "single utterance about religion" on the tapes, he told the jury; "it is pure alien smuggling."[9] To illustrate the dubious motives of the defendants, he brought up once again John Fife's now infamous "bullshit" comment (which had been made in the privacy of his own living room). This time, during the recess, Fife knelt in the hall of the courthouse, and Father Ricardo made the sign of the cross over his head, absolving him of his scatological sin.[10]

The defense came on next, with feeling. As expected, the attorneys told a diametrically opposed story built around two themes: Cruz's debased character and the utter selflessness of their clients. Someone just entering the courtroom might have thought he or she had wandered into a morality play, with all the stereotypical characters of good and evil.

Swinging their wrecking balls at the already razed character of the Mexican spy, the defense attorneys depicted a criminal-turned-snitch, a perjurer who would say anything to avoid prison or deportation. Before he began his remarks, Michael Piccareta set up an easel bearing a huge sign. In letters three inches high, it asked the question "Would you rely on Jesus Cruz in making the most important decision in your life?" This was a reference to the requirement that the jury could convict only if it found the evidence so convincing "that an ordinary person would be willing to make the most important decisions in his or her own life on the basis of such evidence."

"Jesus Cruz transported people into peonage. That's a lot of potential punishment that Mr. Cruz avoided," the curly-haired advocate reminded the jury. "Jesus Cruz has been given 'sanctuary' by the United States government."

In contrast, he said, the church workers "are here because they are good. They are here because they love their fellow man."[11]

Hirsh said that Reno had taken "the story of people helping people and tried to turn it into some evil sinister conspiracy." Yaroshefsky declared that the government had viewed the sanctuary movement "through crime-colored glasses." Through the government lens, she explained, refugees became "aliens," and churches "drop houses." "Take . . . acts of caring, add Jesus Cruz, and you have a conspiracy," said Yaroshefsky.

She noted that in ten of the thirteen incidents involving the transportation of illegal aliens, undercover agents actually did the transporting. Although it had been ruled out as a defense, she reiterated the claim that the defendants had been exercising their First Amendment rights. As part of their normal work and religious activity defendants like Mary K. Espinosa helped people, regardless of the beneficiaries' immigration status. To prosecute such individuals, thereby preventing them from helping a certain class of people, would deprive them of their right to exercise their religion, she argued.

Former prosecutor Bates Butler did not, as he had feared, slip into automatic and become a prosecutor again by asking the jury to "convict these people." In a meticulous, point-by-point rebuttal of the government's case, he stressed how difficult it is to prove all of the elements of a crime under the immigration laws. He concluded with a powerful appeal to the jury. "Send a message to the I.N.S.," he urged. "Never again use somebody like this [referring to Cruz] and turn him loose against people like this." When he emerged from the courtroom following his carefully reasoned argument, sympathetic spectators surrounded him and applauded.

The last to argue were Cooper and Walker. They emphasized the government's failure to call all its agents on the case or to play all but twenty to twenty-five minutes of its ninety-one hours of secretly recorded conversations and argued that that alone was sufficient reason to acquit.

Walker, his voice often raised in anger, also wondered how the government had decided to prosecute these particular eleven people, out of a nationwide movement involving thousands of individuals. "Where did they draw the line?" he asked. He noted that Salvation Army representatives had been present at one allegedly "conspiratorial" meeting. "If there really was clandestine activities going on, perhaps they should've investigated the Salvation Army," he said.

"You are deciding this case for America," he concluded to the jury.

Cooper told the nine women and three men almost the same thing. "American justice will be judged" by this case, he said.

In his rebuttal Reno, too, became increasingly emotional. He immediately tackled the problem of Cruz's credibility. "It would be nice if the government could operate without informants like Jesus Cruz. It would be nice if we could hire a nice, clean-cut choirboy," he said. But such an informant, he went on, would have to be bilingual, be willing to lie to a priest and allow himself to be "absolutely brutalized" by defense attorneys—all for less than six dollars an hour.

Reno then went on to say that he could prove his case without the testimony of the informant he had called his key witness in opening statements. He ended in a passionate plea. "The drafters of the Constitution and this court and the law of this land do not permit people to commit criminal acts and then say it was a religious example," he declaimed. "The law comes from Congress, not from Southside Presbyterian Church. Every nation has the absolute right to control its borders."

He asked the jury "to have the courage and come out, look these people in the eye as I have done and tell them that there is no higher law than that passed by Congress."[12]

Reno had made an earlier comment that caused the courtroom spectators to gasp. In his previous remarks Reno had read from a tape transcript in which the Reverend George Lockwood had said that he was going to go pick up "his own two Central American refugees," a statement Reno used to demonstrate the conspiracy. In their closing remarks, defense lawyers had pointed out that Lockwood had actually said "my own two Central American refugees who are my own children."

Reno read the full sentence in his rebuttal. But then he added:

". . . if they were his own children, why had he left them down there for 14 years?"

Lockwood was devastated. He had been separated from his Costa Rican wife for six years, and she had had the children with her in Central America. Not only had they not been "left there for 14 years"— one was only eleven years old—but he had brought them up for visits four times in the previous five years. After Reno's remarks in open court, which Lockwood had no opportunity to answer, the minister wept publicly, and he did so again in several church meetings when the subject came up.[13]

The treatment of Lockwood, the look-them-in-the-eye comment, and several others drew a last, angry round of motions by defense lawyers. They accused the prosecutor of unethical conduct, of misstating evidence, and of trying to provoke a mistrial so he could retry the case. All their motions were denied.

On April 17 Judge Carroll read the fifty-two instructions to the jury, a process that took fifty minutes, and the jury began its deliberations after a trial "as rancorous, emotional and complex as the immigration issue itself," as the *New York Times* man put it.[14] As the spectators filed out of the courtroom, a red-faced William Walker approached Don Reno and said, "Reno, you are a stinking, dirty dog."[15] It seemed a fitting end to the exhausting, acrimonious proceedings. Reno told his wife, Carole, who was standing beside him during Walker's outburst, that the defense attorney had snarled at him so often that "by now I consider it nothing more than the usual 'Good morning' greeting from Bill." He still thought Walker was the best attorney in the courtroom and claimed that he actually liked him.[16]

Chapter
Thirty-three

O N MAY 1, 1986, the jury went to lunch in the patio of the El
Adobe, a Mexican restaurant in an old colonial house preserved
in the middle of downtown Tucson. Shortly after the meal the beepers
worn by the defendants, their lawyers, and the court officials went off.
Almost sixteen months after the indictments, more than six months
since the beginning of the trial, and after forty-eight hours of deliberations spread over nine days, the jury had finally reached a verdict. One
of the lawyers, walking back to the courthouse, passed a new office
tower that was almost completed, one of several sprouting up in downtown Tucson. He remembered that it had still been a hole in the ground
when he had begun working on the sanctuary trial.

The defendants felt confident as they filed into the windowless courtroom where they had been held captive for so long. At first they had
been concerned when the jury had not returned with a quick decision,
but as the days wore on, they and their supporters had tried to convince
themselves that they would win, that the jury would have to see the
rightness and justice of their cause. In an unusually quiet scene they sat
expectantly as the jury somberly entered the courtroom without glanc-

ing at the church workers. Shortly after 3:00 P.M. the bailiff began to read the verdict.

"Socorro de Aguilar, Count One. Guilty."

Holy shit, we're in for a dark day here, folks, thought Bill Risner.[1]

By the time the alphabetical reading had gotten down to Father Quiñones, Risner's client, it was all over. The jury had voted to convict on eighteen of the government charges. A grim pall settled over the defendants' side of the room. Most of them, sitting in stunned silence, showed more control than some of their lawyers. Nancy Postero was quietly crying, and Bob Hirsh, who hadn't lost a case in four years, briefly slumped over the defense table in a pose of dejection. Eight of the sanctuary workers had been found guilty. Three—Nena Mac-Donald, Mary K. Espinosa, and Jim Corbett—were acquitted of all charges.

Darlene Nicgorski, who had never smuggled anyone into the country, was hit the hardest. As she sat impassively, her chin tilted slightly up toward the jurors, she was found guilty of three felonies—conspiracy and two counts of concealing, harboring, or shielding illegal aliens—plus two misdemeanors. The conspiracy carried a five-year prison term and/or a $10,000 fine; each of the other felonies carried a possible sentence of five years in prison and/or a $2,000 fine. If Judge Carroll decided to throw the book at her, Sister Darlene faced fifteen years in prison.

John Fife was found guilty of the conspiracy charge, of another felony for bringing an alien illegally into the United States, and of a misdemeanor for aiding and abetting the presence of an illegal alien. Philip Willis-Conger was convicted on three counts: conspiracy and two misdemeanors—eluding inspection and aiding and abetting. His frequent partner on the border Peggy Hutchison was acquitted of all but the conspiracy charge.

The "Nogales connection," despite its often bitter differences with Tucson—which the jury knew almost nothing about—was also found to be part of the criminal enterprise. Quiñones and Socorro Aguilar both were found guilty of conspiracy and of one other count each. The fiercely independent Father Clark was acquitted on the conspiracy charge but found guilty of harboring. Finally, Wendy LeWin was convicted of one felony, the crime of driving a refugee within the country. One of the jurors told reporters that after the verdicts had been reached she had gone home and thrown up.

Sentencing for those convicted was set for July 1 in Federal District Court in Tucson. The judge released all those convicted on their own recognizance, and a few minutes later the defendants emerged from the courthouse with family members and their attorneys, singing "We Shall Overcome." More than 150 supporters awaited them, some clutching a quilted banner reading THE TRUTH WILL SET YOU FREE. The crowd erupted into loud applause when John Fife walked out the door with a visibly upset Marianne and one of their two sons. For once the usually ebullient Fife had little to say, and after briefly answering a few questions, the defendants went to the Tucson Community Center for a prayer service.

Corbett, now a completely free man, made one matter-of-fact statement: "We will continue to provide sanctuary services openly and go to trial as often as is necessary to establish . . . that the protection of human rights is never illegal."

Don Reno, for his part, was overwhelmingly relieved. The tension and the hatred in the courtroom, particularly in the last few days of the trial, had taken an emotional toll. During his closing arguments his wife, Carole, had been among the spectators when she heard a woman behind her whisper, "He's lying—they ought to send him to the electric chair!"[2]

In his first press conference since the trial began, Reno declared that "justice was done." He predicted that the verdict would have "a significant impact on those persons who were well-intentioned but misguided." Revealing some of his long-restrained feelings, he attacked what he said had been distorted coverage of the trial and what he characterized as "unusually close personal relationships" among reporters, defendants, and the defendants' attorneys.

Answering critics who wondered why the government would waste so much time and money trying to convict good Christian men and women, Reno, in effect, said that the government, like the sanctuary workers and the refugees, felt it had had no choice.

"What was the U.S. government supposed to do?" he asked. ". . . Was it supposed to look the other way . . . while illegal acts were being committed . . . even in front of cameras like we have here today? Was the United States government supposed to turn their [*sic*] back and indicate to the public that because of the ostensible religious issues, the political issues in this case, that the United States government is faint of heart when it comes to enforcing the law with all persons?"[3]

Reno's remarks anticipated the official statement put out by Alan Nelson, the INS commissioner. "Above all, this case has demonstrated that no group, no matter how well meaning or highly motivated, can arbitrarily violate the laws of the United States. Perhaps now that this case is behind us, those of the sanctuary movement can redirect their energy in a manner within the law."[4]

Unofficially the government's reaction was more combative. When he got back to the U.S. attorney's office, Reno's colleagues gave him a resounding ovation, and one assistant U.S. attorney slapped him on the back and congratulated him for really "kicking ass."[5] And in an interview with the *Star* two days after the verdict, the prosecutor alluded again to the defendants' political activities. "I would love to take 'em on on that," he declared. "I believe I could prove beyond a reasonable doubt, something more than the fact that they were smuggling aliens in," implying that unwittingly or otherwise, the religious workers had been aiding Communist terrorists or insurgents. Asked to substantiate his statement, Reno revealed that the government had found a photograph in Sister Darlene Nicgorski's apartment showing her with "Communist guerrillas down in Central America."[6]

Told of the allegation, Michael Altman, Nicgorski's lawyer, said that he had not seen the photograph and called the insinuation "bizarre." Upon investigation, it turned out that Reno was referring to the photo of the nun with Nicaraguan Interior Minister Tomás Borge. According to Sister Nicgorski, in 1983 she visited fellow nuns who were working in Nicaragua, and they had accompanied another group of visiting North Americans along on an interview with Borge.[7]

For his part, INS Regional Commissioner Harold Ezell, whose enthusiasm had had so much to do with launching the undercover investigation, was outraged about Corbett's acquittal. "The son of a gun who started the whole thing got off scot-free," he complained. "He ought to be behind bars."[8]

Corbett, cool as ever, noted that his supporters, too, wondered how it had happened. "The Quakers in London called after the verdict," he said after the trial, "and asked, 'Why didn't they get Jim?' "[9]

The Arizona press, which had covered the trial almost daily, was divided on the outcome. The *Arizona Daily Star,* which had been sympathetic to the defendants all along, called the verdicts "a blow to justice." Its lead editorial declared: "Sanctuary, the ancient concept of refuge for troubled human beings, took a terrible blow yesterday. So did fairness, hope, and government ethics." The jury never heard the defense, the article went on, for the sanctuary defendants never had "the chance to explain how ordinarily decent, law-abiding church workers could break laws in order to rescue political refugees. . . . The only hope lies in appeals. Other judges on higher planes may find this case abhorrent and give it a just verdict."[10]

The *Arizona Republic* in Phoenix, on the other hand, thought that the "overblown rhetoric" of the defendants had been "deflated" by the guilty verdicts. ". . . the dictates of conscience do not justify civil disobedience," the paper sternly lectured.[11] The two journals' cartoonists mirrored these conclusions; while the *Star* depicted a Statue of Liberty with a tear flowing down her cheek, the *Republic* drew a cleric on a cross smiling down to the TV cameras and asking, "Does my hair look OK?"

Interestingly, the cloistered jurors, who had not seen the publicity surrounding the trial, had much less pronounced opinions on the pros and cons of the sanctuary movement. In a host of posttrial interviews, it became clear that the majority of the jury had been more or less personally sympathetic to the defendants and regretted having to find them guilty. The strongest force for conviction, in the end, had been the forewoman, Catherine Schaefer. It turned out that her purported conversion to the Democratic party had never happened.

After the verdict the prosecutor received a congratulatory telephone call from Lowell Jensen, the second-ranking official in the Justice Department. "He was relatively low-key," Reno later recalled. "But he said that the result was much more than they'd ever suspected it would be."[12] About three weeks later Reno was flown back to Washington, where he had meetings with Jensen, Steve Trott, and the attorney general himself, Edwin Meese III, who had succeeded William French Smith in 1984. Trott was elated by the convictions, according to Reno, and Meese was full of warm praise. During their meeting Reno commented, "You know, Mr. Meese, I felt like every religious organization in the country was opposing this prosecution."

"Yes, I attend church, and one of the sermons during the trial was in support of sanctuary," Meese replied. "They were even soliciting financial support for the defense."

"The National Council of Churches was supportive of the sanctuary movement," Reno added.

"Well, you know what William Buckley said about the National

Council of Churches," Meese responded. "He wrote a column one time in which he was discussing a statement by them in which they were criticizing Jerry Falwell for mixing politics with religion. And Buckley said the National Council of Churches doesn't have to worry about that because they're not involved in the business of religion."[13]

Reno was asked to address a national meeting of district directors of the INS in Washington about how to handle the ongoing activity of the sanctuary movement. His sense of the attitude at the central office of the Immigration Service was that it had just cracked down on the smuggling conspiracy of the decade and didn't need another trial like the one it had just won. If the Border Patrol ran across some more sanctuary workers and caught them red-handed in the middle of a smuggling operation, then there would be no mercy shown. The government had decided, for example, to retry Stacey Merkt in Browns-ville, Texas, for a conviction that had been overturned because of improper jury instructions.*

But Reno sensed that officials at the Immigration Service didn't want to look like a bunch of zealots who were out of control. They had done their job and enforced the law, and protected their public reputation. In the view of INS officials, the sun had already risen and set on the sanctuary movement, and the only way it could keep itself in the public eye was to appear persecuted. Why should the INS give it the opportunity? Washington especially didn't want to create any media martyrs. The INS and the Justice Department decided not to seek tough sentences for those convicted. They would leave the sentencing decision up to the judge.[14]

The movement had already paid a high price for its defiance of Washington. In addition to the disrupted lives, the National Sanctuary Defense Fund spent an estimated $1.2 million on the Arizona trial, most of it raised by direct mail and contributions from major Protestant denominations and small foundations. The defense planned to appeal, a process that could take years and more substantial sums.

---

*In addition to the Tucson trial and the prosecutions of Merkt and Elder, in 1985 the government had also tried Lorry Thomas, a woman who had briefly taken over the directorship of Casa Romero after Elder's conviction. Turning down a plea to a misdemeanor and refusing to promise never to do it again, Thomas pleaded guilty to the felony of illegally transporting an alien, in this case a Nicaraguan, past a Border Patrol checkpoint. For that she had received a two-year prison sentence and served a year and a half, until Christmas Eve 1986.

The government declined to discuss its own costs, but a *Tucson Citizen* reporter estimated that its documented expenses by the time the jury went out totaled $700,000, including $336,600 for trial costs; $200,000 for lawyers representing witnesses and three legally indigent defendants; $30,000 to the two informants, Cruz and Graham; $50,000 to potential jurors; and $78,000 to a Phoenix woman who translated and transcribed the ninety-one government tapes. Not included in this total was the cost of the pretrial investigation; the expense of bringing in, housing, and feeding twenty witnesses from as far away as Seattle and New York City; and the fare for lodging Judge Earl Carroll and his staff in the Santa Rita Hotel in Tucson for months. By the time it was over, the Tucson sanctuary trial had cost both sides a total of $2 million to $3 million.[15]

Reno flew back to Phoenix feeling satisfied and vindicated. He looked forward to a vacation and to getting on with his job; he was sick and tired of "sanctuary" and all its sanctimonious self-righteousness.[16]

Not surprisingly, the mood among the defendants was somber, and a new note of anger and bitterness crept into some of their public comments. They had been spied on, subjected to more than a year of criminal proceedings, and were now branded as felons; this meant, among other things, that unless they succeeded in eventually overturning the convictions, they had lost their right to vote. Psychologically many seemed to be circling the wagons, to see the world even more as "us against them," the good guys versus the bad.

On the evening after the verdict some 250 people crowded into the tiny chapel at Southside, spilling over into the churchyard and playground, a dusty yard containing a half dozen automobile tires planted in the ground, a large drainage pipe painted red and green, and a children's wooden bridge. The crowd was all ages, almost all white, and sedately middle class. One of those who had come from a Presbyterian sanctuary church in Fort Worth, Texas, told a reporter from the *Fort Worth Star-Telegram* that "I work and travel for an insurance company. My wife is a nurse. This isn't like something from the Sixties. We feel it's a part of the church's ministry. I don't think the government has any understanding of that."

Though the sky was still blue and clear at 7:30 P.M., two sets of spotlights had been turned on, and brightly colored paper flowers had been twined into the church's rusting cyclone fence. A steady breeze whipped at the banner stretched across the front of the church, the same one that had been hanging in the media office, proclaiming THE

TRUTH WILL SET YOU FREE. The long-planned service was originally billed as a celebration, but a volunteer at the sanctuary media office told a reporter that after the verdict the "congregation just needs to get together and hug. That is essentially what tonight's service is about."[17]

John Fife was away in New York City, explaining the outcome of the trial to supporters and the national media, and several of the other defendants were scattered around the country on similar missions. The evening's service was really for the troops, the rank and file of the movement.

Three members of the congregation, two playing guitars, sang a hymn entitled "Do Not Be Afraid." There were brief sermons and Bible readings in English and Spanish, and a woman performed a dance to a song about the "disappeared" in Chile. Bates Butler read a passage from Isaiah. At one point in the nearly two-hour service, a basket was passed to collect bail money for refugees being held in detention camps. By the time it reached the back rows, members of the congregation had to hold their hands over the basket to keep the piled-high dollar bills from blowing away.

A sheet of paper was distributed to every member of the audience. It was called a "declaration of shared responsibility," and its four paragraphs read as follows:

The defendants found guilty in federal court, Tucson AZ, 1 May 1986, had heard the cry of the people of Central America. Responding to the persecution of the church and the people of El Salvador and Guatemala, they recognized their obligations under the 1948 Geneva Conventions, the UN Convention and Protocol on refugees, and the 1980 U.S. Refugee Act, to grant safe haven to sisters and brothers fleeing torture and death.

These defendants have now recommitted themselves to continue the ministry of Sanctuary for as long as persecution and death threaten refugees returned involuntarily from our shores to their homeland. This they have done in fidelity to the one God who long ago called an oppressed people out of bondage, and who today calls on all of us to love the sojourner among us because our ancestors were once refugees.

I, undersigned, share their faith and commitment, with a full knowledge that I also place myself in jeopardy. I have no choice.

If they are guilty, so am I.

Most of the congregation, including many of the more than a dozen Protestant ministers attending the ceremony, signed the statement. It did not go unnoticed that virtually no Catholic priests save Father Ricardo were among them.

That weekend there were four refugees—two Salvadorans and two Guatemalans—in sanctuary at Southside Church. On Sunday Fife delivered his first sermon as a convicted felon. Dressed in his long white vestments, with a native Guatemalan cloth over his neck as a surplice, he began with his customary good humor. He joked that he felt a little like the man who had been tarred and feathered and paraded through the town. When someone asked him how he felt, he replied, "Well, I'm honored, but I'd just as soon not be here."*

Fife told his congregation, seated on rows of white folding chairs facing the center of the chapel, that on the Tuesday before the verdict he had picked up the lectionary to see what was prescribed for the sermon that Sunday. He explained that the Presbyterian lectionary suggests to pastors a text from the Bible they are to read and preach from each Sunday. That week's suggestion was the address of Jesus to His disciples before He was taken off, arrested, tried, and crucified.

"I should have known on Tuesday that it was not going to be a good verdict," the preacher joked. He went on to say that Jesus had told His followers to keep His word and to remember what He had taught. "We ministers really have nothing new to say at all," Fife went on. "Our only function is to remind what has been said, what is the Word.[18]

"Immediately after the verdict I flew off to New York to do the usual round of interviews and interpretations, and I was invited to spend the Sabbath with a large Jewish congregation. There was a bar mitzvah; the Torah was brought out, and the Word of God was read to the people. In that congregation were a few survivors of the Holocaust and two families who had been in Argentina during the disappearances. The rabbi said 'Remember. This is the week in which the Jews remember the Holocaust.' The rabbi kept saying, 'Remember, don't you ever forget, and we have with us one of those Gentiles who don't suffer from

*Reverend Fife wasn't the only one able to see the absurd in the situation. On May 6, 1986, the week after the verdict, an ad appeared in a small paper called the *Tucson Weekly*. Under the heading "Ad of the Week," it read: "WANTED: Special agent, must be clean cut, a 'choir boy,' bilingual, and pure as the driven snow with an extensive religious background. Also must be willing to lie to priests in Nogales, and to be put on the witness stand and brutalized during cross examination. The pay is good. Contact Don Reno or Mr. Jim Rayburn at the I.N.S. 629-6228. There is no higher law than that passed by Congress."

amnesia. I've asked him to come because we must remember what is happening in our streets and cities and hemisphere today.' "

Striding down the aisle dividing the seated congregation, his white robes flapping, the six-foot-four Fife let his voice pick up volume and timbre.

"There was no *proof* of any harm done to Jews in Nazi Germany.

"In Argentina there was no *memory* of who was being dragged off the streets, tortured, and murdered.

"Remember the story of the good Samaritan and the folks who passed by. They didn't pass him by because they were hardhearted folks but because they understood *it was against the law to tend to the sick on the Sabbath.*"

The U.S. government accused the sanctuary movement of being political, not religious, the preacher continued. "But Reno had to *stipulate* in court that we were religiously motivated. And then outside the courtroom he said we were political and that he had a picture of Darlene with a 'guerrilla.' That was a lie!

"The government said these people were looking for jobs. After sixteen Central Americans took the stand and talked about torture and death squads and disappearances and bombing—only we couldn't say 'torture,' we had to say 'great physical harm'; and we couldn't say 'death squads' and 'killing,' we had to say 'great tragedy befell'—who could believe these were economic migrants?

"The truth will be told someday," Fife promised, his voice now filled with the passion of an Old Testament prophet, *"and the Don Renos, and the Alan Nelsons, and the Harold Ezells—they'll sound just like Kurt Waldheim does today:* 'I didn't know; it wasn't me; just following orders; doing my duty; the law is the law. . . .' "

That same night a retired U.S. Army colonel, a veteran of World War II, the Korean War, and Vietnam, helped direct the first sanctuary border crossing after the guilty verdicts.[19] He navigated a group of cars over barely passable backwoods trails to an overnight base camp in the mountains near the Mexican border. The night sky, as he drove, reminded the combat veteran of the time he had navigated a tank destroyer outfit by the position of the stars. At dawn the next morning a small party from the camp hiked to the international line where two other sanctuary workers were waiting on the Mexican side with a seventeen-year-old Salvadoran. Suddenly the boy darted out to the barbed-wire fence and scaled it. He was in the United States.

On the way back to the base camp the refugee told the two journalists accompanying the group that he had been picked up in 1984 by security forces for working as a community organizer. He had been held for fifteen days in the central jail and beaten to reveal the names of his "subversive" friends. He had been forced to sign a blank confession and was then thrown in Mariona prison. He languished there for six months before the Red Cross, mobilized by his father, secured his release in March 1985. Soon after, Americans in El Salvador gave him the number of sanctuary workers in Tucson.

The ex-officer, a former aide to General William Westmoreland in Vietnam, told the reporters that he now believed that American involvement in Vietnam had been misguided and that American policy in Central America was leading the country down the same path. "It's a strong term, but our policy is tantamount to state-supported terrorism. We support people that go in and seek out the teachers, the religious workers, community organizers—those who are doing the things that hold the populace together—and kill them." He said that the conviction of the sanctuary workers was the "straw that broke the camel's back" for him and that was why he had agreed to lead a border operation.

Asked if he wasn't concerned that he might be labeled a Communist sympathizer, as the INS had labeled other sanctuary workers, he replied, "The Administration is using—just as Joe McCarthy did—the word 'Communist' as a scare tactic. Even people in Congress who vote against *contra* aid are labeled 'Communist.' All this anti-Communist hype fits into the same picture." The nation's leaders, he said, were trying "to discredit the humanitarian work of good citizens . . . this is my flag too. I wouldn't have served in three wars if I didn't consider myself a patriot."

On the following weekend 500 to 600 sanctuary supporters attended a three-day event in Tucson to "reaffirm their commitment" to the movement. There was a caravan to the U.S.-Mexican border and a demonstration in Nogales, an all-night vigil in front of the Federal Building, a service in St. Augustine's Cathedral, the huge stark-white Catholic church in the heart of the city, and a march through town to Temple Emanu-El, where a daylong conference took place. At most of these events more signatures were sought for the "So am I" declarations, and at the end of the conference, on the afternoon of May 12, a delegation, including Ken Kennon and Pat Corbett, took more than 400 signed statements down to the Federal Building to William Johnston, who was still the officer in charge of the Tucson INS office.

Johnston, who had stayed forty-five minutes after his office normally closed in order to be able to meet the delegation, greeted his visitors, who included a horde of local reporters and camera crews, just outside the door of the modern office building. "Hello, Bill," said the burly, black-bearded Kennon, clad in a white Cuban shirt. "Can I just hand these to you?"[20]

Johnston, tall and trim in a pink shirt, gray slacks, and a silver belt buckle with the initial *J* on it, took the stack of papers several inches high. "That's what I stayed around for," he replied.

"We hope you'll pass these along to your district director."

"Great."

"Thanks."

The two men shook hands. Then, pressed by the reporters to make a statement, Johnston began in a more official vein. "Apparently these are documents relating to sanctuary. We've tried to make it clear that sanctuary is not a concern of the government. The criminal aspects of the immigration law is [*sic*] one thing, . . . but I don't think sanctuary is something the INS is going to pinpoint as a matter of concern in itself."

Pressed further to look at the statement, Johnston quickly skimmed it. "Well, this expresses a concern for refugees, and we have a concern for refugees. . . . The government shares that concern."

"The Refugee Act is not being applied fairly across the board," Kennon said. "We'd like the INS to administer the law fairly so we can get on with other things."

The two men began to argue about facts or, as Kennon put it, "two different perceptions of reality." One of the sanctuary supporters, an older, heavyset man, grew angry and shouted provocatively at Johnston, "Is your conscience clear?"

"You bet," Johnston snapped back, his face tightening.

Kennon left shortly after that exchange, having shaken hands resignedly with Johnston again. As he departed, he commented, "It was people like Johnston and his colleagues, just doing their job, that sent millions of Jews to their deaths in Nazi Germany."

The angry man stayed behind to badger the official a little more. He told Johnston that members of the sanctuary movement were sincere in their beliefs.

Johnston grabbed his arm and pulled him close. "Look me in the eye," he challenged. "You want to know something? I'm sincere, too, and you'd better believe it!" Then he finished with the man. "You want to talk? They got people with cameras over there." He waved his arm in the direction of the office of the Arizona Theater Company across the street. "Go over there; I don't want to talk to you."

The next day, in his office, Johnston dismissed the protest and the sanctuary movement as insignificant.

"How many supporters do you think they have?" he asked rhetorically. "Ten thousand? What's that? I could get ten thousand people to support anything you want—to be against blondes. . . . I was against the Vietnam War in the 1960s. I thought kids were getting killed for nothing. But this sanctuary thing . . . we've just got a bunch of retread hippies here."

Asked what he was going to do with the signatures, the official swung his chair around and contemplated the pile of statements on a shelf behind his desk. "I don't know. Someone asked me if I was going to throw them away. But I said I thought that would be rude."[21]

Chapter
Thirty-four

ON JULY 1, 1986, three days before the nation celebrated the hundredth anniversary of the Statue of Liberty, U.S. District Court Judge Earl H. Carroll sentenced five members of the sanctuary movement to three to five years' probation. On the following day the remaining defendants were also given suspended sentences and probation. There were no martyrs created by the long and bitter trial.

The church workers had fully expected prison terms from the judge who had presided over what Jim Corbett called "a thoroughly rigged trial." Some suspected that in the end Carroll had been swayed by the appeals for leniency that had flowed in from influential quarters. In an unusual move, forty-seven members of Congress, most of them Democrats, had written Carroll and asked him to "consider the underlying circumstances in Central America and the humanitarian motives of the defendants before passing sentence."[1] The judge also received a letter from Senator Dennis DeConcini of Arizona, the man who had nominated him for the federal bench, asking him to consider John Fife's "fine qualities."

Whatever the reasoning behind it, Carroll's decision stunned the court. The room was overflowing, and outside several hundred people waited in the broiling sun for word on the fate of those convicted. The outside walls of the building were draped with banners, including one with the words of the Emma Lazarus poem from the base of the Statue of Liberty: "Give me your tired, your poor, your huddled masses yearning to breathe free. . . ." Across the street from the Federal Building, a local sculptor had hung a life-size figure of Jesus Christ on a wooden cross from a traffic light. As she entered the courthouse, María Socorro Aguilar placed a rose in the figure's crown of thorns.

The sentencing provided the defendants with their first and only opportunity to be heard in the courtroom and to explain their reasons publicly. The first defendant to be sentenced, Peggy Hutchison, rose and delivered a fiery oration, her voice rising and falling with the rhythm of an evangelical preacher. Once again she compared the deportation of Central American refugees to the U.S. refusal to admit thousands of Jewish refugees from Nazi Germany before World War II.

"I stand before this court to proclaim, 'never again,'" declared Hutchison. When she was finished, Carroll sentenced her to five years' probation, with the restriction that she not associate with any individual or group that engages in "transporting, harboring, concealing, or shielding undocumented aliens." Sister Darlene Nicgorski, Philip Willis-Conger, and María Socorro Aguilar received identical sentences, while Wendy LeWin was given a three-year suspended sentence.

At a midday press conference the defendants wavered between relief and anger at the restriction, which they said would force them to leave their churches, religious orders, friends, and relatives active in the movement. Wendy LeWin explained that she was married to a Salvadoran who had been denied political asylum, and she would have to leave him in order to comply with Judge Carroll's order. Darlene Nicgorski said that her order included the support of sanctuary in its constitution and declared that she would rather go to jail than give up her ministry to Central Americans. Others said they would have to refuse to sign Carroll's probation agreement.

Late in the afternoon, in a typical move, Carroll canceled the offending restriction. His final conditions of probation were that the defendants comply with all federal, state, and local laws and that they seek permission from a probation officer before they left the state of Arizona.

In their statements many of the accused found a new and powerful eloquence. Wendy LeWin, the shyest of all the defendants, told the spectators that she had worked for the federal government as an interpreter and in refugee resettlement work. "I was paid then; and now, for doing the same work, I am here awaiting sentencing," LeWin said, with tears in her eyes.

The angry Mexicans voiced newly nationalistic feelings. "I have the impression the refugees are looking for the Promised Land," declared Socorro Aguilar. "I have been a neighbor of the United States for the last 40 years, and I can tell you that everything is better in my Mexico. But these refugees are determined to find justice and political asylum in your country. There is no way to tell them the opposite."

Father Quiñones declared that "one's own soul rebels if one day the public authorities enter on the scene to say that what one has been doing for twenty-six years constitutes a criminal act. . . . Please leave our Mexican priests with their poor and with their persecuted," he implored the American court; "please don't force us to look for authorization to take in those innocent victims . . . into our churches in Mexico."

In conclusion, Quiñones told an ominous story. "A while ago, maybe three weeks ago," he told the judge, "I received a telephone call from Phoenix, from a woman whose name I could make available to you, Your Honor, through my attorney, and she told me the following:

" 'Father Quiñones, I don't know you personally, but because of you I'm going to be deported.'

"I asked her, 'Why?'

" 'When you were in the trial Jesus Cruz came to visit me and he offered me legal papers for the United States for me and my family. And I asked him[,] "In exchange for what?" And he said[,] "Go to Tucson and take the stand against Father Quiñones. Tell them that he brought you here and your family." I told her[,] [*sic*] 'Mr. Cruz, that is not right.' . . .

" 'And he answered[,] "That doesn't matter, nobody in the Court will know it." ' '

"She refused and now she is about to be deported," Quiñones finished.

The longest and most powerful of all the speeches was delivered by Sister Darlene Nicgorski, the defendant who had most wanted to stand up and take her own defense in court. Although only thirty minutes had been allotted for each statement, the nun held the courtroom spellbound for fifty minutes while she told the story of her brutal experience in Central America and her subsequent involvement in sanctuary, complete with a slide show with scenes from refugee camps and detention facilities.

She told how, after her return from Central America, she had served in immigration court as an expert witness, testifying to the general conditions of repression, only to see every asylum case she was involved in rejected.

"What more could I have done?" she asked the judge. "What would you have done, Judge . . . if you knew what I knew?"

She explained that she had been thinking about the crucial difference between justice and the law, between what is just and what is legal. She noted that Kurt Waldheim, forty years later, was being pursued for war crimes. "He is accused because he refused to say *No* to the orders of his commanding officers. Who will be hunted down in 40 years for these crimes against life? Will those who have followed the letter of the law *now* be tried for engaging in a conspiracy . . . ? Is it possible then that some in this country who hide behind a righteous interpretation of the law might someday be branded by the world community as public criminals?

". . . I think most religious people realize that laws are not the totality of the life of a religious or morally upright person," Nicgorski declared. "Laws for the most part are general directions which are subject to change as new circumstances develop. They are not to be absolutized. . . . Law and government are legitimized only by the fulfillment of certain duties for the maintenance of the general welfare of the body politic. Oftentimes the legal system lags behind 'the sense of right and justice' as expressed by the community. I think we are now in one of those situations."

The speeches lasted so long that Carroll had to postpone sentencing the last three defendants until the following day. On July 2, 1986, he gave John Fife and Father Ramón Dagoberto Quiñones five years' probation and Father Anthony Clark three years' probation. Before he was sentenced, Fife told the judge about a fifteen-year-old boy whose family had been massacred in El Salvador and who needed his help. "The thought I could not escape was, if this was one of my boys, what would I want the church to do? I had no choice. None of us had any choice."

Paternal to the end, Carroll chose on the last day in court to lecture the defendants to pursue their objectives legally.

"Admittedly it is time-consuming," he said; "it doesn't have the kind of attraction that a trial such as this has, the media attention, the applause and that kind of thing." But they should have given a system "that has worked for 200 years" a fair chance and "requested that the agencies involved . . . follow the proper procedures."

Some of the defendants stiffened visibly at the judge's words. After all the frustrations and hardships they had endured, now they were expected to sit quietly and be chided by a schoolmaster in judicial robes. One of the lawyers released the mounting rage. When Carroll suggested that one refugee had not submitted an application for political asylum, Ellen Yaroshefsky shouted, "That application was ripped up by the INS!"

With the proceedings finally over, Don Reno strode out the front door and greeted the awaiting press. The victorious prosecutor said that he was never happy to see anyone convicted of a crime, but the defendants had, after all, broken the law. He was "more concerned with the reform of the defendants," he declared, "than with the reform of INS procedures." At that point Phil Willis-Conger, livid with anger, jumped up on a sidewalk bench near Reno and gave the prosecutor a Nazi salute. "I'm acknowledging the good German in front of me," he shouted.[2]

Maurice C. Inman, Jr., the general counsel of the INS and, in Don Reno's view, the high official who had been most supportive of the prosecution of the sanctuary workers, had flown to Tucson for the sentencing. He wanted to be sure that Reno knew how much he appreciated the "herculean, almost super human effort" the prosecutor had expended on the case.[3] Inman told reporters that he thought the convictions would help discourage other sanctuary activities. Even though the judge didn't fine or imprison the defendants, he pointed out, "they can't vote, they can't run for public office, they can't enlist in the armed services. If I were considering doing what they did, I would think twice about it."[4]

. . .

Two days after the sentencing of the sanctuary workers, the nation celebrated the centennial of the Statue of Liberty, in a Fourth of July Liberty Weekend marathon of parties, air and boat races, speeches, and celebration of the nation's hospitality to immigrants and refugees. Grateful new citizens from Eastern Europe and Southeast Asia spoke movingly on national television of their joy in being permitted to become a part of a great and generous nation. On the gala final night 4,000 guests, who had each paid $5,000 a seat, heard Frank Sinatra sing and saw President Ronald Reagan relight the torch of the Statue of Liberty.

The president, who had spent part of the Fourth of July cruising on the battleship *Iowa* with leading members of his administration, including Vice-Admiral John Poindexter, saluted in his weekly nationwide radio address "that beautiful lady, who for a hundred years now had stood watch over New York Harbor and this blessed and free land of ours." He also took the opportunity to associate the patriotic moment with one of his favorite causes: aid to the rebels trying to overthrow the Sandinista government of Nicaragua. He felt "proud," he declared, "that on this Independence Day weekend, America has embraced these brave men and their independent struggle."[5]

The refugees from Central America were not mentioned at the festivities.

Epilogue

B ETWEEN 1982, WHEN the sanctuary movement officially began,
and 1987, 906 applications for asylum were granted to Salvadorans,
while 21,250 were denied. Among those who never found a safe haven
in the United States were the family of Alejandro Gómez. On that same
Fourth of July weekend 1986, while the nation celebrated the hundredth anniversary of the Statue of Liberty, the Salvadoran refugee and
his family fled the United States for Canada.

A few weeks earlier Alejandro and Letitia Gómez were walking back
to the Downtown United Presbyterian Church in Rochester, New
York, where they had been in sanctuary since their journey up from
Mexico in 1984. Suddenly a man stepped up to them and said, "Hello,
Alejandro." He was an INS agent. Gómez was bundled into a waiting
automobile and sped away, while his wife watched helplessly from the
sidewalk.[1]

After several hours of calling, the Gómezes' lawyer finally learned
that the refugee had been taken to a detention center in Buffalo and
placed under a $50,000 bond. The Immigration Service justified his
sudden arrest with a claim that it had just received information from

intelligence sources that Gómez was a "dangerous subversive" and a "national security risk," but it made public no evidence of the allegations.

On the day after the arrest an ecumenical prayer service was held at a Catholic church, and the bail money started pouring into Downtown Presbyterian. Little children came in with crumpled dollar bills, and one man walked in with $10,000 in cash. Another man, a teacher from the Rochester suburbs who had never been involved in sanctuary, came in several times with cash from his cash card, telling church workers that "it wasn't often he had a chance to do something for his faith." By 7:00 P.M. on the day after the arrest the church had the $50,000 in hand, and parishioners took it by caravan to Buffalo, some eighty miles away. One woman riding back to Rochester in the same car with Gómez said he compared the dramatic fund-raising with the biblical story in which Jesus, seeing that His disciples were not catching any fish, told them to cast their nets on the other side of the boat, whereupon their nets were filled with fish.[2]

A sanctuary resolution was pending before the Rochester City Council, and many of its supporters were convinced that the INS move had been timed to intimidate the local government into rejecting the proposal. If so, the strategy backfired. Three days after Gómez was released, the City Council voted to declare the city of Rochester a sanctuary for Central American refugees. Several council members said that the arrest clinched the decision.

A few weeks later Alejandro Gómez finally had his long-awaited hearing for political asylum in the United States. At that hearing he revealed, for the first time, that in 1962, at the age of twenty-two, he had gone to Cuba for a meeting of trade unions and, while there, received training in the use of small arms, machine guns, and grenades. He had been a member of the Communist party in El Salvador from 1963 to about 1968 and had traveled to Eastern Europe, as had his wife, who had studied ballet in Moscow. Gómez denied that he had been a Communist or a member of any political organization for many years, commenting, "I grew in another direction."

Gómez's testimony contradicted a State Department advisory opinion, submitted as evidence at the hearing, that he had returned to Cuba in 1972 for "additional training." The opinion recommended against granting him asylum.

The revelations stunned Rochester, and the uproar helped convince the Gómezes, who were under constant surveillance, that they stood no chance of being allowed to remain in the United States. Although the asylum hearing was scheduled to resume in August, the family decided not to wait any longer. On the Fourth of July they crossed into Canada, where they now live, just across the border from Buffalo.

Gómez's departure meant that the good citizens of Rochester would lose the $50,000 they had put up for his bond. But a few weeks later the immigration judge on the case ruled that the federal government should return the money. The purpose of the bond had been to hold Gómez until it was determined whether he should be deported, the judge held. Since he had deported himself, its purpose had been fulfilled.

· · ·

A year and a half after the end of the sanctuary trial the case of the eight convicted church workers was pending before the U.S. Court of Appeals for the Ninth Circuit in San Francisco. While awaiting the outcome of their appeal, the defendants had, for the most part, resumed their normal lives.

John Fife continued his ministry at Southside Presbyterian, where refugees were still welcomed, and though he had given up the border runs, he was still spending about half his time on sanctuary-related work. He remained an active speaker on behalf of the refugees and in December 1986 received a human rights award presented by former President Jimmy Carter.

Darlene Nicgorski moved to the Dominican Sisters Women's Center in Plainville, Massachusetts, and also continued to speak at numerous symposiums on sanctuary around the country. In 1986 she was named one of *Ms.* magazine's women of the year.

Phil Willis-Conger moved to Berkeley to attend a seminary in San Francisco, training to become a Methodist minister. His and Ellen's first child was born in the summer of 1987.

Peggy Hutchison remained in Tucson and resumed her ministry along the border for the Methodist Church. At Christmastime 1986 she asked for permission to go to El Salvador to deliver gifts for victims of the earthquake. Judge Carroll denied the request.

Father Tony Clark went to Rome for a year of study and returned to his old parish in Davenport, Iowa. He had been given to understand that he was not entirely welcome back in his diocese in Arizona; he had criticized the bishop in Tucson once too often for not sufficiently supporting the sanctuary movement.

Wendy LeWin took training in emergency medical services. After her acquittal Mary K. Espinosa received numerous threatening telephone calls and letters, including anti-Semitic accusations of "siding with the Jews who killed Christ." A few months later her house was destroyed by fire. Her friends and supporters in Tucson organized on her behalf, and the house was rebuilt. Shortly after the family moved back in, her office at Sacred Heart was broken into, and a picture of her children was removed from its frame.

María Socorro Aguilar's house was vandalized shortly after the trial, but she continued her work with Father Ramón Quiñones. The priest launched a project for the homeless and began to raise money for a two-story addition on his church to house at least thirty people. He vowed that his ministry with refugees in Nogales "could never change."

Don Reno moved to Seattle, where he was greeted by a demonstration of sanctuary activists bearing a cake and a key to their church. He was handling the appeal of the sanctuary case but was thinking about leaving government and returning to the private sector.

Jim Rayburn received a citation from the INS for his work on the sanctuary case, although it was printed on the wrong form. He was also given a small Statue of Liberty, in token of the government's appreciation for his work. In 1987 he was transferred to a Border Patrol post in Blaine, Washington, on the Canadian border.

Joel and Gabriela Morelos received political asylum in the United States in November 1986 in Philadelphia, where he found work as a carpenter.

Meanwhile, at the Arizona border the underground railroad was still running regularly, albeit on a reduced schedule. After eight years of war and an estimated 62,000 civilian lives lost, the human rights situation within El Salvador was better than in the darkest days of the early 1980s, but still below civilized standards. By mid-1987 the number of officers tried and convicted for human rights abuses against civilians was zero. The State Department counted 251 civilian deaths in 1986, and human rights advocates reported that civilians were suffering "grievously" from both the armed forces' and the FMLN guerrillas' efforts to control them.[3] In late 1987 the head of the respected, nongovernmental Salvadoran Human Rights Commission was assassinated, and opposition political leaders returning from seven years in exile were immediately targeted by death squads. A small but steady stream of political refugees fleeing such threats was still running north, and sanctuary workers were still helping some 50 to 75 such people a year into the United States.[4]

Leadership of the border work had gravitated back to the tucson refugee support group, or trsg, the little group that Jim Corbett had originally put together, and Corbett himself remained its guiding spirit. Immediately after the trial the Corbetts decided to take a break from the pressures of the trial. They rented a ranch in Aravaipa Canyon, a beautiful and completely remote spot several hours' drive west of Tucson, where they repaired with their goats and geese and an Appaloosa they had been given by Corbett's mother.

There, in a steady flow of speeches and articles, the rancher continued to expound his concept of principled, nonviolent "civil initiative."

Speaking at Harvard University in 1987, Corbett declared: "As civil initiative, sanctuary extends the rule of law by instituting a way for our society to comply with human rights and humanitarian laws when the government violates them, and in doing so it also establishes public space for us to check and balance the new absolutism of the national security state."[5]

Elsewhere he argued, "In its primary current usage, the term 'sanctuary' refers to protective community with people whose basic human rights are being violated by government officials. As a declared practice, it incorporates prophetic witness into protective community; that is, in addition to protecting the violated from the state, the public practice of sanctuary holds the state accountable for its violations of human rights. . . . Sanctuary is . . . a faith practice that is part of what it means for the church to be the church."[6]

A man of deeds as well as words, the quixotic Quaker soon moved back into Tucson, where he resumed his active role in the refugee effort. The trsg established a policy of routinely notifying the INS of its activities—although the actual routes it took with refugees were still kept secret—and the Immigration Service once again seemed inclined to turn a blind eye.

As for public sanctuary, the more explicitly political aspect of the sanctuary movement was almost moribund by the end of 1986. Few refugees wanted to go "public," and many of the 300 to 400 sanctuary churches around the country had no refugees to sponsor. Instead, the churches focused on providing legal representation for refugees seeking asylum and on helping resettle Central Americans trying to return to their homes from camps for displaced people in the region.

This latest effort by sanctuary supporters to work within the system was given impressive moral and legal support by the highest authorities of both church and state in the year after the Arizona trial.

Pope John Paul II, during his 1987 tour of the United States, paid tribute in San Antonio, Texas, to those "among you . . . people of great courage and generosity who have been doing much on behalf of suffering brothers and sisters arriving from the south. They have sought to show compassion in the face of complex human, social and political realities."

The pope's statement was widely interpreted to indicate support for the sanctuary movement, although a senior Vatican official traveling with the pontiff said that "he was dealing with the matter on a moral level and was not referring to any specific group."[7]

More explicit vindication had come earlier in the year, on March 9, 1987, when the Supreme Court ruled that the Immigration Service had been interpreting the asylum provisions of the 1980 Refugee Act too narrowly. In effect, the six-to-three decision supported the sanctuary defendants' argument that the government had not properly enforced its own laws. The justices ruled that the "plain language" of the 1980 Refugee Act indicated that Congress intended a "more generous" standard of proof for seekers of political asylum than the Immigration Service had been applying. The INS's demand that applicants demonstrate a "clear probability" of persecution required extensive documentation and was all but impossible for most Central Americans to meet. Instead, the Court decided, aliens seeking asylum needed only prove that they have a "well-founded fear of persecution."[8]

In the ruling for the majority Justice John Paul Stevens said, "Deportation is always a harsh measure. It is all the more replete with danger when the alien makes a claim that he or she will be subject to death or persecution if forced to return to his or her home country."

Justice Stevens suggested that a person with "a 10 percent chance of being shot, tortured or otherwise persecuted" might qualify for asylum. And because the "well-founded fear of persecution" standard involves a subjective mental state, those who deeply feared persecution might also qualify.

Justice Harry A. Blackmun, in a separate opinion, singled out the "years of seemingly purposeful blindness by the I.N.S., which only now begins its task of developing the standard entrusted to its care."

The decision did not promise an immediate overhaul of INS asylum practices, however, for the attorney general retains the discretion to decide who, of those who qualify for asylum, will actually receive it. But the ruling was enough to encourage more Salvadorans to reopen their cases, and in Arizona at least, thanks in large part to more sympathetic immigration judges, more of the Central Americans were already meeting with success. By the middle of 1987 roughly half of all Salvadoran applicants in the state were being granted asylum.[9]

Attorney General Edwin Meese III continued nevertheless to cling to the old cold war definition of a refugee. In the summer of 1986 he decreed that the Justice Department should presume that anyone fleeing "totalitarian"—that is, Communist—countries automatically met the legal standard for obtaining a safe haven in the United States. Such a presumption favored the claims of Poles, whose Polish-American supporters had complained that only 50 percent of their applications were being approved. The Reagan administration also remained partial to the claims of other Eastern Europeans, particularly athletes. In 1986 immediate refugee status was granted to two Czechoslovakian hockey players who defected to join American teams and two Soviet acrobats, the latest in a long line of Chinese tennis players and Russian musicians and ballet dancers to be embraced by Uncle Sam. One of the Salvadoran refugees in Tucson, still awaiting his fate more than a year after he had applied for political asylum, joked that maybe he should carry sporting equipment or wear a tutu to his asylum hearing.

The principal new beneficiaries of the Reagan administration's enduring anticommunism were the Nicaraguans. Almost a year to the day after the sentencing of the sanctuary workers, Meese, after consultation with the White House, decreed that all Nicaraguans should be presumed to have a "well-founded fear of persecution" and that the INS should therefore consider their asylum claims favorably. The order was expected to benefit as many as 200,000 Nicaraguans who were in the country illegally, and sure enough, in recent months a substantial majority of Nicaraguans requesting a safe haven have been granted it.

The Meese order, which made no mention of other Central Americans, was immediately attacked by members of Congress still trying unsuccessfully to pass legislation to defer the deportation of Salvadorans. "This government is crazy," declared Representative John Joseph Moakley of Massachusetts. "The Reagan administration is playing politics with people's lives. . . . If El Salvador were under Communist leadership, they'd have the welcome wagons out waiting for them to land."[10]

Instead, the Salvadorans were among those likely to suffer most from the new Immigration Reform and Control Act of 1986. Under the new legislation, employers of illegal aliens who had entered the United States after January 1, 1982, would eventually be fined. The measure was expected to cost many if not most of the estimated 400,000 to 600,000 Salvadorans in the country their jobs, for few of those who had arrived before 1982 had any proof of their entry.

The new law threatened to do what the INS, because of budget cuts and a shortage of personnel, was no longer doing: force the Salvadorans back to Central America. Voting with their feet on that prospect, more than 6,000 "bus people," most of them Salvadorans, flocked to the Canadian border in the first weeks following passage of the immigration bill. So many asylum seekers descended on Canadian-American border stations that the Canadian government quickly shut the door and announced that individuals awaiting a review of their refugee status could no longer receive work permits in Canada but had to wait on the other side of the border. In the spring of 1987 American border towns were jammed with desperate men, women, and children, many camped in church basements, awaiting Canadian review of their claims.

Ironically, the new law promised to harm not only individual Salvadorans but the very regime that the U.S. government had been supporting lavishly for the previous eight years. In April 1987 President Duarte of El Salvador asked President Reagan in a confidential letter to grant safe haven to the Salvadorans living illegally in the United States because their return would be disastrous to the small nation's economy. The earnings repatriated by Salvadorans in the United States amounted to from $350 million to $600 million a year, Duarte wrote, a sum that rivaled American military and economic aid, which was running at a rate of $1.5 million a day. The aid had enabled the Salvadoran armed forces and the police to grow from 16,850 in 1981 to 57,000 strong in 1986. But unemployment remained an estimated 25 to 50 percent, and returning exiles who couldn't find work might turn out to be a "destabilizing force," as the one president delicately warned the other.[11]

A few weeks later the Reagan administration rejected President Duarte's appeal. A State Department spokeswoman said that the government wished to avoid setting a precedent. Privately U.S. officials said they wanted to wait and see how many Salvadorans actually returned, but on the face of it, the Reagan administration's hard-line policy toward Salvadoran refugees was totally at odds with its Central

American foreign policy, a pillar of which was support of the Duarte regime.*

Thus, eight years after their suffering had begun, the refugees from El Salvador were still without peace at home or a safe haven in the United States. And although victory had been declared by both sides, in reality the Americans who had battled over the Central Americans' fate had also lost.

Don Reno had proclaimed that the trial verdicts were the "death knell" of the sanctuary movement.[13] Not only was that not true, but the word within the INS was that the convictions had been a Pyrrhic victory: too costly both in terms of resources and in adverse publicity for the government.

Sanctuary supporters, too, could look to disappointing results. To be sure, the movement, according to many independent observers, could take much of the credit for focusing public attention on the plight of the refugees. "Churches across the board, from liberal to conservative, speak with one voice on this," said Dale S. De Haan, director of the immigration and refugee program of the Church World Service, an organization that is sympathetic to but does not advocate sanctuary. "I can go to small towns from Minnesota to Texas, and they are aware of the problem," he added. "Even the National Association of Evangelicals supports the concept that we need to help these people."[14]

Among international lawyers and immigration experts, the concept of temporary safe haven for refugees from civil wars or internal armed conflict, a principle not currently embodied in the international or domestic refugee law, is also gaining ground. The subject is increasingly discussed in knowledgeable circles, thanks in no small measure to the

---

*Speaking in Washington later, President Duarte finally gave the lie to the administration's claim that returning Salvadorans faced no special dangers. On October 15, 1987, he told an audience at the National Press Club: "We are not asking the United States to let our people stay only because of economic and social conditions. There are three violences we have to take into consideration. The first is *structural violence:* social injustice, the poverty, the misery, the lack of education, lack of housing, lack of health. . . . The second is the *institutional violence.* For many years the power and influence has [*sic*] been in a few hands, and they have used this violence. . . . We have reduced the impunity these people have, but they are still there.

"The third is the *violence of war.* A campesino walks in his fields and he loses his leg; he walks in his fields and all of a sudden bullets are all over the place. These people are afraid of the violence and they want to stay here. . . ."[12]

No sanctuary supporter could have said it better.

dramatization of the Central Americans' problems by the sanctuary movement.[15]

Yet the movement has been unable to accomplish its goals, of winning legal protection for the refugees or, more basically, of ending American military involvement in Central America. Hundreds of thousands of dollars that could have gone directly to the refugees' immediate and legal needs had to be poured into legal defense for North Americans. And the divisions and the suspicions created in this country by the controversy over Central America, culminating in contragate, have threatened the American system itself.

In January of 1988 information was revealed about a massive FBI campaign against CISPES, a left-wing solidarity group opposed to American military intervention in Central America and sympathetic to the cause of the Salvadoran guerrillas. The Center for Constitutional Rights released thousands of pages of documents detailing years of official spying and harassment, despite a lack of any evidence that CISPES was engaged in anything other than its constitutional right of free speech and dissent.

The revelations didn't solve the mystery of the break-ins of sanctuary churches. But the allegations of "terrorism" in the Alejandro Gómez affair again raised the specter that under the guise of "antiterrorist" activity, the federal government might be involved in some subterranean "black" campaign against the sanctuary movement. In February 1987 Representative Don Edwards's Subcommittee on Civil and Constitutional Rights of the House Judiciary Committee—the same panel that had investigated the COINTELPRO break-ins by the FBI in the 1970s—finally took up the question in public hearings.

One of the ministers testifying at the hearing was Victor Carpenter, pastor of the Arlington Street Church in Boston, a congregation founded in 1729 and once located in the building where the Massachusetts delegation ratified the Constitution of the United States. Carpenter, a gray-bearded man with the face and the accent of a nineteenth-century New England ship captain, related how, after a long debate, his congregation had decided to support sanctuary. That was on December 26, 1986, and on Sunday, January 4, 1987, Carpenter planned to speak on the decision.

On the night before, all of the church's locked doors were broken through, and all the files rifled. One file marked "Sanctuary" was ostentatiously pulled out and left on a desk. Nothing of value was taken.

"Clearly the purpose was to send the church a message," Carpenter testified. "Another minister said to me, 'Obviously you had a mole.' It causes people to look at each other strangely during coffee hours and suchlike. . . . We regard this as an infringement of our religious liberties."[16]

Gregory Brown, pastor of the Calvary United Methodist Church in Washington, D.C., testified that his church had been broken into on February 1, 1987. All working papers and reports relating to a caravan of Salvadorans touring the United States and talking about conditions in El Salvador were taken. A few weeks earlier the briefcase of the national organizer of the caravan had been stolen.

The Reverend Donovan Cook, the Seattle minister who had offered sanctuary to as many as twenty-seven refugees at one time, including the family of Elba Teresa López, described another mysterious break-in and a strange incident in which a Latin male, with tears tattooed under his left eye, came into Cook's office and offered him a U.S. birth certificate for use by a refugee. Suspecting an attempt at entrapment, Cook sent him away. Later, when the minister was escorting some refugees to Canada, he spotted the same man trying to take a picture of one of them.

"All this has had a chilling effect," Cook testified. "Is there an FBI or intelligence investigation of us [the University Baptist Church of Seattle]? Some inappropriate people have tried to join our church since the indictments, and we find ourselves suspicious of those in our midst."

The FBI stood by its earlier refusals to investigate the break-ins. Oliver B. Revell, the head of investigations for the bureau, testified at the hearings that "such break-ins could not constitute a violation of federal criminal civil rights statutes absent evidence of law enforcement involvement. . . . No information was reported indicating that any entity of the U.S. government was involved in the break-ins, or that any common threads existed linking them. . . . I can categorically state," Revell said, obviously choosing his words carefully, "that there has been no break-in by any FBI agent acting in his official capacity." Later he flatly denied that "any government agency" had been involved.

Some members of the subcommittee were not persuaded that that was all there was to it. Revell had sat on an interagency task force on counterterrorism with Lieutenant Colonel Oliver North, and Revell was asked whether that group might have been involved in some way. He stated that although "some comments might have been made in an off-the-cuff manner [about domestic groups], I have no recollection of any comments with a focus on domestic issues. . . ."

Representative Patricia Schroeder, whose house was broken into several times after her first election to Congress in 1972, by a man later revealed to be a government informant, pressed Revell on whether the burglaries might have been committed by informants who were paid by law enforcement officials for information obtained through burglaries. "We do not ask any assets to conduct illegal activities," Revell responded. He also reassured the subcommittee that the FBI "is not now engaged in any burglaries or illegal activities as an institution."

"Do you do it under cover of law?" asked Robert Kastenmeier, the Democrat from Wisconsin.

"I can't comment on that or on activities that involve foreign counterintelligence," Revell responded.

Under an executive order signed by President Reagan during his first year in office and under subsequent guidelines issued by Attorney General William French Smith, government break-ins are legal if they are conducted under the guise of a foreign intelligence or counterintelligence operation.[17] Edwards commented during the hearings that the government does not even need a warrant before it can infiltrate a domestic organization, including a church. "In this era such a bill cannot be enacted, but the majority of us on this committee feel that the Fourth Amendment calls for it," he declared. Later Revell agreed that "there is a great deal of subjectivity whether one of these activities violates the law."

• • •

The story of sanctuary is, in the end, a story about ourselves, and the damage that inhumane policies, stubbornly pursued, can inflict on the body politic. More than ten years ago, in a letter to the Young Lawyers Section of the Washington State Bar Association, Supreme Court Justice William O. Douglas wrote that the Constitution and the Bill of Rights "guarantee to all of us all the rights to personal and spiritual self-fulfillment.

"But the guarantee is not self-executing," Douglas continued. "As nightfall does not come at once, neither does oppression. In both instances, there is a twilight when everything remains seemingly unchanged.

"And it is in such twilight that we all must be most aware of change in the air—however slight—lest we become unwitting victims of the darkness."[18]

Appendix I

AS EARLY AS the fall of 1981 both the mainline churches and numerous human rights groups had taken up the cause of the Central American refugees, and several, including the Lutheran and Presbyterian churches, had conducted their own independent surveys of their treatment by the government at the border. Their investigations found a pattern of widespread abuse of refugees' rights.

INS district directors and administrative judges had considerable discretion in administering the 1980 refugee law, and some were exercising their authority with sensitivity and humanity. Some field officers treated aliens with respect and dignity. The detention center at El Paso, for instance, was not considered nearly as harsh as El Centro, and some immigration judges were releasing Salvadoran asylum applicants on their own recognizance. Nevertheless, many church establishments concurred with the general conclusion reached in a September 1981 report prepared for the Lutheran Immigration and Refugee Service. "Attorneys, paralegals, long-time advocates of the undocumented from many nations, social workers, church people—all seemed to agree that I.N.S. treatment of Salvadorans, whatever its residual bureaucratic component, was worse than what they observed in terms of other nationality groups," the author stated after a lengthy investigative tour of the border.[1]

Gary MacEoin, who spent weeks investigating the treatment of the Central Americans, found that at the INS processing center in the Federal Building in Los Angeles a web of rules and regulations effectively prevented the detainees from obtaining legal help.[2]

The bonds set on Central Americans rose to unprecedented heights, partly because so many Salvadorans failed to show up for their deportation hearings. But in many instances the levels seemed punitive and predated the phenomenon of no-shows. By late 1981 bonds in El Paso and Laredo had risen to $5,000, $7,500, or more. Marc Van Der Hout, who represented hundreds of Salvadoran applicants for political asylum, had one case involving a twenty-one-year-old woman who was five months pregnant and who had fled El Salvador after her father had been kidnapped by armed men and assassinated. Her bond had been set in El Paso, Texas, at $10,000. It took several bond redetermination hearings and an appeal to the Board of Immigration Appeals to have the bail reduced to $2,000, which was posted by the archdiocese of San Francisco. The girl, named Eva Antonia Juárez, was finally released when she was seven months pregnant.[3]

The office of the United Nations High Commissioner for Refugees, whose mandate is the protection of refugees everywhere, joined the chorus of critics after conducting its own investigation of asylum processing of Salvadorans in California, Arizona, and Texas in the fall of 1981. In a sharply worded report the Washington representative of the UNHCR, a Ugandan, issued a series of harsh conclusions. He found that the large-scale migration from El Salvador had a "direct causal relationship with the internal strife" there, that "there appears to be a systematic practice designed to secure the return of Salvadorans, irrespective of the merits of their asylum claims," and that the "overwhelming majority of those returning are doing so 'voluntarily' without apparently being freely advised of their asylum rights."[4] The report concluded that the overall American response to the refugee crisis "would appear to represent a negation of its responsibilities assumed upon its adherence to the Protocol."

Back in Washington the UNHCR man became an active advocate of Salvadoran asylum seekers. A one-page *aide-mémoire* sent to the U.S. government recommended the suspension of deportations of *all*

Salvadorans. After what one UN official described as a "somewhat rough response" from the Reagan administration, UNHCR headquarters sent another message to the American government. At least, it urged, stop deporting those Salvadorans who seem to face a particular danger upon return.

Another UNHCR communication, dated May 29, 1981, to the chairman of the Standing Conference of Canadian Organizations Concerned for Refugees, went much further. It read:

> *As you are aware, in situations of large-scale influx it is frequently impracticable to resort to an individual determination of refugee status due to the large numbers involved and also to the frequent necessity to provide assistance and protection on an emergency basis. In order to overcome these various difficulties, recourse has frequently been had to what is known as "prima facie group determination." This is based on the assumption that in view of the conditions prevailing in the country of origin, all members of the group should, in the absence of clear indications to the contrary, be regarded as refugees.*
>
> *As regards persons who have left Salvador after the outbreak of the Civil War early in 1980, we considered that the above-mentioned conditions are indeed fulfilled.*

Partly in response to this message, Canada stopped deporting Salvadorans to their native land, and the UNHCR representative in Washington, pessimistic about any change in American policies, began to help Salvadorans arrested in the United States find a safe haven in Canada or elsewhere.

The UNHCR representative also began publicizing asylum cases that he believed were wrongfully being denied by the United States and sent a letter out to immigration attorneys around the country, advising them of the international refugee definition and how that legal standard might apply to their Salvadoran clients. Infuriated, the State Department finally refused to grant the UNHCR access to its files, thereby effectively preventing the organization from exercising its protective function within the United States.[5]

The most serious indictment of the U.S. government came from within the INS itself. During the Carter administration Commissioner Leonel Castillo had had a deliberate policy of assisting people who wanted to file for admission into the United States, and Castillo himself had frequently spoken to church and immigrants' rights groups on how to maneuver their clients through the complicated immigration procedures.* Some of the INS district offices even lent such advocates space where they could prepare the necessary documentation.

In that spirit INS Deputy Commissioner Doris Meissner in 1981 commissioned an internal investigation of the entire asylum process. Meissner wanted to establish a system to handle the sudden deluge of asylum claims fairly and efficiently. The report, released in 1982 after a three-month field investigation and interviews with more than forty people within the INS and State Department, was an authoritative, inside critique of the government's handling of asylum requests.[6]

The report partially explained why so few Salvadorans were being granted asylum in 1981: As of March 1982 the agency had a backlog of more than 100,000 requests, including 9,363 from Salvadorans. Nine to fourteen months or more could elapse between the time of filing and an INS decision on an asylum application.

In a departure from past policy the Reagan administration in mid-1981 decreed that applicants had to spend this long waiting period in detention, unless someone was willing to put up their bonds. That had not been a policy since Ellis Island had closed almost thirty years earlier, in 1954.

The order had been aimed at the Haitian boat people landing all along the Florida coast, but like porpoises caught in a tuna net, the Salvadorans slammed right into it. The internal INS report documented what the Tucson refugee workers had discovered: that a Salvadoran refugee could languish in prison for a year or more and still not have his plea for safe haven seriously considered.

Applications were reviewed by virtually untrained immigration officials. Only those INS officials trained after 1980—less than 2 percent of the entire officer corps—had received any formal instruction in processing asylum claims. And that instruction amounted to less than 3 of the 560 hours in the basic officer training program. None of that meager time was given to actual work with refugees or their applica-

---

*"You have to work at it," Castillo said in a telephone interview in July 1986. "You have to call on the ministers, the archbishops, the rabbis. It's both good humanitarianism and good public relations, and it's good financially. If we help them fill out the forms properly, the papers will be in much better shape and we can process them more efficiently."

tions or to interview techniques for evaluating a person's fear of individual persecution. One officer said that when she was assigned to asylum work, she bought a subscription to *Newsweek* to "learn more about" countries overseas.[7]

The State Department's Bureau of Human Rights and Humanitarian Affairs was required to render an advisory opinion on every application, recommending approval or rejection. Yet the internal INS study found that the department's treatment of asylum applications was as superficial as that of the INS. Worse, it was highly political. Asylum applications from Salvadorans and Guatemalans were almost invariably rejected, regardless of the merits of the case, while Poles, in contrast, were often welcomed regardless of their circumstances. "In some cases, different levels of proof are required of different asylum applicants," the study declared. "In other words, certain nationalities appear to benefit from presumptive status while others do not. For example, for an El Salvadoran national to receive a favorable asylum advisory opinion, he or she must have a 'classic textbook case.' On the other hand, [the State Department] sometimes recommends a favorable action where the applicant cannot meet the well-founded fear of persecution test."[8] The report told how a Polish crewman who jumped ship in December 1981, a week after martial law was declared, was granted asylum in forty-eight hours. He said the reason he feared returning to Poland was that he had once attended a Solidarity rally. He was not a member of Solidarity, had never participated in any political activity, and was among more than 100,000 people at the rally.[9]

The internal INS study reminded immigration officials that "the prime responsibility for asylum adjudication rests with the I.N.S., not the Department of State," and urged them not to accept unquestioningly State's recommendations on individual asylum requests. It recommended, among other things, that a special asylum officer corps be trained to do what the INS had not yet done: implement the asylum provisions of the 1980 Refugee Act.

These recommendations were ignored. An asylum officer corps was never trained, and uniform procedures were never adopted. INS field offices were instructed to make no asylum adjudications without an advisory opinion from the State Department, even though the law permitted the INS to act alone if no State Department opinion was received within forty-five days. Five years later, in 1987, the 1980 Refugee Act was still being administered under interim regulations.

The UNHCR, heavily dependent upon American financial support, stopped short of publicly urging the United States to grant a safe haven to all Salvadorans, but American religious and human rights organizations were not as reluctant to speak out. As early as 1980 they began to urge the U.S. government to grant "extended voluntary departure" (EVD) status to all Salvadorans in the United States, allowing them to remain in the country temporarily until conditions in their homeland were safer.

By law the State Department may ask the attorney general to halt the expulsion of a given nationality, and historically EVD has been granted if the attorney general decides that there is "widespread fighting, destruction and breakdown of public services and order." Since 1960 EVD status has been given to citizens of fourteen countries: Cuba, Czechoslovakia, Cambodia, Vietnam, Laos, Lebanon, Ethiopia, Hungary, Romania, Iran, Nicaragua, Uganda, Afghanistan, and Poland.

Among those appealing for a halt to deportations of Salvadorans in 1981 were the United States Catholic Conference, the archbishop of Washington, and, in a resolution written by Ken Kennon, among others, the General Assembly of the Christian Church (Disciples of Christ).

Senator Edward M. Kennedy (Democrat-Massachusetts), then the ranking minority member on the Subcommittee on Immigration and Refugee Policy, asked then Secretary of State Alexander M. Haig, Jr., to recommend EVD to the Justice Department. The State Department responded with a letter stating that "El Salvador has not suffered the same level of wide-spread fighting, destruction and breakdown of public services and order as did, for example, Nicaragua, Lebanon or Uganda at the time when voluntary departure was recommended by the Department. . . ." The letter argued that individual applications for asylum would protect those with a genuine fear of returning to El Salvador.[10]

The problem with State's position was that virtually no Salvadorans were getting asylum, even though conditions in the tortured country were steadily worsening. ". . . not since *la Matanza,* the 1932 massacre of 30,000 peasants, has the human rights situation in El Salvador been as bad as it is now," concluded a report submitted to the president in January 1982 by two respected human rights organizations.[11]

The report documented the abrogation of the rights to due process of law and to a fair trial; the destruction of independent newspapers (since January 1980 seventeen news office and radio stations had been bombed or machine-gunned, and twelve journalists killed); the routine use of torture in the central headquarters of the National Guard, the Treasury Police, and the National Police (encouraged by an emergency decree permitting convictions based on uncorroborated confessions made in the presence of police, army, or other security personnel); the outlawing of all public meetings and strikes; the repression of peasant organizations and of the church; and a military policy founded on the elimination of bases for guerrilla organizations by depopulating villages, destroying crops, and killing rural populations who might support the opposition. Almost in passing, the report noted that "there hasn't been a fair election in El Salvador for the last 50 years."[12]

The report pleaded to the president to halt all U.S. assistance to the Salvadoran military, which was closely linked to the terrorist death squads. Since 1979, and as the human rights violations accelerated, American military and economic aid had steadily increased, until by 1982 the tiny country had become the fourth-largest recipient of American aid, trailing only Israel, Egypt, and Turkey.*

The rationale for this massive flow of funds was the need to support the government against Roberto d'Aubuisson and his openly fascist supporters on the right and the Marxist-Leninist guerrillas on the left, who, the Reagan administration charged, were backed by the Soviet Union and Cuba. (At the time the stated reason for the administration's escalating campaign against the Sandinista government in Nicaragua was that the latter was sending arms to the Salvadoran guerrillas.) The government was nominally headed by José Napoleón Duarte, a Christian Democratic politician with a long history of opposition to military dictatorship. Privately, however, American diplomats on the scene in San Salvador told reporters that the regime was dominated by colonels and generals, many with fascist ideologies, whose modus operandi resembled that of the Mafia.[14]

For American support to continue, the president had to certify to

---

*In 1981 $86 million in emergency funds and military aid was rushed to San Salvador and less than two months after the new president took office, 56 U.S. military personnel and Green Beret experts in counterinsurgency were in the country: training; assisting in intelligence; helping military commanders; and putting together a new quick-reaction force, the 2,000-man Atlacatl Battalion. A few months later, in December 1981, soldiers from that elite unit murdered nearly 1,000 peasants, primarily women, children, and old people, during a search-and-destroy operation supported by helicopter gunships and heavy artillery.[13] In addition to military assistance, between 1980 and 1982 Washington sent $354.5 million in economic aid to El Salvador.

Congress that El Salvador was complying with the Foreign Assistance Act, which bars military aid and arms sales to countries that fail to meet certain minimal human rights standards. On January 28, 1982, President Reagan, ignoring the copious documentation of abuses by dozens of churches and human rights organizations, certified "that the Government of El Salvador is making a concerted and significant effort to comply with internationally recognized human rights."[15]

That certification, charged Aryeh Neier of Americas Watch and Morton Halperin of the American Civil Liberties Union, is "a fraud."[16]

Appendix II

AT BOTTOM THE dispute between the government and the sanctuary workers was over the fate of the Salvadorans sent back to their country. Did the people deported back to Central America really face torture and possible death, as the sanctuary activists claimed, or did they run no particular risks, as the government maintained, even at the height of death squad activity? Or was there sufficient reasonable doubt about the answer that an alternative to sending the Salvadorans back should be considered?

The truth has important moral implications, for 48,209 Salvadorans were sent back to El Salvador from 1980 to 1986, and a new immigration law jeopardized the jobs and threatened to force the return of several hundred thousand more.[1] If only a fraction of those returned suffered persecution, then the Reagan administration can rightfully be held responsible for significant human rights violations.

The fate of the deported also has important legal implications. As the State Department itself acknowledged in 1981, in a letter dated April 17 to Senator Edward M. Kennedy, as a signatory of the 1967 United Nations Protocol Relating to the Status of Refugees, "the United States is prohibited from undertaking the forced expulsion movement of a

refugee to a country or frontier where persecution is likely to occur."
This is in accordance with the time-honored international principle of
nonrefoulement. The essence of the sanctuary movement's rationale
was that since the government was deporting Salvadorans back into
very probable danger without affording them a fair hearing, it was the
government, not the movement, that was really breaking domestic and
international law.

When the refugee crisis surfaced, the Reagan administration first
maintained that Salvadorans had little to fear back home. As that
argument became untenable in the face of documented human rights
abuses, the argument shifted and became one that the deportees faced
no special dangers just *because* they had been deported from the United
States. In any event, the State Department has argued ingeniously, one
can invoke nonrefoulement only in the case of a refugee. If the deported
person has not been granted refugee status by American authorities,
then nonrefoulement does not apply.[2]

The "truth" in this case is not as verifiable as a law of physics or
mathematics. Neither the government nor the sanctuary workers have
ever had sufficient evidence on their side to silence the debate. Seven
years after it began, the General Accounting Office made it official, in
a report concluding, as its title stated: *Illegal Aliens: Extent of Problems
of Returned Salvadorans Not Determinable.*

Most objective observers agree that most of those fleeing El Salvador
and Guatemala have been displaced by military operations, including
bombing of civilian areas, and by severe internal upheaval. Technically
these displaced people do not fit the "well-founded fear of persecution"
definition of refugee embodied in the 1951 Geneva Convention, the
1967 UN Protocol Relating to the Status of Refugees, or the 1980
Refugee Act of the United States. Nevertheless, many international
lawyers with no connection to the sanctuary movement argue that such
displaced people should not be returned to their homelands and should
be granted at least temporary safe haven.

Moreover, the anecdotal evidence on conditions in El Salvador in the
early 1980s, when deportations were at their height, indicated that
many Salvadoran deportees were classic refugees, with ample reason to
fear for their lives. *They* certainly seemed to think so, and in a quantita-
tive study of the causes of the recent Salvadoran migration to the
United States, William Stanley of the department of political science at
MIT concluded in 1985 that there was strong empirical evidence, based

on close association between the level of political violence in El Salvador and the numbers coming to the United States, that "fear of political violence is in fact the dominant motivation of Salvadorans who migrate here."[3]

When Jim Corbett, John Fife, and their colleagues were beginning their work with the refugees, several cases involving the murder of deportees had already been documented. These few examples were enough to convince those working with Salvadorans that to send them back would be unconscionable. In early 1981, for example, a rumor was circulating along the border about a group of deportees who had been arrested and killed immediately upon their return to San Salvador. It was this rumor that had first prompted Jim Corbett's concern about the Salvadoran hitchhiker.

In an effort to substantiate the story, Marc Van Der Hout, an immigration attorney in Redwood City, California (and the lawyer for some of the survivors of the trek through the Organ Pipe Wilderness), obtained an affidavit on September 16, 1981, from José Rosales, a twenty-seven-year-old who had applied for political asylum in the United States after deserting the Salvadoran armed forces the previous year. Rosales swore:

[I have] strong reasons to believe that the dangers faced by all young male civilians in El Salvador are enhanced for those who are returned to El Salvador after being deported from other countries. I am aware of this increased danger because I was stationed at the San Salvador airport in the latter part of 1979. I recall one particular incident in November, 1979[,] when an airplane arrived carrying, among others, nine Salvadorans being deported from Mexico. The nine deportees were detained at the airport, "investigated" that is, tortured and killed. Pictures of their bodies appeared in the newspaper. During my duties at the San Salvador airport I learned from conversations with superior officers that young men who are returned to El Salvador deported from other countries must be presumed to have left the country in order to avoid military service. This is considered a form of subversion or communism, because of the assumption that a young man who resists entering the army must be in opposition to the government. For this reason, young men deported to El Salvador face extreme danger of being killed, simply by virtue of the fact of having left and been deported.[4]

On December 9, 1981, an open letter to the government in *El Diario de Hoy,* a newspaper in San Salvador, poignantly illustrated Rosales's assertions. In the letter one Valentina Elias Mejia pleaded for help in finding the whereabouts of her grandson, José Humberto Santacruz Elias, "22 years of age, electrician, single, and a resident of Cuidad Delgado." The woman wrote:

> *My grandson, I am certain, does not have any relation with the existing political organizations in this country. I have known that he was captured on January 15 of the current year, at approximately 2:30 P.M. at Comalapa International Airport. It is a fact that my grandson was being deported from the United States and he entered this country on LACSA flight number 641, as is shown by the records at the Customs Offices of the above-mentioned airport.*
>
> *It is such, members of the Revolutionary Government Junta, that since that date I don't know the whereabouts of my grandson, which makes me extremely worried about what might happen to him. . . . I have already gone to all the security forces garrisons and offices, and they have all denied his capture . . . if he has committed any crime I ask for him to be taken to the corresponding courts or, if innocent, that he be freed.* [5]

CARECEN, the Central American Refugee Center, in Washington, D.C., published documents on another case. In June 1981 twenty-four-year-old Santana Chirino Amaya was deported for the second time by U.S. immigration officials, and on September 1, his body and that of a fourteen-year-old boy were found on the edge of a highway some fifty meters from the bathing resort of Amapulapa, San Vicente, El Salvador. Both had been decapitated and tortured. Amaya's uncle, in a statement to authorities, said that he had last been seen leaving the city of Zacatecoluca on August 25 driving a maroon Datsun pickup in the company of the younger boy. The uncle's statement declared that "his nephew did not take part in any political activity, nor had enemies. . . ."[6]

CARECEN argued that there were two possible explanations for Amaya's death. First, he was sought by the authorities for having left the country after his name had appeared on the flight passenger list handed over to Salvadoran airport officials. Or he was a victim of the random violence that afflicted El Salvador. The bodies had been found at a crossroad notorious as the "Road of Death" because of the behavior of the Salvadoran army patrols in the area. CARECEN speculated that possibly because he had been away from the country, Amaya did not realize that he was driving along a dangerous route.

The most intriguing case involving the dangers of deportation was that of Ana Guevara, a thirty-six-year-old Salvadoran woman arrested in Texas in June 1981. The case confirmed the worst suspicions of the refugees and those working with them that the U.S. government did exchange information with the Salvadoran government on suspected leftists among Salvadoran migrants—information that could amount to a death warrant for those who were deported.

At the time of her arrest for illegal entry Guevara was carrying a tape recording of the last mass of Archbishop Oscar Romero and letters of introduction to church activists in Puerto Rico.[7] The Border Patrol turned these "suspicious" materials over to the FBI in San Antonio, which decided that they expressed "classic Marxist rhetoric." The bureau then began a foreign counterintelligence investigation to ascertain Guevara's identity. Confidential FBI sources led the agency to suspect that the woman might be a Salvadoran guerrilla leader named Norma Fidelina Guevara de Grande, known by the nom de guerre Comandante Norma.

The FBI asked the American embassy in San Salvador to obtain Comandante Norma's fingerprints from Salvadoran authorities. The story leaked, and the possibility that the well-known rebel had been apprehended in Texas received a good deal of publicity in the Salvadoran press. The fingerprint comparisons eventually revealed that Ana Guevara was not, in fact, Norma Guevara, but by that time the Salvadoran government had become ominously interested in Ana G. for her own sake. Indicating that possession of "subversive" materials was a crime for which she could be detained upon her return to El Salvador, the authorities asked U.S. officials to send them the date and number of her flight in the event she was deported and asked that copies of the documents in her possession be furnished to the plane's captain for delivery to Colonel Eugenio Vides Casanova, director general of the Salvadoran National Guard.

Colonel Vides Casanova, who later became General Vides Casanova and El Salvador's minister of defense, was the head of the National Guard when death squad activity was at its peak. Three American nuns, a lay church worker, and two U.S. labor advisers were among those allegedly killed by members of the Guard while Colonel Vides was at its helm.

At her deportation hearing on October 8, 1981, Guevara requested political asylum, but she failed to complete her asylum application on the ground that the U.S. government would give any information she provided to the Salvadoran government, thereby placing her in grave jeopardy. The State Department then recommended that she be denied asylum because of a lack of proof for her fear of persecution. The immigration judge denied her application. She appealed to the Board of Immigration Appeals, and in 1983 it, too, denied her request for asylum on the ground that she had failed to meet her burden of proof.

Within a month of that decision, however, and roughly two years after her deportation hearing, the FBI finally released three documents, pursuant to a FOIA request by Guevara, revealing the extent of the two governments' interest in her case. The immigration board reviewed the documents and concluded that they proved only that she "may be questioned or detained in El Salvador in connection with an investigation into whether she is a terrorist subversive, not that she would be executed for her political beliefs." Her motion to reopen the case was denied.

Guevara appealed that decision to the federal courts, and on April 11, 1986, some four and a half years after her legal struggle had begun, the circuit judges concluded that she had made a "prima facie showing of a well-founded fear of persecution." The board's decision was reversed, and her case was remanded with directions that she be permitted to reopen her asylum application before the immigration judge.

The Justice Department in September 1986 filed a writ of certiorari on the case, and as of the spring of 1987 the case of Ana Guevara was pending before the Supreme Court. Ironically, even if Guevara eventually loses her effort to stave off deportation, she will be eligible for legalization under the 1986 immigration reform, by virtue of having been in the country before January 1982.

The Reagan administration's response to cases like Ana Guevara's was summarized in testimony by Thomas O. Enders, an assistant secretary of state, before a Senate Judiciary subcommittee in August 1981. "We have no reason to believe that they [deported Salvadorans] are singled out for mistreatment by their government or for that matter by insurgents."

An increasingly skeptical and concerned Congress pressed the executive branch to produce some hard data to back up such assertions.

Finally, in 1982, the State Department commissioned a study on the fate of those returned.[8]

A random sample of 482 deportees was chosen by the INS, and the names were sent to the American embassy in San Salvador. The embassy first attempted to contact those listed through telegrams or letters, asking them to come into the embassy for an interview. If they lived some distance from the capital, they were informed that an official would be in their area on a certain date and would like them to be available for an interview.

In the end, only 121 of the 482 personally reported no mistreatment upon their return. Another 60 were not at home when the interviewer knocked at the door, but a friend, neighbor, or family member reported that they were not suffering any mistreatment. Thus, about 38 percent of the sample was apparently in no danger.

The fate of the other 62 percent was not clear. Because of incomplete or false names and addresses, 188 of the letters—39 percent of the total—were returned, while 73 others—another 15 percent—could not be interviewed because conditions near their homes were "too dangerous," according to the interviewers, who were headed by a national employee of the U.S. embassy. Of the individuals on the list, 39 were reported to have already returned to the United States, and 1 was reportedly "mistakenly killed in guerrilla conflict."

Needless to say, these results did not reassure those who were concerned about the fate of the deportees. Even the numbers of those who were apparently safe were questioned, on the ground that many Salvadorans would be hesitant to tell a team sent by the American embassy that they feared harm from their government, which was very publicly embraced and financially supported by the American government.

On June 28, 1983, a group of human rights representatives, including Michael Posner of the Lawyers' Committee for International Human Rights in New York, Morton Halperin of the ACLU, and Linda Yannes, an immigration attorney from Brownsville, Texas, paid a visit to Elliott Abrams at the State Department as part of an ongoing effort to persuade the government to stop deporting Salvadorans. Abrams argued that State's study proved that deportees face no danger. "If you can show us otherwise, we'll take another look at it, but we don't believe you can," he told the group. "We think this is a false issue."[9]

When Yannes returned to Brownsville, she found a pile of papers on her desk documenting the death of a young Salvadoran man who had been deported from the United States a few weeks earlier. She sent the material to Abrams. Less than three weeks later, testifying at a House Subcommittee on Human Rights and Western Hemisphere Affairs on August 3, 1983, Abrams stated that he was unaware of any incidents in which deportees had been killed. "I have asked a lot of human rights groups for information and it is a little like Sherlock Holmes' dog that didn't bark. I am at the point now where I think it is quite persuasive evidence that no one produces anything," he declared.

After that incident the ACLU began work on its own study on the fate of the deportees and, in the meantime, put together the information it had on individual cases. The organization gathered affidavits and newspaper reports describing the violent deaths of four more Salvadoran deportees between 1981 and 1983.

Eventually the ACLU received a list of some 8,500 people who had been deported to El Salvador from the United States between March 1981 and March 1983. (In the three fiscal years 1981 to 1983, the INS returned a total of 20,847 Salvadorans.) The names were matched against 15,000 names of persons in ACLU files who were known victims of political persecution in El Salvador. Researchers found 112 likely cases of persecution, including 52 political murders, 47 disappearances, and 13 unlawful political arrests.[10]

The ACLU considered these cases the tip of the iceberg of atrocities. "As to the 8,400 other deportees whose names we obtained, we have no information regarding their welfare or fates," a representative of the ACLU testified before Congress in 1985.[11] The witness, Carol L. Wolchok, director of the organization's political asylum project, told of several additional and more recent cases that had come to her attention, including that of a young father of two American-born children who returned to El Salvador and was immediately abducted, beaten, and held for three weeks by the National Police before he escaped and made his way back to the States. He applied for political asylum, and the State Department recommended against him.

Nevertheless, members of the Reagan administration seized on the ACLU study's finding—that only 1.3 percent of deportees were "likely" cases of persecution—to support its position. In 1984 the State Department launched another effort to support its arguments. It contracted to have a neutral organization monitor the fate of those deported. Somewhat reluctantly the International Committee for Migration, a respected refugee relief organization based in Geneva, took on the task. By 1986 the ICM, which also ran a reception and counseling service at the San Salvador airport for returnees, had conducted four surveys of returnees, reestablishing contact with 81.6 percent of the 6,373 people it had met at the airport.

The ICM data revealed that the large majority of deportees said that they originally left El Salvador primarily because of their poor economic situation.[12] Only 35 of the 5,203 deportees who maintained contact with the ICM alleged that they had security problems in the country. Of these, 10 left the country again by their own means, 9 were deemed to have solved their problems or not to have had any, and 13 were referred to various embassies for resettlement. Of the latter, 11 were rejected on the ground that they were in fact economic cases. One of the 35 was reported a suicide. The ICM could find evidence of only 1 other suspicious death—of an individual reported killed in a crossfire between the army and the guerrillas.

The Reagan administration took these data as conclusive proof that deportees face no special threat to their safety. Among others, however, there is general agreement that the violent situation in El Salvador, while improved since the nightmare years of the early 1980s, remains a constant threat to deportees and the civilian population alike.

Ironically, as conditions have somewhat improved, deportations have slowed down as well, largely because the Immigration Service doesn't have the funds to track down and deport individuals whose applications for asylum have been denied. Unsuccessful applicants have also learned how to challenge their rejections in court. In the spring of 1985 more than 35,000 Salvadorans—71 percent of those arrested in 1981, 1982, and 1983—were still in the legal process.[13]

Of the 13,000 applicants whose claims were denied in 1984, about 9,000 were still in the legal "pipeline" the following year.[14] A 1987 study by the General Accounting Office found that only 2 percent of aliens denied asylum were actually deported. About 80 percent had uncertain immigration status because the INS had not started deportation proceedings.[15]

Thus, to some extent a de facto safe haven has developed in this country for those who can survive underground, illegally, with all the associated difficulties in working and planning for a future. Whether that is an adequate response on the part of the United States to a massive abuse of human rights in this hemisphere remains a subject of dispute.

Notes

INTRODUCTION

1. These estimates are from the *Report of the National Bipartisan Commission on Central America* (Kissinger Commission), 1984, p. 82; and from Peter Shiras, deputy director of the Latin American region for Catholic Relief Services.

2. James LeMoyne, "Salvadorans Stream into U.S. Fleeing Poverty and Civil War," *New York Times*, April 13, 1987, p. A1.

3. *Arizona Daily Star*, quoted in "The Right of Sanctuary," *Washington Spectator*, vol. 12, no. 12 (June 15, 1986), p. 2.

CHAPTER ONE

1. *New York Times*, July 18, 1980, p. A8.

2. May Schmidt, "Deportation Means Death, Survivors Say," *Tucson Citizen*, July 11, 1980, p. 1.

3. Author's interview with Clarence Dupnik, Tucson, May 1986.

4. Schmidt, *op. cit.*

5. Louis Sahagun, "El Salvador Consul Protests Freezeout," *Tucson Citizen*, July 11, 1980, p. 1C.

6. Author's interview with Clarence Dupnik, Tucson, May 1986.

7. Don Skartvedt, "Ten Salvadorans Released to Sponsors," *Arizona Daily Star*, July 12, 1980, p. 1.

8. The details on John Fife's early career come from a series of author's interviews with him, Tucson, April and May 1986.

9. Author's interview with Marguerite Bowden Reed, Tucson, June 1987.

10. Quoted in A. James Reichley, *Religion in American Public Life* (Washington, D.C.: Brookings Institution, 1985), p. 350. As Reichley points out in his excellent study, a surprising number of Protestant laypersons do support their churches' social activism, possibly because they have delegated the sphere of moral behavior to the clergy. In any event, some light was shed on the split within at least one major Protestant denomination in 1980 by a survey that asked Methodists whether they would be willing to "practice civil disobedience in the social witness of the Christian faith." Fully 77 percent of the bishops said yes, compared with 75 percent of national staff, 53 percent of local clergy, and 24 percent of Methodist lay chairpersons.

CHAPTER TWO

1. Carolyn Forche, "The Colonel," from *The Country Between Us* (New York: Harper & Row, 1981), p. 16.

2. Quoted in Raymond Bonner, *Weakness and Deceit* (New York: Times Books, 1984), p. 16.

3. Evidence that close aides of rightist political leader Roberto d'Aubuisson were responsible for the murder, as well as the killing of two American agrarian reform advisers and the head of the Salvadoran land redistribution program in 1981, was released seven years later. See James LeMoyne, "Picture of Death Squads Seen in Key Salvadoran Notebook," *New York Times*, December 2, 1987, p. A1.

4. Gil Loescher and John A. Scanlan, *Calculated Kindness* (New York: Free Press, 1986), p. 209.

5. Arthur C. Helton, "Political Asylum Under the 1980 Refugee Act: An Unfulfilled Promise," *Journal of Law Reform* (Winter 1984), p. 246.

6. Loescher and Scanlan, *op. cit.*, p. 209.

7. *Ibid.*, p. 191.

8. U.S. Congress, Senate Committee on the Judiciary, Subcommittee on Immigration and Refugee Policy, *Hearings on Extended Voluntary Departure Issues*, 99th Congress, 1st Session, April 22, 1985, pp. 71–72.

9. Elizabeth Ferris, "The Politics of Asylum: Mexico and the Central American Refugees," *Journal of Inter-American Studies and World Affairs*, vol. 26, no. 3 (August 1984), pp. 368–70.

10. *Extended Voluntary Departure Issues*, *loc. cit.*, p. 59.

11. Loescher and Scanlan, *op. cit.*, p. 193.

12. A fuller discussion of these points is found in Ronald Copeland and Patricia Weiss Fagen, *Political Asylum: A Background Paper on Concepts, Procedures and Problems* (Washington, D.C.: Refugee Policy Group, December 1982).

13. Author's interviews with Doris Meissner, acting commissioner of the Immigration and Naturalization Service in 1981 and executive associate commissioner from 1982 to 1985, Washington, D.C., June and September 1986.

14. LeMoyne, "Picture of Death Squads Seen in Key Salvadoran Notebook," *loc. cit.*, p. A12.

CHAPTER THREE

1. This anecdote was confirmed in author's interviews with John Fife and Ricardo Elford, Tucson, April and May 1986.

2. The information on Manzo is based on author's interview with Guadalupe Castillo, Tucson, May 1986.

3. Author's interview with Michael Smith, pastor of St. Mark's Presbyterian Church, Tucson, May 1986.

4. Author's interviews with James A. Corbett, Tucson, April and May 1986.

5. This anecdote is based on comments by Jim Corbett to the author, April 1986.

6. James A. Corbett, letter to friends, May 12, 1981; reprinted in *Some Sanctuary Papers, 1981–86*, vol. I, *Borders and Crossings* (Tucson: trsg, 1986), p. 3.

7. *Ibid.*

8. Author's interviews with Jim Corbett and Lupe Castillo, Tucson, April 1986.

9. Author's interview with Jim Corbett, Tucson, April 1986.

CHAPTER FOUR

1. Quoted in James H. Corbett, *The Sanctuary Church* (Wallingford, PA: Rendle Hill Pamphlet 270, 1986), p. 9.

2. This anecdote and the following material on Jim Corbett's background come from author's interviews with him, Tucson, April 1986.

3. Linda Witt, "On the Line," *Chicago Tribune Sunday Magazine*, May 5, 1985, p. 26.

4. Author's interviews with Jim and Pat Corbett, Tucson, April 1986 and June 1987.

5. This story is related by James A. Corbett, "Background for Trsg Discussion of Border Action Procedures," January 1986; reprinted in *Borders and Crossings, loc. cit.*, p. 201.

6. Author's interview with Jim Corbett, Tucson, June 1987.

7. Quoted in Witt, *op. cit.*, p. 29.

8. James A. Corbett, letter to friends, July 6, 1981; reprinted in *Borders and Crossings, loc. cit.*, pp. 7–8.

9. *Ibid.*, pp. 8–11.

CHAPTER FIVE

1. The account of this meeting and the subsequent events related in this chapter are based primarily on author's interviews with several participants, including Ricardo Elford, Tucson, April and May 1986; Jim Corbett, Tucson, April and May 1986; Lupe Castillo, Tucson, May 1986; Tim Nonn, Washington, D.C., September 1986; and Ken Kennon, Tucson, May 1986.

2. A detailed description of the camp and the conditions encountered by the Tucson delegation can be found in Gary MacEoin and Nivita Riley, *No Promised Land* (Boston: Oxfam America, 1982). Their account was echoed in a report on El Centro produced by Fred Tarazon, of Arizona Senator Dennis DeConcini's staff, and in testimony in several lawsuits challenging INS treatment of the Central Americans.

3. James A. Corbett, letter to Delia Combs, August 13, 1985; reprinted in *Borders and Crossings*, *loc. cit.*, p. 179.

4. Author's interview with Ken Kennon, Tucson, May 1986.

5. MacEoin and Riley, *op. cit.*, p. 49.

6. Author's interview with Ken Kennon, Tucson, May 1986.

7. Author's interview with Tim Nonn, Washington, D.C., September 1986.

8. James A. Corbett, letter to Delia Combs, August 13, 1985, *loc. cit.*, p. 179. See also, Louis Sahagun, "Salvadorans Sweat Out Detention," *Tucson Citizen*, July 15, 1981, pp. 1–2A. A prisoner told the reporter that detainees who had signed voluntary departure statements but who wanted to change their minds and file for asylum were not allowed to, but were "dragged out, kicking and screaming."

9. Sahagun, "Salvadorans Sweat Out Dentention," *loc. cit.*, p. 2A.

10. Author's interview with Lupe Castillo, Tucson, May 1986.

CHAPTER SIX

1. The following story is based on author's interviews with Jim Corbett, Tucson, April and May 1986.

2. These details are based on author's interview with Ramón Quiñones, Nogales, April 1986.

3. James A. Corbett, letter written in Santa Rosa, Arizona, November 11, 1981; letter to Delia Combs, August 13, 1985; both reprinted in *Borders and Crossings*, *loc. cit.*, pp. 12–14, 178.

4. Author's interview with Ramón Quiñones, Nogales, April 1986. In an attempt to substantiate these accounts, Father Quiñones's lawyer, William J. Risner, and the latter's law clerk, Jesus R. Romo, visited Nogales on October 28, 1985, and met with the assistant chief of Mexican immigration, Joaquín Figueroa, and a Mexican customs officer named Teodoro Estrada, both of whom verified Quiñones's statements. The two attorneys then spoke with Gary Rehbein, an INS shift superviser at the port of entry. Rehbein told them, as Romo later swore in an affidavit dated November 4, 1985, "that if any Central American refugee were to ask for asylum at the Nogales Port of Entry,

the policy at the Nogales Port of Entry is to inform the refugee that he or she must apply for asylum at the nearest United States consulate in Mexico." Mr. Rehbein also said that he could not think of any refugee who had asked for asylum at the border.

An explanation for this situation was articulated by Ruth Ann Myers, district director for the INS in Phoenix, in author's interview with her, November 1986. She acknowledged that immigration officials in the early 1980s were unprepared for the appearance of refugees at the border. By the time of her arrival in Phoenix in 1984, she said, a person could apply for asylum at the ports of entry, but he or she would have to wait in Mexico until the case was decided. "If all you need to do is apply in order to get a free ticket in, you can see the problem," explained Myers. "Ironically, if you can get in illegally and file in one of our offices, you can stay in."

5. Author's interview with William Johnston, Tucson, May 1986.

6. The account of the following incident was confirmed by both Bill Johnston and Jim Corbett during interviews with the author, Tucson, April and May 1986.

7. Figures used are from Copeland and Fagen, *op. cit.*, p. 45, and are based on INS statistics.

8. Author's interviews with John Fife and Jim Corbett, Tucson, April and May 1986.

9. Author's interview with John Fife, Tucson, May 1986.

10. Leviticus 19:33–34.

CHAPTER SEVEN

1. *Crosby Wilfredo Orantes Hernández et al.* v. *William French Smith, Attorney General, et al.*, District Court for the Central District of California CV82-1197-KN (1982).

2. Author's interview with Laura Dietrich, deputy assistant secretary of state for humanitarian affairs, Washington, D.C., July 1986.

3. Author's interview with Doris Meissner, Washington, D.C., June 1986.

4. *Ibid.* Inman, in a telephone interview, denied having used the term *deep-six*.

5. *Ibid.*

6. Author's interview with John Fife, Tucson, April 1986.

7. *Ibid.* The account of this meeting is based on author's interviews with other participants as well, including Ricardo Elford, Ken Kennon, and Michael Smith, Tucson, May 1986.

8. Author's interview with Jim Corbett, Tucson, May 1986.

9. For an excellent description of the history and legal ramifications of sanctuary, see Ignatius Bau, *This Ground Is Holy* (New York: Paulist Press, 1985).

10. Renny Golden and Michael McConnell, *Sanctuary: The New Underground Railroad* (Maryknoll, N.Y.: Orbis Books, 1986), pp. 57–59.

11. Bau, *op. cit.*, pp. 124–71.

12. Author's interview with Michael Smith, Tucson, May 1986.

13. Author's interview with Ken Kennon, Tucson, May 1986.

14. Author's interview with Ricardo Elford, Tucson, May 1986.

15. James A. Corbett, letter to friends, January 24, 1982; reprinted in *Borders and Crossings*, *loc. cit.*, pp. 15–16.

16. Author's interview with John Fife, Tucson, April 1986.

17. James A. Corbett, letter to friends, January 24, 1982, *loc. cit.*, p. 16.

18. The account of this meeting is based on author's interview with John Fife, Tucson, April 1986.

19. Author's interview with Tim Nonn, Washington, D.C., September 1986.

20. *Ibid.*

21. Author's interview with John Fife, Tucson, April 1986.

22. Randal Udall, "Local Pastor and Church to Defy the Government on Aid to Salvadorans," *Tucson Citizen*, March 19, 1982, p. 1.

CHAPTER EIGHT

1. James R. Wyckoff, "Church Goes Public with Sanctuary Offer," *Tucson Citizen*, March 24, 1982, p. 1.

2. Author's interview with Lupe Castillo, Tucson, May 1986.

3. INS Intelligence Agent Thomas Martin, "March and Ecumenical Service," memorandum, Tucson, March 24, 1982.

4. Author's interview with Leon Ring, Tucson, April 1986.

5. Author's telephone interview with A. Melvin McDonald, October 1986.

6. *Extended Voluntary Departure Issues*, *loc. cit.*, p. 44.

7. Author's interview with Doris Meissner, Washington, D.C., June 1986.

8. George McHugh, Sr., "An Analysis of U.S./INS Statistics on Refugees from El Salvador," Social Justice Committee of St. Raymond's Catholic Church, Dublin, CA, July 22, 1983, p. 6.

9. *Amnesty International Report 1982*. Numerous other human rights groups also reported thousands of killings and disappearances attributed to death squads. Among the victims were student leaders, priests, professors, labor leaders, journalists, opposition party officials, and hundreds of peasants.

10. These statements are based on the field reports of several human rights organizations, notably a report by Americas Watch of November 1982. The report of the Kissinger Commission on Central America, issued in January 1984, reached similar conclusions. The commission found that "in the countryside, they [government security forces] have at times killed indiscriminately to repress any sign of support for the guerrillas."

11. James A. Corbett, letter to friends, January 24, 1982; reprinted in *Borders and Crossings*, *loc. cit.*, pp. 17–18.

12. *Ibid.*, pp. 17–21.

CHAPTER NINE

1. Tony Clark's story and comments are based on author's interviews with him, Nogales, April and May 1986.

2. Author's telephone interview with Joseph McKinney, April 1987.

3. Author's interview with Tony Clark, Nogales, April 1986.

4. Author's interviews with John Fife and Jim Corbett, Tucson, May 1986.

5. Author's interview with Mary Ann Corley, Washington, D.C., September 1986. Corley, like several other prominent members of the CRTFCA, is a former nun.

6. *Ibid.*

7. Golden and McConnell, *op. cit.*, pp. 48–49.

8. Author's interview with Mary Ann Corley, Washington, D.C., September 1986.

9. Golden and McConnell, *op. cit.*, p. 49.

10. This story was related to the author by John Fife, Tucson, April 1986.

CHAPTER TEN

1. Arnold Levinson, "Salvadoran Tells Grim Tale of War," *Rocky Mountain News*, November 28, 1982, p. 16.

2. Jane Juffer, "Sanctuary Movement Lives On . . ." *Pacific News Service*, August 26, 1987, p. 3.

3. Reverend Richard Lundy, "Sanctuary," a sermon preached at St. Luke's Presbyterian Church, Wayzata, Minnesota.

4. Author's interview with John Fife, Tucson, April 1986, and telephone interview with Peter Schey, April 1987.

5. Author's interview with Margaret ("Peggy") Hutchison, Tucson, April 1986.

6. *Ibid.*

7. Figures are from the Immigration and Naturalization Service, Washington, D.C.

8. Author's interview with Peggy Hutchison, Tucson, April 1986.

9. Author's interview with Philip Willis-Conger, Tucson, April 1986.

CHAPTER ELEVEN

1. Quoted in Golden and McConnell, *op. cit.*, p. 47.

2. Beverly Medlyn, "Underground Railroad Still Runs in the Open," *Arizona Daily Star*, December 25, 1982, p. B1.

3. Author's telephone interview with Guadalupe Sanchez, head of the Arizona Farmworkers' Union, October 1986.

4. *United States* v. *Cortez*, 449, 411, U.S. 101 Supreme Court, 690 (January 21, 1981).

5. Author's interview with INS undercover agent John Nixon, Philadelphia, November 1986.

6. Author's interview with James Rayburn, Phoenix, November 1986.

7. *Ibid.*

8. *Ibid.*

CHAPTER TWELVE

1. Information on Jesus Cruz's background is based on a summary of an interview of Cruz by Thomas M. Hoidal, Phoenix, August 27, 1985.

2. Author's interview with James Rayburn, Phoenix, November 1986.

3. Author's interview with John Nixon, Philadelphia, November 1986.

4. Author's interview with Harold Ezell, San Diego, April 1986.

5. *Ibid.*

6. Interview of Mark Kevin Reed by Robert Hirsh and Michael Kimerer, Phoenix, June 7, 1985 (pretrial material, *United States of America* v. *María del Socorro Pardo de Aguilar et al.*, U.S. District Court for the District of Arizona, CR 85-008 PHX EHC. Hereinafter cited as *United States* v. *Socorro Aguilar et al.*), p. 14.

7. Interview of Robert S. Coffin by Robert Hirsh and Michael Kimerer, Phoenix, June 8, 1985 (pretrial material, *United States* v. *Socorro Aguilar et al.*), pp. 6–14.

8. *Ibid.*, pp. 23–24.

9. Hirsh and Kimerer's interview of Mark Kevin Reed, *loc. cit.*, pp. 79–80.

CHAPTER THIRTEEN

1. This description of sanctuary's screening process is based on interviews with numerous members of the movement, including Jim Corbett, Darlene Nicgorski, and Phil Willis-Conger, Tucson, April and May 1986.

2. Author's interview with Tony Clark, Nogales, April 1986.

3. Author's interview with Phil Willis-Conger, Tucson, May 1986.

4. Author's interview with Ramón Quiñones, Nogales, April 1986.

5. *Ibid.*

6. Author's interview with Ricardo Elford, Tucson, May 1986.

7. This anecdote was confirmed by Phil Willis-Conger and Ricardo Elford.

8. The information on Katherine Flaherty is based on author's interview with her, Washington, D.C., March 1986.

9. The following story is based on author's interviews with Katherine Flaherty, Washington, D.C., March 1986, and Phil Willis-Conger, Tucson, May 1986.

10. Charles Chase and Herman Baca, Report of Apprehensions or Seizure (internal Border Patrol document reporting the stop and arrest of Conger and Flaherty), Tucson, March 8, 1984.

11. *Ibid.*

12. This account is based on author's interviews with Phil Willis-Conger, Tucson, May 1986, and Katherine Flaherty, Washington, D.C., March 1986.

CHAPTER FOURTEEN

1. Author's interview with James Rayburn, Phoenix, November 1986.

2. Testimony of James Rayburn, May 23 and 24, 1985, *United States* v. *Socorro Aguilar et al.*, pp. 149–50.

3. Interview of James Rayburn by Robert Hirsh and Thomas M. Hoidal, Phoenix, June 8, 1985 (pretrial material, *United States* v. *Socorro Aguilar et al.*), p. 46.

4. Much of the biographical material on Father Quiñones is from the defense opening statement at the sanctuary trial, November 1985.

5. Author's interview with Ramón Quiñones, Nogales, April 1986.

6. *Ibid.*

7. *Ibid.* In James Rayburn's handwritten notes of the conversation, made after Cruz debriefed him, Cruz "told the padres about group of Guatemalans (9) in Nogales Son."

8. Author's interview with Ramón Quiñones, Nogales, April 1986. According to Agent Rayburn's case notes, after Cruz mentioned the Guatemalans, Quiñones "told I-98 that groups had to enter into underground RR at Tapacula, Chip. Claimed to be awaiting money at Western Union in Nogales Az. Also stated Mexico was holding 70 of their underground RR people. Asked I-98 to come back or call back."

9. James Rayburn's case notes. (Memorandum of investigation, Operation Sojourner, April 16, 1984.) According to William J. Risner, Quiñones's attorney, the priest said something quite different. "He told them . . . that even if they had money, and these people weren't in that category, but those who had access to it couldn't bribe their way out of that prison. For instance, there is no record known to any of us where anyone was able to secure their release that way." (Author's interview with William J. Risner, Tucson, April 1986.)

CHAPTER FIFTEEN

1. Internal INS memorandum on undercover guidelines issues, June 1985.

2. Undercover Operation Request from James A. Rayburn, INS, Phoenix, to INS central office, Washington, D.C., April 24, 1984.

3. *Ibid.*

4. Internal INS memorandum from R. M. Kisor, associate commissioner, enforcement, INS central office, Washington, D.C., to Harold Ezell, regional commissioner, Western Region, and Ernest Gustafson, district director, INS, Phoenix, May 4, 1984.

5. Howard Kurtz, "Stephen S. Trott: No Longer a Highwayman, but a Voice for the Prosecution," *Washington Post*, October 20, 1986, p. A11.

6. Author's interview with James Rayburn, Phoenix, November 1986.

7. This characterization is based on author's interview with John Nixon, Philadelphia, November 1986, and author's telephone interview with Ernest Gustafson, November 1986.

8. Author's interviews with Donald M. Reno, Phoenix, November 1986.

9. *Ibid.*

10. *Ibid.*

11. *Ibid.*

CHAPTER SIXTEEN

1. Author's interview with Tony Clark, Nogales, April 1986.

2. Author's interview with Mary K. Espinosa, Tucson, April 1986.

3. Conversation with Socorro Aguilar by legal assistant John F. Guerra, May 17, 1985, as reported in a memorandum to defense attorneys Brosnahan, Snell *et al.*; summary of interviews with Bertha Benavidez and Julio Benavidez by John F. Guerra, June 12, 1985.

4. *Ibid.*

5. Author's interview with Jim Corbett and the Quaker, who asked to remain unidentified, Tucson, November 1986.

6. Operation Sojourner, Tape No. 22, May 28, 1984, pp. 24–33.

7. Author's interviews with John Nixon and James Rayburn, Philadelphia and Phoenix, November 1986.

8. Operation Sojourner, Tape No. 38, July 11, 1984, p. 30.

9. Author's interviews with Don Reno, Phoenix, November 1986.

10. Agent notes quoted in "Notes on Transcripts," September 10, 1985, p. 67.

11. Operation Sojourner, Tape No. 43, July 26, 1984, pp. 2–4.

12. Statement of Dale S. De Haan, director, Immigration and Refugee Program, Church World Service, in *Extended Voluntary Departure Issues*, *loc. cit.*, p. 79.

13. Operation Sojourner, Tape No. 43, July 26, 1984, pp. 10–15.

14. *Ibid.*, p. 17.

15. *Ibid.*, pp. 23–27.

CHAPTER SEVENTEEN

1. The material on Darlene Nicgorski's background was obtained in a series of author's interviews with her, Tucson, April and May 1986.

2. Stephen Schlesinger and Stephen Kinzer, *Bitter Fruit* (Garden City, N.Y.: Anchor Books, 1983).

3. Author's interview with Darlene Nicgorski, Tucson, April 1986.

4. Material on the activities of the Valley Religious Task Force was obtained in author's interviews with James Oines, Phoenix, May and November 1986.

5. Transcript of tapes obtained in Operation Sojourner, Tape No. 62, September 10, 1984, p. 3.

6. Author's interviews with Katherine Flaherty, Washington, D.C., March 1986, and Phil Willis-Conger, Tucson, April 1986.

7. Author's interview with Phil Willis-Conger, Tucson, April 1986.

8. Author's interview with James Rayburn, Phoenix, November 1986.

9. Information on "Gina Sanchez" obtained in author's interviews with Phil Willis-Conger, Tucson, April 1986, Katherine Flaherty, Washington, D.C., March 1986, and James Rayburn, Phoenix, November 1986.

10. Operation Sojourner, Tape No. 46, August 6, 1984, pp. 1–2.

11. Author's interview with John Nixon, Philadelphia, November 1986.

12. Operation Sojourner, Tape No. 57, August 29, 1987, pp. 5–6.

13. *Ibid.*, p. 8.

14. *Ibid.*, p. 14.

15. *Ibid.*, p. 15.

16. *Ibid.*, pp. 14–18.

17. The offer was verified by both Don Reno and Phil Willis-Conger.

18. Author's interview with John Nixon, Philadelphia, November 1986.

CHAPTER EIGHTEEN

1. Juana Álvarez's story is based on the series "The Road to Refuge," by Carmen Duarte, *Arizona Daily Star*, August 20–24, 1984.

2. Operation Sojourner, Tape No. 54, August 27, 1984, pp. 52–53.

3. John Nixon's handwritten notes, August 28, 1984.

4. James Rayburn's handwritten notes, September 5, 1984.

5. Operation Sojourner, Tape No. 62, September 10, 1984, p. 3.

6. Operation Sojourner, Tape No. 83, October 22, 1984, pp. 14–15.

7. *Ibid.*, p. 18.

8. *Ibid.*, pp. 19–20.

9. *Ibid.*, pp. 21–22.

10. Operation Sojourner, Tape No. 85, October 29, 1984, pp. 15, 30–32.

11. Operation Sojourner, Tape No. 87, November 1, 1984, pp. 5–7.

12. Author's interviews with Don Reno, Phoenix, November 1986.

CHAPTER NINETEEN

1. Author's interview with John Fife, Tucson, April 1986.

2. These comments on the early American colonists were taken from a talk by Robert Bellah, professor of sociology at the University of California, Berkeley, on "The Kingdom of God in America," at Washington Cathedral, Washington, D.C., September 1987.

3. Author's interview with James Oines, Phoenix, May 1986.

4. Author's interviews with Don Reno, Phoenix, November 1986.

5. Author's interview with Gerald Roseberry, Tucson, May 1986.

6. Author's interview with James Oines, Phoenix, May 1986.

7. Operation Sojourner, Tape No. 73, October 1, 1984, pp. 1–10.

8. Operation Sojourner, Tape No. 74, October 1, 1984, p. 3.

9. *Ibid.*, pp. 3–4.

10. Author's interview with Sara Baird, Phoenix, November 1986.

11. Operation Sojourner, Tape No. 74, October 1, 1984, pp. 6–11.

12. *Ibid.*, p. 12.

13. *Ibid.*, p. 13.

14. *Baird* v. *State Bar of Arizona,* 401, U.S. 1 (February 1971).

15. Author's interview with Sara Baird, Phoenix, November 1986.

16. Author's interviews with Don Reno, Phoenix, November 1986.

17. Author's telephone interview with Victor Rostow, January 1987.

CHAPTER TWENTY

1. Operation Sojourner, Tape No. 87, November 1, 1984, p. 15.

2. This comment was not tape-recorded, but John Nixon reported what Fife had said. The minister later confirmed it in author's interview with him, Tucson, June 1987.

3. Author's telephone interviews with Victor Rostow, January 1987, and Mel McDonald, May and November 1986 and November 1987.

4. *Ibid.*

5. This account is based on author's interviews with Don Reno, Phoenix, November 1986.

6. The above account is based on author's telephone interviews with Mel McDonald, May and November 1986 and November 1987. Details of the meeting in Phoenix were confirmed by two others present.

7. Author's interviews with Don Reno, Phoenix, November 1986.

CHAPTER TWENTY-ONE

1. Author's interview with Pat Corbett, Tucson, June 1987.

2. Author's interviews with Kay Kelly, Tucson, April and May 1986.

3. Author's interviews with Jim Corbett, Tucson, June 1987.

4. Author's interviews with Phil and Ellen Willis-Conger, Tucson, May 1986.

5. Author's interview with James Oines, Phoenix, May 1986.

6. Author's interview with Mary K. Espinosa, Nogales, May 1986.

7. Author's interview with Tony Clark, Nogales, May 1986.

8. Author's interview with Ramón Quiñones, Nogales, April 1986.

9. The conversation in Father Quiñones's office was taped and transcribed; a copy of the tape transcript was obtained from Quiñones's attorney, William J. Risner.

10. Author's interview with María Socorro Aguilar, Nogales, May 1986.

11. Author's interviews with Darlene Nicgorski, Tucson, April and May 1986.

12. Author's interview with the person who had helped this family and who asked to remain unidentified for fear of indictment, Tucson, April 1986.

13. Author's interview with Carla Pedersen, Tucson, April 1986.

14. Author's interview with S. Bryan Hehir, Georgetown University, Washington, D.C., November 1987.

15. Quoted in Gary MacEoin, ed., *Sanctuary: A Resource Guide* (San Francisco: Harper & Row, 1985), p. 12.

16. James A. Corbett, "A View from the Border," September 8, 1984, reprinted in *Borders and Crossings, loc. cit.*, pp. 110–15.

17. Author's interview with Mary Ann Corley, Washington, D.C., September 1986.

18. Operation Sojourner, Tape No. 91, January 7, 1985, p. 37.

CHAPTER TWENTY-TWO

1. These anecdotes are from author's interview with Larry Debus, Phoenix, November 1986.

2. Author's interviews with Don Reno, Phoenix, November 1986.

3. Author's interview with Larry Debus, Phoenix, November 1986.

4. The material on Don Reno's background and attitudes is from author's two lengthy interviews with him, Phoenix, November 1986.

5. Author's interview with John Fife, Tucson, April 1986.

6. The material on A. Bates Butler III is from the author's interview with him, Tucson, May 1986.

7. Jana Bommersbach, "Making a Killing with Bob Hirsh," *New Times* (September 1985), p. 7.

8. Author's interview with Phil Willis-Conger, Tucson, April 1986.

9. Author's interview with Bob Hirsh, Tucson, May 1986.

10. Author's conversation with Mrs. A. Bates Butler III, Tucson, April 1986.

11. The incident between Reno and the defense attorneys was confirmed by all parties.

12. Author's interview with Bob Hirsh, Tucson, May 1986.

13. Author's interview with Darlene Nicgorski, Tucson, April 1986.

14. Author's interview with Ellen Yaroshefsky, Tucson, May 1986.

15. Author's interview with Tom Ambroli of the National Sanctuary Defense Fund, Tucson, March 1986.

16. From an address by A. Bates Butler III to the Presbytery de Cristo, Casa Grande, Arizona, January 25, 1985.

17. A. Bates Butler III, "Legal Justification for the Sanctuary Movement: Addendum," remarks presented to the 197th General Assembly of the United Presbyterian Church (U.S.A.), Indianapolis, June 11, 1985.

CHAPTER TWENTY-THREE

1. Author's interviews with Don Reno, Phoenix, November 1986.

2. Government's motion *in limine*, *United States* v. *Socorro Aguilar et al.*, pp. 1–2.

3. *Ibid.*, p. 3.

4. Affidavit from Eva Campbell, sworn on July 9, 1985, in Maricopa County, Arizona, to Peggy Hutchison.

5. Author's interview with James Rayburn, Phoenix, November 1986.

6. *Ibid.*

7. Testimony of James A. Rayburn, *United States* v. *Socorro Aguilar et al.*, May 23–24, 1986, pp. 126–29.

8. *Ibid.*, pp. 91–92.

9. Government's memorandum in response to defense motions to dismiss on grounds of outrageous government conduct, *United States* v. *Socorro Aguilar et al.*, June 6, 1985, p. 2.

10. Infiltration motion, *United States* v. *Socorro Aguilar et al.*, May 23, 1985, p. 9.

11. *Ibid.*, pp. 34, 41.

12. Author's interview with James Oines, Phoenix, May 1986.

13. Hearing on infiltration, *United States* v. *Socorro Aguilar et al.*, May 23, 1985, pp. 60–64.

14. Author's interview with Gerald Roseberry, Tucson, May 1986.

15. Statement in lieu of testimony by J. Philip Wogaman, "Theological and Practical Implications of the Use of Secret Government Informers in Religious Settings," Wesley Theological Seminary, Washington, D.C., May 31, 1985.

16. Government's memorandum in response to defense motion to dismiss on grounds of outrageous government conduct, *loc. cit.*, p. 10.

17. Infiltration motion, *loc. cit.*, pp. 84–86.

CHAPTER TWENTY-FOUR

1. Deborah Anker, affidavit submitted in conjunction with pretrial motion, *United States* v. *Socorro Aguilar et al.*, June 1985. See also J. Friedland and Jesus Rodriguez y Rodriguez, *Seeking Safe Ground* (San Diego, CA: Mexico-U.S. Law Institute, University of San Diego Law School, 1987), for a full discussion of the difficulties facing Central American refugees in Mexico.

2. Motion—Afternoon Session, *United States* v. *Socorro Aguilar et al.*, June 25, 1985, pp. 39–43.

3. Letter from Michael Altman to Don Reno, October 1, 1985.

4. Confidential memo to defense attorneys from Michael Altman re mock trial, August 20, 1985.

CHAPTER TWENTY-FIVE

1. Author's interview with Leon Ring, Tucson, March 1986.

2. Author's interviews with Don Reno, Phoenix, November 1986.

3. Judge's order, *United States* v. *Socorro Aguilar et al.*, October 28, 1985.

4. Author's interviews with Don Reno, Phoenix, November 1986.

5. Author's interview with A. Bates Butler III, May 1987.

6. Author's interview with Michael Piccareta, Tucson, May 1986.

7. Memorandum of Points and Authorities in Support of Motion for Disqualification, *United States* v. *Socorro Aguilar et al.* Undated.

8. *Ibid.*, p. 3.

9. Motion to Dismiss: Selective Prosecution, *United States* v. *Socorro Aguilar et al.*, October 29, 1986, pp. 1–2.

10. Affidavit of Guadelupe Sanchez in Support of Defendants Quinones and Aguilar's Motion to Dismiss for Selective Prosecution, *United States* v. *Socorro Aguilar et al.*, November 8, 1985, p. 6.

11. *Ibid.*, p. 5.

12. *Ibid.*, pp. 7–8.

13. *Ibid.*, pp. 9–11.

14. Jim Rayburn, a fifteen-year veteran of the Immigration and Naturalization Service, could think of no undercover operation ever conducted in Mexico against an Arizona grower. Transcript of proceedings, *United States* v. *Socorro Aguilar et al.*, November 12, 1985, pp. 19–21.

15. Internal report by Border Patrol agent Leon Ring to INS Region, March 26, 1982.

16. Estimates are from the Immigration and Naturalization Service.

17. Author's interviews with Don Reno, Phoenix, November 1986.

CHAPTER TWENTY-SIX

1. Author's interview with John Fife, Tucson, April 1986.

2. Author's interviews with Don Reno, Phoenix, November 1986.

3. Government's opening statement, *United States* v. *Socorro Aguilar et al.*, November 15, 1985, pp. 3–6.

4. *Ibid.*, pp. 8–9.

5. *Ibid.*, pp. 11–19.

6. *Ibid.*, pp. 33–35.

7. Defense opening statements, *United States* v. *Socorro Aguilar et al.*, November 19, 1985, pp. 22–23.

8. *Ibid.*, p. 47.

9. *Ibid.*, pp. 90–91.

10. *Ibid.*, p. 112.

11. Author's interview with John Nixon, Philadelphia, November 1986.

12. Defense opening statements, *loc. cit.*, pp. 151–55.

13. *Ibid.*, pp. 156, 163.

14. *Ibid.*, p. 179.

15. *Ibid.*, p. 186.

16. *Ibid.*, p. 270.

17. *Ibid.*, pp. 266–68.

18. Author's interviews with Don Reno, Phoenix, November 1986.

CHAPTER TWENTY-SEVEN

1. Author's interview with María Socorro Aguilar, Nogales, May 1986.

2. Arizona Sanctuary Defense Fund, weekly update for the sanctuary trial, November 19–22, 1985.

3. *Ibid.*, December 3–6, 1985.

4. Author's interview with John Nixon, Philadelphia, November 1986.

5. Arizona Sanctuary Defense Fund, weekly update for the sanctuary trial, December 10–13, 1985.

6. Author's interviews with Don Reno, Phoenix, November 1986.

7. This story was confirmed by John Fife and Mark Turner, an *Arizona Daily Star* reporter who covered the trial in its early stages.

8. Author's interviews with Don Reno, Phoenix, November 1986.

9. *Ibid.*

10. Testimony of Jesus Maldonado Cruz, *United States* v. *Socorro Aguilar et al.*, December 6, 1985, p. 605.

11. Author's interviews with Don Reno, Phoenix, November 1986.

12. Testimony of Jesus Maldonado Cruz, *loc. cit.*, December 5, 1985, p. 455.

13. *Ibid.*, pp. 878–93.

14. *Ibid.*, pp. 1354–67.

15. *Ibid.*, pp. 1376–77.

16. *Ibid.*, pp. 1677–78.

CHAPTER TWENTY-EIGHT

1. Testimony of Jesus Maldonado Cruz, *loc. cit.*, January 8, 1986, pp. 1646–50.

2. *Ibid.*, pp. 1963–66.

3. *New York Times*, January 19, 1986.

4. Arizona Sanctuary Defense Fund, weekly update for the sanctuary trial, January 14–17, 1986, p. 5.

5. The following account is taken from the offer of proof made by the defense, *United States* v. *Socorro Aguilar et al.*, January 16, 1986.

6. Arthur C. Helton, "Political Asylum Under the 1980 Act: An Unfulfilled Promise," *Journal of Law Reform*, 243 (1984).
In late 1983 the United States had agreed to accept a group of nearly one hundred Salvadorans who were released en masse from prison there. This one-time exception to the rule came in the wake of a visit to El Salvador by Vice President George Bush, who also reportedly warned the regime to crack down on death squad activity and human rights violations within the country.

7. Testimony of Alejandro Gómez, *United States* v. *Socorro Aguilar et al.*, January 16, 1986.

8. Author's interview with Mary K. Espinosa, Tucson, March 1986.

9. Judith McDaniel, *Sanctuary: A Journey* (Ithaca, N.Y.: Finebrand Books, 1986), p. 136.

10. Testimony of Alejandro Gómez, *loc. cit.*, pp. 10–11.

11. Both lawyers stated this to the author in interviews, Tucson, April and May 1986.

12. Transcript of proceedings, *United States* v. *Socorro Aguilar et al.*, January 21, 1986, pp. 3–8.

13. Author's interviews with Don Reno, Phoenix, November 1986.

14. Arizona Sanctuary Defense Fund, weekly update for the sanctuary trial, January 21–23, 1986, p. 4.

15. Transcript of proceedings, *United States* v. *Socorro Aguilar et al.*, January 23, 1986, pp. 9–11.

16. Arizona Sanctuary Defense Fund, weekly update for the sanctuary trial, January 21–23, 1986, p. 7.

17. Testimony of Candida Núñez de Villatoro, *United States* v. *Socorro Aguilar et al.*, January 28, 1986.

18. Testimony of José Rubén Torres, *United States* v. *Socorro Aguilar et al.*, January 28, 1986, pp. 50–61.

19. Testimony of James Rayburn, *United States* v. *Socorro Aguilar et al.*, January 29, 1986, pp. 6–7, 21–22, 50–51.

20. Arizona Sanctuary Defense Fund, weekly update for the sanctuary trial, January 28–31, 1986, pp. 4–5.

CHAPTER TWENTY-NINE

1. Clive Gammon, "This Beast Is a Beauty," *Sports Illustrated* (March 6, 1986), pp. 42–47.

2. Author's interview with María Socorro Aguilar, Nogales, May 1986.

3. Author's interview with Roger Golec, a researcher for the altruistic personality project, Tucson, May 1986.

4. Testimony of José Noe Segovia, *United States* v. *Socorro Aguilar et al.*, February 12, 1986, pp. 39–40.

5. Author's interview with John Nixon, Philadelphia, November 1986.

6. Arizona Sanctuary Defense Fund, weekly update for the sanctuary trial, February 4–7, 1986.

7. Testimony of Francisco Nieto Núñez, *United States* v. *Socorro Aguilar et al.*, January 30, 1986, pp. 97–99.

8. The details of the story were confirmed by the Reverend Henry S. Atkins, Jr., of St. Michael's Chapel of Rutgers University in a telephone conversation with the author, November 1987.

9. Arizona Sanctuary Defense Fund, weekly update for the sanctuary trial, January 29–31, 1986, pp. 5–6.

10. Testimony of Francisco Nieto Núñez, *loc. cit.*, pp. 25–27.

11. *Ibid.*, p. 101.

12. Author's interviews with Don Reno, Phoenix, November 1986.

13. Morelos's story was obtained from his application for political asylum in the United States; from author's interview with him and his wife, Philadelphia, June 1986; and from author's telephone conversations with Walter Walkenhorst III, Joel and Gabriela Morelos's lawyer, in 1986 and 1987.

14. Testimony of Joel Morelos, *United States* v. *Socorro Aguilar et al.*, February 7, 1986, pp. 178–79.

15. Author's telephone interview with Walter Walkenhorst, November 1987.

CHAPTER THIRTY

1. Author's interviews with defendants, particularly Mary K. Espinosa, and defense lawyers, including Bob Hirsh and Nancy Postero, Tucson, April and May 1986.

2. These anecdotes were related to the author by several of the defense attorneys in interviews, Tucson, April and May 1986.

3. Arizona Sanctuary Defense Fund, weekly update for the sanctuary trial, January 7–10, 1986, p. 2.

4. *Ibid.*, December 3–6, 1985, p. 3.

5. *Extended Voluntary Departure Issues, loc. cit.*, p. 63.

6. This and the following incidents were compiled by the Movement Support Network, a project of the Center for Constitutional Rights in New York City, and published in periodic updates in 1986 and 1987.

7. Letter from Kurt I. Klossner, Federal Bureau of Investigation, Phoenix, Arizona, to David A. Myers, December 19, 1985.

8. Letter from Ellen Yaroshefsky to Donald M. Reno, Jr., June 24, 1985.

9. Author's interviews with Don Reno, Phoenix, November 1986. The author also saw copies of some of these replies in an office of one of the sanctuary defense attorneys, who asked to remain unidentified.

10. Letter from Don Edwards to William H. Webster, January 29, 1986.

11. U.S. Congress, House of Representatives Committee on the Judiciary, Subcommittee on Civil and Constitutional Rights, *Hearings on FBI Authorizations Request for Fiscal Year 1987*, 99th Congress, 2nd Session, March 14 and 24, 1986, pp. 14–15.

12. *Ibid.*, p. 12.

13. Author's interviews with Don Reno, Phoenix, November 1986.

CHAPTER THIRTY–ONE

1. Author's interview with George Lockwood, Tucson, May 1986.

2. Author's interviews with Kay Kelly, Tucson, April and May 1986.

3. *Ibid.*

4. Arizona Sanctuary Defense Fund, weekly update for the sanctuary trial, February 11–14, 1986, pp. 5–7.

5. *Ibid.*, pp. 7–8.

6. *Ibid.*, February 18–21, 1986, pp. 1–2.

7. Author's interview with Mark Rosenbaum, Los Angeles, April 1986.

8. Author's interviews with Don Reno, Phoenix, November 1986.

9. Arizona Sanctuary Defense Fund, weekly update for the sanctuary trial, February 25–28, 1986, pp. 3–4.

10. Author's interviews with Don Reno, Phoenix, November 1986.

11. Testimony of John Nixon, *United States* v. *Socorro Aguilar et al.*, March 4, 1986, pp. 132–35.

12. *Ibid.*, March 5, 1986, pp. 326–32.

13. Author's interview with John Nixon, Philadelphia, November 1986.

14. Testimony of John Nixon, *loc. cit.*, February 28, 1986, p. 68.

15. *Ibid.*, March 5, 1986, pp. 292–93.

16. *Ibid.*, March 6, 1986, pp. 464–66.

17. Author's interview with Don Reno, Phoenix, November 1986.

18. Testimony of John Nixon, *loc. cit.*, March 6, 1986, pp. 467–70.

19. *Ibid.*, pp. 472–73.

20. *Ibid.*, pp. 473–74.

21. *Ibid.*, pp. 480–81, 529–30.

CHAPTER THIRTY–TWO

1. Arizona Sanctuary Defense Fund, weekly update for the sanctuary trial, March 11–14, 1986, p. 1–5.

2. *Ibid.*, pp. 5–6.

3. This anecdote was related to the author by several of the defense attorneys.

4. Author's interview with Bates Butler, Tucson, May 1986.

5. Author's interview with James Brosnahan, Tucson, April 1986.

6. Author's interview with Bates Butler, Tucson, May 1986.

7. *Ibid.*

8. Government's closing argument, *United States* v. *Socorro Aguilar et al.*, April 1, 1986, p. 57.

9. Author's notes from sanctuary trial, April 1, 1986.

10. Author's interview with John Fife, Tucson, April 1986.

11. Author's notes from sanctuary trial. The descriptions of the defense closing statements that follow are drawn primarily from the author's notes of the trial.

12. *Ibid.*

13. Author's interview with George Lockwood, Tucson, May 1986.

14. Peter Applebome, "Arizona Jury Deliberating Issue of Church Sanctuary," *New York Times*, April 18, 1986, p. A8.

15. The author was present when this comment was made.

16. Author's interviews with Don Reno, Phoenix, November 1986.

CHAPTER THIRTY-THREE

1. Author's interview with William J. Risner, Tucson, April 1986.

2. Author's interviews with Don Reno, Phoenix, November 1986.

3. Jay Mathews, "Jury Convicts 8 Sanctuary Defendants," *Washington Post*, May 2, 1986, p. 1.

4. Peter Applebome, "Backers Say Guilty Verdicts Aid Alien Sanctuary Drive," *New York Times*, May 3, 1986, p. A6.

5. Author's interviews with Don Reno, Phoenix, November 1986.

6. Daniel R. Browning, "Sanctuary Defendants May Get Another Day in Court," *Arizona Daily Star*, May 3, 1986, p. 7B.

7. Author's interview with Darlene Nicgorski, Tucson, May 1987.

8. Author's interview with Harold Ezell, Washington, D.C., June 1986.

9. Author's interview with Jim Corbett, Tucson, May 1986.

10. "Comment: A Blow to Justice," *Arizona Daily Star*, Tucson, May 2, 1986, p. 16A.

11. Quoted in Mary Reed, "Sanctuary: Overblown . . . Decision," letter to the editor, *Arizona Republic*, May 7, 1986, p. A18.

12. Author's interviews with Don Reno, Phoenix, November 1986.

13. This exchange was related to the author by Don Reno. The reference to William F. Buckley's column was confirmed by William F. Buckley.

14. Author's telephone interview with Maurice Inman, November 1987.

15. Gabrielle Fimbres, "Cost of Sanctuary Trial Cases Past \$3 Million," *Tucson Citizen*, April 17, 1986, p. 1.

16. Author's interviews with Don Reno, Phoenix, November 1986.

17. "Tucson Congregation Wondering When Truth Will Do Its Job," *Arizona Republic*, May 4, 1986.

18. Tape of sermon delivered by John Fife at Southside Presbyterian Church, May 4, 1986.

19. The following account is from Dennis Bernstein and Vince Bielski, "Returned Colonel Spearheads a Nighttime Sanctuary Mission," *In These Times* (May 28–June 10, 1986), p. 6.

20. The author was present at the encounter between Johnston and sanctuary supporters.

21. Author's interview with Bill Johnston, Tucson, May 1986.

CHAPTER THIRTY–FOUR

1. "Hill Letter Backs Activists," *Washington Post*, July 1, 1986, p. 14.

2. Dennis Bernstein and Connie Blitt, "Sanctuary Trial Judgment Day," *In These Times* (July 9–22, 1986), p. 5.

3. Author's telephone interview with Maurice Inman, November 1986.

4. Jay Mathews, "Work Within the Law, Sanctuary Judge Urges," *Washington Post*, July 3, 1986, p. 2.

5. Bernard Weinraub, "Notebook: Reagan in the Hoopla," *New York Times*, July 6, 1986, p. A16.

EPILOGUE

1. The account of Gómez's arrest and subsequent fate is based primarily on author's telephone interview with Isabel Morrison, a member of the Rochester sanctuary organization, November 1987, and on local newspaper accounts. See James Goodman, "Gómez Describes Torture," *Rochester Democrat and Chronicle*, reprinted in *Congressional Record*, July 28, 1987, p. H6716.

2. Author's telephone interview with Isabel Morrison, November 1987.

3. Americas Watch, *The Civilian Toll*, Ninth Supplement to the *Report on Human Rights in El Salvador* (New York: Americas Watch Committee, August 30, 1987).

4. Author's interview with Jim Corbett, Tucson, July 1986.

5. James A. Corbett, Jerome Hall Forum, Harvard University, May 4–5, 1987.

6. James A. Corbett, *The Sanctuary Church, loc. cit.*, pp. 5–6.

7. Roberto Suro, "Pope Lauds Those Who Aid Refugees of Latin America," *New York Times*, September 14, 1987, pp. A1, B10–11.

8. *INS* v. *Cordoza and Fonseca*, U.S., 107 Supreme Court 1207 (1987).

9. This estimate was provided by several church workers involved in refugee legal assistance in Arizona.

10. "Meese Signs Order Giving Nicaraguans Haven in U.S.," *Washington Post*, July 9, 1986, p. 1.

11. Robert Pear, "Duarte Appeals to Reagan to Let Salvadorans Stay," *New York Times*, April 26, 1986, p. A1.

12. Address of President José Napoleón Duarte, National Press Club, Washington, D.C., October 15, 1987.

13. "Alien Sanctuary Movement's State Unclear a Year After Court Case," *New York Times*, July 7, 1987, p. A8.

14. Author's telephone interview with Dale De Haan, May 1987.

15. See, for example, Deborah Penluss and Joan F. Hartman, "Temporary Refuge: Emergence of a Customary Norm," *Virginia Journal of International Law*, vol. 26, no. 3 (Spring 1986), pp. 551–626.

16. The account of this testimony and other statements made at the hearings are taken from the author's notes of the hearings, held in February 1987.

17. Executive Order No. 12333 on United States Intelligence Activities, December 4, 1981, 46 F.R. 59941.

18. *Douglas Letters: Selections from the Private Papers of Justice William O. Douglas*, edited and with an introduction by Melvin I. Urofsky, with the assistance of Philip E. Urofsky (Bethesda, Md.: Adler & Adler, 1987).

APPENDIX I

1. Mary M. Solberg, *A Report on the Salvadoran Situation* (New York: Lutheran Immigration and Refugee Service, September 15, 1981).

2. MacEoin and Riley, *op. cit.*, pp. 26–28. Also, author's telephone interview with immigration attorney Lisa Brodyaga of Harlingen, Texas, December 1987.

3. *Ibid.*, pp. 74–75.

4. *Congressional Record*, February 11, 1982, p. S827.

5. Confirmation of the conflict between the UNHCR in Washington and the State Department was given in author's interviews with Joachim Henkel, UNHCR representative in Washington, D.C., October 1986, and Laura Dietrich, Washington, D.C., June 1986.

6. *Asylum Adjudication: An Evolving Concept and Responsibility for the Immigration and Naturalization Service* (Washington, D.C.: Immigration and Naturalization Service, June 1982).

7. *Ibid.*, p. 33.

8. *Ibid.*, p. 59.

9. *Ibid.*, p. 59.

10. Quoted in *Congressional Record*, February 11, 1982, p. S831.

11. Americas Watch and American Civil Liberties Union, *Report on Human Rights in El Salvador* (New York: Vintage Books, 1982), p. xivii.

12. *Ibid.*, p. xli.

13. Bonner, *op. cit.*, pp. 112–13. Bonner, then a reporter for the *New York Times*, was at the scene of the massacre and talked with survivors three weeks after it occurred.

14. *Ibid.*, p. 64.

15. Americas Watch and ACLU, *op. cit.*, p. vii.

16. *Ibid.*

APPENDIX II

1. All figures are from the Immigration and Naturalization Service, Washington, D.C.

2. Author's interview with Laura Dietrich, Washington, D.C., June 1986.

3. William Stanley, "Economic Migrants or Refugees from Violence?" *Massachusetts Institute of Technology*, March 1985, p. 24.

4. Quoted in MacEoin and Riley, *op. cit.*, pp. 43, 68.

5. American Civil Liberties Union, *Salvadorans in the United States: The Case for Extended Voluntary Departure* (Washington, D.C.: National Immigration and Alien Rights Project Report No. 1, April 1984), Appendix III.

6. Central American Refugee Center, "Stop Deportations of Salvadoran Refugees," Washington, D.C., undated.

7. Information on the Guevara case is based on court documents from *Guevara Flores* v. *INS*, U.S. Court of Appeals, Fifth Circuit, April 11, 1986 (786 FR, 2d Ser., 1242 [5th Cir. 1986].

8. U.S. Department of State, "Survey of 482 Deported Salvadorans" and "Salvadoran Monitoring Survey Methodology," Washington, D.C., 1982.

9. Author's telephone interview with Linda Yannes, November 1986. The substance of the meeting was confirmed by Morton Halperin.

10. American Civil Liberties Union, *The Fates of Salvadorans Expelled from the United States* (Washington, D.C.: ACLU Political Asylum Project, September 5, 1984), Attachment II.

11. *Extended Voluntary Departure Issues*, *loc. cit.*, pp. 116–17.

12. Intergovernmental Committee for Migration, "ICM's Reception and Counselling Program in El Salvador," Washington, D.C., November 12, 1986; also, author's telephone interview with Gretchen Bolton, chief of mission, ICM, Washington, D.C., November 1986.

13. Testimony of INS Commissioner Alan Nelson, *Extended Voluntary Departure Issues*, *loc. cit.*, p. 51.

14. *Ibid.*, p. 60.

15. U.S. General Accounting Office, "Asylum: Uniform Application of Standards Uncertain—Few Denied Applicants Deported," Washington, D.C., January 1987.

Index

About the Author

ANN CRITTENDEN is a writer based in Washington, D.C. For eight years she was on the staff of the *New York Times*, where she wrote on a wide range of subjects, including international economics and finance and world hunger. A graduate of Southern Methodist University and the Columbia University School of International Affairs, she has been a teacher of history, a reporter for *Fortune*, and a foreign correspondent for *Newsweek* in Southeast Asia and South America. Her articles have appeared in numerous publications, including *Foreign Affairs*, *The Nation*, and *Reader's Digest. Sanctuary* is her first book.